Customer Service

Custom Edition

Donna Knapp
Pattie Gibson-Odgers
George Reynolds

DELMAR
CENGAGE Learning

Australia • Brazil • Japan • Korea • Mexico • Singapore • Spain • United Kingdom • United States

Customer Service, Custom Edition
Donna Knapp, Pattie Gibson-Odgers,
and George Reynolds

Vice President, Technology and Trades ABU:
David Garza

Director of Learning Solutions: Sandy Clark

Senior Acquisitions Editor: Stephen Helba

Managing Editor: Larry Main

Marketing Director: Deborah S. Yarnell

Marketing Manager: Kevin Rivenburg

Marketing Coordinator: Shanna Gibbs

Director of Production: Patty Stephan

Curriculum Manager: Elizabeth Sugg

Production Manager: Andrew Crouth

Contract Publishing Content Project Manager:
Takeyce Walter

Sr. Editorial Assistant: Dawn Daugherty

For product information and technology assistance, contact us at
Cengage Learning Customer & Sales Support, 1-800-354-9706
For permission to use material from this text or product,
submit all requests online at **www.cengage.com/permissions**
Further permissions questions can be emailed to
permissionrequest@cengage.com

ISBN-13: 978-1-4283-3688-9

ISBN-10: 1-4283-3688-5

Delmar
Executive Woods
5 Maxwell Drive
Clifton Park, NY 12065
USA

Cengage Learning is a leading provider of customized learning solutions with office locations around the globe, including Singapore, the United Kingdom, Australia, Mexico, Brazil, and Japan. Locate your local office at **international.cengage.com/region**

Cengage Learning products are represented in Canada by Nelson Education, Ltd.

For your lifelong learning solutions, visit **www.cengage.com/delmar**

Visit our corporate website at **www.cengage.com**

Notice to the Reader

Printed in the United States of America
2 3 4 5 6 7 11 10 09

CONTENTS

1

INTRODUCTION TO CUSTOMER-CENTRIC SERVICE

Objectives

◆ Define customer-centric service.

◆ Contrast traditional customer service with exceptional customer service.

◆ Identify required customer service skills and competencies.

Businesses—large or small, industrial or retail, new or established—cannot survive without customers. Customer service is not about fancy products or intricate corporate culture, but about dedicated, trustworthy employees and loyal, satisfied customers. Today, with more and more competitors vying for customers' attention, exceptional customer service is no longer optional—it's essential to staying profitable in business. Although nobody would claim that customer service is simple, the basic foundations and concepts should be.

Service occupations are projected to account for approximately 18.7 million of the 18.9 million new wage and salary jobs generated over the 2004–2014 period. The approach in this book places you in the role of a service provider. If not in your current job, then sometime in the near future, much of your on-the-job success may be influenced by your ability, knowledge, and willingness to provide exceptional customer service.

Chapter 1 begins by describing what customer service is and how a customer is defined. Discussion then moves to identifying what exceptional customer service is and how it has changed. Finally, the goals of customer-oriented organizations and the importance of hiring the right person to perform the role of delivering exceptional customer service are addressed.

DEFINING CUSTOMER SERVICE

Even though every customer is unique, all customers expect three things—a quality product, reliable service, and reasonable prices. In other words, customers want to receive what they feel they have paid for. A customer views you, an employee of an organization, as the company, regardless of what your job description says.

Customer service means different things to different people. In reality, however, the only perspective that matters is the customer's perception of good customer service at the time service is needed and delivered. Here are some examples of good customer service:

- For a busy traveling executive, a flight that leaves on time
- For a harried office manager, working with an office supply store that keeps a good inventory of products on hand and delivers dependably
- For a lonely retiree, conversation and kindness from a waitress when frequenting a neighborhood restaurant
- For a college student entering a new school, competent and caring advice from an advisor on the best course of study

Simply stated, **customer service** is the process of satisfying the customer, relative to a product or service, in whatever way the customer defines as meeting his or her need, and having that service delivered with efficiency, understanding, and compassion.

Whether online or offline, customers now have unparalleled power to research and transact with companies exactly when, where, and how they choose. A new worldview is at work that companies must either embrace or ignore at their peril. The **customer-centric service** worldview simply means that business revolves around the customer. Put another way, a customer-centric organization puts customers first, is service oriented, and thoughtfully develops and satisfies a loyal, repeat customer base.

To be customer-centric does not mean being a doormat. It means being respectful to the customer's point of view and letting the customer know that his or her opinion is heard and valued before making the right decision from both the short- and long-term business perspectives. It means listening with care to the customer's concern, then taking the time to respond to that concern reasonably. Companies that focus on creating a good customer experience will succeed far more than those that do not.

 It has been said that one way to exceed customer expectations is to promise good but deliver great! In other words, go above and beyond what is expected.

TIP

Mission Statement, Values, and Goals of Customer Service

Organizations, like people, require direction and focus in order to achieve stated goals. How many times have you heard that if you don't have any idea where you're going, you

Myth	Fact
1. We are providing good service, but a perception exists outside the organization that we are not.	• You may, in fact, already be providing good customer service, but it is not good enough; you can improve it. More important, if you are providing good service but the customer's perception is that you are not, then you have a problem that needs to be corrected; to the customer, perception is reality.
2. You can't improve service without more people and a larger budget.	• Poor service is far more costly to provide than high-quality service. Eliminating long, repetitive customer interactions and responding to customer complaints more efficiently saves time and money.
3. Why all the concern over customer service? If customers don't like the service we provide, they can try getting it elsewhere.	• A "take it or leave it" attitude is unacceptable. If enough customers receive poor service, they will eventually complain to management or an elected official in a way that can be very uncomfortable for you and/or your organization.
4. You can't provide high-quality customer service when the requirements you must implement force you to tell customers "no."	• Quality customer service is not saying "yes" to everything customers request. People can accept a "no" if it is presented in the right way, but they cannot accept loss of dignity and control.
5. Our customers have conflicting objectives; we will never be able to satisfy them.	• You can do only what legal requirements authorize you to do. However, you cannot let what you cannot do be an excuse for not doing all that you are authorized to do. This includes providing warm, friendly, caring service that is responsive, efficient, and accurate.
6. I don't need to worry about customer service because I don't deal with the public.	• You cannot provide high-quality service to your external customers until you provide high-quality service to your internal customers.

Figure 1–1 Common Customer Service Myths

probably don't know where you've been, are confused as to where you are, and most certainly won't know it when you get to where you ought to be? In like fashion, employees who have no idea where they are going flounder aimlessly, trying to get through the day, with no sense of purpose, loyalty, commitment, or urgency. This is not what customers who buy from organizations have a right to expect.

The quality of customer service that a customer receives is greatly influenced by an organization's mission statement and its vision of doing business. As simple as the statement "Good service is good business" can be, it may say all that is necessary to represent a company's mission statement or general values. Another example of a purpose statement is the Ritz-Carlton Hotel's motto: "We are ladies and gentlemen serving ladies and gentlemen." If employees at this hotel follow the motto to the letter, they provide the finest personal service and facilities for their guests, who will always enjoy a warm, relaxed, yet refined hotel experience.

Companies must have planned goals to ensure that daily decisions, actions, and behaviors are totally customer-focused and are designed to be adaptable as needed to changes in customers' needs, desires, and expectations. Many corporations consider Nordstrom's department store as a premier example of superior customer service. When helping customers, top management at this upscale department store has empowered employees with two simple phrases that reflect its core values: (1) use good judgment in all situations, and (2) there will be no additional rules.

In most cases, when companies ask employees to put themselves in the place of their customers, doing so will guide the employees' efforts to provide the same treatment and service that they would expect to receive if they were the customers. If this sounds like the Golden Rule, "Do unto others as you would have them do unto you," it is. For lack of a stated mission and values statement, many companies use the Golden Rule as a guiding principle when serving customers.

Customer service is not new, but much confusion surrounds its importance and degree of practice in today's marketplace. Figure 1.1 lists some common customer service myths and corresponding facts that speak to an organization's corporate values.

When organizations commit to a way of treating customers by writing down their mission statement, values, and goals, they create a corporate culture that is better understood and lived by all who work there. According to Peggy Morrow, in her book *Customer Service— The Key to Your Competitive Edge*, organizations can take critical steps to create and ensure a customer service culture. Those measures are explained in Figure 1.2.

---

1. Management must make the measurement of service quality and feedback from the customer a basic part of everyone's work experience. This information must be available and understood by everyone, no matter what his or her level in the organization. The entire organization must become obsessed with what the customer wants.

2. Be very clear about specifying the behavior that employees are expected to deliver, both with external customers and with their coworkers.

3. Explain why giving excellent customer service is important—not only for the company but also for the world. What does your company do that makes life easier for everyone? What does your product or service add?

4. Create ways to communicate excellent examples of customer service both within and outside the company. Institute celebrations, recognition ceremonies, logos, and symbols of the customer service culture and its values. This is where you want the mugs, buttons, and banners. Seize every opportunity to publicize the times when employees "do it right."

5. Indoctrinate and train all employees in the culture as soon as they are hired. Disney is famous for this. Disney puts all newcomers through a "traditions" course, which details the company history with customer relations and how it is the backbone of Disney. Your orientation program is a key part of the ultimate success of your customer service efforts. Make sure that it contains more than an explanation of benefits and a tour of the facilities.

6. Encourage a sense of responsibility for group performance. Help employees see how their performance affects others. Emphasize the importance of internal customer service. Help everyone see that, if you don't serve each other well, you can never hope to serve your ultimate customer.

7. Establish policies that are customer-friendly and that show concern for your customers. Eliminate all routine and rigid policies and guidelines. Never let your customer service representatives say, "Those are the rules I have to follow; there's nothing I can do about it." There is always a way to satisfy the customer. You must give your employees the power to do so.

8. Remove any employees who do not show the behavior necessary to please customers. Too many companies allow frontline service representatives to remain on the job when they are not suited to a customer service position. Everyone, from the top down, must believe that he or she works for the customer.

Figure 1–2 Keys to Creating a Customer Service Culture within Organizations
Source: Reprinted with permission from Peggy Morrow & Associates, *Customer Service—The Key to Your Competitive Edge* (Houston, TX: Advantage Plus Publishers, 1995).

External and Internal Customers

To be successful, an organization must first identify its customers and then learn as much about them as possible—including their age, gender, income level, lifestyle, and occupation. This demographic information, once collected, creates a **customer profile** that explains who the customers are and what they want in terms of service. Companies identify their main customers for a very good reason—so they can develop and market the goods and services their customers want.

Most organizations have two main sets of customers: external and internal customers. **External customers** are the customers whose needs we traditionally think of serving, because these customers are the persons or organizations that purchase and use a company's products and services. **Internal customers**, on the other hand, are identified as other people or departments within a company that rely on colleagues to provide the support they need to serve their own internal and external customers. If you work at an organization's computer help desk, for example, your internal customer is anyone who requests your assistance in using the software packages or hardware components on your company's computer network system.

The external customer buys a company's product or service.

Never take for granted the importance of serving internal customers well.

In many firms, unfortunately, internal customers are often ignored or taken for granted—an attitude that compromises the productive flow of work throughout a company. Employees should respect and serve internal customers as if they were paying clients. Typically, the ways in which internal customers are treated translate into how a company is perceived by its external customers.

Employment Growth—Customer Service Representatives

According to the U.S. Bureau of Labor Statistics, employment in professional and service-related occupations is expected to increase at a faster rate than all other occupations, and these sectors will add the most jobs from 2004 to 2014. Office and administrative support occupations are projected to grow about half as fast as other occupations, while jobs in production are projected to decline slightly.

Beyond growth stemming from expansion of the industries in which customer service representatives are employed, a need for additional personnel in this role is likely to result from heightened reliance on these workers. In many industries, gaining a competitive edge and retaining customers will be increasingly important over the next decade. This is particularly true in industries such as financial services, communications, and utilities, which already employ numerous customer service representatives.

As the trend toward consolidation in industries continues, centralized call centers will provide an effective method for delivering a high level of customer service. As a result, employment of customer service representatives may grow at a faster rate in call centers than in other areas. However, this growth may be tempered: a variety of factors, including technological improvements, make it increasingly feasible and cost-effective to build or relocate call centers outside the United States.

Prospects for obtaining a job in the customer service field are expected to be excellent, with more job openings than job seekers. Bilingual applicants, in particular, may enjoy favorable job prospects. Replacement needs are expected to be significant in this field because many young people work as customer service representatives before switching to other jobs. This occupation is well suited to flexible work schedules, and many opportunities for part-time work will continue to be available, particularly as organizations attempt to cut labor costs by hiring more temporary workers. Figure 1.3 shows recent employment projections provided by the Bureau of Labor Statistics, reflecting the occupations with the largest job growth from 2004 to 2014.

UNDERSTANDING THE EVOLVING ROLE OF CUSTOMER SERVICE

The Internet and mobile/wireless technologies, which have become fundamental parts of our lives, have caused an unparalleled shift in the balance of power from companies to their customers. Consumers, armed with instant 24-hour access to information, not only are

1. Management must make the measurement of service quality and feedback from the customer a basic part of everyone's work experience. This information must be available and understood by everyone, no matter what his or her level in the organization. The entire organization must become obsessed with what the customer wants.

2. Be very clear about specifying the behavior that employees are expected to deliver, both with external customers and with their coworkers.

3. Explain why giving excellent customer service is important—not only for the company but also for the world. What does your company do that makes life easier for everyone? What does your product or service add?

4. Create ways to communicate excellent examples of customer service both within and outside the company. Institute celebrations, recognition ceremonies, logos, and symbols of the customer service culture and its values. This is where you want the mugs, buttons, and banners. Seize every opportunity to publicize the times when employees "do it right."

5. Indoctrinate and train all employees in the culture as soon as they are hired. Disney is famous for this. Disney puts all newcomers through a "traditions" course, which details the company history with customer relations and how it is the backbone of Disney. Your orientation program is a key part of the ultimate success of your customer service efforts. Make sure that it contains more than an explanation of benefits and a tour of the facilities.

6. Encourage a sense of responsibility for group performance. Help employees see how their performance affects others. Emphasize the importance of internal customer service. Help everyone see that, if you don't serve each other well, you can never hope to serve your ultimate customer.

7. Establish policies that are customer-friendly and that show concern for your customers. Eliminate all routine and rigid policies and guidelines. Never let your customer service representatives say, "Those are the rules I have to follow; there's nothing I can do about it." There is always a way to satisfy the customer. You must give your employees the power to do so.

8. Remove any employees who do not show the behavior necessary to please customers. Too many companies allow frontline service representatives to remain on the job when they are not suited to a customer service position. Everyone, from the top down, must believe that he or she works for the customer.

Figure 1–3 Occupations with the Largest Job Growth—2004–2014
Source: Data from U.S. Department of Labor, Bureau of Labor Statistics.

reshaping the products that a company offers and the distribution channels it uses, but also are demanding a higher level and quality of service than ever before.

That power shift from companies to their customers underlies the new **customer economy.** What counts in the new customer economy? American businesses are realizing that the depth of their relationships with customers and the loyalty of those customers to the company are increasingly linked directly to profit margins and, ultimately, to their overall sustained existence.

Traditional versus Exceptional Customer Service

The very nature of customer service has changed dramatically over the last decade. In the past, organizations provided what could be called traditional customer service. That is, if customers needed service, they went to the organization's customer service department. The implicit message to the customer was "This department is the only place you'll get customer service in this company."

Today's customers, however, expect something more than traditional customer service. They want a company and its employees to exceed their expectations, demonstrate that the organization cares for them, and work immediately and decisively on their behalf. To be precise, customers today demand exceptional customer service. To that end, a successful company recognizes that its competitors may easily be able to copy its products, its prices, and even its promotions, but competitors cannot copy an organization's employees and the distinctive and exceptional service they provide.

Each time customers come in contact with an organization, they get an impression of service and the overall products they think they will receive. Everyone in an organization touches customers. The employees' behavior and attitudes affect how the customer feels about the company. As the customer service representative (CSR), or frontline person who deals with customers on a day-to-day basis, you come to signify all that your company stands for—both good and bad. To the customer, you are the voice and personality of your organization. Customers who experience exceptional customer service will come back for more. They will be less likely to shop around as a result of how well you treat them.

 Always strive to improve your overall service by focusing on the small details of each transaction. It will mean a lot to the customer and make a difference in total customer satisfaction.

Multichannel Customer Contact Points

As a customer service representative, you will serve customers in several situations, typically known as **contact points**. For example, customer contact occurs in person, on the phone, through written communications, or online. To the customer, it doesn't matter where the interaction takes place. What does matter is that the frontline employee, the CSR, takes ownership of the problem. The CSR must apply the Golden Rule or other course provided by the organization's values statement and must follow it through to the satisfactory outcome expected by the customer. This is not difficult to do, provided that the CSR has all the knowledge, tools, and authority needed to take care of each customer's problem in a positive way.

A caring, friendly atmosphere and quick resolutions to problems create positive points of contact. Clean, neat surroundings—whether in an office, a store, or a restaurant—say, "We pay attention to details because we value them as important to our success." Accurate invoices, prompt shipments, and returned phone calls help convey a positive impression to customers.

On the other hand, examples of negative points of contact include letting your phone ring five or six times before answering it, leaving the customer on hold for two or more minutes, and not replying promptly to an e-mail request for information. This translates to the customer as "We don't value your time." Long lines, out-of-stock items, faded signs, and unclean surroundings are other ways to leave an unfavorable impression about the company and its product or services.

Any successful company strives to make sure that all its points of contact with customers are positive ones. In the final analysis, all customers deserve exceptional service at each point of contact, regardless of the means they use to seek customer service.

Ethics/Choices

Which of these best reflects your views, in general, of dealing with customer service issues: *"I tell the whole truth, all the time"* or *"I play by the rules, but I bend them to my company's advantage whenever I can."*

The Tiered Service System

In years past, most thriving companies gave all their customers special attention, regardless of the size of their purchase. The thinking then was that a customer who makes a small purchase today might make a large purchase tomorrow. Today, however, the mindset of treating customers differently is based on certain criteria—their actual or potential value, for example. This idea is beginning to make economic sense to more and more businesses. In other words, many companies today are asking themselves, "Why invest the same amount of customer service effort and expense in a onetime customer as we would in a customer who has a multimillion-dollar history with our business?"

This increasingly popular approach to serving customers is referred to as a **tiered service system** and is used with a database of customer transaction records, which have been stored and analyzed with the help of computers and customer relationship management (CRM) software. The concept and use of CRM software will be discussed in depth in a later chapter; however, the underlying principle of CRM is that every interaction with a customer is part of a larger relationship that the company should be able to maximize and use in helping increase customer loyalty.

What does tiered service look like? Whether we realize it or not, we are already being served by this concept each time we choose to fly. Airlines, for example, usually place their customers into three tiers of service: basic, or coach-class; enhanced, or business-class; and premium, or first-class. For the customer, the good news is that a tiered service system has a lot more choices on price, convenience, and comfort. Also, consumers have the option of upgrading if they choose to. On the other hand, companies can invisibly identify individuals who don't generate profits for them and may decide to provide them with inferior service.

Although tiered service exists, customers should never feel that they are getting a certain level of service because they are buying a certain level of business. All customers should feel that they are receiving the same level of customer service when it comes to assistance with problems or the handling of complaints.

DESCRIBING THE ROLE OF CUSTOMER SERVICE REPRESENTATIVES

Superior service doesn't just happen; it is a process. Next to a company's product, excellence in customer service is the single most important factor in determining the future success or failure of a company. Regardless of what products or services a company offers, the company is also in the business of providing customer service.

If you look at companies that are not doing well or have gone under, a common thread is failure to deliver superior customer service. Today's successful companies show that they understand and deliver what their customers want. More important, they are believers in the value of hiring the right people and providing customer service training not only for frontline employees, but for management and all other support workers as well.

Top organizations carefully select people to fill the position of customer service representatives. CSRs are trained well and are provided a supportive working environment because CSRs count in these companies. A customer service representative can work in a variety of settings and have any number of job titles. For instance, a CSR might work in a telephone call center, at a help desk, with customers at a counter face-to-face, on the phone in the role of telemarketing, or on the Internet, providing hospitality and technical information to both internal and external clients. Regardless of the setting or job title, the CSR's role, in general, is to answer questions, solve problems, take orders, and resolve complaints.

Ethics/Choices

Assume you are answering a customer's inquiry about a product. After an amicable conversation with you, the customer realizes she cannot afford your product and thanks you. You know that a competitor offers the same product in her price range. What do you do?

Required Customer Service Skills and Competencies

Although the responsibilities of a CSR are many and varied, most companies write the job description to include the following duties:

- Provides in-house support for salespeople whenever a customer requires information or assistance
- Provides communication between levels of management and customers
- Represents the customer's interests, rather than those of a department within the company
- Helps develop and maintain customer loyalty
- Handles customer complaints and strives to have the company set them right

- Alerts upper management to trends or any conditions within the company's products or services that lead to customer dissatisfaction and recommends solutions to problems

The fundamental service skills needed by all customer service professionals involve knowing how to

- build rapport, uncover needs, listen, empathize, clarify, explain, and delight customers.
- handle customer complaints, irate customers, and challenging situations.
- avoid misunderstandings, manage expectations, and take responsibility.
- work in teams and build internal cooperation and communication within the organization.
- show a positive customer service attitude.

Hiring the Right Person

The CSR's task is always to resolve the customer's problem as quickly and completely as possible. This requires three critical skills: (1) exercising judgment, (2) possessing knowledge of the product, customer history, company information, and competitive data, and (3) using that judgment and knowledge, along with common sense.

When hiring customer service professionals, companies should look for a helping attitude. You can teach anyone almost anything, but the feeling of customer service has to come from within a person. First-rate CSRs sense what irritates their customers. For example, seemingly minor issues such as the way a carton is labeled or type of packaging *are not minor*, if they bother the customer.

The most important task in hiring CSRs is to select individuals who fit in with the company's customer service culture and have a demonstrated skill and interest in working with the public. Companies look for a variety of character traits, abilities, and experience levels for customer service jobs. The profile for an exceptional CSR includes the following characteristics.

- **INITIATIVE** Takes the initiative to resolve issues before they become problems; ensures that customer needs are met
- **RESPONSIVENESS** Looks for speedy solutions to problems; goes the extra mile to please the customer; responds quickly and effectively
- **RELATIONSHIP BUILDING** Is friendly and courteous; easy to talk to; tactful and diplomatic; respectful and considerate
- **SENSITIVITY** Shows an understanding of and an interest in customers' needs and concerns

- **OBJECTIVITY** Is open-minded; is respectful to others; treats others equally and fairly; tolerates different points of view
- **RESISTANCE TO STRESS** Works effectively under stressful conditions; remains calm; copes well under pressure
- **RESILIENCE** Is open to criticism; feelings are not easily hurt; tolerates frustration well
- **PROBLEM SOLVING** Provides appropriate solutions to problems; capably handles customer requests; finds positive resolutions to problems
- **POSITIVE ATTITUDE** Is optimistic; maintains a cheerful attitude; looks for positive resolutions to problems

The Workplace Environment

Not too long ago, most customer service representatives worked at retail stores or corporate headquarters. Today, if you work in customer service, you might be located in a retail store or an office, but CSRs are just as likely to work at a remote call center, at a help desk for a computer software company, or for a web-based company. As the number of web-based companies grows almost daily, a need for more CSRs to professionally and accurately take orders, answer questions, handle complaints, and track customer information is growing steadily. You might be called by any of the following job titles: customer service representative, customer care representative, client services representative, customer service specialist, account manager, account service representative, call center representative, claims service representative, help-desk assistant, telesales representative, telemarketer, or by another job title.

A **call center** is a location where groups of people use telephones to provide service and support to customers. Increasingly, this area is also referred to as a contact center, because it uses more technologically sophisticated devices when interacting with customers. **Contact center** representatives don't only answer the phones; they also respond to customers' e-mail messages and participate in chat sessions via a chat room set up for the purpose of live customer interaction.

Focus on Career

Review the following job description for a Customer Service Manager. Then ask yourself, "Is a management position in my future?"

Manages multiple teams of customer service associates and coordinates a large segment of a customer service function. Responsible for staffing as well as CSR training and development. Establishes policies and procedures and monitors for compliance. Implements changes to enhance efficiency and high-quality customer interactions. Involves processes and procedures for fulfilling internal and external customer needs related to products and services offered through a multi-channel contact center environment. Monitors e-mail and call volume levels and trends in order to maximize efficiencies and makes recommendations for improvement. Performs all aspects of management including leadership, performance planning/evaluations, expense planning and control, initiating process improvements, and interacting with customers and associates at all levels. Ensures scheduling and forecasting are completed in a timely manner and schedules communicated to customer service representatives.

Call centers can be inbound, outbound, or both. That is to say, some call centers handle only inbound calls, such as customer orders and questions or complaints about service issues. Others are outbound centers, where CSRs call customers to promote products or services or to conduct polls about anything from product testing to opinions about recent purchases. Some call centers perform both inbound and outbound functions.

At a **help desk,** customer service representatives answer customer questions by phone, fax, e-mail, and the Internet. **Help desk software** automates the help desk and is available to assist CSRs in quickly finding answers to commonly asked questions about particular products and services. Typical functions of this software include call management, call tracking, knowledge management, problem resolution, and self-help capabilities.

The Customer Service Challenge

Customer service begins with putting the right people in place. Teaching customer service skills to employees who don't have a service-oriented attitude is difficult. As the workforce changes, identifying the specific skills employees need to learn about serving customers becomes more important. For instance, simple acts of kindness that we used to take for granted—such as smiling and saying "thank you"—may now have to be taught. A major challenge of customer service today is the shortage of customer-oriented employees.

An additional challenge most companies face is finding and training staff that can keep up with the technology in the industry. Consider the changes in technology that CSRs have seen in the past few years: e-mail, text-based Internet chatting (the ability to hold a real-time conversation over the web by typing back and forth), voice-over Internet protocol (the ability to have a real-time verbal conversation over the Internet), and push technology (the ability to send a specific image over the Internet directly to the customer's computer screen).

With the growth of the Internet and online companies, CSRs must be able to manage digital contacts effectively. Quick, accurate, and appropriate responses by e-mail that adequately address customer concerns can prevent the risk of losing customers to a competitor in seconds with just a few clicks of the mouse. If call center representatives aren't familiar or comfortable with instant messaging, chat rooms, and customer-friendly e-mail responses, they may be left behind in these critical skill areas.

Is it any wonder that customer service training— especially with the new generation of workers—is taking on greater importance? The new breed of CSR will need to be able to handle not only the latest technology, but also the most complex customer interactions— those requiring extensive problem-solving and negotiating skills. Making matters even more challenging, these CSRs will have to be able to communicate both verbally and in writing. Increasingly, companies are realizing that the most significant investment they can make is not in purchasing their databases or computer systems, but in making the best decisions when hiring their customer service staff. Moreover, once customer service representatives are hired, often the challenge is to keep them trained and ready to do their jobs in this technology-driven society.

Business in Action
T-MOBILE

When Sue Nokes joined T-Mobile as the Senior Vice President of Customer Service, the cell-phone company, based in Bellevue, WA, had a big problem. Lousy customer service was driving T-Mobile users crazy. When calling with a question or complaint, they were often placed on hold for what seemed like eons and then spoke with customer service reps who weren't very helpful. J. D. Power's customer-satisfaction surveys ranked T-Mobile dead last in the industry, trailing Verizon, Cingular, Nextel, and Sprint. Nokes launched a total overhaul. The first step was getting T-Mobile's human resources people and its marketing department to sit down and talk. The idea was to revamp the company's hiring practices, thus increasing the odds of picking customer service staffers willing and able to follow through on the marketing mavens' promises. Sounds like common sense, doesn't it? But surprisingly few companies do it.

Source: " For Happier Customers, Call HR," *Fortune* (November 28, 2005): 272.

CONCLUDING MESSAGE FOR CSRS

Marshall Field, founder of the Chicago-based department store Marshall Field and Company, said, "Those who come to me with a complaint teach me. Right or wrong, the customer is always right." He was saying that a complaint gives a service provider the chance to show just how good he or she can really be. Field wasn't saying that the customer is truly always right; some customers are very wrong. What Field meant was that, in dealing with complaints, you're dealing with people's perceptions. Although a customer's perception of a problem may be shortsighted or distorted, in the customer's eyes that perception is right. Most people who complain truly feel they have a legitimate concern.

A customer service representative is often the customer's first impression of the competence, quality, and tone of the company. The CSR serves as the company's first line of defense against an unhappy customer. Further, customers are more likely to listen to reason and to a different perspective of their problem if frontline providers have product knowledge, express understanding, and treat each customer as if he or she were unique. To a consumer, that human touch of being treated as a valued individual is often more important than price.

SUMMARY

- Customer service is the process of satisfying a customer relative to a product or service, in whatever way the customer defines his or her need, and then delivering that service with efficiency, understanding, and compassion.
- The power shift from companies to their customers underlies the new customer economy, in which the depth of relationships and loyalty to customers are critical to an organization's success.
- Regardless of the setting or job title, the customer service representative's duties are to answer questions, solve problems, take customers' orders, and resolve complaints.
- One of the most important tasks in hiring CSRs is selecting an individual who has a service-oriented attitude and a demonstrated skill and interest in working with the public. The new breed of CSR will need to be able to handle the latest technology and the most complex customer interactions—those requiring extensive problem-solving and negotiating skills.

KEY TERMS

call center
contact center
contact points

customer economy
customer profile
customer service
customer service representative (CSR)
customer-centric service
external customers
help desk
help desk software
internal customers
tiered service system

CRITICAL THINKING

1. Give two examples of a customer's concept of good customer service.

2. Why do organizations' mission statements for customer service differ from one another's?

3. In your opinion, which type of customer is more important in the long run to an organization— external or internal customers? Explain.

4. Describe the ways traditional customer service varies from exceptional customer service.

5. Name two advantages to organizations of providing customers with multichannel contact points.

6. If you owned your own business, would you provide your customers with a tiered service system? Why or why not?

7. List five critical skills and competencies a customer service representative must possess.

8. Of the various working environments presented in this chapter, which one would you prefer to work in and why?

ONLINE RESEARCH ACTIVITIES

HANDS-ON
PROJECTS

Project 1.1 Outstanding Customer Service

Assume you are doing a report on the top outstanding customer service organizations in the United States. Use the Internet to research and specifically locate the publications within the past six months from only .com domains. As a result of your search, outline three items (including the URLs) of current information you might use in your report.

Project 1.2 Customer Service Training Topics

Assume Mary Graeff, your supervisor at On-Time Technology Products (OTTP), has asked you to conduct online research to locate at least three outside sources that OTTP can use to provide training on customer service. Consider all types of training materials as possibilities. For example, consider videos on customer service, bringing in an outside consultant to train in-house, and subscribing to magazines that focus on customer service issues.

Use the information from this chapter to evaluate the information on each resource you discover. Fill in the table below with the data you collect.

Source or Website URL	Description of Training Topics	Cost	Advantages
1.			
2.			
3.			

Project 1.3 Customer Service Culture Task Force

Assume you have been asked to participate on a company task force with two co-workers at On-Time Technology Products. The three of you have been asked to come up with ways to improve the customer service culture at OTTP. Using the list of eight items from Figure 1.2 on page 8, prioritize and reach a consensus about the top five methods you feel would represent the approach your company should follow.

Working in small groups, discuss the issue, reach a consensus, and complete the table below.

Methods	Reasons for Supporting Each Method
1.	
2.	
3.	
4.	
5.	

HANDS-ON
PROJECTS

Project 1.4 Tiered Service—a New Approach

Collin MacGibson, President of On-Time Technology Products, recently returned from a Manufacturing Technology Conference in downtown Chicago. As a result of talking with leaders of other companies, he is now considering establishing a tiered service system, an idea he shared with Mary Graeff. Mr. MacGibson's basic thought is to reward the customers who give On-Time Technology Products $100,000 worth of business an end-of-year "thank you payment" that reflects a 5 percent discount on all yearly purchases. In addition, those customers would receive a commitment to next-day turnaround time on the resolution of all customer service problems. Moreover, the customers who purchase $500,000 or more annually would receive a 10 percent discount and a commitment to a four-hour resolution of customer service problems.

Prior to responding to Mr. MacGibson's idea, Ms. Graeff has asked you and the other five CSRs your opinion, because she has some customer service concerns about this new proposal.

1. As a CSR, what is your initial reaction to this new tiered service recommendation by Mr. MacGibson?

_____

_____

_____

2. What would be some advantages of going to a tiered service approach at On-Time Technology Products?

_____

_____

_____

3. What would be some disadvantages of going to a tiered service approach at On-Time Technology Products?

_____

_____

_____

HANDS-ON PROJECTS

Project 1.5 Customer Orders Are Perfect or They Don't Pay

Thunderbird Technology Products president, Darrell Williams, stormed out of his office and said, "Customers' orders are perfect or they don't pay." At first, those in earshot thought he must be kidding, but the seriousness with which he made that statement and his demeanor said differently. Give some thought to this pronouncement and be prepared to discuss the following three questions in a class discussion.

1. In your opinion, can a company literally afford to live by this statement? Why or why not?

2. Can you think of any situations in which an organization may have difficulty honoring such a customer pledge?

3. What are some hidden and actual benefits to the company of setting such a standard?

HANDS-ON PROJECTS

Project 1.6 Customer Service Job Description

Because sales have been increasing over the past few months, On-Time Technology Products is planning to advertise for an additional customer service representative position. As a result, your supervisor has asked you to review the following draft of a job description, which will be printed in the local newspaper early next week. Your opinion has been requested as to its wording and appropriateness in attracting the right applicants for a new CSR at OTTP.

We are currently seeking to hire a superior customer service representative. The ideal candidate must be familiar with technology and computers. In addition, a postsecondary degree or certificate in information technology is a plus. Those who apply should possess an enthusiastic personality, have excellent problem-solving skills, and work well under pressure. As part of the team, responsibilities involve dealing with customers over the phone, providing pricing, technical, and order-processing information. Strong communication and interpersonal skills are a must. Contact Ms. Graeff at (312) 555-0111 for more information.

1. What is your first reaction to the wording of this job announcement?

2. What recommendations to improve the intent and wording would you suggest?

2

COMMUNICATION ESSENTIALS

Objectives

- ◆ Explain each of the elements in the communication process.
- ◆ Identify the behaviors of people who communicate using different communication styles.
- ◆ Compose examples of open, probing, closed, alternative choice, leading, and direct questions.
- ◆ Understand the fundamentals of business writing.

Communication is important to business. Most people spend about 80 percent of their workday communicating— one-half is spent listening, the other half is spent reading, writing, and speaking. In every point of contact with customers, customer service representatives communicate something. As more contact is made with an organization, customers combine their perceptions into an overall impression of the company's customer service. The three basic purposes of business communication are to inform, persuade, and build goodwill. Any CSR who achieves these objectives is comfortable with the communication process.

THE BASICS OF COMMUNICATION

The truth is, great service requires great communication skills. Think of a time you experienced poor customer service. What made the service poor? Did a failure to communicate contribute to the problem?

- If you didn't get what you wanted, did you say so?
- If your expectations were not met, did you communicate that to the service provider?
- If you perceived that you were being treated rudely, did you discuss the service provider's behavior toward you?

As a working definition, we'll consider that **communication** has been successful if there is shared understanding between two or more persons. So what is the result of shared understanding? Put another way, what are the implications of a lack of shared understanding? To answer these questions, we must first have an understanding of communication fundamentals.

The Communication Process

Understanding the communication process can help CSRs become better communicators. The process shows that each communication event is unique—that one mind is different from another mind. Unless the words or other signals used to send a message have the same meaning or frame of reference, communication suffers in some way in the minds of the sender and receiver.

The human communication process follows this pattern: first, a message arrives from a sender, and the senses pick up the message through signals and relay it to the receiver's brain. This is called the **encoding process**. Next, the receiver's brain filters the message and gives it a unique meaning. The meaning triggers a response, and the receiver returns (by voice, writing, or gestures) the shared understanding of this message to the sender. This is the **decoding process**. Finally, a message transmitted back to the original sender is called **feedback**. This cycle may continue as long as the people involved want to communicate.

There are seven elements in the communication model: the sender, the receiver, a message, signals, the brain, shared understanding, and feedback.

1. *The sender.* The sender has an idea to share with another person. That idea is in the sender's mind and the goal is to get it into the receiver's mind.
2. *The receiver.* The receiver is the person or persons with whom the sender is trying to communicate. The receiver has the responsibility of hearing, listening, and providing feedback to the sender.

3. *A message.* The message is not just some words. The message is a combination of thoughts, feelings, words, and meanings.

4. *Signals.* Signals are the means by which the sender encodes a message and broadcasts it to the intended receivers. Signals include more than the sounds of words; they encompass feelings, attitudes, facial and body gestures, and the sender's unique personality traits.

5. *The brain.* All communication is filtered in the sender's and receiver's brains through personality, background, upbringing, culture, and current state of being. When a person is tired, stressed, or in an unpleasant circumstance, communication is that much harder.

6. *Shared understanding.* The degree to which a receiver understands what a sender is trying to communicate depends on many factors. How much alike are they? Do they share any background experiences? Are their language skills, attitudes, and beliefs similar? What assumptions have they made about each other based on stereotypes and previous perceptions?

7. *Feedback.* Feedback is the receiver's reaction sent back to the sender. Each of us has experienced from time to time the feeling, "He doesn't have a clue what I'm talking about." In most cases, we reach this conclusion by interpreting the verbal or nonverbal feedback the receiver is generating.

Communication theory attempts to explain what happens when we communicate successfully. Here is an example of when communication with a customer goes wrong: A company offers a high-quality product at a competitive price. Customer service policies and systems are flexible and user-friendly. Everyone in the organization knows the value of the customer, and all accept the philosophy that the "customer is king"—yet the customer, based on his or her perception, may still not be satisfied. Often, the problem is mixed messages.

Mixed Messages

A **mixed message** is a single communication that contains two meanings. One part of the message—usually the verbal part—is positive, while the other part of the message—usually the nonverbal component—contradicts the verbal portion and is negative. For example, a salesperson says, "Thank you" to a customer as she rings up the purchase, but does so in a hurried tone and with no eye contact. When the verbal portion and the nonverbal portion of a message contradict one another, the nonverbal portion is almost always believed. This is because nonverbal communication is perceived as less conscious, more honest, and harder for people to fake.

Mixed messages cloud the communication process.

Organizations unintentionally send hundreds of mixed messages to customers every day. One example is company policies that claim to be intended for the convenience and protection of the customer, that some customers feel are actually designed to make life easier for managers and their employees. Procedures that require customers to move from one workstation to another to get "taken care of " may provide assembly-line efficiency for the company, but what they communicate to the customer is quite different. When one person sees to our needs, it feels warm and caring. When we interact with many different people, we don't feel nurtured and "taken care of "; instead, we feel processed.

Service-Oriented Communication

What does service-oriented communication look and sound like? Think of a time when you felt you were the only customer the vendor had or when someone went the extra mile for you. In every story you can recall, think about the positive effect communication had when it was factored into the overall buying experience. Service-oriented communication takes on the following ten dimensions:

1. Listening skills that make the other person feel heard

2. Questions framed in a respectful manner

3. A willingness to perform the work needed to reach the desired goal

4. An ability to remain calm and centered, despite chaos or challenge

5. Flawless follow-up by taking full responsibility for bringing communication full-circle

6. A demonstrated understanding of the other person's perspective

7. An ability to anticipate the client's needs

8. A calm and pleasant tone of voice

9. Honest communication with good eye contact

10. Ease with admitting fault and a sincere desire to set right any misunderstanding

TIP

Seek to treat each customer fairly, demonstrate sound business practices, and resolve disputes using effective communication techniques.

CLOSE UP

Focus on Best Practices

The American Management Association® recognizes how hard it is to manage conflict in business so that it doesn't end up managing you. This professional organization offers communication training seminars around the country to improve a person's success in business.

A three-day seminar entitled "Responding to Conflict: Strategies for Improved Communication" is one such opportunity for business professionals who want to better their business communication skills. This seminar teaches participants to understand their own emotions and behaviors when addressing conflict and to find productive ways for managing it. When service professionals become aware of their emotional triggers to prevent explosive situations, they improve their communication performance and ultimately increase the success of customer interactions.

Source : www.amanet.org.

COMMUNICATION STYLES

Good communication skills—both verbal and written— require a high level of self-awareness. By becoming more aware of how others perceive you, you can adapt more readily to their different styles of communicating. This means that you can make another person more comfortable with you by selecting and emphasizing certain behaviors that fit your personality. The selection you make should help you respond naturally to another person's communication style. In business and in our personal lives, we encounter and practice three basic communication styles: aggressive, passive, and assertive.

Aggressive Communication

A person who has an **aggressive communication style** is closed-minded, listens poorly, has difficulty seeing another person's point of view, interrupts other people while they are talking, and tends to monopolize the conversation. Typically, an aggressive communicator feels he or she must win arguments and usually operates from a win or lose position.

Unfortunately, this communication style fosters resistance, defiance, and retaliation. It exacts a high price in personal and business relationships, especially when it comes to satisfying customers. Aggressive communicators express their thoughts and feelings in ways that violate or disregard the rights of others. They tend to

- humiliate and dominate others.
- make choices for others.
- show a lack of respect for others' rights.
- use sarcasm, insult others, and make unfair demands.

Passive Communication

People who communicate using a **passive communication style** tend to be indirect and hesitant to say what is really on their minds. By avoiding or ignoring problems, passive communicators are likely to agree externally, while disagreeing internally. They often feel powerless in confrontational situations because they don't like to make waves or upset anyone.

Passive communicators fail to express their feelings, thoughts, and beliefs, and so, typically give in to others. As a result, they allow others to make choices for them. In general, passive communicators

- believe that other people are more important or more correct than they are.
- are concerned that they will anger someone if they express their true feelings.
- beat around the bush when trying to make a point.
- say nothing is wrong and then become resentful about the situation later.

In this room, which participants are using aggressive, passive, or assertive communication styles?

Assertive Communication

A person who practices an **assertive communication style** tends to be an effective, active listener who states limits and expectations and does not label or judge people or events. By confronting problems at the time they happen, assertive communicators leave themselves open to negotiating, bargaining, and compromising in such a way that everyone involved wins.

The greatest advantage assertive communicators have is the ability to exercise their rights without denying the rights of others. Moreover, they express feelings honestly and directly, while practicing mutual respect for others. Assertive communicators state their message without being blunt or rude and consciously practice good eye contact, while using appropriate hand gestures and other suitable body language.

The assertive communication style is the one to strive for when serving customers. However, the reality is, very few people use only one communication style. In fact, the aggressive style is only essential when

- a decision has to be made quickly or during an emergency.
- you know you are right and that fact is crucial to the outcome for both parties.

The passive style also has its critical applications, such as when

- an issue arises that is much more important to the customer's happiness than to the business's. In this case, passive communication on the CSR's part may be the best option to keep the customer happy.
- emotions are running high, and it makes sense to take a break to calm down and regain perspective about the situation.

Refer to Figure 2–1 for more information about behavior and nonverbal and verbal cues of each communication style.

COMMUNICATING WITH CUSTOMERS IN PERSON

Telecommunications, computerization, and self-service have reduced person-to-person communication to minutes and sometimes seconds. For CSRs to provide superior customer service in this fast-paced, competitive business world, they must be able to gather information appropriately by asking and answering questions. When working with customers, how CSRs pose a question is often as important as what they ask.

Style	Behaviors	Nonverbal Cues	Verbal Cues
Aggressive	• Puts others down • Has a know-it-all attitude • Doesn't show appreciation • Is bossy	• Frowns • Squints eyes critically • Glares and stares • Is critical • Uses a loud tone of voice • Has rigid posture	• "You must (should, ought, or better)..." • "Don't ask why. Just do it."
Passive	• Sighs a lot • Clams up when feeling badly treated • Asks permission unnecessarily • Complains instead of taking action	• Fidgets • Smiles and nods in agreement • Has slumped posture • Speaks in a low volume • Is meek	• "You have more experience than I do." • "I don't think I can.." • "This is probably wrong, but." • "I'll try."
Assertive	• Operates from choice • Is action-oriented • Is realistic in expectations • Behaves in a fair, consistent manner • Is firm	• Has open, natural gestures • Uses direct eye contact • Has a confident, relaxed posture • Uses a varied rate of speech	• "I choose to..." • "What are my options?" • "What alternatives do we have?"

Figure 2–1 Communication Styles

Asking Questions

Time and again, customers call with questions. To answer customers' questions and address their needs, you should ask questions also. Typically, questioning others continues a discussion or pinpoints and clarifies issues when gathering pertinent information.

Asking a question skillfully increases the likelihood of quickly getting a good understanding of the issues. The person doing the questioning is usually in control of the discussion. Therefore, all questions should be asked in a positive way. A positive question is one that the customer is not afraid to answer. By rewording a "you" statement into an "I" statement, you can steer clear of questions that use sarcastic language or a threatening tone.

For example, avoid, "What exactly are you getting at?" or "Could you get to the point a little quicker?" and say instead "I don't understand what you are trying to tell me" or "Could you please try to explain it in a different way so I can understand better?"

Relative to questioning techniques, avoid bombarding the customer with questions or using a multiple-question approach when serving customers.

- *Bombardment approach.* Asks too many questions in a short period of time and puts customers on the defensive. This tactic controls the conversation but may limit the information gained. "Why" questions, if improperly asked, often cause individuals to become defensive.

- Multiple-question approach. Asks many questions wrapped up as one. When a question actually contains several questions, clients may get confused about which one to answer. In addition, individuals from non-Western cultures do not receive rapid-fire questions favorably, and this creates distrust.

To get the response you want, you need to know how to choose the appropriate type of question to ask. During the course of a normal conversation, you will be using all types of questions to gather a lot of data into information you can use. Depending on the situation, use an assortment of open, probing, closed, alternative choice, leading, and direct questions.

1. An **open question** requests information in a way that requires a fuller answer than a simple "yes" or "no." Open questions encourage an individual to talk and elicit maximum information to identify causes so you can work more quickly and effectively toward solutions. Open questions usually begin with action verbs or "How," "What," or "Why." As a result of asking open questions, CSRs are able to gain more information, which makes offering solutions or suggestions to customer problems much easier. Examples are, "Describe the kind of engine noise you are hearing," "How can I assist you?" and "What information were you given when you spoke with the CSR yesterday?"

2. A **probing question** uses information already established to clarify points and ask for more details. Often, these questions promptly follow up a previous question and response, for example, "Whom did you speak with yesterday?" "When did you purchase the product?" "Can you always be reached at this telephone number?" and "Tell me more about how you are feeling."

3. **Closed questions** usually elicit a "yes" or "no" answer. Closed questions can be useful in the concluding minutes of a customer conversation to confirm small details and to make sure that you have covered all the topics concerning the customer's query. These questions elicit specific information and usually begin with "Where," "Are," or "Do." Examples are, "Do you want these items delivered?" and "Are there other questions you have for me at this time?"

4. **Alternative choice questions** provide alternatives for the customer to choose from. These questions can be particularly useful when dealing with difficult customers. The approach is to ask customers what they would like you to do for them, but to limit their responses by providing them with two or three alternatives that also suit you. Examples are, "I could find this information for you and call you with an answer by the end of the morning, or would you prefer me to fax the information later in the day?" and "Would you like me to get our supervisor, or would you like to give me an opportunity to try to help first?"

5. **Leading questions** help speed up interactions with people who find it difficult to make a final decision, and they help the customer confirm information in an easy way. Some examples are, "You would like to receive the catalog updates on a monthly basis, then?" and "So, you would agree on a delivery this coming Thursday, if I can get you a discount?"

6. **Direct questions** can be open or closed; however, all direct questions have two characteristics in common: the name of the other person is always used, and the question is posed as an instruction. Examples are, "Tell me, Mr. Harkins, ... ," "Explain to me, Mr. Siskowski, ... ," and "Describe to me, Ms. Chada, ..." Using the other person's name puts you in a better position to get his or her immediate attention. In phrasing the question as an instruction ("Tell me, ..."), you are giving a subconscious order.

TIP   Don't answer your twentieth question of the day as if it were your twentieth question of the day. Instead, answer your twentieth question as if it were your first question. It may be the twentieth time you hear the same question, but keep in mind, it's probably the first time the customer has asked it.

Answering Questions

Answering customer questions effectively is equally important as asking the right questions. Here are several tips to consider before answering customer questions:

- Understand the question. Pay attention to every word the customer uses when asking a question. Once you understand the question, then respond.

- Decide whether you know the answer. If you are not sure that your response is accurate, do not answer. Although quick responses are preferred, providing correct information is always the first priority.

- Remember, you are an expert. As a CSR, you know your job better than anyone else. If you are certain you are right and you can back up your answer with facts, politely claim the truth of what you say. Again, do not promise something you cannot deliver.

- Take enough time. If a customer needs assistance, don't refuse to help because you are too busy. Also, do not pass the client from person to person.

- Smile. If you've got a cranky customer or one who insists you are not right, bend over backwards to make him or her happy. Be pleasant at all times when answering the customer's questions.

- Never answer a question with a question. Questions should be asked only to clarify the original question; beyond that—answer, don't ask.

- Be careful with your power. Never belittle a customer or criticize a question you receive. Don't say, "Can't you see the sign over the door that says ¼?" or "You mean you don't know?"

- When you don't know, admit it. If you are sure you don't know the answer to a question, say so. Admit you don't know, but make an effort to find someone who does.

Ethics / Choices

Assume you started a new customer service job and after a short time, determined that promising customers products that can't be guaranteed a reasonable delivery was standard procedure. Would you express your concerns or start thinking about finding another job? Explain.

Using Positive Language

Language is an exceedingly powerful tool. Whatever the method of communication, verbal or written, the way you express yourself affects whether the message is received positively or negatively. The impact of unpleasant news can be softened by the use of positive language. **Positive language** projects a helpful, encouraging feeling rather than a destructive, negative one.

No doubt you are familiar with "the cynic," the person who often criticizes ideas or provides reasons why something won't work. If you've ever worked or associated with such a person, you know that this kind of negative communication is very arduous. Additionally, the cynic's constant challenging creates a negative environment and increased confrontational situations.

People who are cynical don't always have negative attitudes. In many cases, they simply use language that gives the impression of negativity. They have not learned to phrase their comments in more constructive, positive ways. **Negative language** conveys a poor image to customers and may cause conflict and confrontation where none is necessary or desired. Its use should be avoided. Falling into the negative language pattern, however, is very easy, and many of us do so without being aware of it. Read the following dialogue that could take place at a business service counter:

> "We regret to inform you that we cannot process your application to register your business name because you have neglected to provide sufficient information. Please complete all sections of the attached form and return it to us promptly."

Note the high incidence of negative words—*cannot* and *neglected*. The message has a tone that suggests that the recipient is to blame for the problem. Contrast this example with the following rewritten, more positive approach:

> "Congratulations on your new business. To register your business name, we need some additional information. Please return the attached form, completing the highlighted areas, so we can send your business registration certificate within one week. We wish you success in your new endeavor."

Notice that the negative example tells the person what he or she has done wrong but doesn't stress the positive things that can be done to remedy the problem. The information is all there, but it sounds bureaucratic, cold, and negative. The positive example sounds completely different; although it contains a lot of the same information, it has a more upbeat and helpful tone. Negative language often has these characteristics:

- It tells the recipient what cannot be done.
- It has a subtle tone of blame.
- It includes words such as can't, won't, and unable to, which tell the recipient what the sender cannot do.
- It does not stress positive actions that would be appropriate.

Positive language displays these qualities:

- It tells the recipient what can be done.
- It suggests alternatives and choices available to the recipient.
- It sounds helpful and encouraging rather than bureaucratic.
- It stresses positive actions and consequences that can be anticipated.

The first task in moving toward more positive communication is to identify and eliminate common negative phrasing. Figure 2–2 lists some familiar expressions that should be avoided whenever possible in communicating with customers. Figure 2–3 offers some examples of conveying the same information with positive phrasing.

Handling Customer Requests

When handling customer requests, special service skills are sometimes required. The best response to a request is "yes," but sometimes "I'm not sure" cannot be avoided, or "no" is even required. Here's how to handle each circumstance:

SAYING "YES" Use a friendly voice tone, combined with positive, cheerful words. Clearly tell the customer what you can do for him or her.

SAYING "NO" Empathize with the customer and help if you can. Explain why you cannot complete the request. Choose words that are calming and soothing. When customers are distracted or emotionally upset, they may not hear what you intended to say, so make every effort to use positive, clear, effective phrases.

SAYING "I'M NOT SURE" Use this phrase when you are not sure if the request can be completed or what options you can offer, or if you don't have the authority to address the request.

 Use creative ways to say "no" to a customer. If you must use the word policy, do so only for matters of legal compliance, ethics, or absolute performance standards, such as employee or customer safety.

TIP

Expressions that suggest carelessness	• "You neglected to specify ..." • "You failed to include ..." • "You overlooked enclosing ..."
Phrases that suggest the person is lying	• "You claim that ..." • "You say that ..." • "You state that..."
Expressions that imply that the recipient is not too bright	• "We cannot see how you ..." • "We fail to understand ..." • "We are at a loss to know..."
Demanding phrases that imply coercion and pressure	• "You should ..." • "We must ask you to ..." • "We must insist that you ..."
Phrases that might be interpreted as sarcastic or patronizing	• "No doubt ..." • "We will thank you to ..." • "You understand, of course, ..."

Figure 2–2 Common Negative Language

• "If you can send us your bill of sale, we will be happy to complete the process for you."

• "The information we have suggests that you have a different viewpoint on this issue. Let me explain our perspective."

• "Might we suggest that you ... [suggestion]."

• "One option open to you is ... [option]."

Figure 2–3 Examples of Positive Phrasing

Sensitive Issues

In the rush of doing our jobs, we sometimes forget that we are not merely serving customers; we are in the business of serving people who have real lives and experiences. When individuals approach us for assistance, we see only a snippet of their existence. We have no way of knowing what challenges or crises they are quietly coping with as they approach us. Providing rude or apathetic service is always bad business, but to provide it to a person who is suffering mental or physical pain is simply bad human behavior.

When serving others, it is safe to assume that some of the customers you encounter on most days are undergoing personal distress. Who these people are or what crises they face will likely never be revealed, but rest assured, your actions will make a positive or negative impact on their outlook for the day. The following are some sobering statistics about various crises people (customers) in America face every day. For each situation, reflect and then ask yourself how you will treat these people when they come to you for service.

- *Death of a loved one.* Each day in America, more than 6,500 people die, and many customers walking around today are dealing with shocking news about the death of a loved one.
- *Suicide.* Today, more than 90 people will take their own lives, and another 1,350 will attempt suicide. This means that sometime today, many CSRs unknowingly have the opportunity to convince these people they are valuable human beings.
- *Divorce.* Today, 3,440 spouses will be served with papers for divorce. For many of them, this will be a surprise causing absolute devastation.
- *Missing children.* Today, more than 2,000 children will be listed as missing. How will you treat their parents when they come to you for service?
- *Death of pet.* Today, more than 16,000 faithful house pets—dogs and cats with an average age of ten years— will die. Losing a loving pet saddens us greatly.
- *Loss of job.* Today, more than 7,000 people will be laid off, fired, or otherwise removed from their jobs. How will you treat these people when they come to you for service?1

Ethics / Choices

How would you react if a customer began talking to you about a faulty product, and suddenly her eyes filled with tears and she was unable to continue?

FUNDAMENTALS OF BUSINESS WRITING

From simple e-mails to formal customer letters, CSRs will need to compose documents that educate, persuade, inform, or enlighten the customer. Writing is an essential element of business communication. The ability to write effectively is a skill you learn; it comes naturally to only a few gifted individuals.

Business writing experts say that the most important strategy behind good written communication is to be clear. Striving for clarity is important, even if the subject is difficult. It is much better to be as honest as you can be, within whatever limits are set by your work, rather than to write around the problem. Second to clarity is the skillful and professional presentation of the written communication. Presentation reflects your company's professionalism, quality, and reputation. The costs of sloppy and poorly written documents with spelling or grammatical errors can be staggering to organizations.

TIP When writing to customers, some important books to have on hand are a good dictionary, a thesaurus, and one or two office handbooks. These reference books are also available in electronic form, either online or as part of a complete word-processing software package, such as Microsoft® Word.

Identify the Audience

Clear writing is essential if you want your message to be understood by the recipient; what makes writing clear will vary and is ultimately dependent on your target audience. Before you write, it is critical to understand whom you are addressing.

When conveying information, put yourself in your audience's shoes. What is important to them? How can you make sure that what you have to say becomes important to the reader? Answering these questions takes an awareness of your audience and an understanding of how people best receive messages. The vocabulary you use and the organizational structure you give the piece of writing depend on whom you are addressing and what your message is.

Write Clearly with a Purpose in Mind

Before writing the first sentence, decide what the message should be. Are you conveying information to an upset customer? Are you following up with a customer to clarify issues from a recent phone conversation? Do you want your reader to *do* something when he or she finishes reading your message? If you aren't sure what your purpose is, your reader won't be either. If you want your reader to take some type of action, clearly state the benefits *he or she* will receive by doing what you ask in terms that are meaningful to this person.

Because most people today spend little time reading, they want the whole picture in concise, easy-to-understand, and grammatically correct language. At the heart of effective writing is the ability to organize a series of thoughts. Once you've identified your true objective, take the time to list and prioritize the key points you want to make supporting that purpose. For some, an outline works best, because it allows writers to visualize their thought processes on paper and in some detail. For others, the best ideas come from using the creative approach of simply jotting down ideas as they brainstorm the major elements of the message they want to convey.

Get to the point by presenting your primary message or call to action as quickly as possible. Few busy people today have the time or patience to wade through long introductory paragraphs before coming to the point of a document. Provide just enough information to capture readers' attention and let them know what is being asked of them.

Use the Proper Tone

Tone is present in all communication activities. The overall tone of a written message affects the reader, just as one's tone of voice in oral exchanges affects the listener. **Tone** refers to the writer's attitude toward the reader and the subject of the message.

BE CONFIDENT Careful preparation and knowledge about the ideas you wish to express instill confidence.

BE COURTEOUS AND SINCERE A writer builds goodwill by using a tone that is polite and sincere. Be respectful and honest, and readers will be more willing to accept your message, even if it is negative.

USE NONDISCRIMINATORY LANGUAGE Nondiscriminatory language addresses all people equally and expresses respect for all individuals. It does not use any discriminatory words, remarks, or ideas.

STRESS THE BENEFITS FOR THE READER A reader will want to know, " What's in it for me?" Your job is to write from the reader's perspective, or with a "you" attitude. It's better to say, "Your order will be available in two weeks" than "I am processing your order tomorrow."

Business in action

TEXT ALERTS

On the edge of a new kind of communication, some innovative companies are providing a text-messaging service to their customers. For example, customers can sign up to receive up-to-date information about their auto insurance policies or banking transactions through text messages sent directly to their cell phones. If they would like, customers can also sign up to receive payment reminders, payment confirmations, and other account information. The beauty of this communication method is that customers get the information instantly, without having to be connected to their e-mail.

CONCLUDING MESSAGE FOR CSRs

How important is practicing good communication skills with customers? More customers leave one company for another because of poor customer service than dissatisfaction with a product. A lost customer is never just one lost sale, or even just one lost customer, but a chain of events that has an impact on a large scale.

One unhappy customer talks to someone who may have been a satisfied customer, but now is not so sure, and so on. Keep in mind that it doesn't matter whether customers are right or wrong; what matters is how they feel when they leave an interaction or a conversation with you, the representative for a company. Before ending an interaction with a customer, always ask, "Is there anything else I can do for you? If you need me, you can reach me by...."

Summary

- The seven elements in the communication process are the sender, the receiver, a message, signals, the brain, shared understanding, and feedback.
- Communication styles vary and include aggressive, passive, and assertive.
- When clarifying issues with customers, consider the information you want to get and choose from among the six types of questions: open, probing, closed, alternative choice, leading, or direct.
- In written communication, understand whom you are addressing, what you want your message to accomplish, and how to incorporate the right tone for the message.

KEY TERMS

aggressive communication style
alternative choice questions
assertive communication style
closed questions
communication
decoding process
direct questions
encoding process
feedback
leading questions
mixed message
negative language
open question
passive communication style

positive language
positive question
probing question
tone

CRITICAL THINKING

1. Recount two situations you participated in or observed this past week in which mixed messages were sent.

2. Describe the behaviors of a person you know who predominately uses a passive communication style; an aggressive communication style; an assertive communication style.

3. Assume that a customer returns an article of clothing or a household item for a refund or credit. Develop six queries a CSR might use in this situation that make use of each type of question: open, probing, closed, alternative choice, leading, and direct.

4. Describe your reaction to a personal or business letter you've received recently that you perceived as having an inappropriate tone. How did it make you feel?

ON LINE RESEARCH ACTIVITIES

HANDS-ON PROJECTS

Project 2–1 Communication Styles

Research a number of websites and locate several articles on communication styles in a working environment. As a result of your research, prepare a short oral presentation (ten minutes or less) entitled "The Impact of Communication Styles on Customer Service," as directed by your instructor.

HANDS-ON PROJECTS

Project 2–2 Popular Word-Processing Features

On-Time Technology Products is in the process of revising its correspondence manual in the Customer Service Department. Mary Graeff has decided to incorporate the use of many of the electronic writing tools in word-processing software packages in revising the current manual.

Go to the websites of Microsoft and Corel® that sell the popular word-processing packages, Microsoft Word and Corel WordPerfect®. In the table below, compare the features listed for each package. If possible, also locate online a consumer report comparing the two packages feature by feature.

Feature	Microsoft Word	Corel WordPerfect
Templates and wizards		
AutoCorrect		
AutoFormat		
Spelling and grammar check		
Research tool		
Mail merge		
Thesaurus		

HANDS-ON PROJECTS

Project 2–3 Language That Makes a Difference

Brainstorm with other students to provide more appropriate responses to each of the negative language statements shown here. *Hint:* Use "I" statements rather than "you" statements.

1. "You didn't do this right."

_____

_____

_____

2. "You are wrong."

_____

_____

_____

3. "Wait here."

_____

_____

_____

4. "It's not my job."

_____

_____

_____

5. "What's your problem?"

_____

_____

_____

6. "You aren't making any sense."

_____

_____

_____

7. "Why are you so upset?"

_____

_____

_____

Project 2–4 The New CSR—Temporary Hire

A temporary, six-month CSR position has just been filled at On-Time Technology Products. The new hire is Abhey Patel, a very nice and bright person, who everyone agrees works extremely hard. Abhey has recently established citizenship in America from his homeland, India. Realizing the need to write to customers using proper English and grammar, the other CSRs have been covering for Abhey, doing his letter writing and e-mail messaging for him. He is trying very hard to learn English, but he hasn't mastered all the fine points yet.

Respond to these questions regarding Abhey's situation:

1. Can you think of ways to help Abhey complete his duties on his own more easily?

_____

_____

_____

2. Do you feel that the supervisor should be informed that Abhey has not yet developed his business writing skills and that others are doing his work for him? Is this practice of covering for Abhey hurting anyone or OTTP?

_____

_____

_____

Project 2–5 "I'll Take That Customer!"

Neal Erwin has a reputation he has always been proud of in the Haskin's Bookstore customer service department. He takes calls from customers that others don't want to deal with. Sometimes when he is on the phone with a customer, he asks coworkers to come near his desk to hear his side of the argument. In the past, he has gotten loud and belligerent with customers and later has even boasted of "winning." Things have changed, however, and Neal is now in trouble with management because of a recent incident.

A loyal 20-year customer, who spoke to Neal last week, has just left the store and expressed in no uncertain terms that she was taking her business elsewhere.

1. In your opinion, should Neal have been allowed to get away with his behavior to customers? Explain.

_____

_____

_____

2. As a coworker of Neal's, would you have any responsibility to report his aggressive communication style to his supervisor?

_____

_____

_____

Project 2–6 "I Understand How You Might Feel That Way"

Doug went into work this morning at On-Time Technology Products and casually mentioned to his fellow CSRs that his wife had just been to a communications in-service training for her company, where she learned the "feel, felt, found" technique for responding to customer questions and concerns. Doug wasn't sure how using this technique would work at OTTP, but he thought it was worth discussing with his coworkers.

According to what Doug's wife told him, the technique works this way: when a customer expresses a concern, the CSR should respond by saying, "I understand how you might feel that way. Others have *felt* that that way too. Then they *found,* after an explanation, that this policy protects them, so it made sense."

1. What is your first reaction to communicating with customers using the "feel, felt, found" approach?

_____

_____

_____

2. How extensively do you think it could be applied to most customer problems and concerns?

_____

_____

_____

3. Identify and discuss with fellow students situations when it would not be advisable to use this approach with customers.

_____

_____

_____

3

NONVERBAL COMMUNICATION, DRESS, AND MANNERS

Objectives

◆ Understand the elements and interpretations of body language.

◆ Recognize the importance of having a dress code in the workplace.

◆ Cite examples of business etiquette and manners.

Stop slouching and sit up straight. Stand with your back flat, your shoulders back, your head held high, and your feet planted firmly on the floor." How many times have you heard this from someone—most likely your mother— over the years? Showcasing our intelligence and professional abilities is as much about presentation, including body language, dress, and manners, as about verbal communication.

Sensing people's needs through nonverbal communication is important, because valuable information can be gained about your customer's state of mind by paying attention to what you see and hear. Customers are also able to read your responses to them by observing your nonverbal signals. Understanding body language in the workplace isn't trivial—it's a career necessity.

CUSTOMER-FRIENDLY BODY LANGUAGE

When we communicate, we send nonverbal messages, called **body language,** that include tone of voice, eye movement, posture, hand gestures, facial expressions, and more. Body language is the oldest and most genuine means of communication in the world. Learning to interpret it will give you a big advantage in all communications. To really understand the full meaning of a message, pay special attention to a person's body language, because nonverbal cues are more immediate, instinctive, and uncontrolled than verbal expressions. They bring attitudes and feelings out into the open.

Clues about a person's character come through in the quality of that person's voice and the expression on his or her face, as well as through posture and hand gestures. However, even though these behaviors are important, they can be interpreted differently from culture to culture.

The Importance of Body Language

Customer service often comes down to one person doing something for another person. One study concluded that when companies lose customers to their competition, 67 percent of the time, it happens because of one incident with one employee. Every contact contributes to customers' impressions of a company. Therefore, each employee's communication skills contribute significantly to those impressions.

Without realizing it, we frequently send messages to customers with posture, facial expression, tone of voice, gestures, and eye contact. Body language communicates our attitudes to customers, and it can either reinforce or contradict our words. Understanding body language can help us strengthen our own verbal messages as well as understand our customers' messages better.

Nonverbal signals constitute a silent language that has about four and a half times the effect of spoken words. Linguists who study the nonverbal elements of a conversation have concluded that these silent elements make up 55 percent of a message, and tone of voice contributes another 38 percent, leaving 7 percent for the words we use.[1] The net result, therefore, is that up to 93 percent of every conversation is interpreted through body language. We react more to what we think someone meant than to the words he or she actually said. For example, you may tell a customer that you are happy to help her, but if you frown, slump, or refuse to make eye contact, the customer, in most cases, will not believe you. This is because people are more likely to believe nonverbal signals, such as a frown, than words.

Because body language is a crucial communication tool for delivering great customer service, Figure 3–1 describes several body language signs and their possible meanings.

---

[1]Carol Smith, "Face to Face with Customers," *Professional Builder* (June 2001): 20.

Nonverbal Behavior	Interpretation
Brisk, erect walk	Confidence
Standing with hands on hips	Readiness, aggression
Arms crossed over chest	Defensiveness
Walking with hands in pockets, shoulders hunched	Dejection
Putting hand to cheek	Evaluation, thinking
Touching, slightly rubbing nose	Rejection, doubt, lying
Rubbing the eye	Doubt, disbelief
Clasping hands behind back	Anger, frustration, apprehension
Resting head in hand, eyes downcast	Boredom
Rubbing hands	Anticipation
Gesturing with open palm	Sincerity, openness, innocence
Pinching bridge of nose, eyes closed	Negative evaluation
Tapping or drumming fingers	Impatience
Steepling fingers	Authoritative
Tilting head	Interest
Stroking chin	Trying to make a decision
Looking down, face turned away	Disbelief
Biting nails	Insecurity, nervousness
Pulling or tugging at ear	Indecision

Figure 3–1 Body Language

Ethics / Choices

A manager says he is very interested in receiving suggestions from you; however, while you try to outline an idea for reducing copier costs, he reads his mail and accepts incoming phone calls. How would you handle this situation? How would this exchange make you feel?

Interpreting Body Signs

Besides communicating an attitude of caring and cooperation, body language conveys professional stature and self-confidence. Listeners consider those who speak with conviction in a calm voice to be competent and trustworthy. The major elements of body language include eye contact, tone of voice, smiling, posture, and gestures.

EYE CONTACT The eyes communicate more than any other part of the human anatomy. For example, staring or gazing at others can create pressure and tension. Rolling your eyes sends the message that you aren't taking the other person's ideas seriously. Shifty eyes and too much blinking can suggest deception, whereas people with eye movements that show they are relaxed and comfortable, yet attentive to the person they are conversing with, are seen as more sincere and honest. Because of increasing diversity in the marketplace, you may encounter customers from other cultures in which direct eye contact is considered offensive. Be sensitive and take your cue from the customer.

TONE OF VOICE You may have noticed that you can "hear" a smile on the phone. The muscles that form your smile also cause your vocal cords to produce a warmer sound. Your tone of voice can sound either interested and caring, or aggressive. Interested and caring works best for most customer situations. Notice the tone of voice others use and the feelings created in you in response. Tone of voice is especially important on the phone, when visual cues are missing from the conversation.

SMILING Show customers you enjoy helping them by smiling at appropriate times. If you smile even when you are not feeling your best, your own brain does not distinguish the difference and sends signals that you are happy. The result can be that you cheer up yourself—and the customer.

POSTURE Slouching and leaning postures send the message, "I'm tired, bored, or uninterested in your concerns." A military stance is unnecessary, but an alert posture reinforces the customer's feeling that you are interested in helping.

GESTURES Gesturing, especially during tense conversations, can mean the difference between sending a message of trust and cooperation and one of suspicion. Placing your hands on your hips typically conveys annoyance. Crossing your arms over your chest suggests distrust. Slamming something down abruptly indicates you are angry.

By paying careful attention to body language and noticing when someone makes a sudden transition from one attitude to another, you'll have a good idea of what the other person is thinking—whether or not that is what he or she is saying. When serving customers, remember these four typical interpretations of noteworthy body language cues:

1. Openness and warmth: open-lipped smiling, open hands with palms visible

2. Confidence: leaning forward in the chair, keeping the chin up, putting the tips of the fingers of one hand against the tips of the fingers of the other hand in a "praying," or "steepling," position

3. Nervousness: smoking, whistling, fidgeting, jiggling pocket contents, clearing the throat, running fingers through the hair, wringing hands, biting on pens or other objects, twiddling thumbs

4. Untrustworthiness or defensiveness: frowning, squinting, tight-lipped grinning, crossing arms in front of the chest, darting eyes, looking down when speaking, clenching hands, pointing with the fingers, rubbing the back of the neck

Understanding other people's body language is not enough—controlling your own non-verbal signals can improve your image and increase your success. If you want to appear confident, open, and in control, then practice the following moves in front of a mirror until they become second nature:

- Walk with a brisk, easy stride and with eyes looking forward.
- Stand evenly on both feet. Keep your arms relaxed and casual. For example, keep one hand in your pocket and use the other one for gesturing as you speak.
- Move slightly closer to others if you want to warm up the relationship. Avoid hostile postures, such as hands on your hips or clasped behind your head. Also avoid defensive gestures, such as turning your body away from the listener or keeping your arms folded over your chest.
- Look at others straight on. Meet their eyes and then occasionally let your gaze drift elsewhere to keep from staring.
- Keep your gestures loose, yet controlled. If those around you seem reserved or nervous, avoid excessively exuberant or frantic movements.

 ## DRESSING TO MAKE A GOOD IMPRESSION

Most of us have heard the expressions, "There's never a second chance to make a first impression," and "First impressions are lasting ones." Whether interacting with fellow employees on the job or meeting with customers, your attire, behavior, and attitude say a lot about you. Those who wish to move ahead in their careers must think carefully about what they wear. Clothing choices can help or hinder those goals.

Workers today don't dress as formally as they once did, yet the concept of dressing for success is just as relevant given the competitiveness of today's workplace. Knowledge and skills are instrumental, but image and appearance still continue to be key factors in moving into better jobs. To achieve success, you must look successful by presenting an image of competency, self-confidence, and professionalism.

focus on Best Practices

Many corporations and industries around the country are passing employee dress codes that ban formfitting, revealing, or ripped and faded clothing. In addition, no body-piercing jewelry, other than on the ears, can be visible at work, and displaying tattoos is prohibited. Employees who don't follow the dress code are being sent home and are not paid for time away from work.

Many workers feel these policies are too strict; however, the majority of people who work full time in an office setting have a dress code, according to a BizRate Research study, with only 26 percent allowed to wear casual work attire. The majority—64 percent—work under a business casual dress requirement.

Dress Code

Whereas employees have to deal with the decision of what to wear to work every day, employers must decide what parameters to put on that decision and how to enforce those guidelines. A generation ago, most professional workers were expected to dress up for work, wearing business suits that demonstrated their conformity with corporate America. Today, most workplaces allow business casual dress, a more relaxed look. This allows workers to express their individuality—and therein lies the problem. What happens when a worker's choices do not conform to the image that the employer wants to project?

Ideally, each company has developed a written description of the types of clothing that are acceptable. Some companies seek legal counsel to ensure that their policies do not discriminate against men or women and that the wording is explicit. By using common sense and exercising good judgment, dressing to make a good impression is easy. Following is a list of suggested dress-for-success guidelines in business today:

- Hair. Your hairstyle should be neat, and your hair color should be natural looking and complementary to your complexion.
- Nails. Long, elaborately decorated nails may be frowned upon in many companies. Short, clean nails in a French manicure or one-tone polish (light pink or earth tones) are always stylish. For men and women, clean and cared-for nails send a positive message to customers.
- Makeup. Your makeup should be subtle and paired to your overall look. Choose shades that are natural and flattering to your complexion.
- Dress. Your clothes should not be too short, too formfitting, or too revealing in the office—that could send a message that you are not serious about your job.

- Footwear. Shoes should be polished and not rundown. Stockings and socks should be traditional and in shades that are compatible to your outfit or your skin tone.

- Jewelry and accessories. Jewelry should always be kept to a minimum in the office. Avoid facial jewelry. Nose jewelry, lip jewelry, or studs in the tongue or eyebrows are generally inappropriate in most businesses. Invest in fun accessories that showcase your individuality. Colorful silk scarves, pins, and bracelets can add a touch of individuality and interest to your wardrobe. Men can select vibrant ties, if the occasion calls for one.

- Perfume and cologne. Use discretion and taste in choosing office scents. Fragrances can linger in a closed office and seem stronger to others than you believe they are. Some people are chemically sensitive to perfume and cologne, and more and more places of business are discouraging their use.

Ethics / Choices

Bonnie, a 19-year-old new hire and community college student, stormed out of the customer service manager's office and belligerently said for all to hear, "She can't tell me what to wear! This is America and I'll wear what I want to work!" In your opinion, is this type of thinking by workers unique to Bonnie, or is this attitude becoming the routine in today's workplace? Discuss.

The Business Attire Issue

It is important to get a clear idea about what is acceptable apparel from your employer. Your choice of work clothes sends a strong nonverbal message about you and can affect the way you work. That's why many employers have mixed feelings about the current trend toward casual business attire.

If CSRs deal extensively with the public, it is fitting for organizations to require certain standards of appearance. If, on the other hand, CSRs have no contact with the public, as in a telemarketing environment, then wearing more casual clothes seems more acceptable. When deciding whether a dress code is appropriate and what it should be, most organizations take into consideration the following three factors:

1. The business's public image

2. The nature of the work performed by the employees affected by the dress code

3. Safety standards

Some employers oppose casual dress because, in their opinion, too many workers push the boundaries of what is acceptable. They contend that absenteeism, tardiness, and flirtatious behavior have increased since dress-down policies began to be adopted. Moreover, and perhaps more important, they feel that casually attired employees turn off some customers.

Regardless of what critics say, employees generally love casual-dress policies. Supporters argue that comfortable clothes and a more relaxed working environment lift employee morale, increase employee creativity, and improve internal communication. Employees also appreciate reduced clothing-related expenses.

The popularity of casual days is increasing in corporate America. Still, among those companies that allow casual dress, there is a need to have some type of appearance standards, as covered earlier. In most companies, employees should go to work well groomed and dressed for a professional work environment. Clothing such as casual shorts, sandals, T-shirts, jeans, and sneakers is not appropriate.

Your industry, age, geographical location, position in the corporate hierarchy, and personality will contribute to determining what is appropriate dress. Regardless of how informal the outfit, clothes should always be clean and pressed, stain- and odor-free, and not ripped, torn, or frayed.

If first impressions count, which CSR would you prefer assist you?

Respect is at the heart of good manners. All good manners are based on thoughtfulness for others and respect for them as individuals of equal value.

TIP

PRACTICING BUSINESS ETIQUETTE AND MANNERS

In the United States, we live in a business casual world, but many people forget the first word is still business. As such, we have to mind our manners. Having good manners will help you regardless of the business you are in. Any time you make contact with a customer, you are making a mini-presentation of yourself, ultimately representing your company, service, and products.

Proper business etiquette goes beyond using the right fork at a lunch meeting, to include developing effective people skills. By definition, **business etiquette** dictates the rules of acceptable behavior that identify the application of correct or polite manners in a general business situation. Considering the welfare of others is all part of having good business manners—a practice that many experts say is missing in the American workforce.

The rules of etiquette can be compared to a common language that all successful professionals must learn to speak. People make choices in the business arena, and they choose to do business with people they like and respect. Etiquette skills can help establish productive relationships with colleagues and clients. Successful relationships begin when you exhibit courtesy, respect, and concern for the comfort of others. Better relationships mean better business.

Practicing good manners makes life more enjoyable for everyone because of the courtesy and respect shown to one another. In today's stress-filled world, coupled with the ups and downs inherent in everyday life, experiencing day-to-day pleasantries is very nice. Good manners are said to be two-thirds common sense and one-third kindness. Experiencing a moment of pleasant kindness can be uplifting. Respecting others is truly empowering as well.

No matter how tired you might be or how abrasive a customer might become, service professionals must practice good manners. An environment in which people treat each other with kindness and consideration is certainly one in which a client enjoys doing business. Learning the rules of business etiquette is not hard to do or costly, and it is the best professional development tool business persons can use to increase their chances of success.

Employers value well-mannered employees because they are a reflection of the company itself. Do people really notice good manners? Even though lifestyles are more informal and relaxed in today's society, good manners are appreciated. Using polite language, turning off cell phones, holding the door, sending a thank you note, offering a smile—these are just a few favors people appreciate. Saying "please" and "thank you," warmly greeting customers and coworkers, and showing patience are essential skills for anyone's success.

A smile seems very simple, but it's amazing how people's moods and words are misjudged because their expressions are often overly serious. A smile shows that you like yourself; you like your current place in the world; and you're happy with the people you're interacting with. A smile says, "I'm approachable and confident."

Some may ask whether **soft skills** like punctuality, positive attitude, and cooperation are more important than knowing how to perform a job. These soft skills, also referred to as people skills, are just as important because they help you become successful. A dependable worker will most likely be given more responsibility, advancements, and pay increases over an undependable coworker. Employees who practice the soft skills of business etiquette and manners will have the ability and confidence to make a better impression. People who display refinement make better impressions, and others want to be around them. Customers do business with people they like; it's that simple.

People with good attitudes usually respect their coworkers, accept responsibility, and accomplish more each day. Your attitude is evident in your body language, the way you complete tasks, your attention to detail, your consideration of those around you, the way you take care of yourself, and your general approach to life. Good manners, attitude, and self-discipline work together to make good things happen for customer service representatives.

Understanding the use of good manners helps you relax and feel confident and capable in your job. Practicing them allows you to appear comfortable and competent to others and builds self-respect in the process. According to a survey conducted by Eticon, a South Carolina–based consulting firm specializing in business etiquette, lack of proper etiquette can have a major negative impact on business. Fifty-eight percent of respondents say they react to rudeness by taking their business elsewhere.[2]

Business in Action
UNIFORMS

Some symbols are world famous, others are less well known. This is also true for the image uniform. When it comes to having a positive corporate identity, employees in distinctive uniforms can be a surprisingly powerful symbol. Companis increasingly understand that public perception of employees is vital to creating and maintaining customer trust. An instantly recognized corporate appearance can result in a competitive edge, so essential in today's marketplace.

There are many advantages to corporate attire. Uniforms project a consistent and unified image for companies that regularly interact with the public, and they allow customers to quickly identify employees for assistance. They permit employers to control the appropriateness and condition of the clothes worn by the employees, who are not required to buy, clean, or repair their own clothing.

An estimated 32 million people in the United States go to work each day wearing a uniform. They are worn by employees in fast-food restaurants, hotels, and major retail stores, such as Target®, Home Depot®, and Wal-Mart®. While uniforms have traditionally been associated with single-color shirts and pants, companies can generally select whatever they choose for their employees. Garments such as aprons or vests promote a more consistent corporate image without requiring each person to be outfitted in the same clothes.

---

[2]Andrea C. Poe, "Mind Their Manners," *HR Magazine* (May 2001): 40.

CONCLUDING MESSAGE FOR CSRs

Customer service representatives should be aware of the impact of their body language on others. To become customer-friendly communicators, CSRs must interpret nonverbal signals from others and become cognizant of their own nonverbal cues. Your total communication— body language, tone of voice, and word choice—helps you deal with each customer situation. As important as your verbal and nonverbal responses to your customers are, don't overlook other important components: dressing appropriately and practicing business etiquette and manners with customers of all types. Behaviors that go against kindness, logic, and efficiency get in the way of good business.

SUMMARY

- Total communication involves sending nonverbal signals, called body language, which include tone of voice, eye movement, posture, hand gestures, and facial expressions. Using appropriate body language is critical when dealing with customers.
- Dressing appropriately and being well groomed make a statement about you and your employer.
- Good manners contribute to a positive first and lasting impression in social and business situations, as well as give you a favorable reputation.

KEY TERMS

body language
business etiquette
soft skills

CRITICAL THINKING

1. Of all the elements that constitute body language, which three would you describe as the most important when serving customers? Explain.

2. If one customer expressed confidence and another expressed nervousness, what types of body language signals would you look for in each instance?

3. In your opinion, what societal factors make it difficult for organizations to establish a proper dress code in today's workplace?

4. When shopping in a retail store, how important is it for service professionals to practice good business etiquette and manners? Explain.

ONLINE RESEARCH ACTIVITIES

Project 3–1 Writing a Dress Code

Research a number of websites and locate several articles featuring appropriate dress for the workplace. Suggested magazines to research include Working Woman, Ebony, and HR Magazine. As a result of your research, develop a simple dress code that would be appropriate in the banking and financial industry. Might this dress code be different for a fast-food worker than for a telemarketing CSR? Explain.

Project 3–2 Soft Skills

Research a career exploration website or a number of websites for large corporations, and locate several job descriptions for customer service representatives and other administrative services positions that have been posted within the last 30 days in a major city near you. Pay particular attention to the descriptions that request soft skills, such as punctuality, positive attitude, willingness to learn, and cooperation.

As a result of your research, prepare a simple poster of the printouts of job descriptions you were able to locate, and highlight the soft skills that are mentioned. Present your poster findings to your class, as directed by your instructor.

Project 3–3 Good Manners Strategies

Manners are being taught less and less. Supporters of this statement believe that knowing and practicing good manners is not a matter of vanity, snobbery, or trying to impress, but simply a matter of being kind and sensitive to the needs of others. The use of good manners creates a considerate, gracious, and respectful atmosphere in which to live and work.

Form a discussion group and discuss some strategies for dealing and communicating with persons who do not use good manners when interacting with others. Report back to your class on the top three strategies your group came up with.

Project 3–4 Manners and Business Etiquette

While eating lunch at the food court in the mall, Keanna, a CSR at a retail store within the mall, witnessed a customer service incident in action. A woman approached the counter with a crushed Styrofoam cup and said, "This cup fell off our table and broke. I need another drink and I need someone to come clean up our table and the floor." The tone of her voice suggested that somehow the restaurant was responsible for her broken cup. At that point, Keanna noticed that the staff quickly gave her a new drink. Then the manager appeared with a smile and said, "I would be glad to clean that up for you." The staff who served the woman were exemplary in their manners and etiquette throughout the service exchange. When Keanna went back to work, she relayed her observations to her colleagues.

1. What do you think the likelihood is of this type of customer service practice in most businesses today? Can you name some businesses you are personally aware of that provide exemplary customer service similar to that shown at the restaurant?

_____

_____

_____

2. In your opinion, what do you think contributes most to staff with manners and etiquette—were they hired with these qualities or were they trained in these behaviors by the restaurant?

_____

_____

_____

3. If you had been the person confronted by the woman who complained, what would have been your first reaction or response? Describe.

_____

_____

_____

HANDS-ON PROJECTS

Project 3–5 Enforcing a Dress Code

Molly Delecki recently went to work for a telecommunications firm in San Francisco as the receptionist and customer service representative. In the first week, several other employees went out of their way to go through the lobby just to see her. She is very attractive, and everyone soon learned she was a former local model.

Molly's image started to create problems within the company. Though Molly was a nice person and didn't appear conceited, her appearance was a distraction to the organization. The office manager discovered that work had slowed down since Molly was hired. For instance, male sales reps were stopping by and spending time chatting with her; female workers were saying catty things behind her back and seemed to be spending more time having negative conversations. Three comments overheard were, "She's too perfect," "She wears heavy makeup," and "She dresses too nice for this place."

Make notes regarding what is happening here. Include the roles in this situation of the receptionist, visitors to the front lobby, other employees, and the office manager. Each person or group is playing a role. Using the questions below as a guide, be prepared to discuss how you would resolve this situation.

1. Do you think the office manager should view this problem as one that will work itself out with time? Why or why not?

_____

_____

_____

2. What steps should be taken to get work back on track? What should the manager say to the other workers? Is Molly to blame at all in this situation?

_____

_____

_____

Project 3–6 Casual Dress Debate

HANDS-ON PROJECTS

Mary Graeff at On-Time Technology Products is becoming increasingly concerned with the way CSRs are dressing. It seems as if the concept and application of casual dress are going from bad to worse, with workers in halter tops, ripped blue jeans, and scuffed and dirty athletic shoes.

Today, Ms. Graeff has called in ten people from various departments to debate the following proposition: business casual dress at On-Time Technology Products will be left up to each employee's interpretation and taste. You are among the ten people on the panel. Brainstorm with others in class to answer the following questions:

1. What are three support statements you could make in favor of this proposition?

_____

_____

_____

2. What are three opposition statements you could make against this proposition?

_____

_____

_____

4

DEVELOPING STRONG LISTENING AND COMMUNICATION SKILLS

In this chapter you will learn:

♦ The characteristics and benefits of active listening

♦ How to avoid the distractions that prevent good listening

♦ How to build rapport and trust with customers who have varying communication styles

Listening and communication skills are two of the most basic and important skills that help desk analysts must possess. Analysts take in information by listening. They use both verbal and nonverbal skills to communicate. These skills are important because analysts must communicate and listen actively when customers provide information about their problems or requests. In return, analysts must respond in ways that give customers a sense of confidence that they are being heard and understood. They must also deliver information in a way that is meaningful to their customers. Good listening and communication skills benefit both of the parties involved in a conversation and can be improved through practice.

Learning to communicate with customers around the world is particularly important to the growing number of help desks that provide global support. Communicating with people of different cultures can be challenging. Languages and rules about proper behavior when communicating may vary from one country to the next. A willingness to learn about cultural differences and make a conscious effort to overcome those differences are keys to communicating with international customers.

When working as a help desk analyst, you must develop strong listening and communication skills so that you can communicate effectively with customers, coworkers, managers, and other service providers, such as internal support groups and vendors. This chapter focuses on how to be an active listener and avoid the distractions that prevent good listening. You will also learn how to be an effective communicator and how to identify and respond to the varying communication styles you may encounter.

THE POWER OF ACTIVE LISTENING

Listening is a skill that is important to many professions. For example, skilled negotiators listen carefully and understand the other party's needs before they make a compromising offer. Top salespeople concentrate on listening to avoid talking customers out of a sale. What does this have to do with customer support? Well, at times in customer support, analysts must be skilled negotiators—remember that can do attitude—and at times analysts must be sales- people. You can't always give customers what they want, but if you listen actively you can at least acknowledge and try to address what customers need.

In a survey conducted by the Help Desk Institute, 94.5% of respondents cited listening as the most important quality for a support person ("Help Desk Institute 2003 Practices Survey," Help Desk Institute, 2003, p. 51). In fact, listening has been ranked the most important quality since the Help Desk Institute began surveying its members in 1990. Why? Because customers are living, breathing human beings and a basic human need is to be heard and understood.

> *You can convey no greater honor than actually hearing what someone has to say.*
> Philip Crosby

Listening, like speaking and writing, is hard work; it requires thought and can be improved through practice. You have to want to listen. Listening is even more challenging when you are facing a difficult situation such as a n upset or angry customer. In difficult situations, you need to stay calm and focused and avoid becoming defensive or offensive.

NOTE

Chapter 13 explores techniques for handling difficult customer situations.

TIP

Self-listening is an important form of listening. If you could assume the perspective of others and hear what you say and how you say it, you might, at times, be appalled. You need to listen to yourself to ensure you are presenting yourself in a positive manner. When others do not respond in the way you expect, you need to honestly assess your words and tone of voice in an effort to become a better communicator.

Whether you are interacting with customers, coworkers, friends, or family members, listening enables you to understand the other person's needs. Only then can you concentrate on fulfilling those needs. Furthermore, it is not enough to just listen, you must listen actively so the other person knows that you are listening.

Being an Active Listener

Listening means making an effort to hear something—paying attention. Analysts with good listening skills can focus on what the speaker is saying to obtain the information needed to handle problems and requests quickly and correctly. They can convey a caring attitude and build rapport with the speaker by using active listening. **Active listening** involves participating in a conversation and giving the speaker a sense of confidence that he or she is being heard. **Passive listening** involves simply taking in information and shows little regard for the speaker. Table 4-1 compares the characteristics of active and passive listening.

Table 4–1   Active versus passive listening

Active Listeners	Passive Listeners
Ask questions and respond to the speaker	Take in information without questions
Verify understanding	Accept information at face value
Pay attention to *what* is being said and *how* it is being said	Show little regard for the feeling with which the information is being communicated

This section explores each active listening characteristic and discusses ways you can demonstrate that you are actively listening.

Ask Questions and Respond to the Speaker.

Customers do not typically contact the help desk because everything is going well. They are calling because they have a problem or because they need information about a product or service. Sometimes, customers can articulate their needs succinctly. Other times, customers aren't exactly sure why they are experiencing a problem or what it is that they need. They just know they can't get their job done. By asking appropriate and relevant questions and by assimilating and acknowledging the information the customer is providing, you can solve the problem or at least determine the next steps to take.

Successful analysts often develop checklists they can use to diagnose problems and methodically identify solutions. In some companies, level two service providers also develop checklists in an effort to enhance the abilities of level one analysts. These checklists help to ensure that analysts have correctly identified the failing hardware, software, or network component. A methodical approach also enables analysts to avoid making assumptions when diagnosing problems. Remember, just because a customer was using Microsoft Word when a problem occurred does not mean that the software package is the failing component. By asking questions and validating the facts given, you can better ensure that you fully understand what the customer needs.

Chapter 14 discusses how to develop problem-solving checklists.

NOTE

Knowing what questions to ask is an important skill for analysts. It is also important to know when to question the answers received. This is because customers occasionally provide information that can be misleading. Customers do not intentionally provide misleading information, they may simply lack the skills to provide an accurate diagnosis. Good listening and tactful questions help you assess your customers' skill level, which in turn helps you determine how to respond or proceed. Tactful questions obtain information without offending customers. For example, asking a customer "Can you describe the steps you took before this problem occurred?" is much better than asking "What did you do?" The latter question has a condemning tone and most likely will make the customer defensive.

Keep in mind, too, that not all customers feel comfortable using technology. Some customers may be just getting started and have not yet mastered the basics. Asking a customer questions such as "Do you have Internet access?" or "Do you know how to download a patch?" is much better than assuming that the customer has Internet access or simply stating that he can download the needed patch from the Internet. On the other hand, some customers may be quite sophisticated and, in fact, may have a better understanding of a product or system than some analysts do. Active listening enables you to avoid asking questions that are unnecessary or too simple. For example, if a customer says, "I looked on your Web site and could not find any information about this problem," you know not to ask the customer if she has Internet access. Asking questions that are too simple will offend a sophisticated customer just as quickly as asking questions that are too complicated will alienate a customer who is just getting started. Asking questions that are too simple may also undermine the analyst's authority and effectiveness in the customer's mind. In other words, the customer may perceive that the analyst is new to the job.

You can get a good idea of customers' skill levels by listening to how they use jargon to describe a problem or request. **Jargon** is the specialized or technical language used by a trade or profession, in this case, the computer industry. For example, a customer who reports in a panicked voice that he has "lost" the report for his boss that he worked on all afternoon will need to hear some assurance that you can help before you begin asking questions in a nontechnical manner. On the other hand, a customer who reports that she is having a chronic, repeatable problem when running a spreadsheet macro, but only in a certain spreadsheet, will need you to acknowledge the detailed information she has given and then proceed accordingly.

How or if a customer uses acronyms can be another indicator of his or her skill. An **acronym** is a word formed from the first letters of a series of words, such as TSC for Technology Support Center. For example, a customer who reports that he is new in the Accounting department and is having trouble logging on to the system will need tactful probing in an effort to determine what system he is trying to use. On the other hand, a customer who calls and indicates that she got a "Cannot Open" message when trying to access a file in the AAS (Advanced Accounting System) is demonstrating a higher level of skill.

 Resist the temptation to make assumptions about customers' skill levels based on their use of jargon, acronyms, and terminology. Customers may be very familiar with the technologies they use on a daily basis, but may be unfamiliar with others. Conversely, many long-term users have a fairly broad base of technical knowledge, but may not have any experience at all with specific systems. It is also important to remember that customers may know and use jargon, acronyms, and terminology that is unfamiliar to analysts. For this reason, it is best avoid language that may be confusing or uncommon to customers.

Good listening also enables you to learn the business language that customers are using to describe their work. When you understand how customers are using the technology you support to do their work, you can then provide useful tips that will help them. You may also identify ways your company's product can be enhanced to better fit your customers' business needs. If nothing else, you can help bridge the gap that can exist between the business needs of your company and the technology used to fill that need. Remember that many customers simply want to *use* technology to do their work. When they have a problem using technology or want to use the technology more efficiently or effectively, they turn to the help desk for support. Good listening enables you to understand and adjust to your customers' needs—no matter what their skill level.

Knowing when *not* to ask questions while still being responsive to customers is one of the nuances of customer service. For example, when customers are angry or in a highly agitated state, it is best to let them vent before asking questions. Customers who are upset have a story to tell. If you interrupt their story with questions they may become more upset.

 In most cases, it is best to curb any tendency you may have to interrupt a speaker. Interrupting is generally considered rude and sends a signal to the speaker that you are unwilling to listen. If you catch yourself interrupting, quickly halt your interruption and say, "Excuse me. Please continue."

 One situation where it may be appropriate to interrupt a customer is if that customer is being abusive, for example, if the customer is criticizing you personally or using particularly foul language. Chapter 13 provides techniques you can use to deal with this type of situation.

When customers are angry or upset, it is best to simply listen, and, in the least intrusive way possible, respond to what the customer is saying. For example, when interacting with a customer face-to-face, maintain eye contact and nod your head to let the customer know you are listening. When interacting with an upset or angry customer over the telephone, use a verbal nod of the head to let the customer know you are listening. Verbal nods of the head include phrases such as "Uh-huh," "I see," "Go on," and "I understand" at appropriate points in the conversation. For example, use the phrase "Uh-huh" or "Go on" when you want to encourage the customer to continue. Use phrases such as "I see" and "I understand" when you understand what the customer is telling you or when you can appreciate his or her point of view. Although you may be tempted to just be quiet and listen, that may cause the customer to become more upset. If a customer asks, "Are you listening?" you are not being responsive enough.

When in doubt, keep asking questions until you feel comfortable that you have the information you need to solve the problem.

Verify Understanding.   One of the most important aspects of active listening is to verify understanding. For help desk analysts, this means verifying that you understand what a customer said and verifying that the customer understands your reply. If you are unsure of the customer's meaning or think they may be unsure of yours, then you can ask a follow-up or clarifying question. For example, when interacting with a customer face-to-face, the customer may furrow his brow or stare vacantly at you, his computer, or something on his desk. In other words, he will look confused. When interacting with a customer over the telephone, you may hear silence on the other end of the telephone. In either situation, the customer may question the course of action you are suggesting by inquiring, "Are you sure?" The following questions will enable you to determine the customer's level of understanding in any of these situations.

> Would you like me to repeat that?
>
> Would you like to go through that again?
>
> How does that sound?

These questions enable you to verify that the customer understands the course of action that you are proposing.

Another good technique for verifying that you understand what a customer is telling you is to paraphrase, or restate, the information given by the customer using slightly different words. Paraphrasing repeats something using new words and enables you to verify the meaning of, or clear away any confusion about, the information you have received.

> **Customer:** I printed the page and the words were okay, but the pictures didn't print right.
>
> **Analyst (paraphrase):** Let me make sure I understand. You printed a document and the text printed correctly but the graphics did not?

When you verify understanding, you not only satisfy the customer by ensuring the customer's needs are being met, you also promote a good working relationship with other service providers. Level two service providers commonly complain that they received a problem from the help desk that they perceive the help desk should have been able to solve or that should have been assigned to a different level two group. Very often this occurs because help desk analysts failed to ask a sufficient number of questions or assumed they knew the answer to an unasked question. For example, when a customer reports that her printer is not working, you may be tempted to send a field engineer to her office to investigate. However, a customer may have trouble printing for a number of reasons, many of which can be diagnosed over the telephone. Asking questions is the only way to determine the actual source of the problem. Again, it never hurts to ask additional questions in an effort to make sure you fully understand your customer's needs. Be sensitive, though, and be aware that customers can become impatient or frustrated if you ask too many questions or if you ask the same question over and over. Choose your questions carefully and actively listen to the responses so that you can quickly determine what your customers need.

Pay Attention to *What* Is Being Said and How It Is Being Said.   Ultimately, your goal as an analyst is to solve a problem a customer is experiencing or to provide the customer with needed information or instructions. This is the "what" component of a conversation for which you need to listen. How the customer is delivering that information is also important. Customers are often experiencing emotion as a result of having a problem or not having what they need to use the products or services you support. For example, they may be confused by the instructions shipped with the software. Or, they may be frustrated that the hardware they purchased is not functioning properly and they have just spent a considerable amount of time trying to determine why. Or, they may be angry because they have experienced this same problem before and they perceive that a solution offered by another member of the help desk did not work. By listening actively, you hear both the problem and the emotion, and acknowledge both. You hear what is being said and how it is being said.

A basic human need is to be understood. When you acknowledge customers' emotions, you address that need. Often, what customers want most is for analysts to say that they understand. When you acknowledge customers' emotions, customers perceive that you care about their well-being and are more willing to work with you to resolve the problem. When you don't acknowledge customers' emotions, the customers may become more upset or angry. Have you ever contacted a company and expressed dissatisfaction with a product or service only to hear, "There's nothing we can do"? Didn't that response make you feel more frustrated or angry than you were to begin with? A much better response would be, "I'm sorry you're frustrated," or "Those instructions can be confusing. Let's walk through them together."

Some help desk analysts have a hard time dealing with emotions and they lack the people skills needed to interact effectively with customers. They are very logical thinkers and just want to solve the problem. Most customers, however, are unable to actively participate in problem solving until the analyst acknowledges their emotion.

Pay attention when you are the customer. Notice how service providers respond when you are upset or angry. Do they acknowledge your emotion? When they do, does it make you feel better? Most likely you will find that it does.

Being a good listener requires concentration. Communicating the fact that you are listening requires thought and caring. If a customer does not perceive that you are listening, you must take responsibility and determine why that is. Are you ignoring what the customer is saying? Are you failing to acknowledge how he or she feels? Determining how you can be more responsive requires that you listen to what the customer is saying. When a customer says, "That doesn't answer my question" or "Let me say this again," you are being given strong cues that the customer perceives you are not listening. Good listeners acknowledge what the customer has said when responding and they respond to both what is being said and how it is being said.

It is important to control your own emotions when interacting with customers. In other words, it is important to pay attention to what you say and how you say it. When a customer is angry or upset, it is neither helpful nor appropriate for you to become angry or upset as well. Chapter 13 provides specific techniques you can use when facing "sticky" customer situations, such as calming an irate or extremely demanding customer or saying "no" to customers while maintaining their goodwill.

It is also important to pay attention, or "listen," when communicating with customers through channels such as e-mail and chat. For example, customers may ask multiple questions in a single e-mail and will quickly become frustrated if each question is not answered—particularly if they have had to wait for a response. Customers may also provide cues as to their emotions by using words, punctuation, and capital letters. For example, customers may include words such as frustrated or disappointed to describe their feelings about a situation. Or, they may use an exclamation point or capital letters to emphasize a point.

Don't assume, however, that you can fully understand the customers' point of view when it is provided in writing. For example, although you may assume that an e-mail written entirely in capital letters was written in anger, the customer may have just mistakenly hit the Caps Lock key. When in doubt and when possible, pick up the telephone and verify understanding.

Chapter 6 explores how to effectively use technologies such as e-mail and chat to communicate with customers.

> *Nothing is ever gained by winning an argument and losing a customer.*
> C. F. Norton

The Benefits of Active Listening

The benefits of active listening far exceed the benefits of speaking. Active listening helps you establish rapport with a customer. The most common way to build rapport is to listen for the customer's name and use it respectfully during the remainder of your conversation.

Listen carefully to how customers provide their name. If a customer uses a title, such as Professor Brown, Dr. Jones, or Ms. Smith, address the customer using that title until the customer gives you permission to use a first name or nickname. When supporting international customers, avoid using first names unless you have been given permission to do so.

Active listening also enables you to determine the customer's emotional state. If a customer is upset or angry, you must acknowledge and address that emotion before you can begin to address the technical problem. Active listening can help you build trust by enabling you to respond in a way that acknowledges your customer's sense of urgency. For example, helping a customer route a presentation she is scheduled to make in an hour to another nearby printer when her personal printer jams will go a long way in terms of building trust. Quick thinking and a viable workaround may not solve the actual problem, but it can satisfy the customer's immediate need. If you do not at least try to satisfy the customer's immediate need—that is, if you do not respond in a way that acknowledges the customer's sense of urgency—the customer may become demanding and challenge you to do more than is possible. When customers understand that you will go the extra mile when they have a critical need, they may not feel the need to be as demanding in the future.

In addition to enabling you to establish rapport, address emotions, and build trust, active listening helps you keep the conversation on track so you can quickly determine the nature and likely cause of the customer's problem or request. If you are not listening carefully, you may miss an important detail or you may have to ask the customer to repeat what he or she said. Either scenario may instill a lack of confidence if the customer perceives that he or she has to repeat information because you were not listening. Active listening will also enable you to determine situations that require management involvement. For example, if a customer is unhappy with the service he received from another department in your company, you need to pass on that information to your manager. It is then your manager's responsibility to relay that information to the manager of the other department.

What is most important, active listening enables you to show customers that they are important and that you want to do all you can to satisfy their needs. This leads to customer confidence, and the customer is left with a positive image of you and your company.

Avoiding Distractions That Prevent Good Listening

At least half of our time is spent listening, and, yet, we're not good listeners (The Business of Listening: A Practical Guide to Effective Listening, Crisp Publications, 2001). In fact, studies indicate that we usually listen using about 25% of our listening capacity and that we ignore, forget, distort, or misunderstand 75% of what we hear. Given that we spend much of our time listening, why aren't we better listeners? In today's society, a lot of things get in the way, including those listed in Figure 4-1.

- Distractions and interruptions
- "Third ear" syndrome
- Jumping ahead
- Emotional filters
- Mental side trips
- Talking

Figure 4-1   Factors that prevent good listening

This section looks more closely at each of these factors that influence your ability to be a good listener.

Distractions and Interruptions.   Whether you work for a large or small help desk, you work in a high-energy environment. In a typical help desk on a typical day, telephones are ringing, electronic reader boards are flashing information and may be sounding alarms, customers and service providers are wandering about talking and perhaps entering your workspace, and all are demanding your attention. Figure 4-2 shows these typical distractions at a help desk. It is easy to lose focus in this dynamic working environment. Good listeners find ways to minimize these distractions by, for example, turning into their workspace when talking on the telephone or working on problems and signaling to visitors when they are already engaged.

Figure 4-2   Distractions and interruptions at a help desk

"Third Ear" Syndrome.   Many analysts believe they can listen to their customers and keep a "third ear" tuned in to what is happening around them. This concept of being aware of what is happening is valid, but must be used appropriately. Few people can truly listen and still do other things at the same time. For example, if you are speaking with a customer and hear a coworker discussing a similar problem, you may want to ask the customer if you can put him on hold while you determine if there is a system-wide problem. On the other hand, if you are speaking with a customer and hear several coworkers talking about their lunch plans, you must focus on your customer's needs and avoid the distraction your chatting coworkers represent.

Jumping Ahead.   The concept of jumping ahead is best explained by the adage, "Listening is not waiting for your turn to talk." Unfortunately, analysts sometimes decide they know the solution to a problem or they have rehearsed a standard response to an inquiry and they are simply waiting for the customer to stop talking so they can begin. Analysts who jump ahead run the risk of missing key information from the customer that changes the nature of the problem. They may waste time diagnosing the wrong problem because they were not listening and missed important information. They may also appear insensitive because they have failed to hear out the customer. As a result, the customer may become defensive or uncooperative. The customer may reject an analyst's solution because she does not feel that she has been heard or understood. Good listeners wait until the speaker has provided all available information before reaching a conclusion.

Emotional Filters.   We all have prejudices that influence our thinking and, as a result, our ability to listen. You may not like a speaker's appearance, voice, race, religion, or nationality. You may not like a speaker's temperament. For example, some people have a hard time dealing with negative people or people who whine. You may simply disagree with what the customer is saying. It is important to remember, however, that as a help desk analyst it is your job to uphold the policies of your company and assist all customers to the best of your ability.

Mental Side Trips.   As a card-carrying member of the human race it is inevitable that your "life" will at times intervene when you are working. It may occur to you that you need to buy your friend a birthday gift or that you have to take your child to baseball practice after school. As these thoughts race through your mind, they make it hard for you to listen. This ability to manage several conversations in your mind at once is because most people can listen to 125 to 250 words per minute, but can think more than 1,000 to 3,000 words per minute ("Sssh! Listen Up!," HighGain Inc., June 2000). Good listeners focus on what the speaker is saying and resist thoughts that sidetrack their attention.

 Consider keeping paper and pen nearby to maintain your personal "To Do" list. Write down items that you don't want to forget to give your mind a sense of satisfaction and enable you to focus your energies on the task at hand.

TIP

Talking.   Talking is a necessary part of communication, but it is possible to talk too much. A common mistake in customer service is delivering too much information. For example, a customer asks you for the status of an outstanding problem and you answer by saying that Joe Brown in the Programming department is working on it. The customer promptly calls Joe Brown and asks him for the status, thus taking him away from solving the problem. Also, the customer now has Joe Brown's name and telephone number and may call him directly in the future, rather than calling the help desk. A more appropriate response is to let the customer know the problem is being worked on and that you will give the customer a call when the problem has been solved. Or, if the problem is critical, promise the customer you will provide periodic updates. Then, make sure you do!

In Western cultures, silence is perceived as negative and so people often feel compelled to fill quiet moments by talking. People tend to speak first, listen second, and observe third. If you are working or visiting abroad, a better approach is to observe first, listen second, and then speak. Seek to understand the varying approaches to communication that you encounter and make an effort to avoid misunderstandings and appear rude.

Knowing when not to talk too much is also an important part of communication. This is because it is sometimes necessary to listen for cues that the customer is following your instructions. For example, if you asked a customer to restart her computer, you can listen for the Microsoft jingle to know the restart is underway. There is sometimes the tendency to engage in idle chatter during a lull in the problem-solving process, but remember, you cannot listen if you are talking too much. It is better to stay focused on working with the customer to solve a problem. For example, rather than simply chatting while a customer is restarting her computer, you may want to describe for the customer what steps you will be taking once her computer has restarted. Use the active listening techniques described earlier in this chapter to verify that the customer is following the plan of action.

Knowing What to Listen For

Listening requires concentration and it helps to know what you are listening for and how to record the information you receive. Begin by taking note of the key points the customer is making. If your company has a incident tracking or problem management system, record the information directly into that system, so that you do not have to handle the information again when you finish your conversation with the customer. If your company does not have a system, the system does not facilitate real-time logging of information, or you are simply not in a position to log information (for example, you are at a customer site), take notes as neatly and precisely as possible. Be as specific as possible so you can restate, using the customer's words when appropriate, the information the customer provides. A good guideline is to note who, what, when, where, and how. That is, who is experiencing a problem or has a request? What product or service is involved? When is the problem occurring, for example, chronically, intermittently, and so forth? Where is the problem occurring, for example, where is the failing device located or on what server is the failing software installed? How severe or widespread is the problem or how is the problem affecting the customer? Why the problem is occurring is determined once a solution is identified.

When taking notes about a problem or request, capture details such as who, what, when, where, and how.

When listening to customers, your ultimate goal is to determine their needs. It is important to remember that customer needs can go beyond obtaining details about a technical problem or request. It is also important to remember that you and your company can learn a lot by listening closely to customers. Challenge yourself to comprehend and retain as much as possible when communicating with customers. Skillful listening will enable you to:

- Detect any emotion the customer is experiencing that you need to acknowledge and address.
- Obtain the details of the customer's problem or request.
- Graciously receive any complaints the customer has about your company, its products, or its services.
- Detect any misconceptions the customer has about your company and its products and which you or others in your company such as the Sales or Marketing department need to clarify.
- Learn ways that your products and services can be enhanced and improved.
- Gain insight about your customers that will enable you to improve the quality of your services.

Remember, too, that listening involves keeping your eyes open as well as your ears. When interacting with customers face-to-face, watch their face and body language. Speakers often deliver information through nonverbal cues, such as folded arms, a furrowed brow, or poor eye contact. These cues may indicate that the customer is having a hard time understanding or believing what you are saying. If a customer rubs her eyes or scratches his head, it may be because they are confused and need you to slow down or restate your instructions.

In the Americas and most of Europe, steady eye contact is considered a sign of trust and respect. In Asia, eye contact is considered a personal affront and is kept to a minimum.

When interacting with customers over the telephone, remember that silence can be very telling. If a customer is unresponsive or fails to comment on the information you are delivering, the customer may be confused or may disagree with what you are saying. Although there is nothing wrong with a brief interlude of silence (for example, the customer may be processing what you have said), you want to avoid the temptation to view that silence as acceptance. A tactful clarifying question, such as "Would you like for me to repeat that?" or "Is that acceptable to you?" will enable you to avoid incorrect assumptions.

Good listening requires discipline and begins with a willingness to fully comprehend and retain everything that customers are saying, both in terms of what they are saying and how they are saying it. Also, good listening does not begin and end with the conversations you have with customers. Listening is a skill that you can use and apply on a daily basis in all areas of your life.

COMMUNICATING WITH CUSTOMERS

<u>**Communication**</u> is the exchange of thoughts, messages, and information. It requires skills such as listening, speaking, and writing. It also requires the desire to convey information in a meaningful and respectful way. Technology is helping us to communicate faster and with a larger audience, but it cannot help us formulate the information we transmit. Knowing what to say and how to say it when communicating with customers takes practice and patience.

Chapter 4 explores ways that analysts can improve their writing skills.

NOTE

Building Rapport and Trust with Customers

What you say is a simple matter of knowing and selecting the right words to use for a given situation. The words you choose should also communicate to customers that you appreciate their business and want to assist them in any way you can. *How* you say it is much more complex and requires an understanding of how people communicate. Figure 4-3 illustrates the factors that influence customer perception when people are communicating face-to-face and over the telephone (*Effective Telephone Communication Skills,* 1995, pp. 6, 7).

It is easy to see from this chart that communicating with customers over the telephone requires a very different approach than communicating face-to-face. When communicating over the telephone, "how people say it" makes all the difference.

Customers will sometimes say things over the telephone that they would never say in person. Customers may also tend to come on strong if they think their request is going to meet with resistance. This can cause analysts to become defensive because the analysts perceive they haven't even been given the opportunity to try to help. A better approach is for analysts to remain calm and avoid overreacting. Controlled breathing is an excellent way for analysts to release tension and reduce any symptoms of anxiety or panic. Breathing techniques analysts can use to relax and stay in control are discussed later in this chapter.

NOTE

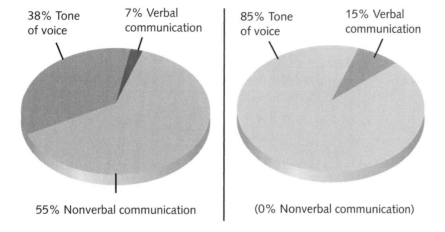

38% Tone of voice

7% Verbal communication

55% Nonverbal communication

85% Tone of voice

15% Verbal communication

(0% Nonverbal communication)

Figure 4-3 How people communicate

Verbal Communication

Verbal communication is the exchange of information using words. The words you choose to use can greatly influence the response you receive from customers. If you speak in a straightforward manner using everyday language that customers can understand, then your message will be well received. If you speak in riddles or use technical language that customers cannot understand, you can alienate customers. If you acknowledge customers' emotions and let them know that you will do all you can to help, then most customers will be willing to open up and tell you their problem. If you use phrases, such as those listed in Figure 4-4, you can quickly turn even a reasonable, calm customer into a charging bull. These phrases tend to provoke customers and should be considered forbidden phrases.

There may be times when you are faced with the need to deliver the message these forbidden phrases represent. However, even when you have to deliver bad news to customers, you can present it in a positive, respectful way. Look at how these "forbidden phrases" can be replaced with more positive statements.

■ **"It's against our policy."** This is a tough one because what your customer is asking for may very well be against your company's policy. Rather than state the negative, try stating your response as a positive. For example, "Our policy states. . . . " Or, if the policy enables you to offer the customer options, let the customer know what those options are. For example, "According to our policy, what I can do is. . . . "

■ **"That's not my job."** It may not be your job, but it is your job to determine who can assist the customer. Here's where you put your can do attitude to work. Phrases such as "What I can do is transfer you to the person who handles that area" or "What I can do is give you the telephone number of the company that supports this product" enable you to keep the customer's goodwill even when you are unable to assist the customer directly.

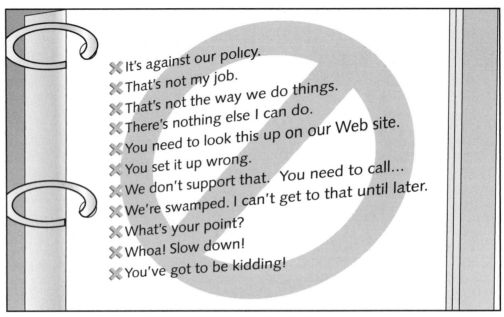

Figure 4-4   Forbidden phrases

- **"That's not the way we do things."** This phrase rejects the customer's request without offering an alternative or positive option. Rather than state the negative, turn this phrase into a positive statement that addresses the customer's request. "I need you to fill out a form and obtain your manager's signature, and then I can assign those rights to your account."

- **"There is nothing else I can do."** This phrase, and its counterpart, "I don't know what else I can tell you," rejects the customer's request and implies you are unwilling to explore other ways to meet the customer's needs. It also undermines your credibility. Remember that there is always something you can do. When in doubt, offer to let the customer speak with your manager. Although you do not want to engage your manager in every conversation you have, there are times when management involvement is needed to satisfy the customer.

- **"You need to look this up on our Web site."** This phrase begs the response "I don't need to do anything!" A better way to approach this situation is to ask "Have you tried finding a solution to this problem on our Web site?" Also, a good technique is to replace "you" with "Let me" or "Let's." For example, "Let me show you how to locate that information on our Web site." Although customers may prefer you simply give them the answer, this technique enhances their self-sufficiency while acknowledging their need to get information quickly.

- **"You set it up wrong."** There is nothing to be gained by pointing out the fact that a customer has made a mistake. Here is another example of where the "Let's"

technique can be used. "Let's look at the system parameters and make sure they are set up correctly." If the customer figures out that he made a mistake, offer empathy. Giving the customer an encouraging "It happens to the best of us" response will go a long way in restoring the customer's confidence.

- **"We don't support that. You need to call. . . . "** Stating the negative disempowers you and may alienate the customer. Remember that there is always something you can do. A more appropriate response would be "What I can do is give you the telephone number of the group that supports this product." Using a positively stated phrase leaves the customer with the impression that you have helped. And you have! You have directed the customer to the best possible source of help.

- **"We're swamped. I can't get to that until later."** We are all busy. The fact that you are busy is not the customer's fault nor does the customer really want to hear about it. Although it is appropriate to let the customer know that there are other customers who also are waiting for service, the best thing to do when you can't respond to a customer's request immediately is give an honest estimate of how long it will take to satisfy the request. When an SLA is in place, you may want to communicate the terms of that agreement. For example, "Per our SLA with your department, this request will be completed within 48 hours."

- **"What's your point?"** A more appropriate way to ask this question would be "Let me make sure I understand" or "Would you explain that again? I'm not sure I understand." Remember that you are the one not getting the point or you wouldn't be asking that question. If you don't understand, ask the customer in a respectful way to clarify what she means.

- **"Whoa! Slow down!"** You may be tempted to use this phrase when a customer is speaking very quickly. Although it is appropriate to let the customer know you are having trouble following the conversation, a more appropriate approach would be to get the customer's attention (for example, call the customer's name if it has been given), and then respectfully ask the customer to slow down. "Mr. Lee, could I ask you to slow down just a bit so that I can be sure I am getting all of your information correctly?"

- **"You've got to be kidding!"** This is where the golden rule comes into play. How would you feel if a service provider said this to you? There will be times when you are amazed by what a customer says or requests, but you must always be respectful. Consider the customer's request and positively and respectfully let the customer know what you can do. For example, "What I can do is take control of your system and work on this problem remotely. That will save the time it would take a technician to travel to your home office."

Choose your words carefully when communicating with customers. The wrong words not only can alienate your customer, they also can disempower you and undermine the credibility of your entire company. Practice using phrases that are positive and respectful.

TIP
When you support a global customer community, it is a good idea to know a few words—such as "Hello," "Could you hold please?", and "Thank you"—in each of the primary languages that your customers speak. This way, you can politely place on hold any customers who do not speak English while you obtain translation services.

ANN COOK

AMERICAN ACCENT TRAINING

AUTHOR/DIRECTOR

VALENCIA, CALIFORNIA

WWW.AMERICANACCENT.COM

One of the things that analysts may find difficult in a customer support setting is understanding people who have accents. Conversely, customers sometimes have difficulty understanding analysts who have accents. When you add technical jargon to the equation, communication can quickly break down. Ann Cook, author of *American Accent Training,* answers a few questions about accents, particularly as they relate to American English. Ann Cook is the Director of American Accent Training, an international program that teaches people who speak English as a second language how to speak standard American English. She has developed a diagnostic speech analysis that identifies each aspect of a person's accent and pronunciation.

Question: What is an accent?

Answer: An accent is how we deliver a particular language. An accent has three main parts: the speech music or intonation, word connections, and the actual pronunciation of each sound. If you don't have speech music, your speech will sound flat and monotone: "He. Is. In. A. Dark. Room." With intonation, you'll be able to say, "He is in a DARK room" (developing photographs) or "He is in a dark room" (the room is dark). With intonation, you can also indicate how you feel about something. Think of the difference between "I should CALL him" and "I SHOULD call him." In the first case, it is likely that you will pick up the telephone; in the second case, you are indicating some degree of reluctance.

How you run words together, or make word connections, is also very important. A sentence that looks like "He is in a meeting room" actually sounds like "heezina meeding room."

Finally, pronunciation is the difference between phrases such as "I like tennis" and "I like Dennis."

Question: How do people get an accent?

Answer: People learn their original accents in infancy. Babies hear the speech rhythms of the people around them and mimic those rhythms, long before they acquire grammar and vocabulary. When they learn a second language in adulthood, they bring those patterns and pronunciations with them, and that results in a "foreign" accent. For instance, in languages other than American English, the R sounds like a D, the T always sounds like a T, and there are only five vowel sounds. In American English, the R is a kind of growly semi-vowel (ARRR), the T is frequently pronounced as a D ("meeting" sounds like "meeding"), and American English has 14 vowel sounds. The result is that when a person who was not born in America says, "Eet eess hoeddeebel," they are trying to say, "It is horrible." In American English, it would come out "Idiz horrabul."

Question: What perceptions do people have about people who have accents?

Answer: To a large extent, it depends on the accent. If a person's accent is very light, people frequently respond positively. If an accent makes communication difficult, however, the response can be extremely negative, to the point of considering the speaker less capable or less intelligent. Americans and Europeans generally understand each other's accents, as they all speak western languages. Asians, on the other hand, tend to have difficulty both speaking and understanding western languages.

Question: Are there any stereotypes associated with people who have accents?

Answer: Quite sadly, people think that someone with nonstandard speech is speaking with an accent on purpose or isn't quite bright enough to talk "right." Many age-old notions about people from other countries arise, in large part, from the fact that foreign-born people don't use intonation the way a native American English speaker does. For example, to a native speaker, the sentence "Ben has a red pen" can be inflected many different ways:

- BEN has a red pen (not Sue)

- Ben HAS a red pen (he already has it, so don't offer him one)

- Ben has a RED pen (not a blue one)

- Ben has a red PEN (but no pencils)

A non-native American English speaker will frequently say BEN HAS A RED PEN, so the listener has to try to imagine which interpretation to make. Also, most other languages don't use the words "A" and "THE," so words that are important in American English may be left out. Think about the difference between:

- A teacher bought a book (an unspecified teacher bought an unspecified book)

- The teacher bought a book (a specific teacher bought an unspecified book)

- A teacher bought the book (an unspecified teacher bought a specific book)

- The teacher bought the book (a specific teacher bought a specific book)

Given all of those possible interpretations, it is easy to see that if a person were to say, "Teacher bought book," the American listener would have to struggle to interpret what the speaker meant.

Question: What techniques can people use to better understand people who have a strong accent?

Answer: To better understand people who have a strong accent:

1. Speak slowly and clearly, but not loudly.

2. Acknowledge and accept that their speech isn't "perfect."

3. Don't sweat the details: try to grasp their main idea, as opposed to trying to understand each and every word they are saying.

4. Don't try to correct them, even if inadvertently. (Oh! THE teacher bought THE book.)

5. Listen for a key word, no matter how it's pronounced.

6. Don't interrupt. Make notes and go back to the problem point when the person finishes speaking. The calmer you are, the calmer the other person will be.

7. Avoid colloquial, or conversational, speech. Foreign-born speakers are usually more familiar with longer words rather than the short words Americans prefer. For instance, "postpone" would be more familiar to someone who does not speak American English than "put off," and "arrange" would be more familiar than "set up." When you think about English verbs and prepositions, it's mind-boggling. With the word "get" alone, you have "get up," "get over," "get away," "get away with," "get off," "get on," "get through to," and many, many more. These are very difficult for foreign-born speakers.

Question: Is there one most important thing that people can do to better understand people who have an accent?

Answer: It's like learning a new dance—try to catch the rhythm without being judgmental of how it "should" be.

Question: How is interacting over the telephone with a person who has an accent different than interacting face-to-face with that person?

Answer: There is so much more information available face-to-face. You can point to things, hand things back and forth, and use facial expressions and body language to communicate. Over the phone, you are limited to the sound of the other person's voice.

Question: What techniques can people use to reduce their accent?

Answer: To reduce an accent:

1. Focus on the rhythm of an entire phrase instead of word by word.

2. Learn to "hear." Listen to the radio and write down exactly what the person says based on pronunciation, not spelling. For example, the word "water" would be "wahdr," not "wa-ter."

3. Don't worry about sounding fake—Americans don't tend to notice if a foreign-born person speaks with a heavy American accent. They'll just think that your English has improved.

4. Don't sound too perfect—native American English speakers don't talk that way. Let all your words run together. "I'll get it" should sound like "I'll geddit." This is not slang; it's perfectly standard colloquial American speech.

5. Take a course that is specifically oriented to "accent training" or "accent reduction," rather than grammar or vocabulary based.

Question: Is there one most important thing that people can do to reduce their accent?

Answer: Imitate and learn the American intonation. One way to do that is to listen to and repeat ballads and children's books on tape.

Question: Is there anything else that you think it is important for students to know about accents?

Answer: For a person to have an accent means that they communicate perfectly in a entirely different language—not that they are deficient in their second language, which is English. Also, English is the hardest language in the whole world. It has more synonyms than any other language. Think of the difference between to tap, to rap, to pat, to pet, to stroke, to caress—these are all very similar words for using your hand to touch something, but look how different and specific each one is.

Nonverbal Communication

Nonverbal communication is the exchange of information in a form other than words. Nonverbal communication can say as much as words and includes qualities such as facial expressions, body language, and even clothing. When communicating with customers over the telephone, by e-mail, or by chat, these nonverbal qualities have no impact whatsoever. When communicating face-to-face, however, they make up over half of our conversation. This is because people read meaning into nonverbal cues. For example, if you wink while telling a story to a friend, he knows that you are kidding or teasing. If you avoid eye contact and tightly fold your arms across your chest when speaking with a customer, she may perceive that you are not listening or that you are rejecting what she is saying. If you dress sloppily or do not practice good grooming, people may perceive your thinking is sloppy as well and may resist your ideas.

To communicate effectively, learn to use your nonverbal vocabulary in the same positive way you use words. Be respectful, be attentive, and "listen" to what the speaker is telling you with his or her nonverbal cues. If a customer steps back when you approach him to discuss a problem, you may be standing too close. Allow the customer to establish a distance that feels comfortable. You can also observe and consider emulating the nonverbal techniques used by someone that you believe is an excellent communicator. Also, be aware of the culture at the company where you work. Although some companies allow a more casual dress code, there is such a thing as too casual. A neat appearance and good grooming always serve you well.

TIP People in the United States are much more casual in terms of how they speak and dress than are people in other countries. When interacting with a customer, an effective technique is to mirror that customer's behavior. If the customer's manner is formal, respond in a formal manner. If the customer's manner is more casual, you can relax a bit. However, it is your responsibility to remain professional at all times. When traveling for business, ask people who have been to the country you are visiting, or ask your coworkers who live in that country, for guidance on how to make a good impression.

Tone of Voice

Figure 4-3 illustrated the dramatic difference tone of voice makes when you are interacting with customers face-to-face and even more so over the telephone. A number of factors, including those listed in Figure 4-5, make up your tone of voice.

- Energy
- Rate of speech
- Volume and pitch

Figure 4-5 Factors that influence tone of voice

We all have different voices and we can change our voices by controlling the energy, rate of speech, volume, and pitch we use when we speak.

Energy.   Enthusiasm is contagious and the energy in your voice often reflects your personality and your attitude. Answering the telephone with a bored "Yeah" will not impress and instill confidence in customers. Facial expression mirrors mood, and mood mirrors facial expression. One technique that works well is to approach all interactions with customers as if they were standing in front of you. In other words, even if you are speaking to a customer over the telephone, put a smile on your face, focus your attention on what the customer is saying, and be as responsive as possible. Don't overdo it, however. False enthusiasm can be just as offensive and distracting as no enthusiasm. Be yourself! And remember, some days it can be tough getting excited by the prospect of handling one problem after another. Stay focused on the fact that you chose the field of customer support because you enjoy helping people. Hang inspiring quotes in your office or place a funny picture on your desk that will help you put a smile back in your voice on even the toughest days.

> *Everyone smiles in the same language.* Author Unknown

TIP   To monitor your facial expressions and posture, place a mirror on your desk at eye level. Placing the mirror at eye level ensures that you are sitting straight and practicing good posture. By taking a quick look in the mirror before you answer the telephone, you can ensure you have a relaxed and pleasant facial expression. You can put a smile on your face, give the customer (who you pretend to see in the mirror) your full attention, take a deep breath if needed to get focused, and then answer the telephone. Give it a try!

Rate of Speech.   A normal rate of speech is about 125 words per minute. Speaking too quickly or too slowly can be distracting to customers and affect their ability to listen. A good technique is to determine your normal rate of speech. You can do this by placing a tape recorder next to you to record yourself while you are conversing or reading aloud casually from a book. The trick is to forget about the tape recorder so you get a more accurate reading of your rate of speech. You can then replay the tape, marking time with a stopwatch, to determine the number of words you speak per minute. Once you have determined your normal rate of speech, strive to adapt your pace to the needs of your customer. Factors to consider include your customer's rate of speech and the information you are delivering. For example, if you tend to speak quickly and a customer is speaking slowly, you may want to slow your speech slightly as well. Or, if you are walking the customer through an important set of instructions, you may want to slow your speech slightly. You may also want to slow down a bit if you are speaking to a customer in his or her second language. On the other hand, if you are asking a routine set of questions or simply validating information, you can pick up the pace a little.

Speaking too quickly at any point in a conversation can cause confusion or alienate the customer. This is particularly true when you are wrapping up a call. There is often a temptation to rush through the closing and move on to the next call. Unfortunately, you can undo any goodwill you have created by hanging up before the customer is satisfied. Take your time and listen to your customers; their needs will help you adapt and adjust your pace.

Volume and Pitch.   The volume of your voice should always be loud enough that your customer and any of the other people involved in your conversation can hear you. The volume of your voice should not, however, be so loud that it disturbs the people around you.

Help desks can get loud. All analysts must do their best to be courteous and respectful in terms of keeping the volume of their voice at an appropriate level and utilizing speaker-phones appropriately. If things get too loud on any given day, don't be afraid to politely signal coworkers that they need to keep it down. Graciously accept and respond to any such signals you receive from coworkers.

Pitch refers to the highness or lowness of vocal tone. Generally speaking, high-pitched voices are viewed as weak. We also tend to associate a high-pitched voice with someone who is excited, possibly even in a state of panic or out-of-control. Low-pitched voices are typically viewed as strong, and we tend to associate a low-pitched voice with someone who is confident and in control.

Voice pitch is influenced by the way you hold your head and by the way you breathe. For example, if you tend to have a high-pitched voice, practice lowering your head slightly when you speak. If you tend to have an exceptionally low-pitched voice, practice raising your head slightly when you speak. Your posture could also be influencing the quality of your voice. Good posture enables you to project your voice and makes it easier for customers to understand what you are saying. You can improve your posture by making sure you have a good chair that enables you to sit up straight and by making sure your workspace is ergonomically aligned.

You can also influence the pitch of your voice by learning to take long, slow, deep breaths, especially when you are under pressure. Most people become shallow breathers when they are under pressure. When this happens, your vocal cords tend to tighten, making your voice go up and sound strained. By slowing down your breathing, you lower the pitch of your voice and create a calmer tone.

Coupled with the right words, the tone of voice you use can dramatically change the message you communicate to a customer. Consider the differences between the following two phrases:

Stated using a frustrated tone of voice: What do you expect me to do about it?

Stated using a calm tone of voice after taking a deep breath: How would you like to see this situation resolved?

Both questions ask how the customer would like to see the situation resolved. The first example not only fails to engage the customer, it also fails to have the speaker take responsibility for the customer's satisfaction. The second example encourages a dialogue with the customer and at the same time avoids false promises. By selecting positive words and using a calm tone of voice, you communicate a completely different message—one that is much more empowering to both you and your customer.

Customers recognize and respond to your "words," whether they are spoken or communicated through nonverbal cues or your tone of voice. Practice using each of these techniques to establish rapport with your customers and gain their trust. Understanding the communication style of your customer is another tool you can use to enhance communications.

Identifying and Understanding Customer Communication Styles

Becoming an effective communicator requires that you acknowledge the fact that customers are people, and people are different. They have different personalities, different ways of handling change and stress, and different communication styles. To communicate effectively, you must first identify the communication style of your customer. You can then respond, rather than react, to your customer in a way that is meaningful. Figure 4-6 lists some of the most common communication styles you will encounter.

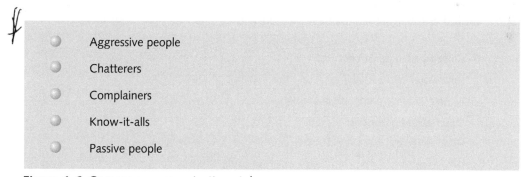

- Aggressive people
- Chatterers
- Complainers
- Know-it-alls
- Passive people

Figure 4-6 Common communication styles

You determine every customer's communication style by listening to the information they provide and to the responses they give when you ask questions. Use the following techniques to determine which communication style your customers exhibit and how to respond to them.

Aggressive People.   Aggressive people like to be in control. They are usually unwilling to engage in social conversation and want to get to the point immediately. Aggressive people may be quick to inform you that they "don't have time for this." They can become hostile and will often try to bully and intimidate people, or they will make a scene in order to get their way. For example, an aggressive person may challenge you to "Get someone out here right away" or "Put your supervisor on the phone." When interacting with aggressive people, give them time to tell their story and then jump into the conversation when they pause or ask you a question. You can also try to get their attention and then take control of the conversation. For example, respectfully call out their name and then state specifically what you can do. Always restate the information that aggressive people give you and their opinions of the problem. This technique enables aggressive people to feel that they have been heard.

Chatterers.   Chatty customers can be fun, but they can also be a challenge when you are busy. The first way to deal with a chatty customer is to avoid encouraging them. For example, resist the temptation to ask a chatty customer how his vacation was. You are asking for a prolonged answer. When a chatty customer asks you a question that lends itself to a prolonged response, reply with a minimum response. For example, if a customer asks if you are busy, you can politely respond "Yes, very. How can I help you?" Another great technique is to take control of the conversation by asking closed-ended questions. **Closed-ended questions** prompt short answers such as "yes" and "no." Once you have taken control, you can ask open-ended questions as needed to obtain more information. **Open-ended questions** cannot be answered with a "yes" or "no" response.

> **Closed-ended questions:**
>
> Have you ever been able to access this system? [Yes/No]
>
> Is there another printer close by that you can use? [Yes/No]
>
> **Open-ended questions:**
>
> What other applications did you have open when this problem occurred?
>
> When was the last time you were able to use this device?

Complainers.   Complainers whine and object but cannot always identify reasons why a solution will not work. They cannot or will not take responsibility for problem solving and often deflate the creativity or optimism of others. When interacting with complainers, empathize but do not necessarily sympathize with the customer's complaint. For example, it is okay to acknowledge that computers can be frustrating, but agreeing that they should all be banished from the face of the earth is probably not a good idea. Also, when interacting with complainers, paraphrase their main points and make sure you understand the specific nature of their complaint. Try not to waste time talking about generalities. You can also ask complainers how they would like things to turn out. By empowering them to participate in developing a solution, you enhance their self-sufficiency and increase the likelihood that they will be satisfied with the final outcome.

Know-It-Alls.   Know-it-alls believe they know everything and tend to resist advice or information they receive from others. They may go to great lengths to convince you that they are right. They can be condescending and pompous and in extreme cases take pleasure in making other people feel stupid. When interacting with know-it-alls, suggest alternatives without attacking their opinions. For example, avoid phrases such as "That won't work," which tend to be perceived negatively. Instead, use positive phrases such as "In my experience, this will work." Also, be respectful when asking questions and acknowledge the customers' knowledge. When appropriate, use phrases such as "What if . . ." and "Let's try this." These phrases will engage customers in the problem-solving process without rejecting their perspective.

Passive People.   Passive people avoid controversy at all costs and they often cannot or will not talk when you need information. They never volunteer opinions or comments and will tend to go along with suggestions from other people whether or not they feel those suggestions are correct. When interacting with passive people, ask open-ended questions in an effort to encourage a prolonged response rather than a "yes" or "no" response. Also, do not feel you have to fill the silence when waiting for a passive person to respond. If you have posed a question, wait for them to answer. Resist the temptation to jump in and put words in their mouth. Listen responsively when passive people are talking. If they perceive you are not listening, they may resume their silence.

Although these are the most common communication styles, they represent only a handful of the different kinds of people that you will encounter during your career in the support industry. It is also important to remember that people can use different communication styles depending on the situation they are facing or the response that they are receiving. For example, a customer who is getting pressure from his boss may tend to be much more aggressive than he normally would when he is experiencing a problem. Or, a customer who perceives that you have been rude may suddenly become very passive and unresponsive. The more carefully you listen and strive to understand the different ways that people communicate, the more effective a communicator you will become.

Speaking the Customer's Language

It may not have occurred to you before, but you and your customers are bilingual. You may not speak French or Spanish in addition to English, but you do speak Business and

Technology. Customers tend to speak Business. Analysts tend to speak Technology. Table 4-2 lists some examples of how customers and analysts speak different languages.

Table 4–2 Sample translations between Business and Technology languages

Customers say	Analysts hear
I can't log on.	The system is down.
I can't print.	The printer is down.
Analysts say	**Customers ask**
FPS1 (File and Print Server #1) is down.	Why can't I print?
The mainframe will be unavailable this weekend.	Does this affect Payroll?

To keep communications on track, and to avoid alienating your customers, avoid jargon and acronyms that they may not understand, or worse, may think they understand but actually do not. When customers do use jargon or an acronym, ask clarifying questions to avoid making an invalid assumption that they fully understand what they are saying. We all know it is possible for two people to have a conversation, walk away thinking they agree, only to find out later that they did not communicate. The excessive use of jargon and acronyms increases the likelihood that this will occur.

Remember that most people consider technology a tool. They typically are using it to do something, not just for the sake of it. The best way to serve your customers is to understand their business and learn to speak its language. You can then translate that language into your language, the language of technology.

CHAPTER SUMMARY

❐ Listening is the most important skill for a support person. Active listening involves participating in a conversation by asking questions, responding to the speaker, and verifying understanding. Good listening requires discipline and begins with a willingness to fully comprehend and retain everything that customers are saying both in terms of *what* they are saying and *how* they are saying it. Listening brings many benefits and is a skill that you can use and apply daily in all areas of your life.

❐ Communication is the exchange of information. It requires skills such as listening, speaking, and writing. It also requires the desire to convey information in a meaningful and respectful way. What you say—the words you choose to use—greatly influences the response you receive from customers. How you say it—the nonverbal ways you communicate and your tone of voice—can say as much as your words because people can read meaning into your nonverbal cues.

❐ You can determine and influence your customers' response by listening and by learning to speak their language. Most people consider technology a tool. They typically are using it to *do* something, not just for the sake of it. The best way to serve your customers is to understand their business and learn to speak its language. You can then translate that language into your language, the language of technology.

KEY TERMS

acronym — A word formed from the first letters of a series of words.

active listening — Listening that involves participating in a conversation and giving the speaker a sense of confidence that he or she is being heard.

closed-ended questions — Questions that prompt short answers, such as "yes" and "no."

communication — The exchange of thoughts, messages, and information.

jargon — The specialized or technical language used by a trade or profession.

listening — To make an effort to hear something; to pay attention.

nonverbal communication — The exchange of information in a form other than words.

open-ended questions — Questions that cannot be answered with a "yes" or "no" response.

paraphrase — To restate the information given by a customer using slightly different words in an effort to verify that you understand.

passive listening — Listening that involves simply taking in information and shows little regard for the speaker.

pitch — The highness or lowness of vocal tone.

verbal communication — The exchange of information using words.

REVIEW QUESTIONS

1. What is the most important skill a support person must possess?

2. What is a basic human need?

3. You have to _____ to listen.

4. Why is active listening important?

5. What is active listening?

6. What is passive listening?

7. How can analysts use checklists?

8. What are tactful questions?

9. What can you learn about a customer by listening to how the customer uses jargon?

10. When is it inappropriate to ask questions?

11. What are two ways to let a customer know you are listening when you are interacting face-to-face?

12. What is a verbal nod of the head? Provide two examples.

13. How can you obtain the information you need to solve a problem?

14. What are three cues that a customer may give when confused or unsure?

15. What is paraphrasing?

16. What two things should you listen for when interacting with customers?

17. Why is it important to acknowledge a customer's emotion?

18. What must you do if a customer indicates he or she does not perceive you are listening?

19. List six benefits of active listening.

20. What percentage of our listening capacity do we normally use?

21. List the six distractions that prevent good listening.

22. What should you do if you are speaking to a customer and hear one of your coworkers discussing a similar problem?

23. What are three risks you run when you jump ahead?

24. What information should you capture about a customer's problem or request?

25. What can silence tell you when you are interacting with a customer over the telephone?

26. What factors influence customer perception when communicating face-to-face?

27. What factors influence customer perception when communicating over the telephone?

28. What is a good substitute for "forbidden phrases?"

29. What are three nonverbal ways that people communicate?

30. Name the three factors that influence your tone of voice.

31. What is a normal rate of speech?

32. What three factors influence your voice pitch?

33. How can you lower the pitch of your voice?

34. How can you determine the communication style of your customer?

35. What is an open-ended question?

36. Which language do you need to speak—Business or Technology? Explain your answer.

DISCUSSION QUESTIONS

1. In today's busy world, people often pride themselves in their ability to multitask. For example, a person might work on the computer while talking on the telephone, or check instant messages while in a meeting. Can people really do two things at one time and still be an active listener?

2. Many technical support providers believe that customers need to become more technical, and so they use jargon and acronyms in an effort to teach customers. Conversely, many customers believe that technical support providers could avoid jargon and acronyms, but they just don't want to. Who is right?

3. Have you ever forgotten someone's name within minutes of meeting them? Why does that happen?

HANDS-ON PROJECTS

Project 4-1

Assess your listening skills. Table 4-1 compares the characteristics of active and passive listening. Review these characteristics and identify the active listening characteristics that you possess. Discuss these characteristics with at least three of your friends or family members. Ask them to provide feedback in terms of what kind of listener you are. Review your list, consider the feedback you received, and then prepare a list of ways you can become a more active listener.

Project 4-2

Discuss the pitfalls of passive listening. Assemble a team of at least three of your classmates. Discuss each of the characteristics of passive listening. Discuss the ramifications of these characteristics in terms of meeting customer needs. Write a brief summary of your conclusions and then discuss them with the class.

Project 4-3

Practice becoming a better listener. Two common traits of poor listeners are (1) assuming you know what a person is about to say or that you understand the point he or she is trying to make, and (2) interrupting. For the next 21 days—at which point these techniques will become habit—pick one or more good listening techniques and apply it at least once a day. Techniques you may want to practice include using a verbal nod of the head, paraphrasing, and halting your tendency to interrupt. Prepare a one-page report describing your efforts and observations.

Project 4-4

Pay attention when you are the customer. Over the course of a week or two, pay close attention when you are the customer. Keep a list of any situations where you experienced emotion, such as confusion, frustration, or anger, as a result of a customer service encounter. For each situation, answer the following questions:

❏ How did the service provider treat you?

❏ Did the service provider acknowledge your emotion?

❏ How did that make you feel?

In addition, write a paragraph describing the conclusions you can draw from your experiences.

Project 4-5

Avoid distractions. Review the list of distractions that prevent good listening. Select two distractions that you can honestly say have influenced you in the past or continue to affect you in your current job, hobby, or home life. Prepare a list of three things you can do to minimize the impact of each distraction.

Project 4-6

Collect and rewrite forbidden phrases. During the next week, pay close attention to the service you receive (see Project 4-4) and keep a list of any "forbidden phrases" that you hear. Refer to Figure 4-4 for a sample list of forbidden phrases. For each phrase, state a more positive, respectful way of delivering the message. Share your list with three classmates and have them critique your restatements.

Project 4-7

Determine your rate of speech. Place a tape recorder next to you while you converse or read aloud casually from a book. If you don't have a tape recorder, simply read aloud casually from a book. Determine the number of words you speak per minute. Is your rate of speech faster or slower than the average rate of 125 words per minute? Prepare a list of situations in which you may want to adjust your rate of speech.

Project 4-8

Assess the effectiveness of nonverbal communication. Over the course of a day, take note of the various nonverbal ways that people communicate. Write a paragraph describing two or three nonverbal cues that you found to be particularly effective. Conversely, write a paragraph describing two or three nonverbal cues that you found to be particularly ineffective or annoying. Write a final paragraph describing any conclusions you can draw from your observations.

Project 4-9

Determine your voice pitch. Record your voice and replay the recording, listening for the pitch of your voice. If you do not have a tape recorder, leave a voice mail message somewhere that you can play it back. Do you have an exceptionally low- or high-pitched voice? Prepare a list of ways that you can adjust the pitch of your voice to project confidence and strength. Practice changing the pitch of your voice. Record your voice again and replay the recording. Have you improved the pitch of your voice? Consider asking a classmate to listen to your recording and provide feedback.

CASE PROJECTS

1. Diagnose Printer Problems

Your boss has asked you to develop a problem-solving checklist that can be used to diagnose printer problems. She has asked you to "keep it simple" and list only a half a dozen questions. Prepare a list of three open-ended and three closed-end questions that can be used to determine why a customer may be having trouble printing a report.

2. Coach an Analyst to Keep It Positive

You are the team leader for a large internal help desk. Your boss recently overheard an analyst ask a customer, using an incredulous tone of voice, "You want it by when?" He asks you to provide the analyst with some coaching. Speak with the analyst (choose a classmate) and help the analyst determine a more positive, respectful way to respond to a customer's seemingly unreasonable request.

3. The Business of Listening

This exercise illustrates how to be an effective communicator and a good listener.

1. Select volunteers who are willing to read out loud to the class.

2. Students who are not reading must close their books and prepare to listen.

3. Volunteers read from an article in one-minute sequences.

4. As a class, discuss how effectively each volunteer communicated, and how well the students listened. For example:

   ❏ Was the volunteer's tone of voice energetic?

   ❏ How was the volunteer's rate of speech? Fast? Slow?

   ❏ Did the volunteer read as fast or slow as the class perceived?

   ❏ How was the volunteer's volume?

   ❏ How was the volunteer's pitch?

❐ Did any factors influence the students' ability to be good listeners? If so, what factors?

❐ What were the students listening for?

5. As a class, discuss the main points of this article.

4. One-Way Communication

This exercise illustrates how analysts and customers benefit when they can ask questions and receive responses. In other words, they engage in two-way conversation as opposed to one-way communication, which does not allow the exchange of questions and answers.

1. Select one volunteer to describe a diagram to the class.

2. Other students place a clean sheet of paper in front of them and prepare to listen. Students are not allowed to ask questions or communicate in any way with the volunteer. Students must remain silent throughout this entire exercise.

3. The volunteer describes the diagram to the class. The volunteer must use only words to describe the diagram. The volunteer cannot use any nonverbal techniques to communicate, such as facial expressions, hand movements, or body movements. The volunteer cannot ask the students if they understand the information that is being communicated.

4. Students draw the diagram the volunteer is describing on their clean sheet of paper. Remember, students cannot ask clarifying or follow-up questions.

5. Once the volunteer has finished describing the diagram to the class, reveal the diagram. Compare the students' drawings to the original diagram.

6. As a class, discuss how effectively the volunteer communicated, and how well the students listened. For example:

❐ How explicitly did the volunteer describe the diagram?

❐ Did the volunteer use any jargon that the class did not understand?

❐ Did the volunteer go too fast or too slow?

❐ Did any students become confused or frustrated and just quit listening? Why?

❐ Why was the one-way communication difficult to follow?

❐ If the students had been allowed to speak, what questions would they have asked the volunteer?

7. As a class, discuss the benefits of being able to engage in two-way conversation. Also, discuss ways to become better listeners and communicators.

5

WINNING TELEPHONE SKILLS

In this chapter you will learn:

◆ The power of the telephone

◆ How to handle calls professionally

◆ How to avoid the most common telephone mistakes

◆ How to place callers on hold and transfer calls in a positive, professional way

◆ How to continuously improve your telephone skills

◆ How to consistently convey a positive, caring attitude

For many help desks, the telephone is the primary way that customers obtain service. According to a survey conducted by the Help Desk Institute, 71% of its membership indicated that customers request services through the telephone versus nearly 16% whose customers use e-mail, and 9% whose customers use other channels such as the help desk's incident logging system and the Internet ("Help Desk Institute 2003 Practices Survey," Help Desk Institute, 2003, p. 33). Although e-mail and Internet-based support services have increased in recent years and will continue to increase, the telephone will always play a role in customer service. Professional telephone skills help to ensure that the help desk handles customer requests in a prompt, courteous, and consistent manner. Consistency is particularly important because it builds trust between the analyst and customer, and it teaches customers what they can expect during the call so they know how to prepare.

To communicate effectively with customers over the telephone, you must understand how to handle calls professionally and how to avoid the most common call-handling mistakes. You must also let your caring attitude and personality shine through and use your telephone skills to send a positive, proficient message to your customers. How you answer the telephone and handle telephone calls greatly influences how customers feel about your entire company.

CREATING A POSITIVE TELEPHONE IMAGE

Two characteristics of excellent customer support discussed earlier—responsiveness and a caring attitude—are fundamental to a positive telephone image. How long it takes analysts to answer the telephone and the energy and enthusiasm they convey can greatly influence a customer's perception of the analysts and their entire company. Although conducting business over the telephone can be frustrating and impersonal for both analysts and customers, when handled properly, the telephone can be an efficient, effective way to deliver support.

Understanding the Power of the Telephone

The telephone is one of the most common ways that businesses and customers communicate today. At a help desk, analysts may handle incoming calls (calls received), such as calls from customers, or they may handle outgoing calls (calls they make), such as follow-up calls to customers or calls to vendors. Telephone technology automates and facilitates many of these activities. The most common telephone technologies are listed in Figure 5–1.

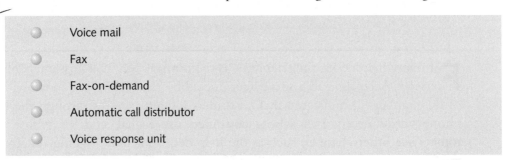

- Voice mail
- Fax
- Fax-on-demand
- Automatic call distributor
- Voice response unit

Figure 5–1 Common telephone technologies

Help desks use telephone technologies that range from simple voice mailboxes to highly complex, automated systems. Which telephone technologies a help desk selects are determined by a number of factors, such as the help desk's size, the company's goals, the nature of the company's business, and customer expectations. For example, smaller help desks may opt to use a simple set of telephone technologies, such as voice mail and fax. Larger help desks and those in high-technology industries tend to use more sophisticated technology, such as automatic call distributors and voice response units. The technology a help desk uses affects how customer contacts are directed to analysts and how analysts' performance is measured.

Voice Mail

Voice mail is an interactive computerized system for answering and routing telephone calls, for recording, saving, and relaying messages, and sometimes for paging the user. According to a survey conducted by the Help Desk Institute, nearly 90% of its members use voice mail ("Help Desk Institute 2003 Practices Survey," 2003, p. 21). For customers to view voice mail positively, they must be given an idea of when their call will be returned, and then customers must receive that return call within the promised time frame. The best companies diligently manage voice mail messages and promptly return all customer calls, even if only to let the customer know that (1) the call was received, (2) it has been logged in the company's incident tracking or problem management system, and (3) it is being handled. In other words, acknowledging the voice mail is not the same as resolving the customer's problem or request. The first step is to simply let the customer know that their voice mail message has been received and logged. In some companies, voice mail messages are logged and acknowledged via e-mail. Analysts may also contact customers who have left a voice mail message to verify the accuracy of the customers' information or to gather additional information.

TIP The voice mail recording customers hear should list the specific information they should provide when leaving a message, such as their name, a telephone number where they can be reached, their account number or personal identification number (PIN) when applicable, the product they are calling about, and a brief description of their problem or request.

Voice mail requests are typically logged in the help desk's incident tracking or problem management system in the same way as a telephone call. Most incident tracking and problem management systems automatically assign a ticket number or unique identifier to logged customer requests.

NOTE The term *ticket* is a throwback to the days when customer requests were recorded on paper forms or tickets. Today, of course, customer problems and requests are logged electronically, but the term ticket is still widely used. Tickets may also be called cases, incidents, logs, and records. Incident is the most commonly used term and is the term used by the Information Technology Infrastructure Library (ITIL). Recall that ITIL is a set of best practices for IT service management.

TIP An excellent practice is to provide customers with their ticket number as assurance that their request will not be lost or forgotten. Also, inform customers that they can reference the ticket number when calling to check the status of a problem or request. If the help desk's Web site provides the capability, inform customers that they can use the ticket number to obtain a status update online.

Fax

A fax is an electronic device that sends or receives printed matter or computer images. Some companies allow their customers to fill out forms or write letters requesting service and then fax the form or letter to the help desk. Occasionally, a help desk analyst may ask a customer to fax information, such as a report that has an error message, to the help desk so that the analyst can see the error and better diagnose the problem. Faxed requests are typically logged in the help desk's incident tracking or problem management system in the same way as a telephone call.

Fax-on-Demand

With fax-on-demand, customers use their touch-tone telephone to request that answers to FAQs, procedures, forms, or sales literature be delivered to the fax machine at the number they provide. Help desks encourage analysts, when appropriate, to inform customers that this type of system is available. Analysts are then free to work on more complex issues, and customers can quickly receive the desired information at their convenience, even if it is after hours and the help desk is closed.

NOTE   In lieu of using a fax, many help desks provide forms that customers can complete and submit electronically through the help desk's Web site or by e-mail. The information captured using these electronic forms typically corresponds to the problem entry screen of the company's incident tracking or problem management system. Once the electronic form has been completed, the information is automatically logged in the incident tracking or problem management system. A benefit of using electronic forms is that once the information is logged in the incident tracking system, an e-mail that acknowledges the customer's request and provides a target response time can automatically be sent to the customer. Most companies also have paper forms that can be used as a backup if the system goes down.

Automatic Call Distributor

An **automatic call distributor** (ACD) answers a call and routes, or distributes, it to the next available analyst. If all analysts are busy, the ACD places the call in a queue and plays a recorded message, such as "We're sorry, all of our service representatives are currently assisting other customers; your call will be answered in the order it has been received." Some companies provide an estimate of the time customers can expect to wait for the next available analyst, and may let customers choose between waiting in the queue or leaving a voice mail message. According to the Help Desk Institute's 2003 Practices Survey, 57% of its members use ACDs and another 9% plan to add ACDs within 12 months.

NOTE   A **queue** is, quite simply, a line. In terms of an automatic call distributor, the term *queue* refers to a line of calls waiting to be processed. The term *queue* can also be used to refer to a list of tickets waiting to be processed in an incident tracking system or a list of e-mail messages waiting to be processed in an e-mail response management system (discussed in Chapter 6).

ACD software determines what calls an analyst receives and how quickly the analyst receives those calls. Analysts use an ACD console to perform ACD functions (discussed in the following bullet points). Figure 5–2 shows a sample ACD console.

Figure 5-2 Sample ACD console

An ACD console, like the one shown in Figure 5–2, enables analysts at their desks to:

- Log on at the start of a scheduled shift each day and place the telephone in an available state. An available state means the analyst is ready to take calls.
- Log off anytime they leave their desk for an extended period of time and log on when they return.
- Log off at the end of a scheduled shift each day.
- Answer each call routed to them within a certain number of rings, as specified by help desk policy, to avoid an idle state. An idlestate means the analyst did not answer a call routed to his or her telephone within the specified number of rings. When an idle state occurs, the ACD transfers the call to the next available analyst.
- Correctly use **wrap-up mode,** a feature that prevents the ACD from routing a new inbound call to an analyst's extension. Help desk analysts use this wrap-up time to finish documenting the customer's request after they have hung up, to escalate a call, and to prepare for the next call. Many companies establish guidelines for how long analysts can stay in wrap-up mode before making themselves available to take the next call.

The terminology used to describe these ACD functions and states varies slightly from one ACD system to the next.

NOTE ACDs provide a wealth of statistical information that the help desk can use to measure individual and team performance. Also, some ACD systems enable companies to use this tool to queue and manage e-mail, voice mail, fax, and Internet inquiries along with traditional telephone calls. This feature is very attractive to companies because it enables them to use a single tool to produce statistics about their workload.

ACDs can integrate with and use other technologies to deliver information to analysts and customers. For example, when integrated with an announcement system, an ACD can inform customers about the status of a system that is down. An announcement system is a technology that greets callers when all help desk analysts are busy and can provide answers to routine questions or promotional information. The ACD can use caller ID data (discussed later) to provide the help desk analyst with the name of the caller. ACDs also can use the caller's telephone number or information collected from the caller such as an account number or a PIN to route the call. This information can be captured in a number of different ways, such as an automated attendant, a voice response unit, or automatic number identification, (all of which are discussed later in this chapter).

ACDs also may come with advanced features. Two common ACD advanced features are automated attendant and skills-based routing.

An **automated attendant** is an ACD feature that routes calls based on input provided by the caller through a touch-tone telephone. Systems that have speech-recognition capability allow customers to speak their input, rather than key it in through their telephone keypad. A basic automated attendant prompts the caller to select from a list of options or enter information, such as the extension of the party the caller wants to reach, and then routes the call based on the caller's input. Automated attendants can be much more sophisticated. They can also be integrated with other technologies to enhance functionality. For example, automated attendants can use caller ID or automatic number identification data to identify the customer and then route the caller to an appropriate analyst or group of analysts.

Skills-based routing (SBR) is an ACD feature that matches the requirements of an incoming call to the skill sets of available analysts or analyst groups. The ACD then distributes the call to the next available, most qualified analyst. Skills-based routing determines the call requirements from the customer's telephone number or information collected from the customer or from a database. This information is obtained from services such as caller ID and automatic number identification, or from a voice response unit. Companies that use SBR require analysts to create and maintain a skills inventory that correlates the products, systems, and services supported by the help desk to each analyst's level of skill. Then, calls can be routed to an analyst who has the skill needed to handle the customer's problem or request. For example, with SBR, a call concerning a spreadsheet application can be routed to an analyst who has a depth of experience supporting spreadsheets.

Voice Response Unit

A **voice response unit(VRU),** which may also be called an interactive voice response unit (IVRU), integrates with another technology, such as a database or a network management system, to obtain information or to perform a function. A VRU obtains information by having callers use the keys on their touch-tone telephone, or, when speech recognition is available, speak their input into the telephone. For example, a VRU can collect a unique identifier, such as a customer's employee ID or PIN, and then use it to verify that the customer is entitled to service. A VRU can prompt customers to specify the nature of their inquiry or the type of product they are using and then route the call to an analyst skilled in that product. Some companies also use a VRU to automate routine tasks, such as changing a password or checking the status of an order. Other companies use a VRU to provide access to a reduced set of help desk services during nonbusiness hours. For example, after normal business hours a VRU can enable a customer to hear system status information, leave a voice mail message, or page an analyst if the customer is experiencing a critical problem.

NOTE

Many of us have experienced the frustration of reaching a company and being prompted to select an option from a long list of choices. To increase customer acceptance, the optimum number of choices for a VRU menu is four options that lead to no more than four additional options. Optimally, one of the options enables customers to speak with an analyst. To avoid confusion and frustration, VRUs should also be programmed to provide callers with the ability to repeat the menu options, return to the main menu, and cancel input by, for example, using the asterisk key. A well-designed VRU enables callers to feel that they are in control of calls and that they have options, rather than feeling that the company is simply trying to avoid human interaction.

When poorly implemented or when used improperly, telephone technology can lead to customer frustration and be perceived negatively. When customers mistrust or dislike technology, it affects how they interact with help desk analysts and how analysts receive their work. For example:

- Some companies fail to respond to voice mail and fax messages in a timely fashion. As a result, customers may mistrust that technology and choose to wait in the queue instead. This means that help desk analysts are required to be on the telephone for extended periods of time.

- Some companies are not staffed properly, causing customers to spend an extended time waiting in the queue. When customers finally reach an analyst, they may be more upset at having to wait than they were about the problem they were originally calling to report.

- Some companies offer long VRU menus with a number of confusing options. Because there may not be any way to reach a human being who can help, customers select the option they think most closely matches their need. As a result, help desk analysts occasionally receive calls from disgruntled customers or calls that they are not qualified to handle because a customer inadvertently selected the wrong option or was unsure of which option to select.

- Some companies fail to provide customers with the ability to leave a message or reach a human being. As a result, customers are forced to either wait in a queue, hang up and call back later, or seek an alternate form of support.

These negative effects are a result of telephone technology that has been poorly implemented. By listening to customers and help desk analysts and implementing the technology in a way that both perceive is useful and beneficial, companies can minimize these negative effects.

Telephone technology is not a substitute for help desk analysts. Implemented correctly, it is a powerful communication tool that can enhance the services a help desk offers and benefit help desk analysts. For example, tools such as voice mail and fax offer flexibility to customers and time away from the telephone to analysts. Automatic call distributors can broadcast messages at the beginning of the call that inform customers about, for example, a virus that is affecting the network, thus reducing the number of calls that analysts must handle. Automatic call distributors and voice response units can also use caller ID data or automatic number identification data to provide the analyst with the name of a caller. **Caller identification (caller ID)** is a service provided by your local telephone company that tells you the telephone number of the person calling. **Automatic number identification (ANI)** is a service provided by your long distance service provider that tells you the telephone number of the person calling. ACDs and VRUs can also use the caller's telephone number or information collected from the caller through automated prompts to route the call to the analyst best suited to handle the customer's request. As a result, analysts receive only the calls they can handle, which reduces their stress.

Many companies use computer telephony integration to further enhance the services offered via the telephone. **Computer telephony integration (CTI)** links telephone technology with computing technology to exchange information and increase productivity. Companies use CTI at the help desk to perform functions such as screen pops and simultaneous screen transfers. CTI can also facilitate fax server transmissions and outgoing calls which means that people can send faxes or dial an outgoing call right from their computer.

A **screen pop** is when information about the caller appears, or pops up, on an analyst's monitor based on caller information captured by the telephone system and passed to a computer system. Figure 5–3 illustrates how the telephone system can use caller ID to determine the caller's telephone number and the computer system can look up the number in the company's customer database to find additional information, such as the caller's name and address. The computer can add this information to the telephone number and create a new ticket that pops up on the screen of the analyst taking the call.

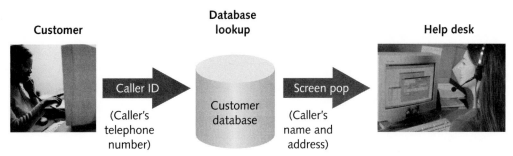

Figure 5–3 Computer telephony integration

The analyst can quickly verify the customer's information and then ask questions and add details of the customer's incident to the ticket. A history of the caller's previous problems and requests can also pop up on the screen. The analyst can then use that history to diagnose the customer's problem or provide a status update. A screen pop reduces the amount of data that an analyst must gather to create a ticket and enables the analyst to quickly verify the customer's information and begin determining the customer's need. A screen pop also ensures that the data collected is accurate and complete because much of the information is entered automatically, rather than by an analyst.

When working in a help desk, you must understand the telephone technology that is available and strive to use it properly. Regardless of the technology that is available, there are proven techniques that can facilitate faster and smoother telephone transactions. These techniques enable you to present a positive image to customers and leave them feeling confident that their call has been handled professionally.

Handling Calls Professionally from Start to Finish

Jan Carlzon, former president and CEO of Scandinavian Airlines (SAS) refers to service encounters as "Moments of Truth" for a company (*Moments of Truth*, 1989). This means that to be excellent, customer service providers must view each and every customer encounter as critical to the success of the company. This is particularly true when interacting with customers over the telephone. Over the telephone, customers cannot see an analyst's body language to know that the analyst is ready to assist them or is listening. They cannot see that the analyst is using a tool to determine an answer to their question. All they have to go on is what the analyst says and how the analyst says it. Figure 5–4 lists some of the most common "Moments of Truth" that occur in the course of a call to a help desk.

Each of these moments contributes considerably to how customers perceive an analyst and the entire company. The use of a script, or standard set of text and behaviors, is a common help desk practice that is particularly useful when providing technical support. Using scripts and turning them into a habit enables analysts to focus their energy on solving problems and handling unique situations. Analysts may use scripts when they need to find a positive way to say something they do not feel comfortable saying, such as "No," to a customer.

- Answering the telephone
- Handling calls about unsupported products or services
- Taking a message
- Closing the call

Figure 5–4 "Moments of Truth" during telephone calls

Scripts also enable customers to perceive that help desks deliver services consistently. By learning and applying the following proven techniques, you can feel confident that you are providing the best service possible, regardless of the situation.

> *Customer service should flow smoothly, almost effortlessly. Everything about the business is touched and nourished by it. It's not a department, it's an attitude.*
> Author Unknown

Answering the Telephone

How you answer the telephone sets the tone for the entire conversation. Grunting your last name into the telephone, a common practice followed by some technicians, is not good telephone etiquette. When answering the telephone, pick up the telephone promptly, but with composure. Customers like timely service but they also like working with someone who is composed and in control. Put a smile on your face and, if you have one, glance in a mirror to ensure you appear willing and ready to assist the customer. Remember that your smile, energy, and enthusiasm are communicated to the customer through your tone of voice. Take a deep breath so the customer perceives you are relaxed and in control.

NOTE   Most companies have a guideline or goal that reflects how quickly the telephone should be answered. For example, most companies strive to answer the telephone within three rings. Companies that have telephone technology that places customers in a queue if an analyst is not available may strive to answer the telephone within a goal time, such as 20 seconds.

Answer the telephone using your company's standard script. This ensures that customers are greeted in the same, consistent way. Many companies use the following approach:

1. **Announce the name of your company or department.** This lets customers know they have reached the right place. Some companies place a greeting such as "Hello," "Thank you for calling," or "Good Morning" in front of the department name. This is because customers very often do not hear the first word or two that is stated and so the first thing they do hear is the department

or company name. Be careful when using greetings such as "Good Morning" and "Good Afternoon." If you state the time of day incorrectly or if the customer is in a different time zone, the customer may perceive that you are inattentive or insensitive. The best practice is to keep it simple.

> *Quality is never an accident; it is always the result of high intention, intelligent direction, and skillful execution. It represents the wise choice of many alternatives.*
> Will A. Foster

2. **Give the caller your name.** Say your name slowly, so it can be understood. Providing your name is a simple courtesy and it lets customers know that you are taking ownership (discussed later) of their problem or request. Your company's policy will dictate whether you provide your first name or your title and surname.

3. **Ask the first question.** By asking the first question, you take control of the call and begin gathering needed information. Your company's policy and the technology you use will determine the question you ask. For example, some help desks must determine if customers are entitled to service before they begin handling a call. In this case, you may ask customers for a customer ID or a product serial number. You can then use their response to look up information in the company's incident tracking or problem management system. Some help desks simply ask customers how they can help. Resist the temptation to ask personal questions or questions that can veer the call off track. This is a common mistake that analysts make when they know customers personally or have established a high degree of rapport. Greeting a customer with a hearty "Hey, Jan, how was your vacation?" will elongate the call and may offend a customer who is experiencing a severe problem and needs immediate help. The best practice is take care of business first and keep personal conversation to a minimum.

The following are a few examples of standard help desk greetings:

Help Desk, this is Carmen. How may I help you?

Help Desk, this is Sue. May I have your name please?

Hello, Options Unlimited, this is Leon. May I have your customer ID?

After greeting the customer, listen *actively* to the customer's request. When asking the customer for the information you need to log the request, ask every customer for the same information *in the same order every time*. For example, if you must determine a customer's name, location, and employee ID in order to log the request, ask for that information in the same order every time. Over time, customers learn what information they need to provide when they call. Customers can then be prepared and often begin to volunteer the information before being asked. As a result, you will be able to quickly and easily log the customer's request.

If you speak with a customer regularly and know, for example, his address or telephone number, a good practice is to verify the information rather than skipping over that step and assuming that what you have is correct. For example, ask, "Julian, do you still live at 123 Main Street?" You want to verify the information because the customer may have moved or some information may have changed. This also ensures that the customer knows the call is being logged and manages the customer's expectation of how calls are handled no matter who answers the call. Remember that you are usually not the only person on the help desk. Although it may seem that you are making it easier for the customer by skipping steps and failing to ask questions, you are actually doing the customer and your coworkers a disservice. A customer who has gotten used to speaking with you may be dissatisfied when your coworker follows the standard procedure. As a result, the customer may ask to speak with only you in the future. Although this seems like a compliment, it actually is not in the customer's best interest because you may not always be available when that customer needs help. The help desk is a team setting; by being consistent you communicate your company's policies and you convey to customers that anyone on the help desk can assist them.

Handling Calls about Unsupported Products or Services

Few companies are in a position to be "all things to all people." This means that few companies can support every product or service their customers may conceivably use. The costs would simply be too high. As a result, many companies define a list of supported products and services. In an internal help desk setting, the help desk supports those products that are most commonly used by the company's employees and those products that most directly contribute to the company's goals. In an external help desk setting, the supported products and services are limited to those developed or sold by the company, or those the help desk has been contracted to support. Most external help desks do not support products and services that are developed or sold by another company unless they are being compensated to do so. The help desk receives training, documentation, and procedures related to the products and services it does support. It also typically has a copy of supported software and may have access to a lab environment that contains supported hardware that it can use to replicate and diagnose problems. Thus, the help desk is able to deliver high-quality support.

Help desk analysts often have a hard time referring customers to another group or company when customers need help with unsupported products or are requesting unsupported services. In other words, they have a difficult time saying "No" to customers. This is particularly difficult for help desk analysts who may be familiar with the product the customer is calling about because they supported that product in the past. Analysts want to help. It is important to remember, however, that the number of analysts assigned to the help desk is determined by the help desk's projected workload, which is based on the list of supported products and services. When help desk analysts assist customers with problems related to unsupported products, they are undermining the ability of the entire team to handle work that is within its scope of responsibility. This is why it is the policy of most help desks to simply refer the customer to the correct group or company, rather than contacting that group or company for the customer. Then, help desk resources can be devoted to assisting customers who call about supported products and services. Analysts may also try to help customers only to realize that they lack the ability or authority to handle the problem. This is a disservice to customers because time and effort have been wasted working on the problem, finding a solution has been delayed, and the customer may need to start over with another group or company. Assisting a customer with an unsupported product also leads the customer to expect that she can contact the help desk about this product in the future. The customer will become dissatisfied if another analyst refers her to the correct group or company.

 NOTE   Referring a customer who needs help with an unsupported product or service to another group or company is different than escalating a problem to a level two support group. Typically, the help desk does not retain ownership of problems relating to unsupported products. This means that the help desk does not follow up to ensure the problem is resolved to the customer's satisfaction. It lets the other group or company assume that responsibility.

Remember that while your help desk may not support some products and systems, there is always something you can do for the customer. Many help desks develop scripts that analysts can use to advise customers of their options.

> What I can do is provide you with the telephone number of the company that supports that product. They will be able to help you.
>
> What I can do is transfer you to the group that supports that product. They will be able to help you.

Sometimes you may not know who supports a product. In that case, let the customer know you will look into the matter and get back to them with an answer.

> What I can do is research this matter and call you back with the name and telephone number of someone who can help.

Although uncommon, a few companies allow an exception to this scenario by establishing a "best-effort" policy. **A best-effort** policy means you do your best to assist the customer within a predefined set of boundaries, such as a time limit. For example, you may try to assist the customer, but if you cannot resolve the problem within 15 minutes, you refer the customer to the correct group or company. This practice is sometimes found in companies that support PC-based off-the-shelf products. **Off-the-shelf products** are personal computer software products that are developed and distributed commercially. Because these products, particularly Microsoft Windows–based products, function similarly, help desk analysts can sometimes assist customers even though they have not received specialized training on a given product. By setting a time limit, the help desk can assist customers while minimizing wasted effort. A good practice is to let the customer know in advance that you are working under a time constraint or that there is a possibility you will have to refer them to another group or to a vendor.

> This product is supported by Superior Software Solutions, Inc., but what I can do is work with you for 15 minutes to see if we can resolve the problem. If we can't, I can give you Superior Software's telephone number and they will be able to assist you. Would you like to continue working on the problem or would you like to contact Superior Software?

If your company does not have a policy of giving "best-effort" support, or if you feel you do not have the ability or authority to resolve a customer's problem or request, the best practice is to quickly refer the customer to the correct group or company. Even though it may seem like you are not supporting the customer when you refer them to another group or company, you are actually helping them obtain assistance from the people who are best suited to support the products or services in question. You are also contributing to the goals of your team by resisting the temptation to devote time and effort to support services that are outside the scope of your mission.

Taking a Message

There may be times when a customer calls the help desk and asks to speak with a specific analyst. If that analyst is unavailable, let the customer know, and ask who is calling. Then, in an effort to ensure that the customer receives service as quickly as possible, ask the customer if you can do anything to help.

Inform the customer of the analyst's availability before asking for the customer's name. If you state that the analyst is unavailable after asking for a name, the customer may perceive that the analyst is available but avoiding his or her call.

TIP

When communicating to a customer the fact that an analyst is not available, explain the analyst's absence in a positive way. Also resist the temptation to give out too much information. For example, rather than informing the customer that the analyst is meeting with a supervisor, simply say that he stepped away for a couple of minutes or that the analyst is currently not available. Avoid saying things the customer may perceive negatively, such as "I don't know where he went" or "She hasn't shown up yet today."

TIP

In the best help desks, any analyst can assist a customer even if that analyst did not handle the customer's problem or initial request. For example, if the customer is inquiring about the status of an outstanding problem, you can look up the ticket in the incident tracking system and give the customer a current status. If the customer is calling to provide information, you can log that information in the ticket. If the call is personal, or concerns a matter that requires a particular analyst, such as a special project, or if there is nothing you can do to assist the customer, offer to take a message or transfer the customer to the analyst's voice mailbox.

TIP

> When transferring a caller to a voice mailbox, be careful to dial correctly so that the call is not disconnected during the transfer. When appropriate, provide the customer with the telephone number of the person to whom you are transferring the call so that the customer can reach that person directly in the future. Make sure that providing a direct telephone number is, however, an acceptable policy at your company. Also, learn what you can do in the event a call is inadvertently disconnected. For example, if you have the caller's telephone number, you may want to call him or her back and ensure a successful transfer. Or, you can contact the person the caller was trying to reach and leave a message with the name, and, when available, telephone number of the caller.

When taking a message, write down all of the important information. For example, obtain the caller's name, telephone number, the best time for the analyst to return the call, and any message the caller chooses to leave.

> Joyce has stepped away from her desk. May I ask who is calling? (Get caller's name.) Mr. Brown, Joyce should be back in 10 minutes. In the meantime, is there anything that I can help you with? (If not...) I can take a message for you, or I can transfer you to Joyce's voice mailbox. Which would you prefer? (If a message is preferred, record all important information. Read it back to the customer.) Okay, Mr. Brown, I have written that you would like Joyce to call you at 555-1234 before the end of the day about your printer problem. Is there anything else that I can help you with today? (If not...) Thank you for calling, Mr. Brown. Feel free to call anytime.

Read the information back to the caller and verify that you have gotten everything correct. Place the message where the analyst will see it upon his or her return. You may also want to relay the message to the analyst via voice mail or e-mail on behalf of the customer. If the message is urgent and the technology is available, you may want to page the analyst, send an instant message, or contact the analyst by cell phone.

Closing the Call

There is always something to do in technical support and a help desk can be a particularly busy place. Because of this, there is often a temptation to rush the closing of a call in an effort to take the next call or move on to the next problem. Trust and customer confidence comes, however, by taking a little extra time and making sure that the customer is comfortable with the steps you have taken, before you hang up the telephone. Ending the call on a positive note leaves the customer with a lasting, good impression.

> *Be quick but do not hurry.* John Wooden

Figure 5–5 lists some points to consider when ending the call. Each of these items is important and helps close the call effectively and professionally.

> 1. Recap the call.
>
> 2. Repeat any action steps that you are going to take.
>
> 3. Be specific about the time frame within which the customer can expect a resolution or a status update.
>
> 4. Share any information that will enable the customer to be more self-sufficient in the future.
>
> 5. Ask the customer if there is anything else you can do.
>
> 6. Thank the customer for calling.
>
> 7. Let the customer hang up first.

Figure 5–5 Steps for closing a call effectively

The next sections look at each of these steps in more detail.

Step 1. Recap the Call.   Take a moment to ensure that you have collected all the information needed to log the customer's problem or request and any information that may be required by level two service providers. Verify that all the information you have collected is accurate and complete. Provide the customer a ticket number and let the customer know that she can use that number if she calls in the future for a status update.

Step 2. Repeat Any Action Steps That You Are Going To Take.   Provide the customer an overview of what you are going to do. For example, "I need to try to duplicate this problem in our lab" or "I need to check with our Accounting department to verify the correct policy." If the problem must be escalated to level two, let the customer know that. Remember to resist the temptation to impart too much information. The customer usually does not need to know the name of the person who will be working on the problem. You may not even know that yourself. Keep it simple.

> Dr. Rogers, I'm assigning this ticket to the network administration group. They will be able to make this change to your account.

Step 3. Be Specific About the Time Frame Within Which the Customer Can Expect a Resolution or a Status Update.   This is one of the greatest challenges you will face in technical support. On one hand, customers do not want vague time frames, such as "We'll get to it when we can" or "We'll get to it as soon as possible." On the other hand, level two support groups are sometimes hesitant to commit to deadlines that they may not be able to meet. This is not a problem you can solve. It is up to your management team to establish SLAs that clearly define the time frame within which problems must be resolved. Then you can state these guaranteed times to your customers. As shown in Table 5–1, most companies establish guidelines for target resolution times that consider the problem severity and the combined efforts of service providers in level one, level two, and level three that may be called upon to resolve the problem. A **target resolution** time is the time frame within which the support organization is expected to resolve the problem. **Severity** is the category that defines how critical a problem is based on the nature of the failure and the available alternatives or workarounds. The help desk analyst and customer typically work together to determine a problem's severity.

Severity	Definition	Example
1	System or device down, critical business impact, no workaround available, begin resolution activities immediately, bypass/recover within four hours, resolve within 24 hours.	A network device is not working and many customers are affected. The only printer that can print checks or special forms is malfunctioning. A real-time critical application, such as payroll or the company's Web site, is down.
2	System or component down or level of service degraded, potential business impact, alternative or workaround available, resolve within 48 hours.	A slow response time on the network is severely affecting a large number of customers. The network is down but customers can dial in to do their work. A product is usable; however, its use is restricted due to memory constraints.
3	Not critical, customer can wait, a workaround is possible, resolve within 72 hours.	A printer is down, but customers can route their output to a similar printer down the hall. One of many registers in a retail store is down at a slow time of the month.
4	Not critical, customer can wait, a workaround is possible with no operational impact, time to resolve negotiated with customer.	A "how to" question or a request for one-on-one help using a product. Intermittent errors that the customer can work around. One of two speakers attached to a PC is not working.

Table 5–1 Sample severity definitions

NOTE

A **workaround** circumvents a problem either partially or completely, usually before implementing the final resolution. For example, helping a customer route his report to a printer down the hall when the printer in his office is jammed is an excellent workaround. The jammed printer must still be repaired, however, as a workaround is available, the problem is less severe, and therefore the target resolution time is greater.

TIP   Make sure you understand the problem severity definitions for any company where you work. More importantly, make sure you understand the target resolution time associated with each severity so that you can be specific when telling a customer when he or she can expect a resolution or a status update. Promising a swift resolution may make a customer happy in the short term; however, he or she will become dissatisfied and distrusting if the support organization cannot deliver a resolution in the time promised.

In the absence of SLAs, you can work closely with your level two support groups to gain an understanding of their workload. Then, even if you can't provide the customer an estimated resolution time, you can let him know where his request stands in the backlog. That is, how many requests the support group must handle before they get to this customer's request. If nothing else, you can offer to call the customer at an agreed upon time with a status update. Another approach is to provide the customer a time frame within which level two will contact him to schedule a time to work on the problem or request.

> Someone from the field services group will contact you within the next two hours to schedule a time when they can come out and work on your PC.

Step 4. Share Any Information That Will Enable the Customer to Be More Self-Sufficient in the Future.   Although the help desk's role is to support customers, help desk analysts best serve their customers when they enable them to help themselves. When appropriate, let customers know that they can use resources such as online help or the Internet to find answers to FAQs or solutions to common problems. You can also let the customer know that there are alternate ways to request support. For example, the customer may not know that she can use e-mail to submit inquiries or that she can download and electronically submit forms from a Web site. If the customer does not have the time to discuss these options, let the customer know that you will send an e-mail message or fax/mail a brochure that describes alternative ways to obtain support.

Step 5. Ask the Customer If There Is Anything Else That You Can Do.   Analysts are sometimes hesitant to ask if they can do more for a customer because they are afraid the customer will say "yes." This is particularly true in a busy help desk where calls are stacking up in the queue. The only alternative is to have the customer hang up and call back. This is neither practical nor good customer service. Although difficult, don't worry about the next call until you have fully satisfied the current customer. If the customer does have another request, politely ask the customer to wait for a moment while you complete the first ticket. Then handle the next request as a new ticket. If the customer has a problem or request that is beyond the help desk's mission, for example, the customer may ask you to have someone come out and repair the soda machine in the break room near his office, use the techniques discussed in the "Handling Calls about Unsupported Products or Services" section of this chapter to direct the customer to the group or company that can handle his request.

Step 6. Thank the Customer for Calling.   Remember that whether you are supporting internal customers or external customers, they are indeed customers, and you have a job because they need your help. Always thank your customers for calling, and let them know that they should not hesitate to call if they need help in the future.

Step 7. Let the Customer Hang Up First.   We've all experienced the frustration of getting cut off mid-sentence. This frustration is even greater when we must work our way through a series of menu options or wait in a queue to get back to the service provider. By letting the customer hang up first, you avoid rushing the customer or cutting the customer off. If the customer seems to be waiting for you to hang up, tactfully ask, "Is there anything else?" If there is not, then go ahead and hang up the telephone. As a courtesy to the customer, make sure the line disconnects before you begin talking to yourself, a coworker, or another customer.

The following examples demonstrate how to close a call that the analyst has not been able to resolve as well as how to close a call that the analyst has resolved.

> **After searching unsuccessfully for an answer:** Liz, I have logged your request and your ticket number is 40304. I am going to assign this ticket to the database administration group. You can expect this problem to be resolved within two hours. Is there anything else that I can help you with today? (If not ...) Thank you for calling the help desk. If you need further help, please call us again.
>
> **After finding the answer and giving it to the caller:** Kevin, did you know that you can find similar information on our Web site? (If the customer did not ...) The address of our Web site is www.supportdesk.com. Other information you'll find includes answers to FAQs and information about our other products. Is there anything else that I can help you with today? (If yes ...) Okay, please give me a moment while I save your first request. (Update and save the ticket.) Now, what else can I help you with?

When possible, log all important information in the ticket before you hang up the telephone or, if necessary, immediately after you hang up the telephone. Use the first couple of moments after you hang up the telephone to update the ticket and, if necessary, escalate the call properly. Again, this can be difficult when there are other calls in the queue or other customers waiting, but this is time well spent and it ensures that the customer receives the best possible service.

TIP A common misperception is that help desk analysts and people whose job consists primarily of handling telephone calls are the only ones that must develop professional telephone skills. Managers and level two service providers, particularly highly specialized technicians, often believe that they do not need telephone skills because it is the help desk's job to handle calls. Not true. On any given day, anyone may receive telephone calls and may need to place a caller on hold or transfer a caller to another person or group. In today's business environment where telephones are a common communication tool, excellent telephone skills are indispensable regardless of your position.

Avoiding the Most Common Telephone Mistakes

Two things that most frustrate customers are being placed on hold for an extended period and being transferred repeatedly. Pay attention when you are the customer. How do you feel when someone asks, "Can you hold please?" and then puts you on hold without waiting for a response? How do you feel when you have given a service provider a detailed explanation and they transfer you to someone else who asks, "May I help you?" and you have to begin again. When working in a help desk there will be times when it is appropriate to place a customer on hold or transfer the customer to another service provider. The proven techniques that follow enable you to conduct these transactions in a way that engages your customer and minimizes frustration.

Putting a Customer on Hold

At times it will be necessary to put a customer on hold while you look up information or determine if another service provider is available. You may need to put a customer on hold if another customer is in front of you demanding your attention or if another call is coming in, for example, on the help desk's emergency line. Remember that it takes only a little extra time to put customers on hold in a professional manner that instills confidence. It is also important to let customers decide if they would prefer to have you call back rather than being placed on hold. Figure 5–6 lists some points to remember when placing a caller on hold.

1. Ask the customer if you can put him or her on hold.

2. Tell the customer why he or she is being put on hold.

3. Tell the customer approximately how long he or she can expect to be on hold. Be realistic when estimating time it will take you to complete a task. If you tell the customer it will take you "Just a second," the customer will immediately mistrust your estimate. A good guideline is to never ask a customer to hold if you are going to be longer than three minutes.

4. Wait for the customer to respond. *This is very important.* If the customer does not want to be placed on hold, ask what he or she would prefer. If a call back is preferred, set a time when it is convenient for the customer and when you know you will indeed be able to call.

5. When placing a customer on hold, use the Hold button on your telephone. Resist the temptation to simply set your headset or telephone down on your desk. The customer may want to read or think while on hold and may find the background noise distracting. The customer may also hear you asking questions or interacting with other customers or service providers who have come into your workspace and perceive that you are neglecting his or her problem.

6. When you return, thank the customer for holding. Resist the temptation to say, "I'm sorry to keep you holding." Customers may consider such a comment insincere because if you were really sorry, you would not have kept them on hold in the first place.

Figure 5–6 Steps for putting customers on hold

The following example demonstrates how to use all of these points to put a customer on hold.

> Tim, may I put you on hold for approximately two minutes while I obtain more information? (Wait for an answer.) Okay, I will be back with you in a minute or two. (...forty-five seconds pass.) Thank you for holding. What I have learned is that the next release of that product will be available in two months.

If you find it is going to take you longer than expected to handle a particular task, return to the customer and give the customer an update on your progress and the option of either continuing to hold or receiving a call back. The important thing is to stay in control and remain sensitive to your customer's needs. If you have one customer on hold for an extended period of time and another customer who is receiving only half of your attention, it is likely that neither customer will be satisfied. The best practice is to focus your energies on one customer at a time.

Knowing When and How to Transfer Calls

There are a number of reasons why you may need to transfer a caller to another person or group. The customer may ask to speak with a particular analyst, she may have a problem or question that requires the help of a subject matter expert, or he may simply have called the wrong number and must be transferred to another department. Figure 5–7 lists a number of different ways to transfer a caller. The method used will depend on the type of call and the needs of the caller.

- Hot transfer (conference call)
- Warm transfer
- Cold transfer

Figure 5–7 Telephone transfer techniques

A primary consideration of which technique to use when transferring calls is the amount of information you have received or given until the point when you determine a transfer is needed. The following examples demonstrate when and how to use the hot, warm, and cold telephone transfer techniques.

Hot Transfer (Conference Call).   A hot transfer, or conference call, occurs when you stay on the line with the customer and the service provider whom you are engaging in the call. A conference call may be appropriate when:

- You can continue to contribute to the resolution of the customer's request.

- You can benefit from hearing how the problem is resolved by another help desk analyst or by a specialist from another group. For example, the problem being described by the customer has been occurring frequently, and you want to learn how to solve it in the future.

- Time allows; that is, there is no backlog of incoming calls or work in the queue.

Before you establish a conference call, inform the caller that you would like to engage another service provider and ask if it is okay. This is very important. If the customer does not want to stay on the line, ask what she would prefer. If a call back is preferred, set a time that is convenient for the customer. Make sure you clearly communicate to the other service provider the customer's expectation of when she wants to be contacted.

When establishing a conference call, put the customer on hold and place a call to the person whom you want to engage in the call. Briefly explain the problem to the service provider along with how you feel he can contribute to the resolution of the problem. Ask the service provider for his permission to bring the customer on the line.

Use common sense when engaging another service provider. If the problem is critical and requires immediate attention, make sure the service provider knows that. If the problem is not critical, ask the service provider whether this is a good time or whether you could schedule a more convenient time for a conference call. Being considerate is in the best interest of your customer and will also enable you to maintain a good relationship with other service providers.

When permission is granted, bring the customer on the line and introduce the customer and the service provider. As a courtesy to the customer, explain the reason for the conference call and relay to the service provider any information the customer has given you thus far in the call. Include any problem determination steps you and the caller have already tried. This is very important. Resist the temptation to have the customer repeat everything she has told you as this could leave the customer with the perception that you were not listening. You can, however, engage the customer in the call by asking her to let you know if you restated any information incorrectly. You can also encourage the customer to jump in if she would like to contribute additional information. Let the customer and the service provider know you plan to stay on the line. Stay on the line until the call is completed to the customer's satisfaction. Close the call as you normally would.

When working in a help desk, you can avoid embarrassment and customer frustration by understanding how to use your company's telephone system to put customers on hold and transfer customer calls. Follow available procedures or, when necessary, request the training you need to feel confident that you will not inadvertently disconnect your customers. Also, when transferring the customer to another department, make sure you let the customer know if there will be a wait in a queue or perhaps a voice mailbox.

Using someones name

Warm Transfer. A **warm transfer** occurs when you introduce the customer and the service provider to whom you are going to transfer the call but you do not stay on the line. A warm transfer may be appropriate when:

- There is no perceived value to be gained or given by staying on the line. For example, you do not feel that you can continue to contribute to the resolution of the customer's request. Or, you do not believe you can benefit from hearing how the problem is resolved by another help desk analyst or by a specialist from another group.
- Time does not allow you to stay on the line. For example, there is a backlog of incoming calls in the queue or you need to attend a meeting.

Before you warm transfer a call, inform the caller that you would like to transfer him to another service provider and explain why. For example, the service provider may be a subject matter expert who is best suited to answer the customer's question. Or, the service provider is a security administrator and has the authority to provide the customer with the requested access to a confidential system. Ask the customer for permission to transfer him or her to the service provider. This is very important. If the customer does not want to stay on the line, ask what he would prefer. If a call back is preferred, set a time that is convenient for the customer. Make sure you clearly communicate to the other service provider the customer's expectation in terms of when he wants to be contacted.

Your company's policy and the role of the service provider to whom you are transferring the call will determine whether you place the customer on hold first, or simply transfer the call. If there is a possibility that the service provider will either not be available or not be in a position to assist, put the customer on hold and place a call to the service provider to whom you want to transfer the call. Ask the service provider for her permission to bring the customer on the line. When permission is granted, bring the customer on the line. If you know the service provider is available and in a position to assist the customer, simply bring the service provider on the line.

Once you have both parties on the line, introduce the customer and the service provider. As a courtesy to the customer, explain the reason you are transferring the call and relay any information you have been provided thus far in the call. Include any problem determination steps you and the caller have already tried and explain how you think the service provider can assist. As was the case when establishing a conference call, resist the temptation to have the customer repeat everything he has told you. This could leave the customer with the perception that you were not listening. You can, however, engage the customer in the call by asking him to let you know if you restated any information incorrectly. You can also encourage the customer to jump in if he would like to contribute additional information. Let the caller and the service provider know that you will not be staying on the line.

> Mrs. Higgins, I understand your urgency in this matter. Would you mind if I transferred you to our spreadsheet expert for immediate assistance? (Wait for answer.) Great. Let me see if I can get her on the line.

Once you feel confident that you have relayed all important information and both the customer and service provider have what they need to proceed, give the customer and the service provider the ticket number assigned to the customer's request for follow-up purposes. Encourage both the customer and the service provider to let you know if there is anything else that you can do and then hang up.

Cold Transfer.   A cold transfer occurs when you stay on the line only long enough to ensure that the call has been transferred successfully. A cold transfer is appropriate when:

- The customer asked to be transferred.
- You quickly realize that the caller has dialed the wrong telephone number or that the caller should be transferred to another person or department.

A cold transfer is not appropriate when the customer has provided detailed information about the nature of her request. For example, if a customer is upset and begins venting as soon as you pick up the telephone, you want to listen actively and collect as much information as you can. When the customer has provided detailed information, use either the hot or warm transfer technique described previously.

When a cold transfer is appropriate, acknowledge the customer's request to be transferred and let her know that you are going to transfer her to the correct department. This is very important. If the customer indicates that she does not want to be transferred, ask what she would prefer. If a call back is preferred, set a time that is convenient for the customer. Make sure you clearly communicate to the other service provider when the customer wants to be contacted.

TIP   When appropriate, provide the customer with the telephone number of the person or group to whom you are transferring the call so that the customer can reach that person or group directly in the future. Many companies, particularly those that provide toll-free numbers, take this approach in an effort to manage the high cost of calls to the help desk. Make sure that providing a direct telephone number is, however, an acceptable policy at your company. Some companies prefer not to give out the direct telephone numbers of employees. Rather, customers are encouraged to contact a department, such as the help desk, when they need support.

Transfer the call, making sure you dial carefully so the customer is not cut off.

Please hold one moment while I transfer you to the Benefits department.

Handling a customer call and placing a customer on hold or transferring a customer to another service provider requires the use of common sense and sensitivity. Pay attention when you are the customer so that you can gain an appreciation of how it feels when these techniques are and are not used appropriately. By applying these techniques appropriately, you can ensure that every customer feels that you have fully respected his or her time and needs.

> *To give real service, you must add something which cannot be bought or measured with money, and that is sincerity and integrity.* Donald A. Adams

FINE-TUNING YOUR TELEPHONE SKILLS

Telephone skills, like any other skills, need to be honed. You can always learn new techniques and you can periodically rekindle your skills by attending a refresher course. New best practices are constantly emerging that you can use to improve your skills. Also, sometimes analysts just need to get back to the basics of excellent service: being responsive; demonstrating a caring attitude; and acknowledging the fact that customers are living, breathing human beings who have called because they need your help. This last point is particularly important when interacting with customers over the telephone, a technology that can be viewed as very impersonal.

Continuously improving your skills enables you to feel more comfortable and confident as a service provider, and also enables your customers to know that you care and that you sincerely want to help. As listed in Figure 5–8, there are a number of techniques you can use to fine-tune your telephone skills.

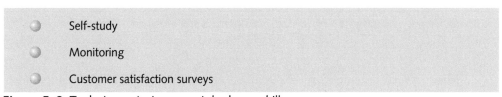

- Self-study

- Monitoring

- Customer satisfaction surveys

Figure 5–8 Techniques to improve telephone skills

SPEAKERPHONE ETIQUETTE

A speakerphone is a telephone that contains both a loudspeaker and a microphone. It allows several people to participate in a call at the same time without the telephone receiver being held. In some help desk settings, the use of speakerphones is discouraged for a number of reasons. First, many people don't feel comfortable talking on a speakerphone because they do not know who else may belistening. Second, the quality of some speakerphones makes it difficult for the customer and the analyst to understand everything that is being said. Last, speakerphones can be disruptive to coworkers and may make it difficult for them to hear other customers. There are times, however, when speakerphones are appropriate, for example, when the team is working together to solve a problem or when the team is holding an informal meeting to exchange new information or a new set of procedures. In these cases, steps can be taken to minimize the noise that the conversation being held via speakerphone generates. The following techniques can be used to minimize the negative effects of using a speakerphone:

- If possible, use the speakerphone behind closed doors.

- Ask all callers for permission before using a speakerphone.

- Introduce each person who is present.

- Briefly explain why each person is present.

- Participants who are speaking for the first time or who are unfamiliar to other callers may want to identify themselves before they speak.

Speakerphones enable multiple people, regardless of their location, to work together. They minimize the problems that can occur when information is relayed second hand. Speakerphones also free people to use their hands to take notes, consult reference materials, and so forth. Used properly, speakerphones are an effective communication tool.

Many of these techniques can be used to improve all of your skills—business, technical, soft, and self-management—not just your telephone skills.

Self-Study

There are literally hundreds of books, videotapes, and audiocassettes available that you can use to improve your telephone skills and your skills in general. When you work at a help desk, take advantage of any training programs that are offered. Bring to the attention of your supervisor or team leader any training possibilities that you think will help. You can also engage in a self-study program by checking out books or tapes from your local library.

Monitoring

Recall that monitoring is when a supervisor or team leader listens to a live or recorded call, monitors an analyst's data entry and keystrokes during an e-mail or chat session, or sits beside an analyst to measure the quality of an analyst's performance during a customer contact. Used properly, monitoring is an excellent training technique because analysts receive specific feedback on how they can improve their call handling. Monitoring also promotes the consistent handling of telephone calls and provides employees and supervisors specific guidelines that they can use when measuring performance. Some companies use monitoring only for training purposes. Others use monitoring both as a training tool and as a way of measuring performance.

NOTE Varying techniques and technologies are used to monitor help desk calls. For example, managers may simply walk around and observe calls being handled, or they may sit side-by-side with a particular analyst to monitor not only what the analyst is saying, but also how the analyst is following established procedures and using available systems. Some managers can plug in a headset when sitting next to an analyst, making it possible for them to hear the customer's side of the call along with the analyst's. Monitoring systems make it possible for managers to silently monitor calls from their office or review recorded calls at a later time or date. Voice and screen monitoring systems enable help desk managers to remotely review the conversation between a customer and an analyst as well as the keystrokes the analyst used while logging and handling the call. Voice and screen monitoring systems are highly complex and expensive and are typically found in only large help desk and call center settings.

To be effective, a monitoring program must be implemented carefully and analysts must perceive they are being given the opportunity to be successful. Most companies involve the help desk staff when designing their monitoring program so the staff is comfortable with the program and participates willingly. For example, management and staff may jointly define guidelines for how and when employees will be monitored. They may agree to monitor only recorded calls or to silently monitor live calls five times each month. Other guidelines include agreeing not to monitor partial calls or personal calls and placing a higher weight, or importance, on items in an effort to ensure analysts are focusing on the right things. For example, companies may assign a higher weight to delivering the correct solution than they assign to transferring a call correctly.

One of the keys to a successful monitoring program is providing analysts with a checklist or scorecard that describes the specific criteria that supervisors or team leaders are using to measure the quality of a call. As shown in Figure 5–9, this checklist typically reflects all of the "Moments of Truth" that occur during the course of a telephone call. For example, checklist items may include using the help desk's standard script when answering the telephone or waiting for customers to respond before placing them on hold. Checklist items may also include items such as analysts' tone of voice, posture, use of knowledge resources, and so forth, as all of these items influence analysts' ability to deliver great service. Without a checklist, analysts are unsure what supervisors and team leaders are looking for when they monitor calls, and therefore may perceive the results as subjective.

Used properly, monitoring enables you to put yourself in the customer's shoes and objectively assess the quality of your service from the customer's perspective. An effective monitoring program provides specific feedback that you can use and apply day to day.

Customer Satisfaction Surveys

A necessity for today's help desk is to solicit feedback from customers by conducting customer satisfaction surveys. Recall that customer satisfaction surveys are a series of questions that ask customers to provide their *perception* of the support services they received. The two most common customer satisfaction surveys are event-driven surveys and overall satisfaction surveys. **Event-driven surveys** are customer satisfaction surveys that ask customers for feedback on a single recent service event. **Overall satisfaction surveys** are customer satisfaction surveys that ask customers for feedback about all calls they made to the help desk during a certain time period.

Help desk managers use survey responses to measure the performance of the help desk team and to identify improvement opportunities. Survey responses, particularly responses to event-driven surveys, can also be used to measure individual performance and identify training needs. The feedback that customers provide via event-driven surveys is particularly useful to individual analysts because it represents feedback about a specific event that the analyst handled. Analysts can use this feedback to improve their telephone skills.

If the help desk where you work does not have a monitoring program or it does not conduct customer satisfaction surveys, you can still receive feedback. You can listen actively to your customers when you are providing support. For example, if a customer begins to raise her voice, check your tone of voice to ensure that you are remaining calm and making positive statements. You can also ask a trusted coworker or your team leader to provide feedback. Ask for feedback not only when you need to improve but when you handle a situation efficiently and effectively as well.

One of the best ways to improve your telephone skills is to record and review your calls. If the technology is available, ask to review recorded calls on a periodic basis. If not, place a tape recorder on your desk and record your calls so you can hear how you sound and determine ways to improve.

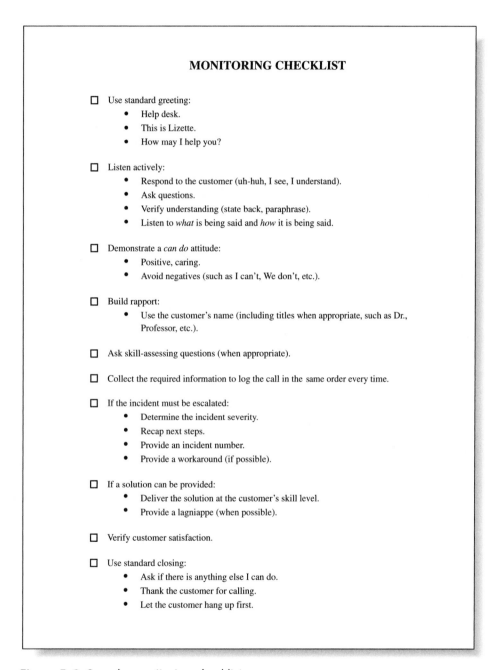

MONITORING CHECKLIST

☐ Use standard greeting:
  • Help desk.
  • This is Lizette.
  • How may I help you?

☐ Listen actively:
  • Respond to the customer (uh-huh, I see, I understand).
  • Ask questions.
  • Verify understanding (state back, paraphrase).
  • Listen to *what* is being said and *how* it is being said.

☐ Demonstrate a *can do* attitude:
  • Positive, caring.
  • Avoid negatives (such as I can't, We don't, etc.).

☐ Build rapport:
  • Use the customer's name (including titles when appropriate, such as Dr., Professor, etc.).

☐ Ask skill-assessing questions (when appropriate).

☐ Collect the required information to log the call in the same order every time.

☐ If the incident must be escalated:
  • Determine the incident severity.
  • Recap next steps.
  • Provide an incident number.
  • Provide a workaround (if possible).

☐ If a solution can be provided:
  • Deliver the solution at the customer's skill level.
  • Provide a lagniappe (when possible).

☐ Verify customer satisfaction.

☐ Use standard closing:
  • Ask if there is anything else I can do.
  • Thank the customer for calling.
  • Let the customer hang up first.

Figure 5–9 Sample monitoring checklist

Regardless of the method used to obtain feedback, analysts can use the feedback their customers and coworkers provide to identify their weaknesses and determine ways they can improve. It is important to remember that your recollection of an event and another's perception of an event may represent different perspectives. When working in a help desk, you must follow the policies of your company while being sensitive to the needs of your customers, service providers, and coworkers. If a customer perceives that you were rude or disrespectful, you must accept that and determine a more positive way to communicate in the future. If a service provider perceives that you did not relay all important information before you transferred a call, you must accept that and vow to slow down and be more thorough in the future. By working hard, being consistent, and keeping a positive attitude, you can let your caring attitude shine through.

LETTING YOUR CARING ATTITUDE SHINE THROUGH

It is difficult to handle problems and enthusiastically answer questions day in and day out. Some days it seems as if you have to drag the facts from customers who want their problems solved NOW! It is even harder to be "up" for each call, but that is what is required if your goal is to be excellent. Providing superior customer support is a habit—a state-of-mind that requires enthusism and passion. You have to work at it every day and you have to take care of yourself in the process. Practice relaxing and surround yourself with positive reminders of your commitment to customer satisfaction.

NOTE   Chapter 12 explores techniques you can use to maintain your energy and enthusiasm and minimize the stress that may take away from your ability to enjoy working in a help desk setting.

Using scripts is an excellent habit-building technique and ensures consistent "Moments of Truth" when customers call the help desk. Scripts are not meant, however, to make you behave like a robot, never deviating from predefined remarks. Try to avoid rushing through scripts or using a tone of voice that implies tedium or boredom. When appropriate and allowed, change the phrasing of your script slightly to make it sound fresh and enthusiastic. For example, rather than always saying "Feel free to call us if you need help in the future," you can say "Give us a call if there is anything else you need." What you say is important and the words you use must be positive, but how you say it is equally as important. Be enthusiastic!

TIP   Become familiar with all of the scripts used at the help desk where you work and, when needed, suggest additional scripts.

It is also important to remember that help desks that respond to calls in a consistent manner are perceived as more professional than those that do not. When help desk analysts respond to calls in different ways, customers may be uncomfortable during the call handling process, or they may begin to mistrust the responses they receive. When working in a help desk, you must understand your company's policies and resist the temptation to deviate from those policies, even when you perceive that doing so is in your customer's best interests. If you feel a policy needs to be changed, provide your team leader or supervisor with the reasons why you believe a change is needed and suggest reasonable alternatives. Until the policy is changed, be a team player, and support the policies of your company in a positive way that acknowledges the needs of your customers. Remember that there is always something you can do.

CHAPTER SUMMARY

❒ The telephone is one of the most common ways that businesses and customers communicate today. Telephone technologies used by help desks range from simple voice mail boxes and fax machines to highly complex, automated systems, such as automatic call distributors (ACDs) and voice response units (VRUs). Implemented properly, these technologies benefit customers and help desk analysts.

❒ To be excellent, support providers must see each and every customer encounter, or "Moment of Truth," as critical to the success of the organization. "Moments of Truth" that occur in the course of a typical help desk call include answering the call, taking a message, and closing the call. Handling calls about unsupported products is also important and represents an excellent opportunity to demonstrate your can do attitude.

❒ Two things that frustrate customers most are being placed on hold for an extended period of time and being transferred repeatedly. Placing customers on hold or transferring them to another service provider requires the use of common sense and sensitivity. You can minimize customer frustration by listening to your customers' preferences and carefully managing their expectations.

❒ Telephone skills, like any other skills, need to be honed. Techniques you can use to fine-tune your skills include self-study, monitoring, and customer satisfaction surveys. You can use each of these techniques to obtain feedback that you then can use to improve your skills. You can also record and listen to your calls or you can ask a trusted coworker or your team leader for feedback. Ask for feedback about what you do well along with what areas you can improve.

❒ Providing superior customer support is hard work. You have to work at it every day and you have to develop good habits. Scripts are an excellent habit-building technique and ensure consistency when customers call the help desk. It is also important to take care of yourself, stay relaxed, and let your caring, can do attitude shine through!

KEY TERMS

announcement system — A technology that greets callers when all help desk analysts are busy and can provide answers to routine questions or promotional information.

automatic call distributor (ACD) — A technology that answers a call and routes, or distributes, it to the next available analyst.

automated attendant — An ACD feature that routes calls based on input provided by the caller through a touch-tone telephone.

automatic number identification (ANI) — A service provided by your long-distance service provider that tells you the telephone number of the person calling.

available state — An ACD state that occurs when an analyst is ready to take calls.

best effort — A policy that states analysts do their best to assist a customer within a pre-defined set of boundaries, such as a time limit.

caller identification (caller ID) — A service provided by your local telephone company that tells you the telephone number of the person calling.

cold transfer — A way of transferring a telephone call when you stay on the line only long enough to ensure that the call has been transferred successfully.

computer telephony integration (CTI) — An interface that links telephone technology with computing technology to exchange information and increase productivity.

event-driven survey — A customer satisfaction survey that asks customers for feedback on a single recent service event.

fax — An electronic device that sends or receives printed matter or computer images.

fax-on-demand — Technology that enables customers to use their touch-tone telephone to request that answers to FAQs, procedures, forms, or sales literature be delivered to the fax machine at the number they provide.

hot transfer — A way of transferring a telephone call when you stay on the line with the customer and the service provider whom you are engaging in the call; also known as a conference call.

idlestate — An ACD state that occurs when an analyst did not answer a call routed to his or her telephone within the specified number of rings.

off-the-shelf product — A personal computer software product that is developed and distributed commercially.

overall satisfaction survey — A customer satisfaction survey that asks customers for feedback about all calls they made to the help desk during a certain time period.

queue — A line.

skills-based routing (SBR) — An ACD feature that matches the requirements of an incoming call to the skill sets of available analysts or analyst groups. The ACD then distributes the call to the next available, most qualified analyst.

screen pop — A CTI function that enables information about the caller to appear, or pop up, on an analyst's monitor based on caller information captured by the telephone system and passed to a computer system.

script — A standard set of text and behaviors.

severity — The category that defines how critical a problem is, based on the nature of the failure and the available alternatives or workarounds.

speakerphone — A telephone that contains both a loudspeaker and a microphone.

target resolution time — The time frame within which the support organization is expected to resolve the problem.

voice mail — An interactive computerized system for answering and routing telephone calls, for recording, saving, and relaying messages, and sometimes for paging the user.

voice response unit(VRU) — A technology that integrates with another technology, such as a database or a network management system, to obtain information or to perform a function; also called an interactive voice response unit (IVRU).

warm transfer — A way of transferring a telephone call that occurs when you introduce the customer and the service provider to whom you are going to transfer the call but you do not stay on the line.

weight — A rating scale of importance.

workaround — A way to circumvent a problem either partially or completely, usually before implementing the final resolution.

wrap-up mode — A feature that prevents the ACD from routing a new inbound call to an analyst's extension.

REVIEW QUESTIONS

1. What do professional telephone skills ensure?

2. Why is important that calls are handled consistently?

3. What two characteristics of excellent customer support are fundamental to a positive telephone image?

4. List four factors that influence the telephone technologies used by a help desk.

5. What two things must be done for customers to view voice mail positively?

6. What technologies are some companies using in lieu of a fax machine to make forms available?

7. Do you need to log customer requests that are received via voice mail and fax?

8. List four of the capabilities that ACDs provide.

9. How is skills-based routing different from normal ACD routing?

10. A VRU integrates with another technology to do what? Provide one example.

11. How does a VRU obtain information?

12. What is a screen pop?

13. Describe three of the benefits that help desk analysts receive when telephone technology is implemented properly.

14. What are "Moments of Truth?"

15. How can scripts be used by help desk analysts?

16. What are two techniques you can use before you answer the telephone to ensure you are ready?

17. What three pieces of information should you provide or ask when answering the telephone?

18. What should you do when customers provide their name?

19. Why should you ask customers for the information you need to log calls in the same order every time?

20. When there is more than one person in the help desk, why should you avoid encouraging customers to speak with only you?

21. Why are help desks able to deliver high-quality support for supported products and services?

22. Describe four pitfalls of assisting customers with problems relating to unsupported products.

23. What should you do if a customer asks to speak with an analyst that is unavailable?

24. What are four important pieces of information that you should obtain when taking a message?

25. List the seven steps you should follow when closing a call.

26. How long should customers be kept on hold?

27. What is an important point to remember before you put customers on hold?

28. Briefly describe the differences between hot, warm, and cold transfers.

29. After you hot or warm transfer a call, why should you resist the temptation to have customers repeat everything that they already told you?

30. List two ways you can improve your telephone skills through self-study.

31. What does monitoring promote?

32. What can you learn from customer satisfaction surveys?

33. What three things can you do to obtain feedback if your company does not have a monitoring program or they do not conduct customer satisfaction surveys?

34. How may customers respond when analysts handle calls inconsistently?

35. What do you do when there is nothing you can do?

DISCUSSION QUESTIONS

1. Generally speaking, do companies that use sophisticated telephone technologies implement them in a way that benefits the company, its customers, or both? Explain your answer.

2. A customer calls on a cell phone and you can barely hear her. What should you do?

3. Monitoring calls can be perceived positively or negatively by analysts. Some analysts feel it is a form of spying, or a way to catch them doing something wrong. Other analysts feel it is an excellent way for them to receive feedback and improve their skills. What factors do you think influence how an analyst feels about monitoring? How do you feel about monitoring?

HANDS-ON PROJECTS

Project 5–1

Track telephone technology usage. For one week, keep a record of every time you encounter telephone technology when conducting personal or work-related business. Jot down the name of the company, the technology that you encountered (if you can tell), and a grade (such as A, B, or C) that reflects how well you perceive the company used the technology and the techniques discussed in this chapter. For example, if you were prompted to leave a voice mail message, were you given an indication when your call would be returned? Briefly comment on any ways these companies could improve their use of telephone technology. Share the results with your classmates.

Project 5–2

Discuss the pros and cons of VRUs. Assemble a team of at least three of your classmates. Discuss the different ways you use VRUs in the course of going about your day. The indictor that you are using a VRU is having to input information by using the keys on your touch-tone telephone or speaking into the telephone. For example, you may use a VRU at your bank to determine your current balance or whether a check has cleared. Or, you may use a VRU to register for classes at your school. Develop a list that describes the positive benefits of using this technology and the negative or frustrating experiences that you and your teammates have had. Write a brief summary of your conclusions and share them with the class.

Project 5–3

Answer the telephone with a smile. It has been said that if you do something for 21 days, it becomes a habit. For the next 21 days, practice putting a smile on your face before you answer the telephone, both at work and at home. To remind yourself to smile, place a note or mirror by your telephone. Strive to convey energy and enthusiasm in your tone of voice. Share with your classmates any feedback you received from callers.

Project 5–4

Explain an analyst's absence in a positive way. Review the following phrases and suggest ways the statements can be made more positive. Prepare a list of revised statements along with a brief explanation of your suggested revision.

1. I don't know where Jim is. I'll have him call you when he gets back.
2. I think she has gone to the restroom. Can I have her call you back?
3. He's probably still at lunch.
4. I think Louisa is coming in tomorrow. I'll have her call you if she does.
5. Judy went home early today. Can I have her call you tomorrow?
6. Mr. Sanchez has not come in yet. Would you like to try again in an hour or so?
7. Deborah is really busy right now. Would you like to leave a message?

Project 5–5

Take complete messages. When you are required to take a message for someone, whether at work or at home, collect all of the information discussed in this chapter. Ask the recipient of the message for feedback on the completeness of your message.

Project 5–6

Look for a "thank you." For the next 24 hours, note how many service providers and customers thank you for your business or for your help. Service providers can include the clerk at a local retail store or the waiter at a restaurant where you dine. Customers can be internal or external to the company where you work, or they can be coworkers or classmates that you are helping with a project. Write a brief summary of your observations.

Project 5–7

Pay attention when you are the customer. During the next two weeks, pay attention any time you are put on hold or transferred to another person or group. Note any situations wherein you experience frustration as a result of the way your call was handled or any times you were cut off. If your call was transferred, determine whether a hot, warm, or cold transfer was used. Note whether you were asked to repeat any information when your call was transferred. Write a brief summary of your experiences.

Project 5–8

Learn about the importance of telephone skills. Interview a friend, family member, or classmate, who uses the telephone extensively at work. (It does not have to be a help desk.) Ask this person the following questions:

◻ Which of the telephone technologies are used at your company?

◻ How do you perceive the effectiveness of each of these technologies?

- Do you use scripts when answering the telephone, placing customers on hold, and so forth? If yes, what are the scripts?
- What techniques do you use to improve your telephone skills?
- What techniques are used to measure your telephone skills (for example, monitoring or customer satisfaction surveys)?
- In what ways do you find the feedback derived from these techniques useful?
- What habits have you developed that enable you to have positive telephone interactions with customers?

Write a brief report that summarizes what you learned from this person. Share your conclusions with the class.

CASE PROJECTS

CASE PROJECTS

1. WRK Systems, Inc.

You have been hired as a consultant to help a new help desk develop scripts and call handling procedures. The help desk has an incident tracking system that uses the customer's PIN to retrieve the customer's profile. The help desk manager wants analysts to request this information when answering the telephone. Develop a script that analysts can use when answering the telephone. Propose the script to the help desk manager and explain the benefits of having analysts say what you are suggesting.

CASE PROJECTS

2. Shoe String Budget

You work for a help desk that has a very limited budget. Your boss asked you to determine what books or tapes can be used to improve the telephone skills of your team. Go to your local library or search the Web to prepare a list of available books and tapes you would recommend. Explain why you selected each one.

CASE PROJECTS

3. Miller Brothers, Inc.

You are the supervisor for a help desk that supports the internal customers of Miller Brother's Inc., a small manufacturing company that has recently opened a new facility in a different state. Other than the Benefits department, the help desk is the only department that has a toll-free telephone number. As a result, you are beginning to see an increase in the number of transferred telephone calls. Develop a set of step-by-step instructions that your staff can use to perform hot, warm, and cold transfers.

6

TECHNICAL WRITING SKILLS FOR SUPPORT PROFESSIONALS

In this chapter you will learn:

◆ The impact of technologies such as the Internet, e-mail, instant messaging, and knowledge management systems on the help desk and its customers and on the role of the help desk analyst

◆ The most common help desk documents used by help desks to convey information

◆ The characteristics of good technical writing and proven techniques to improve your writing skills

The technical support industry has undergone a dramatic change in the past decade in terms of how it collects information and delivers support. Most companies have implemented incident tracking and problem management systems that enable help desk analysts to log and manage customer problems and requests. Technologies such as the Internet, e-mail, and instant messaging (IM) are complementing the telephone and on-site services as ways to communicate with customers and other support professionals. Support professionals are more often using and developing online knowledge bases that contain answers to FAQs, solutions to known problems, and policies and procedures that customers can use as well. All of these changes have prompted the need for support professionals to add technical writing to their list of required skills.

Good writing skills enable you to communicate technical information accurately, completely, and comprehensively to customers, managers, and coworkers. Customers, managers, and coworkers have varying skill levels, and good writing communicates information in a way that each can understand. Because written communication conveys emotion just like verbal communication, your "tone of voice" is important when you write, just as it is when you speak. It is also important to be concise and consistent so readers can quickly obtain the information they need.

TECHNOLOGY-DELIVERED SUPPORT

Historically, customers called the help desk on the telephone or perhaps walked in to the help desk area when they needed assistance or information. Although that still happens, companies are now providing additional ways for customers to obtain support. Customers may send an e-mail message or fax a form to the help desk. Customers and other support providers may use IM systems to communicate. Companies are also establishing Web sites that customers can use to obtain support without having to wait to speak with a help desk analyst. Technology-delivered support services enable the help desk to anticipate and proactively meet its customers' needs. These alternate ways of delivering support enable the help desk to reduce the overall cost of delivering support, better prioritize and manage its workload, and, ultimately, improve help desk services.

NOTE A common misconception is that cost-cutting measures invariably result in lower quality services. Reducing the overall cost of support services by, for example, providing robust Web-based self-services can, however, result in increased customer satisfaction. The key is to ensure that technology-delivered services are quick and convenient for customers, not just cost effective for the company.

Because of the Internet, e-mail, and other technologies, help desks are completely rethinking the way they deliver support services. Successful companies understand that effective use of these technologies is not just a matter of installing hardware and software. It also requires that they must diligently capture and deliver high-quality information. For most help desks, this means rethinking not only the skills that help desk analysts must possess, but also the skills and knowledge that customers must possess.

Used effectively, technology empowers both customers and help desk analysts. Used improperly, technology can frustrate everyone and can alienate customers. Telephone, Internet, e-mail, and IM technologies all play a role in customer support. As we move into the future, no one technology will replace the others. Technologies such as the telephone and IM provide immediacy and the ability to interact with a human being. Customers will continue to use these technologies when they do not want to wait for an e-mail response or do not have the ability or the desire to access Web-based services. For example, customers will use the telephone or IM when they are experiencing a critical problem or when they have questions that need to be answered before they order a new product. They may also turn to the telephone or IM when Web-based services are not available or the network is down, or to IM when a dial-up service being used to connect to the Internet is tying up their telephone line.

Alternately, e-mail provides the ability to send and receive detailed information. Customers will continue to use e-mail when they do not require an immediate response or when they want a written reply. For example, they'll use e-mail when they want a detailed set of instructions or when they have a general inquiry, such as when the next release of a product is due out.

Web-based services provide customers with the ability to perform functions, such as filling out forms, resetting passwords, and downloading software, in addition to interacting with help desk analysts. Web-based services will continue to be used by those customers who feel comfortable using Web technology and by those who find it useful. For example, they'll use the Web when they want to have a workspace set up for a new employee or when they want to obtain answers to FAQs. Customers who want to work at their own pace and on their own schedule also will rely on Web-based services. Help desk analysts must feel comfortable communicating via all of these methods and must possess or develop the different skills that each of these technologies require.

The Help Desk Analyst's Role in a Technology-Centric World

The availability of technology has dramatically changed the role of help desk analyst. Today's analysts must be extremely flexible in their ability to continuously learn new technologies and adapt those technologies to their work. They need to understand and use myriad technologies, including the telephone, e-mail, and Web-based services, to support their customers and communicate with their coworkers. Also, analysts are required to record the results of their efforts, typically in an incident tracking and problem management system. All of these technologies extend the help desk's ability to gather, organize, and use information. **Information** is data that are organized in a meaningful way. **Data** are raw facts that are not organized in a meaningful way.

The best companies view information as an extremely valuable resource. They rely on their help desk analysts to capture, or collect, the high-quality data needed to create accurate and useful information. Consequently, help desk analysts must recognize and embrace the important role they play in capturing data and sharing knowledge. Gone are the days when simply solving a problem is good enough, or when people in a help desk setting could hoard their knowledge or relay knowledge by word of mouth. Today, help desk analysts must capture data that can be reused by customers and other analysts to solve similar problems and that can be used to produce the information needed to prevent problems from recurring. At a minimum, analysts must capture the data needed to reduce the time it takes to solve problems if they recur.

Analysts are expected to log tickets, document solutions, develop procedures, and exchange information in a way that can be easily used by customers, managers, and coworkers. As a result, writing skills and typing—or **keyboarding**—proficiency are important assets in the help desk. People with good writing and keyboarding skills can quickly, easily, and accurately capture needed data. Because they are more proficient, they may be given a wider range of responsibilities and offered greater opportunity. For example, people with good writing skills may be asked to prepare recommendations that lead to product improvements, or they may be asked to manage or contribute content to the help desk's Web site. By developing good writing skills, you can position yourself to seize these opportunities when they arise. After all, good writing skills not only enable you to communicate efficiently and effectively with customers, they enable you to communicate your abilities to management as well.

Enabling Customer Self-Service

In our busy society, people have become accustomed to using self-services, such as vending machines, voice mail, ATMs, and online banking or banking by telephone. **Self-services** are services that enable customers to help themselves. Customers appreciate services that enhance their self-sufficiency and enable them to accomplish tasks at their own pace. Given proof that a new way of obtaining service works, customers will embrace and then demand services that free up their most valued commodity—time. Enabling self-service for technical support is no different.

Many companies are embracing this self-service concept and using technologies, such as fax-on-demand, automated e-mail response management systems, and Web technology, to enable customers to help themselves. Customers use these technologies to order products, obtain product information, and find solutions to problems without speaking with a help desk analyst. Software publishing companies are also refining the design of their products in an effort to enable and encourage self-service. For example, many companies are providing robust and interactive online help with their software programs that customers can then access and use to answer questions and obtain step-by-step assistance. Hardware manufacturers and software publishers are also embedding diagnostic software in their products that customers can use to troubleshoot and potentially solve problems on their own.

Both customers and help desk analysts benefit from self-services. For example, customers benefit from self-services, such as lists of FAQs, because they do not have to speak with an analyst to receive the information they need. When lists of FAQs are published, help desk analysts are free to work on more complex problems and contribute to product improvements. Simple self-services, such as providing customers with the ability to submit requests via e-mail, are appreciated by customers because customers can use a familiar tool to request service. These simple self-services also reduce the time it takes analysts to handle requests—and therefore reduce the cost to handle requests—because customers are documenting the preliminary customer and incident data themselves (often by using online forms provided by the help desk). This data can then be logged automatically into the company's incident tracking and problem management system.

Today's demanding customers have come to expect self-services. Customers appreciate self-services because these services save them time and reduce their frustration. In fact, customers often view companies that fail to provide self-services as out-of-touch and inefficient. For example, aren't you surprised when, in this day and age, you call a company and the telephone rings unanswered? We expect to interact with some technology. At a minimum, we expect to hear a message with the company's business hours. Additionally, we want the ability to leave a voice mail message. We are suspicious when companies do not provide this "basic" service. Customers also expect companies—particularly companies that provide technical support—to use Web technology to enable self-services.

Customer Support Via the Internet

The Internet has dramatically changed the way customers expect support services to be delivered. Today's savvy customers expect external help desks to have a Web site that they can reach via the Internet. The **Internet** is a global collection of computer networks that are linked together to provide worldwide access to information. Some companies that provide external support may give customers access to secured information via an extranet. An **extranet** is a Web site that is accessed via the Internet—that is, it can be accessed by the general public—but requires a password to gain entry to all or parts of the site. Internal help desks often enable their customers to access a Web site via their company's intranet. An **intranet** is an in-house collection of linked computers that provide a company's employees and other authorized people, such as customers, access to secured information. In other words, an intranet is a secured portion of the Internet that cannot be accessed by the general public.

Self-services that help desks may offer customers via their Web sites include:

- Answers to FAQs
- Tips, techniques, and helpful hints
- Schedules for company-sponsored training classes
- Instructional videos and online demonstrations
- Information about new and planned products and services
- The ability to update customer profile information, such as address information and customer preferences
- Online forms to submit problems and requests
- Current status reports (available without calling the help desk)
- A current list of standard products
- Purchasing policies and information
- A database of solutions that customers can use to solve problems on their own
- The ability to download software, software patches, and upgrades
- The ability to reset or change a password
- E-mail links to submit requests and comments
- A link to live text chats with help desk analysts
- An icon to request a call back
- A forum to submit questions and exchange ideas with other customers
- Customer satisfaction surveys
- Links to other useful Web sites

NOTE A link, or hyperlink, is colored and/or underlined text or a graphic. Clicking a link might open a pop-up window with a definition, instructions, a still picture, or an animated picture. A link can also run an audio or video clip, or jump to a Web page.

Functionality and ease of use are the keys to a successful help desk Web site. When accessing a support Web site, customers are not looking for a simple billboard with a telephone number to call for support. They are looking for a way to obtain the information they need, when they need it. Figure 6–1 shows a sample help desk Web site.

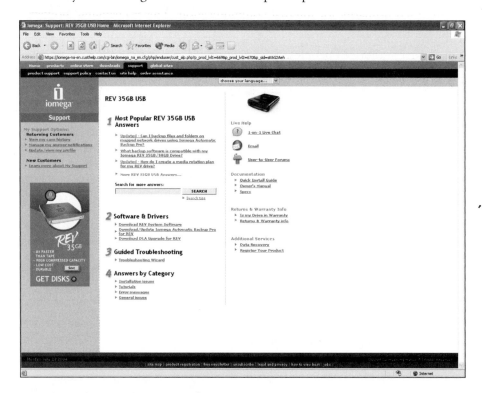

Figure 6–1 Iomega Support Web site

Well-designed Web sites offer customers a variety of options, including a searchable knowledge base, FAQs, tutorials, troubleshooting wizards, and so forth. When customers cannot find the information they need, they want to obtain assistance easily. Again, customers want options including telephone, e-mail, chat, and user forums. The best sites offer customers the ability to personalize their support experience by, for example, specifying a language, creating personalized home pages, and signing up for e-mail alerts and newsletters.

Web sites enable companies to cost-effectively deliver support to their customers 24 hours a day, 7 days a week. Even when the help desk is closed, a Web site can offer access to frequently requested information and basic services such as the ability to contact the company via e-mail.

Using E-Mail Effectively to Communicate with Customers

It is fairly common for help desk analysts to use e-mail to communicate with their coworkers and managers. Help desks may use e-mail internally to communicate the status of projects and promote awareness of changes to existing procedures, or they may use e-mail to communicate schedule changes and notify staff of upcoming system changes. According to a Help Desk Institute study, 93% of help desks use e-mail, but only 16% of help desks provide their customers with the ability to use e-mail to submit requests ("Help Desk Institute 2003 Practices Survey," Help Desk Institute, 2003, pp. 19, 33). This implies that e-mail is currently used primarily for internal communication. This is changing, however, as companies realize that e-mail is a fast and easy way to communicate with customers.

Some companies use e-mail simply to inform customers about the status of outstanding problems and requests, while encouraging customers to submit those requests via the telephone or their Web site. Increasingly, companies encourage customers to use e-mail to submit problems and requests. Often, these companies provide online forms that prompt customers for information specific to their concern. They may also automatically acknowledge that the customer's e-mail has been received, logged, and assigned a tracking number. A growing number of companies use e-mail to conduct customer satisfaction surveys. E-mail can also be used to simultaneously inform large numbers of customers about a virus, product change, or new release that might affect them.

It is important to remember that although e-mail is an easy way to communicate with customers, it does not provide many of the capabilities that an incident tracking and problem management system provides. For example, e-mail cannot be used to automatically create trend reports and it cannot be used as a knowledge base. For this reason, help desk analysts typically log all e-mail requests received from customers in their company's incident tracking and problem management system. Analysts must also record all status updates related to a customer problem or request in the incident tracking and problem management system, not in e-mail messages that may be lost or forgotten.

NOTE

Companies that use e-mail and the Web as their primary communication channels with customers are increasingly using e-mail response management systems. Recall that e-mail response management systems such as Kana (**www.kana.com**) and RightNow Technologies (**www.rightnow.com**) enable help desks to manage high-volume chat, e-mail, and Web form messages in much the same way that ACDs enable help desks to handle telephone calls. For example, these systems enable help desks to route messages to queues; run real-time reports to determine such statistics as how many e-mails are received per hour, per day, and so forth; prioritize messages; and categorize messages so help desks can report on the types of messages being received. These systems also provide analysts with the ability to search and review customer messages and view a history of a customer's activities on the support Web site. In other words, help desk analysts can see the different Web pages, FAQs, and so forth that a customer examined prior to submitting his or her message.

Many incident tracking and problem management systems now integrate with most standard e-mail packages to allow automation of common tasks. For example, e-mail messages from customers can be automatically logged as tickets. The incident tracking and problem management system can then automatically send a return e-mail message to inform customers that their call was logged and to provide a ticket number. Some companies automatically send e-mail messages to customers each time the status of their problem or request changes. Other companies automatically send e-mail messages with a detailed description of the final resolution when the ticket is closed. A customer satisfaction survey requesting feedback may accompany the final resolution.

One downside of e-mail is that it can be perceived as impersonal. Another downside is that analysts sometimes find that using e-mail lengthens the problem-solving process. For example, if the help desk receives an e-mail that does not contain sufficient information, an analyst may try to contact the customer by telephone. If the customer and analyst do not connect, the analyst must send back an e-mail message that requests the needed details. The analyst must then wait for a response before being able to solve the problem. If the analyst does not communicate effectively and the customer misunderstands the analyst's message, the problem-solving process may take even longer. To minimize these downsides, help desk analysts must use common sense and courtesy when using e-mail to communicate with customers.

NOTE

The section "E-Mail Best Practices" in this chapter provides specific techniques for using e-mail effectively.

The effective use of e-mail will gain you the respect of customers and coworkers, and, like excellent telephone skills, will serve you well throughout life. Common sense, care, good judgment, and good writing skills will enable you to make the most of this powerful communication tool. These same characteristics will enable you to make the most of tools such as chat and IM.

Using Online Chat and Instant Messaging to Facilitate Communication

Online chat and IM are extremely popular methods of communicating in both personal and work settings. This is because both are cost-effective, simultaneous ways to communicate. Unlike e-mail where there can be a delay of several minutes or more between when a message is sent and received, online chat and IM are instantaneous. They are essentially text versions of a phone call.

A **chat**, or online chat, is a simultaneous text communication between two or more people via a computer. During the 1980s and early 1990s, chat rooms became extremely popular. A **chat room** is a virtual room that provides users the ability to converse (or chat) real time with one or more other users on a local area network (LAN), on the Internet, or via a Bulletin Board Service (BBS). In other words, a chat room enables two or more people to participate in a discussion online. On the Internet, chat rooms are available from Internet service providers (ISPs) such as America Online (AOL) and Microsoft MSN, or they may be available on individual Web sites.

Companies that provide customers the ability to chat via an online support forum, for example, typically have someone from the company monitor the forum. Monitoring ensures that people using the forum are respectful to each other and the company, do not use the forum to promote other companies, do not use profanity or objectionable language, do not post personal information, and so forth. Most online forums have "forum rules" that describe the criteria that posting to the forum must meet. Postings that do not meet these criteria usually will be deleted or relocated by the forum monitor.

In a help desk setting, chat rooms may be used for team meetings, project team meetings, and trouble-shooting sessions with subject matter experts. Chat rooms also enable customers to interact with other users of a product or service.

Chat rooms are typically set up to handle group discussion, although two people can opt to break off and chat in a private room. Conversely, IM typically involves a conversation between two people, although the two people can invite others to join in. **Instant messaging systems** enable two or more people to communicate in real time on the Internet. People can send an IM by typing on a computer keyboard or on a wireless device such as a cell phone or a PDA. Unlike e-mail where you can send a message even if a recipient is not online, IM requires that all parties be online at the same time. The most popular IM services are AOL Instant Messenger, MSN Messenger, and Yahoo! Messenger.

IM is quickly surpassing e-mail as a preferred method of communication in the business world. Gartner estimates that by 2005, IM will surpass e-mail as the primary way in which consumers interact with each other electronically ("Instant Messaging: The Sleeping Giant," Gartner, Inc., April 2001).

According to the Help Desk Institute, 33% of its members use IM, up from 14% in 2002 ("Help Desk Institute 2003 Practices Survey," Help Desk Institute, 2003, p. 20). An additional 17% plan to add this capability within 12 months. In a help desk setting, help desk analysts use IM primarily to communicate with level two service providers about an ongoing problem. For example, a field service representative may use IM to inform a help desk analyst that he or she has arrived at a customer site to begin work on a high severity problem. Or, a help desk analyst may use IM to communicate with a member of the network support group about a network outage. Like e-mail, IM does not provide the capabilities of an incident tracking and problem management system, so analysts are typically required to record any status updates obtained via IM in the help desk's system. Following this procedure ensures that all parties who access the incident tracking system and problem management system have the latest information, not just the parties who are sending and receiving messages. For this same reason, most help desks currently limit IM communication with customers. For example, a help desk analyst may use IM to communicate the status of a problem to a customer that has an outstanding (logged) incident. Or, a help desk analyst may use IM to communicate with a customer whose telephone line is in use by a dial-up service. Typically, analysts must then record these IM communications with customers in the help desk's incident tracking and problem management system.

Several factors are causing companies to look more closely at using IM to communicate with customers. These factors include the following:

- Customers are increasingly demanding real-time communication.
- Analysts can often handle multiple conversations simultaneously, making IM an efficient and cost-effective way to deliver support services.
- Companies are integrating IM into other systems such as incident tracking and problem management systems, e-mail response management systems, and Web-based knowledge management systems. This integration allows help desk analysts to simultaneously use these resources when interacting with customers. A help desk analyst may, for example, use IM to send the answer to an FAQ or direct the customer to a solution in the company's knowledge base. This integration also enables the help desk to keep a record of and monitor these transactions for quality purposes.
- For many companies that do business via the Internet, channels such as chat, e-mail, and online help are the primary ways they interact with customers. By integrating these channels, help desks are able to maximize their technological resources while reducing the overall cost of delivering support.

Although these factors are compelling, it is likely that companies will work hard to establish guidelines for IM usage in an effort to manage customer expectations relative to IM use. These guidelines will address the cost, legal, security, training, and management challenges that companies face as they implement IM technology. For example, companies must spell out the types of interactions that are appropriate for IM. Failing to due so could result in customer dissatisfaction, or worse, a lawsuit. Companies must also staff this channel appropriately. Failing to do so could result in customers waiting in a queue to chat with an analyst just as they currently wait to speak with an analyst on the telephone. Companies must also ensure they can create a written transcript of communications between analysts and customers. This written transcript ensures that important customer data are captured, and provides the ability to monitor IM communications for quality.

Nancy Flynn
FOUNDER AND EXECUTIVE DIRECTOR
THE ePOLICY INSTITUTE
COLUMBUS, OHIO
WWW.EPOLICYINSTITUTE.COM

Instant messaging (IM) brings many costly business and legal challenges to the workplace. Nancy Flynn, author of *Instant Messaging Rules* (Amacom, 2004), answers a few questions about IM in the workplace and how employers and employees can make the most of this increasingly popular tool. Nancy Flynn is founder and executive director of The ePolicy Institute and the author of *Instant Messaging Rules, E-Mail Rules, The ePolicy Handbook,* and several other books. She has been featured in *U.S. News & World Report, Fortune, The New York Times, The Wall Street Journal,* and on CNBC and National Public Radio.

Question: Why is instant messaging so popular?

Answer: Instant messaging is popular because it delivers speed. E-mail is a powerful communication tool but it simply isn't speedy enough for fans of instant messaging. Instant messaging appeals to users who want to communicate instantaneously with colleagues, clients, and other third parties. Instant messaging can do anything e-mail can do, including transmit text, images, and files. It also offers a few capabilities that e-mail does not, such as chat rooms and Web conferencing, screen sharing and whiteboards, access to content, and the ability to multitask.

Question: Is instant messaging being used in business?

Answer: Absolutely. Instant messaging is quickly replacing e-mail as the electronic communications tool of choice in offices worldwide. It is estimated that 90% of businesses already are engaging in some level of instant messaging. That includes some 25 million U.S. business users who, according to The Yankee Group, are instant messaging on a public network without management's knowledge or authorization. That makes instant messaging risky business.

Question: What are the risks of using instant messaging in business?

Answer: Instant messaging poses a broad range of potential risks to business users. The greatest IM challenges are controlling security system breaches, monitoring written content, retaining and archiving business records, ensuring employee productivity, and managing user IDs. Security is a top concern as the majority of corporate use takes place across public networks, which lack built-in safeguards against Trojan horses, worms, viruses, and other destructive and malicious intruders. This makessensitive business information vulnerable to malicious hackers, cyberthieves, and eavesdroppers. The greatest risks, however, fall under the categories of content concerns and records retention. Because of its instantaneous nature, many users think instant messaging—more so than e-mail—is a throwaway medium that permits casual off-the-cuff content. On the contrary, IM creates information that must be retained as a business record, or, that can be retained as a business record without your knowledge. The fact that IM and e-mail messages may be considerably more casual and conversational than traditional paper records does not diminish their significance in the eyes of litigators, regulators, and the courts. As evidence, electronic records hold as much weight as paper records.

Companies must teach all employees to distinguish electronic business records (IM or e-mail) that must be saved, from insignificant business or personal messages that can be deleted. They must inform employees about the risks and costs the organization can face when electronic business records are not retained, and when IM and e-mail evidence is not preserved properly. Employees must also understand that they should not expect any privacy when it comes to instant messages, e-mail messages, and other electronic records created, stored, transmitted, or received using company resources. Instant messaging belongs to the employer, not the employee, and so companies are increasingly monitoring IM and e-mail transmissions to ensure they contain appropriate content.

Question: What is appropriate content for business IM transmissions?

Answer: Simply put, good IM content for business is businesslike. More specifically, companies are increasingly developing written policies that instruct employees to compose instant messages that adhere to guidelines such as the following:

Employees must abide by the Company's IM content and language guidelines. Using language that is obscene, vulgar, abusive, harassing, profane, suggestive, intimidating, misleading, defamatory, or otherwise offensive is a violation of the Company's instant messaging policy and can lead to disciplinary action or termination. Jokes or inappropriate commentary related to ethnicity, race, color, religion, sex, age, disabilities, physique, or sexual preference are also prohibited.

Such guidelines help employers keep their organizations out of harm's way, while giving employees access to a cutting-edge, productivity-enhancing tool. Employees must guard their own privacy as well. As part of their employee education efforts, many companies suggest that employees protect themselves, their families, and friends by strictly separating their business and personal lives.

Question: What advice can you offer to people using instant messaging in the workplace?

> **Answer:** The most effective tone for electronic business correspondence is professional, yet conversational. To achieve that tone, I suggest you take the colleague, customer, and competitor test. Imagine that you are in an elevator crowded with colleagues, customers, and competitors. What tone would you use? What would you say? What information would you reveal, and what would you keep under wraps? If you wouldn't say it aloud while sharing close quarters with the people you work for, with, and against, don't write it in an instant message, which might be retained and later revealed publicly—to the embarrassment of you and your employer.

Technologies such as e-mail, online chat, and IM are fast and easy ways for customers to contact the help desk with problems and requests. Knowledge bases make it possible for help desks to quickly and consistently respond to customers' problems and requests.

Using and Creating Knowledge Bases

Few, if any, companies have the resources to re-create a solution each and every time a problem occurs. Also, because technology is increasingly complex and changing very rapidly, many companies are unable to give analysts adequate training. When training is provided, it may not occur when analysts need it most—before the technology is introduced. Consequently, just as customers can use self-services to help themselves, analysts must help themselves by learning to use and create online knowledge bases. Recall that a knowledge base is a collection of information sources, such as customer information, documents, policies and procedures, and problem solutions.

A knowledge base can be built using sophisticated technology or it can simply be a collection of books and documents used to solve problems. For example, most help desks make available the following knowledge resources:

- Class notes, such as those you take at a training class.
- Internet sites that you can access via bookmarks.
- Online help.
- Product manuals.
- An incident tracking and problem management system that you can use to look up similar or related problems.
- Coworkers and other service providers.

Referring to class notes and product manuals can be time-consuming, and consulting coworkers and other service providers can be costly. Consequently, companies are trying to consolidate their knowledge resources and maximize their human resources by implementing sophisticated expert and knowledge management systems. These systems capture human knowledge and make it readily available to others who are involved in solving problems and requests. An expert system is a computer program that stores human knowledge in a knowledge base and has the ability to reason about that knowledge. A knowledge management system combines the reasoning capability of an expert system with other information sources, such as databases, documents, and policies and procedures. Although a knowledge management system is, in fact, an expert system, the support industry more commonly uses the term knowledge management system.

Search Retrieval Technologies

Much of the flexibility and power of a knowledge management system comes from the search retrieval technology that it uses to retrieve data and the quality of the data available. Search retrieval technologies include:

- Case-based reasoning
- Decision trees
- Fuzzy logic
- Keyword searching
- Query by example

These retrieval technologies allow users to specify search criteria, which is then used to retrieve similar cases. A **search criteria** is the question or a problem symptom entered by a user. Some of these retrieval technologies do very simple data matching while others use highly sophisticated artificial intelligence.

Case-Based Reasoning

Case-based reasoning (CBR) is a searching technique that uses everyday language to ask users questions and interpret their answers. CBR prompts the user for any additional information it needs to identify a set of possible solutions. CBR finds perfect matches based on user queries but also retrieves cases that are similar to the perfect match. Possible solutions are ranked in order of probability from most likely to least likely to solve the problem.

Decision Trees

A **decision tree** is a branching structure of questions and possible answers designed to lead an analyst to a solution. Decision trees work well for entry-level analysts because they can walk through a methodical approach to solving problems. Senior analysts often feel that decision trees take too long to identify a solution.

FUZZY LOGIC

Fuzzy logic is a searching technique that presents all possible solutions that are similar to the search criteria, even when conflicting information exists or no exact match is present. Fuzzy logic requires that some part of the search criteria specified is valid. In other words, as long as *part* of the search criteria is valid, fuzzy logic can find a match because it presents all possible solutions.

KEYWORD SEARCHING

Keyword searching is the technique of finding indexed information by specifying a descriptive word or phrase, called a keyword. Keywords must be indexed to be located and an exact match must be found. For example, if a user specifies the keyword "computer," only records that contain the keyword "computer" are located. Records that contain the keyword "PC" would not be located.

Some systems provide the ability to create a synonym table. A **synonym** is a word with the same or very similar meaning to another word. For example, the words "monitor," "screen," and "computer terminal" are often used interchangeably. When a synonym table exists, the system uses the synonym table to find records that match the specified word and its synonyms when searching against text fields. In other words, if you search the database for records with "monitor" in a text field, the system also looks for records that contain "screen" and "computer terminal" in that field.

QUERY BY EXAMPLE

Query by example (QBE) is a searching technique that uses queries, or questions, to find records that match the specified search criteria. Queries can include **search operators,** connecting words such as AND, OR, and NOT. QBE can also find records that *do not* contain the search criteria, or that contain a value less than, greater than, or equal to the specified search criteria, for example, a date range.

Today's sophisticated search retrieval technologies have value only if the data stored in the knowledge base are complete and accurate. The expression "garbage in, garbage out" is appropriate: If inaccurate or incomplete information (garbage) is stored in the knowledge base, then inaccurate or incomplete information will be delivered when a search is performed. These systems are useful only if you enter quality data.

Expert and knowledge management technology has advanced considerably in recent years, and its use has become more widespread in the support industry. This is primarily because many of the incident tracking and problem management systems used by help desks can be purchased with embedded knowledge management systems. In other words, if a company acquires a leading incident tracking or problem management system, that system either comes with a built-in knowledge base, or a knowledge base can be purchased as an add-on product and integrated with the base product.

Some companies do, however, purchase and implement standalone knowledge management systems. Leading knowledge management systems include ASK.ME Pro by KnowledgeBroker (**www.kbi.com**), Knowledgebase.net by KnowledgeBase Solutions (**www.knowledgebase.net**), and Primus Answer Engine by Primus Knowledge Solutions (**www.primus.com**).

Knowledge management systems can be used to record newly found solutions and retrieve known solutions and procedures, or they can be used to access existing knowledge bases. Help desks that support custom applications often use these systems to collect and retain their in-house knowledge. Help desks that support standard industry applications from companies such as Microsoft, Lotus, Novell, Netscape, and others can purchase commercially available knowledge bases. Commercially available knowledge bases contain solutions to known problems and can be purchased on a subscription basis. Subscribers receive regular updates that are typically delivered on CD-ROM. Leading commercial knowledge bases include KnowledgeBases by KnowledgeBroker (**www.kbi.com**), Knowledge-Paks by RightAnswers (**www.rightanswers.com**), and TechNet by Microsoft (**www.microsoft.com**).

Much of the information about standard industry applications can be obtained free of charge on the Web. For example, most hardware and software vendors post answers to FAQs and solutions to known problems on their Web sites. Many help desks add links from the help desk Web site to vendor Web sites, making it easier for analysts and customers to quickly access the vendor information they need.

Knowledge management systems benefit help desk analysts considerably because the information they need is available online whenever they need it. They do not have to wait for a coworker to get off the telephone or for the resident "expert" to return from vacation or training to access that person's knowledge. Many knowledge management systems can also lead an analyst through troubleshooting steps that help resolve complex problems, which then improve the analyst's problem-solving skills.

The practice of building a knowledge base and using all available knowledge resources is not meant to imply that humans are unimportant and we can get by without them. Quite the opposite. Companies want to free human resources to work on unique and complex problems rather than wasting time answering routine questions. Furthermore, most people would prefer to work on interesting new problems rather than handle the same boring problem over and over.

Given the rapid pace of change in today's business world, continuing to hold on to knowledge that may soon be obsolete is one of the worst things you can do. By contributing to and using your company's knowledge base, you can expand your knowledge and free yourself to learn new skills.

TIP

Many companies designate a knowledge base administrator (KBA) or **knowledge engineer,** to maintain their knowledge management systems. A knowledge engineer develops and oversees the knowledge management process and ensures the information contained in the help desk's knowledge base is accurate, complete, and current. It is the knowledge engineer's responsibility to ensure that all available information sources are added to the help desk's knowledge base. The knowledge engineer may also provide training in an effort to ensure that analysts can quickly and easily retrieve information when needed.

In smaller companies, a help desk analyst with excellent writing skills may perform this role on a part-time basis. Larger companies may have one or more full-time knowledge engineers. In larger companies, these individuals are often degreed technical writers. This position is becoming increasingly more important and is emerging as a highly valued position in many organizations.

The steps taken to implement and administer a knowledge management system are similar to those taken when implementing and administering a content management system. Simply put, a content management system (CMS) is software used to manage the content of a Web site. In reality, the software is only one small part of what goes into publishing useful information via the Internet. Both knowledge management and content management involve collecting, editing, formatting, and publishing information in a way that the target audience can quickly and easily locate and use.

NOTE

Today, companies want people who share their knowledge, cross-train their coworkers, and continuously develop new skills. Storing knowledge online enables analysts to achieve all of these goals. In addition, it reduces the time that help desk analysts spend answering routine and repeated questions. Analysts are then free to work on more complex problems and pursue new skills, such as improved writing skills.

WRITING HELP DESK DOCUMENTS

The amount of writing done by help desk analysts varies from one company to the next. However, a number of documents are common to all help desks. Figure 6–2 lists some of the most common documents help desk analysts prepare. Each of these documents has a different audience and purpose. Before writing a word, it is a good practice to ensure you understand the audience's needs and how they plan to use the information. Regardless of the type of help desk document, the primary goal of help desk writing is to accurately convey technical information in an interesting way that can be understood by readers.

Trouble tickets

E-mail messages

FAQs

Knowledge base solutions

Reports

Policies and procedures

Figure 6–2 Common help desk documents

The amount of documentation analysts write depends on the technology available to their help desk and the size of their help desk. Analysts at most help desks log trouble tickets and send and receive e-mail messages. They may also be asked to prepare some of these other documents. On the other hand, some help desks have technical writers who prepare FAQs, reports, policies and procedures, and other documents; analysts have little involvement.

The section "Improving Your Writing Skills" later in this chapter, provides best practices you can use when you prepare these help desk documents.

NOTE

Trouble Tickets

Recall that a ticket is a description of a customer's problem or request. Help desk analysts typically log tickets electronically in an incident tracking and problem management system at the time the request is received. Tickets may also be called records, cases, incidents, or logs. Figure 6–3 shows a sample problem entry screen that help desk analysts may use to log a problem or request.

Well-written tickets provide other analysts and service providers with the information they need to solve problems quickly. They also provide a historical accounting of the steps taken to solve a problem.

When documenting problems and requests in a ticket, analysts should clearly record all of the information the customer provides. They should also include all of the steps they have taken to diagnose and resolve the problem. Analysts sometimes leave out problem-solving steps that they perceived to be obvious. Unfortunately, if an action is not explicitly stated, coworkers or service providers have no choice but to assume the step was not taken. For example, if a ticket does not mention that you verified the customer's monitor was powered on and then you escalate the problem, the field service engineer will most likely ask that question before going on-site. This not only wastes the field service engineer's time, it can also frustrate and even anger the customer who must answer the same question multiple

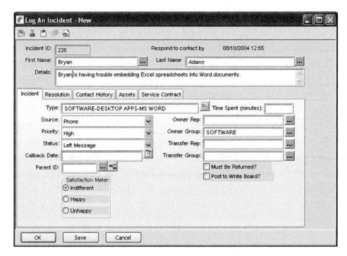

Figure 6–3 Sample trouble ticket

times. Sometimes all of the problem-solving steps are part of an existing checklist; in that case, it is appropriate for analysts to simply state that they completed the checklist and then summarize the results.

When documenting problems and requests, collect details such as who, what, when, where, and how.

TIP

Most tickets are made up of two basic parts: data fields and text fields. A **data field** is an element of a database record in which one piece of data is stored. Most systems can validate data as it is entered into data fields and enforce a standard in terms of what data is entered. This means the system can ensure that a Date field accepts only correctly formatted dates, as opposed to words. For example, in the United States, dates typically conform to a MM/DD/YY (for example, 11/27/07) format. In Europe, dates typically conform to a DD/MM/YY (for example, 27/11/07) format. Again, when data fields are used, the system enforces the standard in terms of how the data is entered. A **text field** is a field that accepts free-form information. Text fields are used to collect detailed information such as descriptions, status updates, and solutions. Text fields cannot typically validate data as it is entered in the system. In other words, the system cannot enforce a standard in terms of what data are entered.

Many companies establish standards for how to enter certain words or phrases into text fields. For example, a standard may direct analysts to use the term "reboot," as opposed to "cold boot," "warm boot," or "power off and on." Although the system cannot enforce the use of these standards in a text field, the presence of the standard helps analysts write more consistently and minimizes the confusion that can result from inconsistent terms.

NOTE   Reports are usually created using the data entered into data fields because the data can be validated. As a result, the person creating the report can predict what data will be present in a data field.

When working in a help desk, strive to understand how the data you collect is being used in a effort to ensure that you are entering information as accurately as possible. For example, many incident tracking and problem management systems have a Date Resolved field. Analysts sometimes simply enter the current date and time, even though the problem was resolved earlier in the day or week. This field, however, is often used to determine whether the problem was resolved within the target resolution time. Recall that target resolution time is the time frame within which the support organization is expected to resolve the problem. If an inaccurate date and time is entered, this ticket appears on a report as late, even though it may not have been.

TIP   Accuracy is important and takes only a few seconds more.

Another reason accuracy is important is that help desks are increasingly providing their customers with the ability to check the status of outstanding tickets, usually through the help desk's Web site. This customer access has heightened awareness within the support industry of the need to document requests accurately and professionally, and maintain tickets on as close to a real-time basis as possible. Remember that even when customers cannot access trouble tickets directly, the trouble ticket data are often automatically forwarded to the customer in an e-mail message, so it is important to be accurate and professional.

The data documented in tickets is also used by other help desk analysts and service providers to diagnose and solve problems, and by management to create management reports and analyze trends. Effective trend analysis can eliminate recurring problems, thus saving valuable time and, ultimately, increasing customer satisfaction. Many companies use the data captured in their incident tracking and problem management system to justify resources and to measure performance of both the help desk team and individual analysts. You may perceive that it takes too much time to create complete and accurate tickets. Remember, however, that management analyzes ticket data to more fully understand your workload and your contributions. They also rely on this information to institute improvement opportunities that may save time in the long run.

E-Mail Messages

Every day, more help desks are using e-mail to communicate with customers. Well-written e-mail messages are as clear and concise as possible, while conveying a positive, friendly tone. When e-mail messages are too long, readers may become bored or miss an important detail. When e-mail messages are too succinct or impersonal, readers may consider the messages abrupt or even rude.

The section "E-Mail Best Practices" in this chapter provides specific tips you can use to prepare well-written messages.

Ultimately, e-mail messages should provide as much of the needed information as possible the first time and not prompt additional messages to be sent back and forth. Try to anticipate follow-up questions a customer may ask and volunteer the information. If lengthy discussion is needed, it may be best to make a telephone call or schedule a meeting.

FAQs

A common business practice that is particularly relevant to help desks is publishing lists of **frequently asked questions (FAQs),** well-written answers to the most common customer queries. These answers are then made available to customers. For example, they can be posted on a company's Web site, published in the help desk's newsletter, incorporated into documentation, such as a user's manual, or distributed at a training class. Some companies list the top ten FAQs for a given month, for a specific product, or for a certain type of user, such as those who are new to a product.

It is important to update FAQs regularly as issues become obsolete, new topics arise, and best practices evolve.

The key to a well-written FAQ is to state both the question and answer clearly and in a language that is appropriate to the audience. In other words, phrase the question the way that customers do when they contact the help desk, then explain the answer in language that customers can understand. It is okay to use jargon and technical terms in the answers, as long as you define those terms for the reader.

FAQs are a basic self-service and enable help desks to proactively address their customers' needs. Analysts can also develop FAQs that provide their coworkers with answers to common questions about their area of expertise. FAQs satisfy customers and coworkers because they are able to find solutions and answers to questions on their own. Many people prefer FAQs because they can find answers to questions they may be reluctant to ask or are afraid may seem silly.

Knowledge Base Solutions

Today's sophisticated knowledge management systems have value only if the information stored in the knowledge base is accurate and complete. Unfortunately, if analysts perceive that the information in a knowledge management system is inaccurate or incomplete, they become hesitant to use the system and may return to the practice of seeking out a human who can assist. To be effective, a knowledge management system must be carefully developed and maintained.

An effective knowledge management system serves as a repository for reusable solutions that are developed by analysts and service providers, such as the network management group and development groups. A **solution** is a definitive, permanent resolution to a problem, or a proven workaround. In most systems, solutions are stored as records in a separate file than trouble tickets. This enables the use of one solution to solve many trouble tickets (referred to as a **one-to-many relationship**), as illustrated in Figure 6–4. In other words, the same solution can be used each time a problem recurs without being retyped or cut and pasted into each trouble ticket.

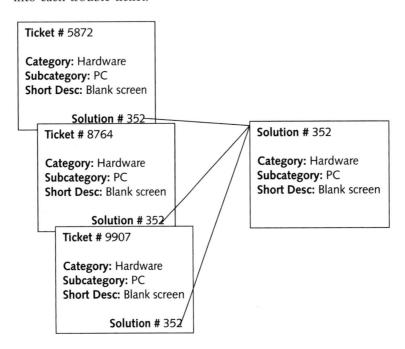

Figure 6–4 One solution to many trouble tickets

Solutions do not describe things to *attempt* when diagnosing problems or responding to inquiries. Checklists and tip sheets can be used to provide this type of information. A solution represents the known answer to a problem. Solutions also do not contain the details of a single specific problem, such as names, dates, and so forth. These specific data elements would make the solution unusable if the same problem happens in the future. By developing a "generic" solution—one that does not contain specific details—the solution is reusable. Thus, one solution can be used to solve many problems.

Many help desks develop standards that describe how to write solutions. Creating a standard solution format serves many purposes. Analysts with varying skill levels can obtain information at the level of detail that they need. Solutions are presented in a consistent format, so the human mind can quickly and easily pick out key data elements, such as commands and variables. A standard solution format also makes the writing process easier because analysts know how to present information when documenting solutions. For example, analysts know how to specify words or phrases that may be similar or confusing, such as "program" as opposed to "software" or "application." Figure 6–5 shows a sample format for a standard solution.

Sample Standard Solution Format

Consider the following guidelines when categorizing solutions:

- <u>Category:</u> Use care when specifying this field. Specifying a very generic category can result in a solution being presented a greater number of times than is appropriate.
- <u>Subcategory:</u> Use care when specifying this field. Specifying this field in too detailed a fashion can result in the solution rarely being presented.
- <u>Solution Short Description</u>: Provide a brief, symptom-oriented description of the solution that is not incident specific.
- <u>Solution Description:</u> Provide a "reusable" description of the solution. Reusable means that details relating to a single specific incident such as names, dates, and so forth are not included in the solution. While the need for those details may be referenced in the solution, the actual details should reside in the trouble ticket. Include:
    - A technical solution that offers an experienced technician a brief summary
    - A detailed solution that offers a less-experienced technician a more step-by-step approach

The following documentation standards have been developed in an effort to achieve consistency when documenting Solution Descriptions:

- Enclose variable data in brackets, for example, [**xxxxxx**].
- Enclose specific commands in quotation marks, for example, **"xxxxxxx"**
- When attaching another document, specify "See ***att:document.doc*** for additional information"—where *att:document.doc* represents the name of an attachment.
- When referencing a manual or user's guide, specify "Refer to the ***Word Users Guide*** for additional information"—where *Word Users Guide* represents the complete and accurate name of a reference document. Include the manual's release, version, or volume number when appropriate.
- When appropriate, indicate customers or other service providers to be notified when this solution is implemented.

Figure 6–5 Sample standard solution format

Standard solutions contain two types of information:

1. Fields that are used to index the solution and link it to the type of problem being solved.
2. Text that describes the solution.

The description of a solution may contain links to online documents, or a multimedia presentation of some kind, such as a video or audio clip. This enhances the usability of the information and enables people who are visual learners to receive the information in a meaningful way. Table 6–1 shows a solution that was written using a standard format.

Table 6–1 Solution with a standard format

Technical Solution	Detailed Solution
Delete print jobs with SunOS lp commands	1. rsh as root to the server where the print queue resides
	2. Type **"lpq -P[xxx]"** where 'xxx' is the queue name
	3. Find the print job to kill, note the job # and the user name
	4. Type **"lprm -P[xxx] [job#] [username]"**
	5. Use the line printer control utility (lpc) to bring the queue down, restart it, and bring it back up again as follows: **"lpc down [xxx]"** where 'xxx' is the queue name **"lpc restart [xxx]"** **"lpc up [xxx]"**

When working in a help desk, strive to use all available knowledge resources and contribute to the creation of your company's knowledge management system. By doing so, you can considerably expand your ability to solve problems and you can help others solve problems by sharing what you know. Respect the fact that your coworkers and other service providers are just as busy as you are. Rather than interrupting their work to ask a routine question, look in the knowledge base for the answer. If you have difficulty finding a solution or using your company's knowledge management system, seek help from someone who is involved in administering or maintaining the system.

Reports

Entry-level analysts do not typically prepare reports, but senior analysts and managers often do. Although in smaller help desks, where analysts tend to be "jacks-of-all-trades," anyone may be asked to prepare a report. Reports may be statistics or detailed accountings that are produced from the data collected in an incident tracking and problem management system. Creating this type of report requires knowledge of the system, the available data, and knowledge of the reporting package used to pull the data out of the system. Reports may also reflect the results of a study, the status of a project, or the analysis of statistics. For example, a report may describe why the volume of calls goes up on Thursdays, or why the number of PC-related problems has gone down in the past two months. Preparing these reports requires writing skills and an understanding of the recipient's expectations. Some common reports a help desk analyst may create include:

- **Progress report.** A progress report provides an update on activities, such as a project. Typically a progress report states:
  - Activities completed during the current period (for example, this month).
  - Activities to be completed during the next period (for example, next month).
  - Activities that are overdue and why those activities could not be completed on time.
  - Considerations and concerns that require management attention.

  Management will usually designate the time frame of progress reports.

- **Requirements report.** A requirements report typically provides:
  - An assessment of the current environment.
  - A description of requirements that will result in an improved environment.
  - Considerations and concerns that require management attention.
  - Recommendations.

  A **requirement** is something that is required—a necessity. For example, a customer requirement is a service that customers expect the help desk to offer. Requirements can also be associated with technology. For example, a company must identify its requirements for a new incident tracking and problem management system before it begins looking for one. Without determining the requirements, the selected system most likely will not meet the company's needs in the long term. Gathering and documenting requirements is usually the first step taken at the start of a new project.

- **Feasibility report.** A feasibility report explores a proposed project such as implementing a new system or offering a new service, and typically provides:
  - The viability of the proposed project.
  - The risks and benefits of starting or continuing with the project.
  - Possible alternatives.

The first time you are asked to prepare a certain type of report, find out exactly what is expected in terms of format and content. Ask to see a copy of a similar report that you can use as an example. Prepare an outline of the report you plan to prepare and then ask for feedback and approval of the outline before you begin preparing the actual report. These are all ways you can avoid wasted time and effort. Also, be open to feedback. Few reports are perfect the first time. Ask for specific, constructive feedback so you can continuously improve.

Policies and Procedures

Companies more than ever are involving the help desk staff in the development of policies and procedures. These policies and procedures may be used by customers, the internal support organization, or simply within the help desk. A procedure is a step-by-step, detailed set of instructions that describes how to perform a task. Many companies develop a standard format, or template, as illustrated in Figure 6–6, that is used to prepare procedures. This ensures that procedures have a consistent look and feel and are therefore easier to read.

Insert Procedure Title

Introduction	Insert description of procedure.
Special Instructions	Insert any special instructions or information to be considered before users begin performing this procedure.

- First consideration
- Second consideration
- Third consideration

⊃ Note: Use the notes icon to highlight pertinent or key information about a procedure.

❗ Important: Use the important text icon if you want to emphasize, qualify, or clarify information.

💣 Warning: Use the warning icon to highlight circumstances in which you can lose data if you perform an action.

✪ Best Practice: Use the Best Practice icon to highlight a particular procedure as the most beneficial or efficient.

Procedure   Follow these steps to… Insert actual procedure.

1. Step One
2. Step Two
3. Step Three

Figure 6–6 Sample standard procedure format

When writing procedures, you must state every step explicitly. Do not assume readers will know that they have to log on to the network before they can retrieve their e-mail. Although a step may seem obvious to you, it may not be at all obvious to your readers. It is also a good idea to state the result readers can expect when a task is complete. For example, let readers know that they can proceed when the message "Logon Complete" appears. You can also let the readers know what to do if the message does not appear.

> *"If any single force is destined to impede man's mastery of the computer, it will be the manual that tries to teach him how to master it."* William Zinsser

When writing procedures, it is appropriate to include information about what not to do. For example, you can inform customers that restarting their PC may not be the best way to solve a problem. Explain that it could result in the loss of data or it could erase the conditions needed to diagnose a problem. Another good practice is to include detailed warnings as needed that communicate important instructions. Figure 6–7 shows a sample warning message.

> WARNING: Documents can contain viruses that can "infect" computer files and have harmful side effects. Always scan your disks to find and remove viruses before transferring documents to the network.

Figure 6–7 Sample warning message

Many help desks create and maintain a Help Desk Analyst's Guide. Some help desks refer to this document as a Technician's Guide or Procedures Guide. Figure 6–8 shows a sample table of contents for a Help Desk Analyst's Guide.

A Help Desk Analyst's Guide spells out the policies and procedures of the help desk and contains information that help desk analysts need to do their work. A Help Desk Analyst's Guide ensures that the knowledge and experience of help desk management and key help desk staff members is available, even when the managers or staff members are not. In other words, analysts can first consult this guide to determine how they should handle a given situation. A Help Desk Analyst's Guide is often used to orient new help desk staff members in obtaining an understanding of the help desk's policies and procedures. A Help Desk Analyst's Guide should be considered a "living" document that is updated regularly. Many organizations maintain this guide online to make it more accessible and easier to revise. Help desk analysts often help to create the Help Desk Analyst's Guide because they are the ones that will be using it day in and day out. Helping to create a Help Desk Analyst's Guide is an excellent way to practice and improve your writing skills.

Each of the help desk documents discussed in this section have a specific purpose and a target audience. To prepare these documents, you must adapt your writing to the style of document and to the needs of the target audience. Learning the rules of writing will provide you the foundation needed to write any document and to make a positive impression with your writing.

Sample Help Desk Analyst's Guide - Table of Contents

HELP DESK MISSION x
- Help Desk Mission x
- Help Desk Goals x
- Help Desk Analyst's Personal Goals x

TRAINING/DEVELOPMENT x
- Help Desk Training Plan x
  - Training Objectives x
  - Training Activities x
  - Training Schedule x
  - References (e.g., Books, Tapes, Magazines) x
- Current Skills Inventory Matrix x

CALL MANAGEMENT x
- Scripts.....
  - Answering the Phone .....
  - Terminating a Call.....
  - Miscellaneous Customer Service Tips.....
- Important/Emergency Phone Numbers .....

CUSTOMER PROFILES .....

PROBLEM MANAGEMENT.....
- Problem Management Introduction.....
- Problem Management Process Owner .....
- Problem Management Indicators and Objectives .
- Problem Management Roles and Responsibilities
- Problem Management Process Flow .....
- Problem Escalation/Notification Guidelines.....
- Problem Management Related Procedures .....
  - Adding a Problem Record.....
  - Assigning a Problem .....
  - Resolving a Problem .....
  - Verifying Customer Satisfaction.....
  - Closing a Problem.....
- Problem Management Reports (e.g., Daily, Week

CHANGE MANAGEMENT x
- Change Management Introduction x
- Change Management Process Owner x
- Change Management Indicators and Objectives x
- Change Management Roles and Responsibilities x
- Change Management Process Flow x
- Change Categories x
- Change Flow By Category x
- Change Management Related Procedures x
- Change Management Reports (e.g., Daily, Weekly, Monthly) x

INVENTORY MANAGEMENT x
- Standard/Recommended Hardware and Software x
- Keyboard Mappings x
- Obtaining Inventory/Configuration Information x

AFTER-HOURS PROCEDURES x
- After-Hours Call List x
- Determining What Is an Emergency x

DISASTER RECOVERY x
- Incident Tracking System x
- Phone System x
- Workstation (Toolkit) x

VENDOR MANAGEMENT x
- Service Contract Specifics x

APPENDIX A - GLOSSARY OF TERMS AND ACRONYMS x

APPENDIX B - FREQUENTLY ASKED QUESTIONS x

APPENDIX C - TROUBLESHOOTING TIPS AND TECHNIQUES x

APPENDIX D - SERVICE LEVEL AGREEMENTS x

Figure 6–8 Sample Help Desk Analyst's Guide Table of Contents

IMPROVING YOUR WRITING SKILLS

No matter what type of help desk document you are writing, the quality of writing is important. Well-written materials are simpler to comprehend, provide needed information, and leave a good impression. Writing, like any other skill, improves and becomes easier with practice. Another way to hone writing skills is by paying attention when you are reading, just as you can improve your customer service skills by paying attention when you are the customer. There are also a number of excellent books and classes available. In fact, many universities and community colleges offer classes in technical writing.

Technical Writing Best Practices

Help desk analysts need good writing skills whether they are logging a trouble ticket in the company's incident tracking and problem management system, sending an e-mail, preparing a report, or preparing content for the help desk's Web site. Regardless of the type of document, good technical writing requires a coherent, precise style. The best practices listed in Figure 6–9 will help you develop an effective writing style and improve your writing skills.

- Know your audience.
- Use the active voice.
- Use simple language.
- Be concise.
- Be specific.
- Avoid or define jargon, technical terms, and acronyms.
- Break up your writing with lists and short sections.
- Be consistent.
- Check your work for accuracy and completeness.
- Check your grammar, punctuation, and spelling.

Figure 6–9 Technical writing best practices

These best practices become second nature when practiced consistently. After mastering these principles, you can focus on the important part of writing—your content.

Know Your Audience.

To communicate clearly, you must determine the skill and education level of the intended readers. This is particularly true with technical subjects. Help desk analysts typically prepare written materials that are geared to a particular audience. For example, analysts may use e-mail messages to communicate with customers, problem tickets to communicate with coworkers, and reports to communicate with management. Customers, coworkers, and managers all have varying skill and education levels, and your writing must address each reader's needs. Ultimately, every reader should be able to understand your main ideas. For example, regardless of the document and its intended audience, it is appropriate to use technical terms, as long as you define those terms the first time you use them. Strive to strike a balance between a very simplistic writing style and one that is highly technical. Either extreme can alienate your audience.

TIP When preparing documents, it is important to know how much information your reader wants and needs. This is particularly true when preparing reports and other potentially lengthy documents. For example, when reporting the results of a feasibility study to the requesting committee, you will provide all available details. However, it is common to also prepare a summary, or Executive Summary, of the report for management. The summary typically refers the reader to the actual study for any details he or she may choose to review.

Use the Active Voice.

Active voice is when the subject of a sentence causes or does the action. When you use active voice, it is clear who is doing the action. Passive voice is when the person or thing performing the action is acted upon. When passive voice is used, it is unclear who is doing the action. Active voice makes your writing style seem more vigorous and your sentences more concise. Active voice also creates the impression the activity is ongoing.

> **Passive voice:** Our Web site is updated every Tuesday.
>
> **Active voice:** Our help desk analysts update our Web site every Tuesday.

Use Simple Language.
Simple language communicates more efficiently and effectively than complex language laced with technical terms. It is becoming more acceptable to use a relaxed, conversational style with customers and coworkers, but, if you would not use a phrase during a normal conversation, do not use it in written documents. Keep it simple. Remember that the ultimate goal is to communicate, not confuse.

> **Complex:** By applying the enclosed instructions, you can remedy the situation.
>
> **Simple:** You can use these procedures to fix the problem.
>
> **Formal:** It is unfortunate that I was unavailable when you visited the Help Desk two days ago.
>
> **Informal:** I'm sorry I missed you the other day.

Be Concise. The fewer words you use, the better. Unnecessary words waste space, take more time to read, and inhibit comprehension. Reread your first draft, and eliminate any words, sentences, or phrases that do not add value to your meaning.

> **Wordy:** Apparently, this problem has happened before and was not resolved correctly. Repeated attempts to resolve the problem have not been successful.
>
> **Concise:** Attempts to resolve this recurring problem have not been successful.

Be Specific. By its very nature, technical writing must deal in specifics, not generalities. When customers and managers read a problem description or report, they seek detailed information, such as facts, figures, data, recommendations, and conclusions. Being vague can severely weaken the impact of your writing and the value of the information you are producing. Do not be content to say something is good, bad, fast, or slow when you can say how good, how bad, how fast, or how slow. Use words that are specific and concrete.

> **Vague:** We respond to e-mail messages as quickly as possible.
>
> **Specific:** We respond to e-mail messages within four hours.

Avoid or Define Jargon, Technical Terms, and Acronyms. Good technical writers use terminology that is compatible with their readers' technical background. If a technical term is appropriate and most readers will understand it, use the term. But avoid jargon and technical terms when a simpler word will do just as well. If you must use technical terms or if you want to introduce an acronym, define the term or acronym the first time you use it.

> **Technical:** Maximize the visible spectrum on your CRT.
>
> **Nontechnical:** Turn up the brightness on your monitor.
>
> **Undefined acronym:** Many help desks use an ACD to manage incoming telephone calls.
>
> **Defined acronym:** Many help desks use an automatic call distributor (ACD) to manage incoming telephone calls.

Break Up Your Writing with Lists and Short Sections.   Readers want to acquire needed information quickly and tend to have a short attention spans. Short sentences and paragraphs help them read and grasp information rapidly. Numbered sequences or lists arranged in a logical order also work well.

Numbered sequence:

Check the following when a customer has a blank screen:

    1. Is the monitor plugged in?

    2. Is the monitor powered on?

    3. Is the screen saver turned on?

Bulleted list:

Consider the following when establishing a help desk:

- Your company's goals.
- Your customer's expectations.
- Your commitment to customer satisfaction.

 Use numbered sequences only when a specific order is required.

TIP

Be Consistent.   In fiction, varying word choice is appropriate. In technical writing, however, inconsistencies cause confusion. To avoid confusion, once you have used a name or title for something, do not use a different name or title to refer to the same thing.

Inconsistent: A field service representative will be on-site tomorrow afternoon. The technician will fix your printer and your monitor.

Consistent: A technician will be on-site tomorrow afternoon. The technician will fix your printer and your monitor.

To increase the readability of a list, use the same grammatical construction for each item in a list. When lists are presented in a consistent way, readers find the list easier to understand and remember.

Inconsistent grammatical construction:

Reasons companies establish a help desk include:

> To provide customers a single point of contact.
>
> Minimization of support costs.
>
> Minimize the impact of problems and changes.
>
> Increasing end-user productivity.
>
> Customer satisfaction enhancement.

Consistent grammatical construction:

Companies establish a help desk to:

> Provide customers a single point of contact.
>
> Minimize support costs.
>
> Minimize the impact of problems and changes.
>
> Increase end-user productivity.
>
> Enhance customer satisfaction.

Check Your Work for Accuracy and Completeness. Accuracy is extremely important in technical writing because people use the answers, solutions, and procedures to do their work, use software, and operate hardware. Inaccurate or incomplete information may cause your customers or coworkers to waste time or experience additional problems. When documenting solutions and procedures, include each and every step a customer or coworker must follow, even ones that seem obvious or intuitive to you. Ask a coworker or subject matter expert to review complex documents for accuracy and completeness. They can catch typographical errors and may question invalid assumptions you have made in the document.

Check Your Grammar, Punctuation, and Spelling. Grammar, punctuation, and spelling are important. As a final step, proofread every document to eliminate any grammar, punctuation, and spelling errors. Readers may catch errors you missed, and perceive that you are lazy or uncaring when it comes to your work. The time it takes to make your documents error-free pays off in the reader's trust of the information and leaves the reader with a positive perception of you and your company.

TIP Many technologies provide spelling- and grammar-checking utilities that can catch some errors. However, still reread your documents. Some words may be spelled correctly but used inappropriately. For example, the words *knew* and *new* are frequently confused, as are the words *their, there,* and *they're.*

When in doubt about grammar, punctuation, or spelling rules, check a style guide or dictionary, or ask an experienced coworker for feedback.

Good writing skills will serve you well regardless of the technology you are using, the type of document you are preparing, or the audience you are trying to reach. Good writing skills also enable you to promote your ideas and enhance your opportunities by completing a greater variety of assignments.

To improve your writing skills, write regularly, ask for feedback on your writing, and identify and work to fix your writing weaknesses.

Writing is an important and increasingly necessary skill in today's business world. It is particularly important when communicating via e-mail, as your writing represents the first impression you and your company make on your readers.

E-Mail Best Practices

E-mail has transitioned from an informal way to communicate to a serious business tool. This is evident by the overwhelming volume of e-mail that companies receive on a daily basis and the pressure placed on companies to respond to e-mails quickly and professionally. E-mail also absorbs a significant amount of time during the typical workday. According to a survey conducted by the American Management Association, the average respondent spends a quarter of the workday (1 hour and 47 minutes) on e-mail, while 31% spend more than 2 hours and 8% spend more than 4 hours ("2003 E-Mail Rules, Policies and Practices Survey," American Management Association, 2003).

An e-mail is a written document and so the technical writing best practices discussed in the previous section apply. The best practices listed in Figure 6–10 provide additional techniques you can use to make the most of this tool at the help desk.

The next sections explore these tips for using e-mail effectively in more detail.

Manage Customer Expectations.   Some help desks view the telephone as the primary way of receiving customer requests. Because e-mail is a secondary method, they check it infrequently and sporadically, or they check it only periodically, such as twice per day. Other companies now view e-mail as their primary communication channel and check continuously for new messages. If customers don't know how the help desk treats e-mail messages, they may be disappointed with the help desk's response. Therefore, it is important that the help desk communicate its e-mail policies to customers. For example, the help desk must indicate the priority it places on e-mail requests and the time frame within which e-mail requests will be addressed. These terms may be dictated by a Service Level Agreement.

○   Manage customer expectations

○   Acknowledge the person

○   Be practical and be patient

○   Check your grammar, punctuation, and spelling

○   Be forgiving

○   Avoid lengthy discussions and debates

○   Avoid negative and derogatory comments

○   Use special characters, emoticons, and acronyms appropriately

○   Use forms and templates to save time

○   Verify your distribution lists periodically

○   Standardize your signature

Figure 6–10 E-mail best practices for help desk analysts

Whatever your help desk's policy is, communicate it clearly to customers so they know what to expect. Some companies publish a Help Desk Quick Reference Card or Newsletter that communicates their e-mail policy. A Help Desk Quick Reference Card can also spell out the information that customers must provide when using e-mail to submit a request. Figure 6–11 shows a sample Help Desk Quick Reference Card. This card or newsletter may be made available to customers via hard copy, an e-mail, or the Web.

Help desks must refine their e-mail policy as needed to meet their customer's needs. For example, because some help desks are seeing the volume of e-mail requests increase, they are beginning to have analysts check for new messages regularly throughout the day, as opposed to just periodically. The key is to respond promptly.

NOTE   It is important for analysts to encourage customers to send messages to the help desk's e-mail box, as opposed to their personal e-mail box. This helps to ensure that every e-mail request is logged and addressed in a timely fashion, regardless of an individual analyst's workload or schedule.

Acknowledge the Person.   Because e-mail supports a level of anonymity, people sometimes say things in an e-mail message that they would never say in person. Other times they ignore e-mail messages or fail to respond in a timely fashion. Remember, however, that when you send or receive e-mail, you are conversing with another person. Think about and acknowledge that person just as you would if you were interacting in person or over

HELP DESK QUICK REFERENCE CARD

This handy booklet explains the services provided by the help desk and also suggests better ways to interface with the help desk.

GIVE US A CALL...
(123) 456-7890

Please be advised that our peak times are between 8:00 – 9:30 A.M. and 1:30 – 2:30 P.M. During peak times, our call volumes are greater and callers may encounter a delay before reaching an analyst.

SEND LOW PRIORITY E-MAIL MESSAGES TO...
help.desk@ company.com
E-mails are answered within 4 business hours.

24 HOURS MONDAY ➤ FRIDAY

NOTE: Coverage provided on weekends by data center operations.

WHAT SERVICES DOES THE HELP DESK PROVIDE?

The help desk:

- Monitors all systems and network lines to ensure availability.
- Serves as a central point of contact for you to report any hardware or software problems.
- Assists with your User ID (cancel, print, status, routing, etc.) related tasks.
- Broadcasts information about upcoming changes and scheduled or unscheduled system outages.
- Logs all incoming calls and facilitates problem resolution to your satisfaction.
- Contacts the proper source to correct any problems that we cannot directly solve and provides you with a solution in a timely manner.
- Communicates with all IT departments to maintain a high level of system availability.

WHEN CONTACTING THE HELP DESK...

- Please give us your name and extension.
- Identify the PC you are working at by reading the number on the white label posted in the lower-right corner.
- Check your screen for any error messages that may help us determine the cause of the problem.
- Give us an estimated time factor when you are experiencing a response time problem (10 seconds, 2 minutes, none).
- Indicate which system or software package you are encountering a problem with (e.g., Payroll, WordPerfect, etc.).
- Give the model number of the failing device for hardware-related problems.

HOW DOES THE HELP DESK MANAGE CALLS?

The help desk manages calls in accordance with its business impact, or severity.

Severity definitions are:

1 - System or component down, critical business impact, no alternative available, notify management immediately, bypass/recover within 4 hours, resolve within 24 hours

2 - System or component down or degraded, critical business impact, alternative or bypass available, resolve within 48 hours

3 - Not critical, deferred maintenance acceptable, circumvention possible with no operational impact, resolve within 72 hours

NOTES:

_____

_____

_____

_____

_____

_____

_____

_____

_____

_____

_____

_____

Figure 6–11 Sampe Help Desk Quick Reference Card

the telephone. Be considerate. Be respectful. Include only those things you would say if that person were standing in front of you.

Remember, too, that writing an e-mail to a customer is different than writing an e-mail to a friend or family member. Figure 6–12 shows an e-mail that is so succinct, it will likely be perceived as terse.

To: joe.smith@workmail.com
From: jlk@techsupport.com
Subject: Re: #63476

Joe, go to http://66.182.92.20 to download the correct drivers
Thanks for contacting Technical Support

Figure 6–12 Poorly written e-mail message

In business, it is best to take a more formal approach. For example:

- **Use a meaningful subject line.** Recipients typically scan the subject line and determine if they should open, forward, save, or delete an e-mail message. An e-mail with a generic subject line such as "Important, Read Immediately!" may get mistaken for unsolicited e-mail, or spam, and be deleted either by the recipient or by an automated e-mail filter. A subject line such as "RE: #335262" does not tell the recipient what the message is about. A clear and meaningful subject line lets the customer know right away that the message is a response to his or her inquiry.

RE: Backing up your data (ticket 335262)

- **Personalize Your Response.** Use the customer's name respectfully. It is best to use a more formal greeting such as "Dear Mr. Lecavalier" rather than "Hi Vincent" or "Hi Vinny." Recall that if a customer uses a title, such as Professor, Dr., or Ms., address the customer using that title until the customer gives you permission to use a first name or nickname.

Dear Ms. Boyet

Dear Professor Levy

Dear Rae

TIP

When in doubt, use the exact name the customer provides in their closing. For example, if a customer signs their message "Chris" and it is unclear whether Chris is a male or female, the greeting "Dear Chris" is appropriate.

- **Personalize Your Closing.** When closing a message, use a positive tone and make it easy for the customer to obtain additional assistance in the future. Unless your company's policy directs otherwise, always include your full name and department.

Your ticket number is 58026. Please refer to that number if you need to contact us again concerning this matter.

If we may be of further assistance, please contact us by e-mail or by phone at 1-800-555-4567 between 7 a.m. and 9 p.m. Central Standard Time.

Sincerely,
Karen Dingman
Customer Support Help Desk

NOTE

Personalizing your e-mails does not mean you make each and every e-mail 100% unique. Most help desks provide prewritten responses and closings that can be used to save time and ensure consistency. These prewritten responses and closings can then be edited to avoid sending customers a generic response that does not acknowledge their specific problem or request.

Figure 6–13 shows the e-mail from Figure 6–12 presented in a more formal, professional manner. Although the message in Figure 6–13 is still succinct, it is much more positive and personal.

To: joe.smith@workmail.com
From: jlk@techsupport.com
Subject: Re: Driver not found (Ticket #63476)

Dear Mr. Smith,

We are sorry that you were unable to locate the correct driver for your external CD-RW driver.

Please go to www.cdcompany.com/support/drivers to download the correct driver. Click the link next to the make and model of drive you purchased. Follow the instructions on your screen to download and install the driver.

Once the driver is installed, we suggest you uninstall and reinstall the software that came with your drive. When you reinstall the software, the driver will be located.

You can use the manual that came with the product or visit www.cdcompany.com/support/userguide to learn how to use your new drive.

If you need additional assistance, please do not hesitate to contact us by e-mail or phone at 1-800-456-1234 between 8 a.m. and 9 p.m. Eastern Standard Time.

Sincerely,

Bill Richards
Customer Support Help Desk

Figure 6–13 Well-written e-mail message

Be Practical and Be Patient.   There are times when e-mail is not the best way to communicate. Use common sense. If a customer immediately needs information that you have, pick up the telephone and call. Even if you prefer to send an e-mail message because the information is detailed, consider calling to let the customer know it is on the way. Remember, too, that not everyone is online throughout the day, and so a customer may not respond immediately to an e-mail message. Also, if you send a message to someone in another country, it may be delivered outside of business hours or during a holiday in that person's country. If you don't receive an immediate response to an e-mail, be patient. Resist the temptation to re-send the message or perceive you are being ignored. If an immediate response is needed, e-mail may not be the way to go.

Check Your Grammar, Punctuation, and Spelling.   Unless you are corresponding with a friend or family member, form and accuracy both matter. The quality of an e-mail message constitutes a "first impression"; people will judge the appearance of your e-mail messages just as they would your appearance if you were standing in front of them and form an opinion about your competence. Remember, every message you send to a customer also represents your entire company. Take care to avoid errors that will reflect poorly on you or your company or leave a bad impression. Resist the temptation to hastily send a response without regard for grammar and punctuation. Always check your spelling. Customers may mistrust or discount an entire response if they find typographical errors.

TIP   A good habit is to proofread every message to a customer twice before you click the Send button. If you are sending an important message that contains detailed or complex information or a message to a large number of people, ask a coworker to also proofread the message for you.

Be Forgiving.   Just as you do not want someone to misjudge you if they find a typographical error in one of your messages, be forgiving when you find errors in others' messages. If you believe that you misunderstand the person's point or that you need additional information, simply ask for clarification or for the missing details. If you receive a copy of a message that a coworker sent to a customer or manager that contains an error that you feel could damage the reputation of your coworker or the company, tactfully bring the error to your coworker's attention and suggest specific ways the coworker can improve the message.

Avoid Lengthy Discussions and Debates.   E-mail communication sometimes requires sending several messages back and forth to resolve an issue. This can be compounded if one of the parties is not "listening" or misunderstands the information.

When writing e-mails, it is best to limit the number of subjects in the message, or clearly distinguish a change in subjects, for example, by leaving a blank line or by numbering the items. This is particularly important when you are requesting responses to different subjects. For long messages, consider restating your requests at the end of the message so the recipient does not need to continuously reread the message to uncover your questions or requests.

Conversely, respond carefully when replying to an e-mail message. Verify that you have answered all of the customer's questions in the order they were presented. You may want to restate each question and follow it with the answer. Optimally, anticipate any additional questions the customer may ask and provide the information needed to fully satisfy the customer's request.

It is best to avoid attachments unless they are essential for a number of reasons: (1) They can transmit viruses. (2) They take time to download. (3) They take up space on the recipient's computer. (4) Increasingly, companies are blocking incoming e-mail messages that contain attachments and may remove prohibited attachments before allowing outgoing e-mail messages to be delivered. Some ISPs, for example, simply delete incoming e-mail messages that contain attachments without informing the sender or the recipient. If detailed information must be sent, let the recipient know how to retrieve the information. For example, a common practice is to include a link to a directory or Web site.

There are times when direct conversation is needed. If a lengthy discussion or an intense problem-solving session seems needed, pick up the telephone or schedule a meeting. Remember that when communicating with customers, it is your responsibility to communicate clearly and effectively. If a customer misunderstands you, it is you who must clarify your position or clear up the misunderstanding.

Avoid Negative and Derogatory Comments.   What you say and how you say it is just as important when using e-mail as it is when communicating in person or over the telephone. Perhaps this is even more so with e-mail because customers may misinterpret your words or interject an inappropriate emotion. In other words, they may perceive that you are being rude, even though that is not your intent. Furthermore, if you are rude, they can forward the message to your boss or print it out and hold you accountable. You also want to avoid saying negative things about your coworkers or your company. Again, because e-mail messages can be easily forwarded, you may find that negative comment making its way to someone you would prefer not see it. If you do not want the world to see something, you should not be putting it in an e-mail message. Let your caring, can do attitude shine through and you can't go wrong.

According to a study conducted by the American Management Association, 22% of respondents have terminated an employee who violated the company's e-mail rules and policies. Furthermore, 14% of respondents have been ordered by a court or regulatory body to turn over employee e-mail related to workplace lawsuits, a 5% increase over 2001 ("2003 E-Mail Rules, Policies and Practices Survey," American Management Association, 2003).

Use Special Characters, Emoticons, and Acronyms Appropriately.   Relaying emotion and emphasizing a point are two of the most difficult things to do when communicating in the written form. Special characters and emoticons, symbols used to convey feelings, can help when used appropriately. In the absence of formatting features such as bold and underline, you can use special characters, such as asterisks surrounding a word, to emphasize a point.

> Passwords must be at least six characters long and *are* case sensitive.

Include emoticons such as a smiley face—☺—or a frowning face—☹—sparingly, and take care to use them appropriately.

> **Appropriate:** Placing a smiley face at the end of a message that indicates you are looking forward to meeting a customer at next month's user group meeting.
>
> **Inappropriate:** Placing a smiley face at the end of a message that delivers bad news.

Resist the temptation to be overly cute or to use obscure emoticons or acronyms. Recall that an acronym is a word formed from the initials of a name. In e-mail and IM conversations, acronyms such as LOL (laugh out loud) are often used within sentences or alone as shortcuts. Remember, however, that customers may not understand what you are trying to communicate or they may misinterpret your message. Furthermore, some of the acronyms that are popular on the Internet are simply not appropriate for business communications.

TIP

When in doubt, leave out special characters, emoticons, and acronyms.

NOTE

Capital letters can be used to emphasize a point, but try not to overdo it. CAPITALIZING MANY WORDS OR AN ENTIRE SENTENCE IS GENERALLY PERCEIVED AS SHOUTING. Conversely, exclusive use of lowercase letters can be difficult to read. It is best to follow standard capitalization rules.

Use Forms and Templates to Save Time.   Help desks are increasingly using forms and templates to customize their e-mail messages and to distribute and collect information electronically. These forms may be used to request information, report problems, request new products and services, and so forth. A **form** is a predefined document that contains text or graphics users cannot change and areas in which users enter data being collected. Forms save time for customers and analysts. Customers save time because they know what data they must provide to submit their request. Analysts save time because they get the data they need to begin working on the request. Forms often correspond to the problem entry screen of the incident tracking and problem management system so that analysts have the data needed to quickly log customer requests. Some e-mail and incident tracking and problem management systems interface so that requests are logged automatically. A **template** is a predefined item that can be used to quickly create a standard document or e-mail message.

Templates save analysts time because they can save text and items such as custom toolbars and links to Web sites and quickly reuse those items to create documents and e-mail messages. The time it takes to create forms and templates pays off in time saved down the road.

Verify Your Distribution Lists Periodically. Checking for new e-mail messages and responding to messages that you receive on a daily basis can be a challenge. Receiving unnecessary e-mail can be frustrating. To avoid being a source of frustration for your customers, periodically verify your distribution lists. For example, you may be sending a message to someone who no longer works for a company or who has moved into a new position and no longer uses your company's product or services. Conversely, a person who should be receiving your information may not be on the list. Make sure you are sending messages to the correct recipients.

NOTE E-mail users have seen a tremendous increase in the amount of spam they receive in recent years. Companies that send legitimate e-mails, for example, to announce the release of new products or to inform customers about viruses, must diligently manage their distribution lists in an effort to maintain customer goodwill. Many companies provide easy ways for customers to opt out of mailing lists and specify their preferences with regard to marketing e-mails and technical alerts. Many companies are also rethinking the practice of having customers use their e-mail address to logon to their Web sites, because customers are increasingly hesitant to post their e-mail address online where it may fall into the hands of spammers.

Standardize Your Signature. Most e-mail packages now provide the ability to automatically insert a signature into an e-mail message. A good practice for a help desk is to use a standard format for all analysts' signatures that includes all the ways to contact the help desk. This consistency lends a professional air to messages and ensures customers know alternate ways to get help. Figure 6–14 shows a sample help desk e-mail signature. Remember to put the help desk's telephone number and e-mail address in your signature, as opposed to your personal telephone number or e-mail address, so customers cannot contact you directly.

Mary Jane Smith
Help Desk Analyst
The Super Software Company
"Working hard to keep you working!"
Web: www.thesupersoftwarecompany.com
E-mail: help.desk@thesupersoftwarecompany.com
Phone: (816) 555-HELP (4357)
Fax: (816) 555-3255

Figure 6–14 Sample help desk e-mail signature

Although it may seem you are providing personalized service by having customers contact you directly, you are actually doing the customer and your coworkers a disservice. This is because you may be out of the office on a day when the customer needs assistance and his or her request will go unanswered. Furthermore, you fail to leave the customer with the impression that anyone at the help desk can assist.

Help desks are increasingly using e-mail to communicate with customers, coworkers, and managers on a daily basis. E-mail best practices ensure that help desk analysts use e-mail in a consistent, professional manner. It is also important that analysts communicate in a way that is respectful to recipients regardless of their location or native language.

Writing for a Global Audience

The Internet and e-mail make it possible for help desks to interact with customers worldwide at any time of the day or night. When writing for global customers, it is important to remember that how you use expressions, dates, times, and even numbers can confuse your customers. Figure 6–15 lists two techniques you can use to minimize any confusion.

> Avoid idioms.
>
> Internationalize dates, times, and numbers.

Figure 6–15 Writing techniques for a global audience

This section describes each of these techniques in greater detail.

Avoid Idioms.   When writing for a global audience, it is best to avoid idioms. An **idiom** is a group of words whose meaning is different than the meanings of the individual words. In other words, an idiom is a phrase or expression that cannot be taken literally. Idioms may be derived from historical references, sports, books, television, or movies; all of which tend to be culturally specific. For example, the expression "Let's touch base in a couple of days" is a reference to the American sport of baseball.

Many idioms have become so commonplace that we use them without realizing they may be confusing to someone from another country. For example, a person in the United States may say that he was "blown away" by the new technology introduced at a trade show, meaning that he was amazed or astonished by the technology. If you look at the words literally, however, you can understand how a non-native English speaker may be confused.

Strive to edit idioms out of your documents and e-mails in an effort to avoid any confusion. For example, rather than say a request has "fallen through the cracks," simply say that it was misplaced. Although stating that a customer can reach the help desk "24/7" may make sense to you, stating that the help desk is available 24 hours a day, 7 days a week will make sense to everyone.

Internationalize dates, times, and numbers.   Dates, times, weights, measurements, and temperature are expressed differently from one country to the next. For example, the international standard for expressing dates is year/month/day. In the United States, however, the date is typically expressed as month/day/year. Most countries other than the United States use the metric system. Many countries use the Celsius temperature scale, as opposed to the Fahrenheit temperature scale used in the United States.

Strive to remember these differences when communicating with global customers. To avoid confusion, be specific. For example, when you give someone the hours that the help desk is available, make sure you specify the time zone. You may also want to consider giving measurements and temperatures, for example, in all applicable forms. For example, "the daily temperatures at the conference are expected to be around 60° Fahrenheit (15° Celsius)."

Remember that whether your customers are in another part of the country or on the other side of the world, learning about and respecting their culture will always serve you well. It is also best to use plain language and a polite, positive tone.

Writing is an acquired skill that becomes easier when you know the rules. If you do not enjoy writing, consider taking a writing class so that writing becomes easier. You may find that you enjoy it more. If nothing else, you will be able to write faster and thus have more time for the things you do enjoy. The ability to write well is an important skill that technical professionals must possess. In today's digital age, good writing is quickly becoming a critical success factor. Remember that all it takes is practice, practice, practice.

CHAPTER SUMMARY

❐ Technologies such as the Internet, e-mail, and instant messaging (IM) are increasingly complementing the telephone and onsite services as a way to communicate with customers. These technologies extend the help desk's ability to gather, organize, and use information. They also enable companies to provide self-services that customers can use to obtain the information they need, when they need it. Information is an extremely valuable resource, and people with good writing skills are able to capture it easily and accurately.

❐ When working in a help desk, good writing skills are needed to log trouble tickets, send e-mail messages, develop answers to frequently asked questions (FAQs) and knowledge base solutions, prepare reports, or prepare policies and procedures. When preparing these documents, always be aware of the document's target audience and purpose. Before you write a word, ensure you understand the audience's needs and how they plan to use the information. Learning the rules of writing will provide you the foundation needed to write any document and to make a positive impression with your writing.

❐ Writing, like any other skill, improves and becomes easier with practice. It also helps to know the rules. Technical writing best practices help you develop an effective writing style and improve your writing skills. E-mail best practices help you use e-mail in a consistent, professional manner. The ability to write well is an important skill thattechnical professionals must possess. In today's digital age, good writing is quickly becoming a critical success factor. Remember that all it takes is practice, practice, practice.

KEY TERMS

capture — To collect.

case-based reasoning (CBR) — A searching technique that uses everyday language to ask users questions and interpret their answers.

chat — A simultaneous text communication between two or more people via a computer; also called online chat.

chat room — A virtual room that provides users the ability to converse (or chat) real time with one or more other users on a local area network (LAN), on the Internet, or via a Bulletin Board Service (BBS).

content management system (CMS) — Software used to manage the content of a Web site.

data — Raw facts that are not organized in a meaningful way.

data field — An element of a database record in which one piece of data is stored.

decision tree — A branching structure of questions and possible answers designed to lead an analyst to a solution.

emoticon — A symbol used to convey feelings.

expert system — A computer program that stores human knowledge in a knowledge base and has the ability to reason about that knowledge.

extranet — A Web site that is accessed via the Internet—that is, it can be accessed by the general public—but requires a password to gain entry to all or parts of the site.

form — A predefined document that contains text or graphics users cannot change and areas in which users enter data being collected.

frequently asked questions (FAQs) — Well-written answers to the most common customer queries.

fuzzy logic — A searching technique that presents all possible solutions that are similar to the search criteria, even when conflicting information exists or no exact match is present.

hyperlink — See link.

idiom — A group of words whose meaning is different than the meanings of the individual words.

information — Data that are organized in a meaningful way.

instant messaging system — Technology that enables two or more people to communicate in real time over the Internet by typing on a keyboard.

Internet — A global collection of computer networks that are linked together to provide worldwide access to information.

intranet — An internal collection of linked computers that provide a company's employees and other authorized people, such as customers, access to secured information.

keyboard — To type.

keyword searching — The technique of finding indexed information by specifying a descriptive word or phrase, called a keyword.

knowledge engineer — A person who develops and oversees the knowledge management process and ensures the information contained in the help desk's knowledge base is accurate, complete, and current.

knowledge management system — A system that combines the reasoning capability of an expert system with other information sources, such as databases, documents, and policies and procedures.

link — Colored and/or underlined text or a graphic, which when clicked might open a pop-up window with a definition, instructions, a still picture, or an animated picture; run an audio or video clip; or jump to a Web page; also called hyperlink.

one-to-many relationship — One solution that solves many trouble tickets.

procedure — A step-by-step, detailed set of instructions that describes how to perform a task.

query by example (QBE) — A searching technique that uses queries, or questions, to find records that match the specified search criteria.

requirement — Something that is required—a necessity.

search criteria — The question or problem symptom entered by a user.

search operator — A connecting word such as AND, OR, and NOT.

self-service — A service that enables customers to help themselves.

solution — A definitive, permanent resolution to a problem, or a proven workaround.

spam — Unsolicited e-mail.

synonym — A word with the same or very similar meaning to another word.

template — A predefined item that can be used to quickly create a standard document or e-mail message.

text field — A field that accepts free-form information.

REVIEW QUESTIONS

1. True or false? A dramatic change in how the help desk collects information and delivers support has prompted the need for support professionals to add technical writing to their list of required skills.

2. Describe four ways that technology-delivered support services benefit the help desk.

3. What role does the telephone play in delivering support?

4. What role does e-mail play in delivering support?

5. What role does instant messaging play in delivering support?

6. What role does the Web play in delivering support?

7. How are information and data different?

8. How do good writing and keyboarding skills benefit people working in a help desk?

9. Describe five ways that companies such as hardware manufacturers and software publishers are enabling customers to help themselves.

10. True or false? Customers often perceive that self-services take too much time.

11. What is an intranet?

12. What are the keys to a successful help desk Web site?

13. Describe three ways that companies can provide customers the ability to customize their support experience.

14. List four ways that companies can use e-mail to communicate with customers.

15. A(n) _____ is a simultaneous text communication between two or more people on a computer.

16. True or false? You can send an instant message even if a recipient is not online.

17. Why do most help desks currently limit IM interactions with customers? Explain your answer.

18. List three reasons that analysts must learn to use and create knowledge bases.

19. What is a knowledge base?

20. Describe the relationship that exists between an expert system and a knowledge management system.

21. List three ways that knowledge management systems benefit help desk analysts.

22. What is the role of the knowledge engineer?

23. What factors influence the amount of documentation that help desk analysts write?

24. Should you include all of the steps you have taken to diagnose a problem when creating a trouble ticket?

25. How is a data field different than a text field?

26. Name four users of the data entered in a trouble ticket.

27. What are FAQs?

28. What is the key to a well-written FAQ?

29. What is a reusable solution?

30. List three benefits of having a standard format for solutions.

31. What should you do if you are asked to write a type of report that you have never written before?

32. True or false? You do not have to explicitly state every step when writing a procedure.

33. What is a "living" document?

34. List three techniques you can use to improve your technical writing skills.

35. What do you need to know about your readers to communicate clearly?

36. When is it okay to use technical terms in your writing?

37. What is the best style to use when writing about technology?

38. What are the benefits of using simple language when you write?

39. When should you define a technical term or acronym?

40. When should you use a numbered list?

41. What is a style guide?

42. Name two things that customers need to know about a help desk's e-mail policy.

43. Why is it important to check your grammar, punctuation, and spelling when sending an e-mail message?

44. What should you do if you want to send a customer detailed information via e-mail without using an attachment?

45. Why is "how you say it" important when communicating in the written form?

46. When should you use characters such as asterisks in an e-mail message?

47. Why do you want to avoid capitalizing entire sentences in an e-mail message?

48. A(n) is a predefined item that can be used to quickly create a standard document or e-mail message.

49. Should you put the help desk's telephone number or your personal telephone number in your standard signature? Why?

50. True or false? Taken literally, an idiom makes perfect sense.

Dicussion Questions

1. What are the pros and cons of using IM to communicate with customers?

2. Companies that offer Web-based support services increasingly are making it difficult for customers to contact the company via the telephone. For example, some companies do not have a telephone number listed on their Web site or they charge a fee for telephone-based support. The company's perspective is that it has made a tremendous investment in its Web site and wants to maximize that investment. What is your perspective as a customer?

3. Prepare a list of the various channels that help desks use to deliver support services such as the telephone, e-mail, and so forth. Prepare a second list that represents the various situations in which customers need support. For example, they are experiencing a problem using a software package, they want to order a new hardware device, and so forth. For each situation in which customers need support, discuss what would be the most appropriate channel from the customer's perspective and then from the help desk's perspective.

HANDS-ON PROJECTS

Project 6–1

Identify support options. Select a software or hardware product that you use regularly. Identify all of the ways you can obtain support from the vendor. For example:

❑ Is telephone support available?

❑ During what hours is telephone support available?

❑ Is e-mail support available?

❑ Does the vendor guarantee a response to e-mails within a stated time frame? If yes, what is the time frame?

❑ Does the vendor have a Web site?

❑ Are FAQs available on the Web site?

❑ What other ways, if any, can you obtain support?

Prepare a short summary of your findings.

Project 6–2

Identify self-service options. Visit the Web site of a large software or hardware vendor, such as Microsoft, Cisco, Dell, or Gateway. Explore its Web site and identify any self-services it provides in support of its products. Prepare a brief paper describing your findings.

Project 6–3

Document a problem and its solution. Briefly describe a technical problem that you recently encountered or were asked to help with. Include details such as who, what, when, where, and how. Develop a solution for this problem using the solution guidelines described in this chapter.

Project 6–4

Prepare a list of FAQs. Prepare a list of at least five questions and answers that you are frequently asked about an aspect of your life, such as school, your job, a hobby, or a sport that you enjoy.

Project 6–5

Prepare a progress report. Prepare a brief progress report about an important activity you are involved in, such as a project at school, at work, or an upcoming event that you are planning, such as a wedding or a vacation.

Project 6–6

Write a procedure. Write a procedure for a simple task, such as tying a shoe or brushing hair. Pair up with a classmate, and then have the classmate follow your procedure exactly to see if he or she can successfully complete the task. Ask the classmate to give you feedback on your writing. For example, is the procedure accurate, complete, and easy to understand? Refine your procedure based on any observations you made while your classmate was following the procedure and based on his or her feedback. Have the classmate follow or review your refined procedure and provide any additional feedback.

Project 6–7

Assess your writing skills. Select a report or paper that you have written recently. Read through the report and, given what you have learned in this chapter, note any changes you could make in terms of style to improve the quality of the report. Briefly summarize your findings. Rewrite the report or a few pages of the report using what you have learned in this chapter. Read through the report again. Briefly summarize how the changes you have made improve the readability of the report.

Project 6–8

Develop a standard signature. Using the format suggested in this chapter, develop a standard e-mail signature. Use telephone numbers and addresses related to your job or school.

Project 6–9

Substitute idioms with a less confusing expression. Working with a group of two or three classmates, prepare a list of at least 10 idioms that you use in everyday language. Exchange lists with another group in your class. Replace each idiom on the list with a less confusing expression. Share your results with the class.

CASE PROJECTS

1. Requirements Report

Your school's help desk manager has hired you as a consultant. The manager wants to enhance the help desk's Web site and provide students with the ability to use self-services. Your job is to determine the students' requirements for an improved Web site. Ask three to five of your classmates how the school's Web site can be improved in an effort to provide self-services. Prepare a one-page Requirements Report that describes your findings.

CASE
PROJECTS

2. Research Knowledge Bases

Your help desk manager wants to implement a commercially available knowledge base that can be used to support industry-standard applications. Your help desk supports products from Lotus, Microsoft, and Novell. Your manager has asked you to provide her with information about the products that are available and to describe the benefits of implementing this type of product. Search the Web for three products that offer knowledge bases that contain answers and solutions for the products you support. Briefly describe the features and functionality that each product offers. Also, list the benefits of implementing this type of product to both help desk analysts and customers.

CASE
PROJECTS

3. Unsupported Product

Your company is discontinuing support for a software program that is supported by the software publisher. Create a template that can be used to respond to customers who request support for this product. Use the tips and techniques discussed in this chapter and don't forget your can do attitude.

7

BUSINESS SKILLS FOR TECHNICAL PROFESSIONALS

In this chapter you will learn:

◆ How to acquire and use business skills in the workplace

◆ How to use business skills to identify and justify improvement opportunities

◆ How to use presentation skills to communicate

◆ Advanced business skills for technical professionals such as managing projects, conducting a cost benefit analysis, and calculating return on investment (ROI)

In the support industry, technical professionals are increasingly being challenged to do more than simply support technology. They are being challenged to ensure that technology is useful and that it is enabling workers to be productive. In other words, they are being challenged to ensure that a company's technology enables its employees and customers to achieve their business goals.

To do this, technical professionals must acquire business skills. Recall that business skills are the skills people need to work successfully in the business world, such as the ability to understand and speak the language of business and the ability to analyze business problems and identify improvement opportunities. Merely identifying improvement opportunities, however, is not enough. Individuals must also be able to communicate the benefits of their ideas in financial terms and use presentation skills to market their ideas to management.

This chapter introduces technical professionals to some of the business topics and disciplines they may encounter when they join the workforce. This chapter also describes advanced business skills that managers are increasingly requiring more senior technical professionals to acquire and use, such as project management, cost benefit analysis, and return on investment (ROI) calculations.

ACQUIRING AND USING BUSINESS SKILLS IN THE WORKPLACE

Whether a person works for a small company or a large corporation, some business skills are useful and increasingly required. One reason is that the business world is extremely competitive. CIOs and hiring managers increasingly expect technical professionals to think like business people and to possess at least some business skills. Another reason is that trends such as automation and outsourcing mean that companies have fewer job positions and are being very selective about who they hire. People who have a mix of skills—including business, technical, soft, and self-management skills—create the greatest opportunities for themselves.

NOTE
Of the IT professionals who participated in a 2003 *Computerworld* survey, 75% say academia is not preparing graduates for the IT jobs of today or the next few years ("The State of IT Education," Computerworld online survey, August 2003). According to survey participants, top skills that colleges and universities need to be teaching their IT students, which they are not teaching now, include communication and people skills, business skills, real-world and hands-on experience, troubleshooting, project management, analytical skills, and systems integration skills. As a result, a growing number of academic institutions are working hard to incorporate these skills into their computer science curriculums.

Some business skills, such as those listed in Figure 7-1, are particularly relevant to technical professionals. It is important to note, however, that these skills are useful regardless of the profession you enter. You can acquire some business skills by simply observing and inquiring about the activities that occur where you work. Your business skills will also grow as you acquire education and experience.

Many of these skills are discussed in other chapters of this book or in the sections that follow.

■ **Customer service.** Skills such as understanding the importance of meeting customers' needs and knowing how to manage their expectations, discussed in Chapter 10, are imperative in today's competitive business world. The need for people who understand the characteristics of excellent customer service—responsiveness, a caring attitude, and skill—is great and on the rise.

■ **Process management.** Processes, discussed in Chapter 10, are an integral component of every help desk. Common processes such as problem management (discussed in Chapter 4), request management, knowledge management, and service level management are vital to the success of the help desk. People who understand processes can suggest improvments that save time and money by eliminating bottlenecks and unnecessary tasks. The growing acceptance of ITIL is also increasing the need for people who have experience developing, documenting, and continuously improving processes.

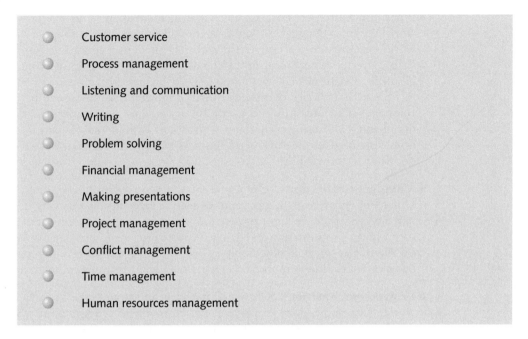

- Customer service
- Process management
- Listening and communication
- Writing
- Problem solving
- Financial management
- Making presentations
- Project management
- Conflict management
- Time management
- Human resources management

Figure 7-1 Business skills relevant to technical professionals

- **Listening and communication.** Listening and communication, discussed in Chapter 4, are two of the most basic skills needed in today's fast-paced business world. Knowing what to say and how to say it takes practice and a willingness to understand the varying communication styles of customers, managers, and coworkers. Good listening and communication skills benefit all areas of your life and can be improved with practice.

- **Writing.** Discussed in Chapter 6, writing is an increasingly important business skill. This is because an ever greater number of communications occur via technologies such as the Internet, e-mail, and IM. Help desk analysts are also regularly required to use writing skills to prepare documents such as trouble tickets, knowledge base solutions, reports, policies, and procedures. The need for strong writing skills grows as a person advances in his or her career.

- **Problem solving.** Problem-solving skills, discussed in Chapter 14, are imperative in the support industry and valued regardless of a person's profession. Knowing how to methodically gather data, determine the probable source of problems, and develop solutions to problems are skills that improve with practice and experience.

- **Financial management.** Financial management skills range from being able to work within a budget—a must-have skill in today's cost-sensitive business world—to preparing a budget for a project or department. The need for these skills increases as technical professionals advance to team leader or supervisory positions. Financial management skills also include being able to communicate the financial benefits of improvement opportunities (discussed in the Using Business Skills to Identify and Justify Improvement Opportunities section later in this chapter) and using techniques such as cost benefit analysis and ROI calculations (discussed in the Advanced Business Skills for Technical Professionals section later in this chapter).

- **Making presentations.** Using presentations to communicate (discussed in the Using Presentations to Communicate section later in this chapter) is an important business skill, because presentations are an accepted and effective way to communicate information and gain acceptance for ideas. Presentations are also an excellent way to build credibility. The use of presentations to communicate becomes increasingly important as a person advances in his or her career.

- **Project management.** Change is constant and imperative in today's business world. As a result, most employees will be involved at some point with a project. For example, technical professionals are often involved in projects such as hardware or software rollouts. An understanding of project management concepts (discussed in the Advanced Business Skills for Technical Professionals section later in this chapter) makes it possible for a person to be effective whether he or she is a member of a project team or responsible for planning and managing a project.

- **Conflict management.** Conflict is a normal part of human interaction. Knowing how to manage conflict in a constructive way (discussed in Chapter 12) is an important skill, particularly when working in a team setting such as a help desk. Conflict management is an excellent life skill that can be improved with practice.

- **Time management.** Time management, discussed in Chapter 12, is a critical business skill that enables people to feel in control and stay motivated during today's "do more with less" times. Good work habits, such as getting and staying organized, make it possible for people to feel job satisfaction and avoid stress and burnout. Like conflict management, time management is an excellent life skill that can be improved with practice.

- **Human resources management.** Human resources management involves activities such as interviewing prospective employees, coaching team members, and conducting performance appraisals. In some team settings, team members provide feedback about their teammates' performance (discussed in Chapter 12) and may be involved in interviewing prospective employees. These skills become more important, and are typically required, as technical professionals advance to team leader or supervisory positions.

Many of these skills such as listening, communication, and writing are basic business skills that can be learned on-the-job, through self-study, or in the classroom. These skills, along with skills such as customer service, problem solving, project management, conflict management, and time management, are relatively universal and can be used regardless of a person's chosen profession. Skills such as financial management and human resources management are also important and become even more important as people advance in their careers.

NOTE

An understanding of ethics is another increasingly important business skill. Ethics are the rules and standards that govern the conduct of a person or group of people. Such rules and standards dictate, or provide guidance, about what is considered right and wrong behavior. Ethical behavior is behavior that conforms to generally accepted or stated principles of right and wrong. The policies of a department or company dictate what is right and wrong behavior and may vary from one department or company to the next. For example, some companies permit limited personal use of the company's e-mail system, whereas others restrict the use of e-mail to work-related correspondences. Recent financial scandals in the business world and dilemmas such as the ease with which Internet sources can be plagiarized have prompted an increased awareness of the need for ethics in business

TIP

Hundreds of books ranging from basic to advanced have been written about business. Furthermore, these books span a broad range of topics. To learn more about business skills, go to your local library or bookstore and search general topics such as "business" and "workplace skills" or more specific topics such as "listening" and "time management." Books, tapes, and videos can also be purchased at Web sites such as **www.bizhotline.com**, **www.amanet.org**, and **www.careertrack.com**.

The business skills required for a help desk job vary, depending on the industry in which the company is engaged and the job category (such as level one analyst, level one specialist, help desk supervisor, or help desk manager). The specific skills a company requires are determined by the company's job description.

Most employers do not expect technical professionals to have fully developed business skills when they first join the workforce. Some basic knowledge, such as service industry knowledge, and a willingness to learn are viewed as a positive. **Service industry knowledge** is knowledge of the customer service and support industry. Companies that don't require this kind of experience at least consider it highly desirable. Many employers scan candidates' résumés for previous service experience or job experience that involves helping people.

Relevant fields include teaching, sales, social work, and healthcare. These fields are relevant because people in these fields must be able to recognize that they are delivering a service and that their "customers" look to them for help.

Some companies also desire business skills that are unique to the industry or profession the help desk supports, such as accounting or banking. These skills are called **industry knowledge.** Some help desks seek to hire people who understand the specific industry in which the company is engaged, such as manufacturing, retail, or financial. This industry knowledge makes it easier for an employee to understand the company's goals and contribute accordingly. Many help desks recruit from within the company to find candidates who are already familiar with the company and its goals. Help desks also often value candidates who have skills and knowledge that pertain to the product or service being sold. For example, a company that sells accounting software may seek help desk personnel who have an accounting background. Such knowledge enables the help desk analyst to understand the customer's needs and appreciate the impact on the customer's business when a product fails to perform properly.

Increasingly, managers are requiring technical professionals who want to advance in their careers to hone and use business skills. People applying for help desk management positions are also expected to have more advanced business skills and experience. The absence of business skills may not hinder a technical professional as he or she pursues a career. The presence of business skills will, however, increase the opportunities available to a technical professional and speed up advancement.

> *In today's knowledge-based economy, what you earn depends on what you learn.*
> Bill Clinton

Employers often receive hundreds of résumés from people who have technical skills and certifications. Developing and demonstrating business skills is an effective way to differentiate yourself from the competition and increase your opportunities. Furthermore, if you are looking to advance your career, business skills are essential.

NOTE   People who want to advance to a higher technical position or into a management role often find it difficult to "give up" their technical skills to acquire business skills. They are used to being the experts and may enjoy having others look up to them and seek them out for assistance. In time, however, individuals who want to advance must move from knowing how to fix technology to how to use technology to achieve business goals.

Industry Knowledge - Only deals with customer service

Learning and mastering business skills takes time and training. Technicians who want to advance their ideas and their careers can begin by striving to understand their company's goals. They must then acquire the skills needed to understand and present in business and financial terms how technology can be used to achieve those goals. To do this, technical professionals must first learn to understand and speak the language of business.

Understanding and Speaking the Language of Business

The term *business* has many meanings and encompasses a broad range of disciplines. By definition, a business is a commercial enterprise or establishment. A commercial enterprise or establishment has profit as its chief aim. The term **business** may also be used to describe a person's occupation, work, or trade. For example, "He is in the computer business" or "She is in the accounting business."

NOTE   The term *business-within-a-business* is often used to describe a company's IT or Customer Service department. This term illustrates that although these departments may or may not have profit as their chief aim, they are responsible for delivering products and services to their customers in the most cost-effective way possible. Many companies that subscribe to the business-within-a-business concept challenge managers to think like entrepreneurs and run their departments as they would a small business.

Some companies are not commercially motivated. **Nonprofit** companies, also known as not-for-profit companies, are established for charitable, educational, or humanitarian purposes rather than for making money. Although the objectives of a nonprofit company are different than those of a for-profit company, the business skills required to work for both are similar.

A good way to learn more about business is to first learn about your company (or a company where you want to work), its mission, the industry that it is in, and its competitors. Study the words that are used to describe your company, its mission, and its goals. Gaining this "big picture" perspective will typically help you understand why, for example, certain technologies or data are viewed as highly important (strategic) or why certain projects are viewed as essential to the business (mission critical).

TIP   To learn more about your company, go to its Web site and click the About link. You may also want to review your company's Annual Report or simply observe and interview workers in other areas of the company. The more you tap into why your company operates the way it does, the more successful you can be.

Companies are increasingly striving to ensure that information technologies support corporate goals and objectives, a process known as **IT and business alignment.** Learning about business in general, and your business more specifically, will help you as a technical professional determine ways technology can help your customers achieve their goals. Admittedly, technology is critical to today's business. However, the focus of business continues to be on the business, not on the technology. Technical professionals who understand that focus can help business people understand available technologies and how best to use them. They can also ensure that new technologies, when introduced, offer real value to the business.

USING BUSINESS SKILLS TO IDENTIFY AND JUSTIFY IMPROVEMENT OPPORTUNITIES

People working in a help desk hear day-in and day-out from customers who are having trouble using technology. They have a unique opportunity to support the goals of business by working hard to eliminate or minimize the impact of business problems and identify improvement opportunities.

The following sections discuss how help desk professionals can use data and techniques such as trend and root cause analysis to analyze business problems and identify improvement opportunities. They must also justify improvement opportunities by communicating the benefits of their ideas in financial terms.

Using Data to Identify and Quantify Improvement Opportunities

It is difficult to find a book or article about help desks that does not describe the tools and technologies that enable help desk analysts and managers to do their work. Such tools and technologies are useless, however, if they do not provide and produce meaningful information. For example, it is a waste of time for help desk analysts to log every problem in an incident tracking and problem management system if they cannot search the system in the future and retrieve historical information about the problems they logged. Similarly, managers must be able to use the incident tracking and problem management system to run reports and produce charts that show problem trends. These trends can then be used to identify opportunities for problem prevention and product enhancement. Problem trends also often influence future technology purchasing decisions.

People working in a help desk must understand clearly that the data they collect on a daily basis becomes information. This information is not just used to track outstanding problems and requests. It is also used to measure their personal performance, the overall performance of the help desk, and, what is more important, customer satisfaction with the company. Failing to record events and activities accurately and completely can have very negative results for the company, the help desk, and the help desk employee. Figure 7-2 shows a sample of the types of data and information collected and used by help desks.

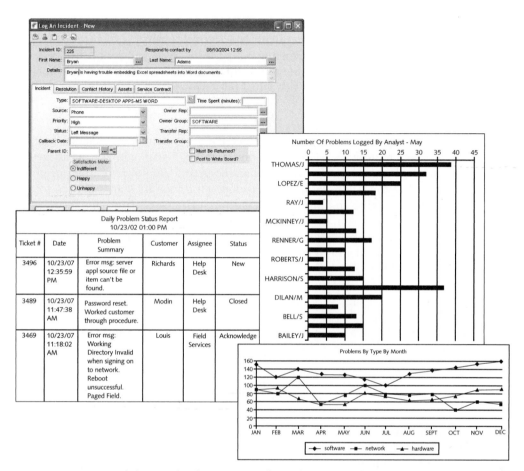

Figure 7-2 Types of data and information collected and used by help desks

Help desks that capture information divide that information into various data categories. These data categories tend to be similar from help desk to help desk because most help desks perform similar processes. Each help desk captures additional data categories specific to its business or industry. Figure 7-3 lists the most common data categories captured by help desks.

Figure 7-3 Common data categories

These data, typically captured through fields in the help desk's incident tracking and problem management system, enable help desks to track problems and requests; measure team, individual, and process performances; and perform trend and root cause analysis (discussed in the Using Business Skills to Identify and Justify Improvement Opportunities section later in this chapter). Be aware that the actual field names used in the data categories vary from one help desk to the next.

Customer Data.   Recall that customer data are identifying details about a customer, including the customer's name, telephone number, e-mail address, department or company name, address or location, customer number, and employee number or user ID. Recall also that all of the fields that describe a single customer are stored in a customer record in the incident tracking and problem management database. Customer records are linked to problem records, which are also stored in the incident tracking and problem management system, by a unique key field such as customer name or customer number. These fields can be used to quickly identify a customer contacting the help desk and to research a customer's history of problems.

NOTE   In some incident tracking and problem management systems, customer records are linked to incident records, which are also stored in the system. Incident records typically contain a field that is used to specify the type of incident being reported, such as problem, request, question, and so forth. The data fields that analysts are required to enter may vary based on the incident type specified. For example, because questions are typically answered quickly, often using solutions from the help desk's knowledge base, a reduced set of data fields may be required.

Problem Data.   Recall that problem data are the details of a single problem. They include the problem category (such as hardware or software), affected component or system (such as a printer or monitor), symptom, date and time problem occurred, date and time problem was logged, analyst who logged the problem, problem owner, description, and severity. Recall also that all of the fields that describe a single problem are stored in a problem record in the incident tracking and problem management system. These fields can be used to research and track trends or to search the knowledge base for solutions. Figure 7-4 shows a sample trend report that uses the problem category field.

Status Data.   **Status data** are details about a problem that are used to track problems not resolved at level one. Status data include problem status (such as assigned, awaiting parts, resolved, closed), the person or group assigned, date and time assigned, and priority. These data are stored in fields in the problem record in the incident tracking and problem management system. After a problem record is created, that record is continuously updated as new data—such as status and resolution data—becomes available. These fields can be used to report on the status of outstanding problems and to monitor SLA attainment. Figure 7-5 shows a sample problem aging report that is used to ensure that outstanding problems are

Problems by Category — May

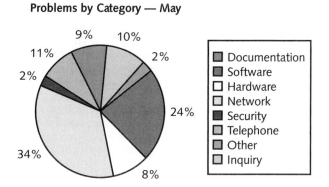

Figure 7-4 Sample problem category report

being resolved within their target resolution time. Many companies use this type of report to monitor adherence to an SLA goal, such as: "Resolve 95% of problems within their target resolution time."

Assigned To	<1 Day	2-3 Days	4-5 Days	6-10 Days	>10 Days	% Within Target
Field Services	24	6	3	1	2	98
Network Support	54	23	15	9	13	94
Development	76	54	8	2	1	87
Vendor	93	27	3	4	12	75

Figure 7-5 Sample problem aging report

Resolution Data.   **Resolution data** describe how a problem was resolved. They include the fields required to track service level compliance and perform root cause analysis, such as the person or group who resolved the problem, resolution description, date and time resolved, customer satisfaction indicator, date and time closed, and root cause. These data are stored in fields in the problem record in the incident tracking and problem management system. When resolution data becomes available, they are added to the problem record created when the problem was reported.

NOTE   Most companies distinguish between resolving a problem and closing the problem. A problem is *resolved* when a level one or level two analyst delivers a solution. The problem is *closed* only after the problem owner verifies that the customer is satisfied with the resolution.

NOTE Some problems are resolved by creating a request. Customers occasionally report problems that are not actually problems. Rather, they represent a desire on the part of the customer to change how the product functions. For example, a customer may report that a product cannot perform a particular function when, in fact, that function was intentionally left out when the product was designed. Conversely, that particular function may have been overlooked when the product was designed and, as such, represents a valid enhancement opportunity. Companies handle this type of situation differently. For example, some companies resolve the problem, create a request, and close the problem only when the request is completed. Other companies open a request and simply close the problem with a reference to the request. When a request is opened, ownership of the problem is transferred to the group responsible for completing the request.

Help desk analysts and managers use these customer, problem, status, and resolution data fields to create detailed tracking and summary reports. In addition, managers use these data fields to calculate many team and individual performance measures.

NOTE Common help desk team performance measures are discussed and defined in Chapter 12.

Forward-thinking companies use the data they capture at the help desk to spot trends and discover the root cause of problems. By getting a good grasp of problem trends and root causes, companies can increase customer satisfaction, enhance productivity, improve the quality of products and services, increase the efficiency and effectiveness with which services are delivered, and create new products and services.

People working in a help desk have the opportunity to continuously capture the data and information needed to determine customers' wants and needs. Successful help desks seize this opportunity by designing and implementing processes and technologies that enable them to capture and use customer information efficiently. People interested in a support-industry career must learn how to interpret data and share and add value to information. They can do this by learning to identify trends and the root cause of problems.

Performing Trend and Root Cause Analysis

Simply capturing data does not prevent problems or make it possible for companies to monitor and improve their services. To do so, analysts must study the data using techniques such as trend and root cause analysis.

Performing Trend Analysis.   Recall that trend analysis is a methodical way of determining and, when possible, forecasting service trends. Trends can be positive, such as a reduction in the number of "how to" questions the help desk receives after an improved training program, or trends can be negative, such as a dramatic increase in call volume after a new product appears on the market. Trend reports provide help desk management and staff with the information needed to formulate improvement plans and communicate achievements. Figure 7-6 illustrates that trend reports can also be used to monitor and measure performance.

	Problem Count	Resolved @ Level One	% Resolved @ Level One	Avg Monthly Volume
Dec	534	265	50	534
Jan	635	295	46	584
Feb	601	234	39	590
Mar	556	241	43	597
Apr	710	319	45	622
May	735	356	48	648

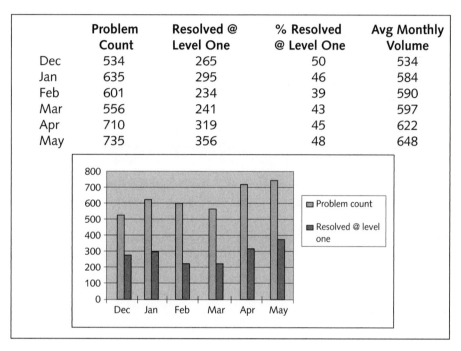

Figure 7-6 Sample trend report

This report shows a consistent rise in the number of problems logged by the help desk. A positive trend worth noting is that the help desk has been able to steadily increase the number of problems resolved at level one, despite an increase in its workload. This may be the positive result of recent training efforts or the addition of improved diagnostic tools. If the percentage of problems resolved at level one was decreasing, as opposed to increasing, it could mean that the level one help desk is understaffed and, as such, does not have adequate time to diagnose problems. It could also mean that a new product has been introduced and the help desk has not received adequate training. Complementary reports, such as the types of problems being reported to the help desk and the types of problems that must be escalated to level two, can be used to validate analysts' findings and identify ways the help desk can continue to improve.

Used effectively, trend analysis involves looking at a set of data—such as the problems reported during a given month—and viewing it from different angles in an effort to identify a trend. For example, Figure 7-7 shows a breakdown of the top 10 hardware problems for a given month by device.

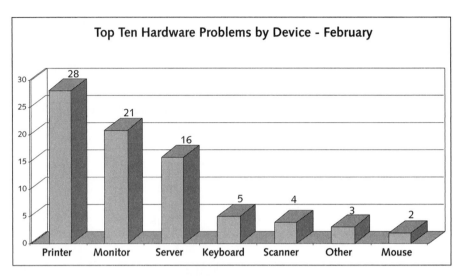

Figure 7-7 Sample top 10 hardware problems report

A comparable report could show a breakdown of software problems for a given month by system. Or, a report could show a breakdown of problems reported by department or division.

Top 10 reports are an excellent way to identify problem trends that require immediate action. Many companies use top 10 reports to determine the types of problems that warrant root cause analysis.

NOTE

Trend reports make it possible to determine the most common and frequently occurring problems and also make it possible for analysts to identify anomalies. An **anomaly** is a deviation or departure from the average or the norm. For example, printer problems tend to be fairly common in most organizations. An exceptional number of printer problems should, however, prompt additional analysis. In such a case, additional trend analysis or root cause analysis can be used to determine the cause of the anomaly. For example, Figure 7-8 shows a breakdown of the printer problems identified in Figure 7-7 by root cause.

This report reveals that a high percentage of printer problems are caused by hardware failures. Such a statistic should prompt the company to revisit its product evaluation process and perhaps select a different brand of printer. This information can also be used to show printer manufacturers the extent of the problems the company is experiencing. A complementary report might be arranged by model or manufacturer and show a breakdown of printer problems caused by hardware failures. The company may also decide that additional root cause analysis is needed.

Performing Root Cause Analysis. Root cause analysis is used to determine why problems are occurring so that the company can take steps to prevent similar problems from occurring in the future. Recall that root cause analysis is a methodical way of determining

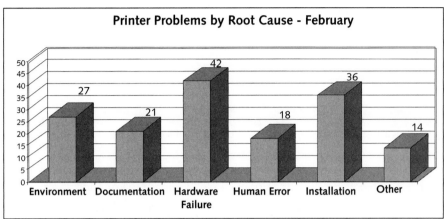

Figure 7-8 Sample printer problems by root cause report

the root cause of problems. Recall also that root cause is the most basic reason for an undesirable condition or problem, which, if eliminated or corrected, would prevent the problem from existing or occurring.

When customers contact the help desk with a problem, they are typically experiencing a symptom. Using the information that the customer provides, the help desk analyst diagnoses the problem in an effort to determine the probable source and a possible solution. The root cause of the problem cannot be identified until a solution to the problem is found, implemented, and proven successful. In other words, the root cause cannot be identified until the problem is solved.

Determining the root cause takes a little extra time and it requires analysts to look beyond the obvious and seek an answer to the question, "Why?" A failing of some analysts is that they think of root cause only in terms of technology. For example, if a customer experiences a problem using a word-processing package, the analyst may indicate that the root cause of the problem was software related. The actual root cause may be that the customer has not received adequate training and is using the word-processing package incorrectly. Until the root cause is identified and eliminated—that is, until the customer receives training—it is likely that the customer will continue to experience problems.

> *The measure of success is not whether you have a tough problem to deal with, but whether it's the same problem you had last year.* John Foster Dulles

Root cause is captured in a data field when problems are closed and is typically supplied by the person who identified the resolution. For example, if the help desk resolves a problem, an analyst will enter the root cause. If level two resolves a problem, the level two service provider will enter the root cause. Figure 7-9 provides a short list of common root cause codes for technology-related problems.

Root Cause: The most basic reason for an undesirable condition or problem, which, if eliminated or corrected, would prevent the problem from existing or occurring.	
Code	**Description**
Communications Failure	For example, network or telephone line down
Configuration Error	PC/System configured incorrectly
Database Problem	For example, database full or generating errors
Environment	For example, power outage
Hardware Failure	Hardware malfunction
Human Error	Problem caused by human error
Incorrect Data	Incorrect input produced incorrect output
Incorrect Documentation/Procedures	Inaccurate or incomplete documentation/procedures
Incompatible Hardware	Incompatible/nonstandard hardware
Incompatible Software	Incompatible/nonstandard software
Installation Error	Hardware/Software installed incorrectly
Insufficient Resources	For example, memory
Lack of Training	For example, for use with "how-to" type inquiries
Other	For use when no other response is appropriate
Planned Outage	For example, customer is unable to access a system due to a planned outage
Procedure Not Followed	Complete and accurate procedure not followed
Result of Change	Problem caused by a change to the system/device
Request for Information	For example, for use with inquiries
Software Bug	Incorrect software code
Unknown	Problem could not be duplicated

Figure 7-9 Sample root cause codes

Notice that many of the root cause codes listed are not related specifically to hardware products or software systems. They are related to how people are implementing or using the technology. In many companies, the technology itself is actually quite stable. The bulk of the problems that help desks handle are caused by changes made to the technology or factors such as inadequate training and insufficient documentation. Root cause analysis provides the information needed to address these issues.

NOTE Most companies that use codes in fields such as root cause include an "other" code that is used when no other response is appropriate. Misuse of this code can considerably reduce a company's ability to do trend and root cause analysis. The best companies use the "other" code to determine what, if any, additional codes are needed and what codes need further explanation. Excessive use of the "other" code may also signal the need to provide additional training to a specific analyst.

Root cause analysis enables analysts to determine ways to reduce costs and prevent problems by eliminating or correcting the "real" reason the problems occur. When performing root cause analysis, many companies subscribe to the "80/20 rule." Relative to problem management, the 80/20 rule means that 20% of the defects or failures that occur cause 80% of the problems. The challenge is then to identify and eliminate the root cause of the most common defects or failures, and therefore considerably reduce the number of recurring problems. As illustrated in Figure 7-10, many companies prepare reports that show the percentage of problems that are caused by a particular root cause. This report shows a breakdown of problems by root cause for a given month and is arranged by problem category. Such a report makes it possible for companies to focus on eliminating the problems that are the most costly to the organization and that have the greatest impact on their customers.

Closed Problems by Root Cause From: January 01 To: January 31			
Category	**Root Cause**	**Problem Count**	**% By Root Cause**
Hardware	[All]	20	100%
	Hardware Failure	14	70%
	Installation Error	6	30%
Software	[All]	102	100%
	Insufficient Resources	54	54%
	Configuration Error	36	36%
	Incompatible Software	10	10%
	Human Error	2	2%

Figure 7-10 Sample root cause report

Trend and root cause analysis work hand-in-hand. They can be used together either reactively to minimize the impact of problems or proactively to identify improvement areas. Help desks that use trend and root cause analysis only reactively rarely have the resources needed to handle problems efficiently and effectively. They simply do not have the information needed to predict their workload. Help desks that use these analysis techniques proactively are able to justify and acquire the resources they need, when they need them. They are also able to better manage their workload, and even reduce their workload, by eliminating problems. Root cause analysis is the more difficult of the two disciplines, and so not all companies determine and document root cause. These companies fail to take the extra time needed to determine why the problem occurred once they have "fixed" it. Unfortunately, by not capturing and then eliminating root cause, these companies put themselves at risk for the problem to happen again. As a result, they may waste time rediscovering a solution or retrieving and implementing a solution from the knowledge base. Remember, just because there is a solution in the knowledge base does not make it okay for a problem to recur. Ultimately, customers would prefer that problems be prevented.

TIP Charts and graphs are an excellent way to organize data and present information. They help the audience to visualize, compare and contrast, and analyze the information you are presenting. Types of charts and graphs include line, bar, and pie. The type of chart or graph you use depends on the information you are presenting. For example, if you want to show how parts relate to a whole, pie charts work well. If you want to show how data varies over time, a line or bar graph is best. Effective charts and graphs share three main characteristics: they are easy to understand, they are visually memorable, and, most importantly, they are accurate.

To solve problems efficiently, effectively, and permanently, the help desk must be diligent in its efforts to capture and use information. This means that help desk analysts must log all problems and capture accurate and complete data about those problems, including the root cause. Without the data captured by help desk analysts, trend and root cause analysis is not possible. When trend and root cause analysis is not performed, it is likely that existing problems will recur and that new problems will appear. When trend and root cause analysis is performed, recurring problems are eliminated, problems are predicted, and, in turn, problems can be prevented. As a result, analysts are freed to work on more complex problems and pursue new skills.

Given the rapid pace at which technology changes, it is unlikely that trend and root cause analysis will enable a company to prevent *all* problems. However, this analysis will enable the help desk to eliminate common problems and avoid major problems by addressing problems when they are minor. This analysis will also aid the help desk in determining and communicating the cost savings that can occur when problems are prevented.

Communicating the Financial Benefits of Improvements

Help desk managers are under increasing pressure to demonstrate the value of help desk services and to justify the funds and resources the team needs to deliver those services. Members of the help desk team who have ideas about how to improve products and services, even great ideas, must learn to justify and quantify the benefits of their ideas in financial terms.

Successful continuous improvement involves determining what improvements are needed, what improvements will enable the help desk to meet its goals, and what improvements can be made without depleting the current help desk budget. A **budget** is the total sum of money allocated for a particular purpose (such as a project) or period of time (such as a year). Good budgeting ensures that the money does not run out before the goal is reached or the period ends.

Typically, the help desk management team prepares the help desk budget with input from the help desk team. The management team also obtains input from other departments because the help desk's budget is tied to other departments' initiatives. For example, in an internal help desk, if another department is installing a new software product, the help desk budget must reflect the tools, training, and so forth that analysts need to support that product. In an external help desk, if the company is introducing a new or enhanced product, analysts must have what they need to support that product as well. It is rare that the individuals involved in preparing a budget anticipate every expense that may arise in the course of a given period of time. Circumstances change and opportunities are identified that can affect the budget. For example, a business slowdown may prompt management to place a hold on nonessential spending. Conversely, a new technology may be introduced that could considerably benefit the help desk and its customers. When improvement opportunities such as a new technology are identified, they must be justified and prioritized in light of other budget expenditures.

Justifying improvement initiatives typically involves stating the expected benefits in the form of goals or objectives and expressing those goals as metrics. The metrics can then be used to compare the expected results of a project to the actual results. Metrics typically assess characteristics such as:

- **Cost.** An amount paid or the expenditure of something, such as time or labor.
- **Customer satisfaction.** The difference between how a customer perceives he or she was treated and how the customer expects to be treated.
- **Efficiency.** How quickly services are delivered.
- **Effectiveness.** How completely and accurately services are delivered.
- **Employee satisfaction.** How satisfied an employee is with his or her job.
- **Quality.** How well services meet customer expectations.

Note that some of these characteristics such as cost and efficiency are quite **tangible**, or capable of being measured precisely. In other words, it is possible to measure exactly how much something costs or how long it takes to complete a task. **Intangible** characteristics such as customer satisfaction, employee satisfaction, and quality are more difficult to measure precisely. This is because intangible characteristics reflect perception and are therefore more subjective. For example, customer satisfaction (or dissatisfaction) with a company's products and services can impact its bottom line. However, because many other factors can also influence a company's bottom line, the impact of customer satisfaction alone is typically hard to measure.

NOTE Employee satisfaction can also be viewed as tangible and intangible. For example, companies often focus on employee satisfaction in an effort to maintain a low turnover rate. **Turnover rate** is the ratio of the number of workers who had to be replaced in a given period of time to the average number of workers. While some turnover is normal, an excessively high turnover rate can be quite costly. When costs such as lost productivity, recruitment costs, training costs, and new hire costs are taken into consideration, the cost of turnover can equal 75% to 150% of an employee's salary. These costs are fairly easily measured, and therefore tangible. On the other hand, the effect that employee satisfaction has on morale can be difficult to measure, but is no less important. For example, losing a key employee to a competing company can negatively affect the morale of an entire team. As a result, companies often work hard to retain peak performers. Conversely, losing a disruptive and unproductive employee can positively affect morale. As a result, companies must ensure that an effective performance review program enables them to weed out poor performers.

Both tangible and intangible goals are important. As illustrated in Figure 7-11, goals can be like a seesaw. In other words, placing an emphasis on one goal or taking emphasis away from one goal may cause another goal to go up or down. When both tangible and intangible goals are established with goals such as quality and customer satisfaction as primary objectives, companies can achieve a more balanced, customer-oriented result.

Figure 7-11 Balanced help desk goals

Cost effectiveness, for example, ensures a proper balance between the cost of service on one hand and the quality of service on the other. Balanced goals are important because many performance goals influence each other. Placing too great an emphasis on any one goal can produce unintended results. For example, emphasizing efficiency can reduce the average duration of calls but could cause customer dissatisfaction because customers feel they are being rushed off the phone. On the other hand, emphasizing effectiveness by having analysts devote an extensive amount of time to research may produce high-quality solutions, but might cause customer dissatisfaction because customers have a long average response time to e-mails.

NOTE When an improvement project begins, it is important to capture a starting point, or **baseline** metric, that can be used to demonstrate the success of improvement efforts. For example, prior to adding Microsoft Word-related FAQs to the help desk's Web site, the help desk's incident tracking and problem management system can be used to create a baseline metric that shows the number of Word-related "how to" questions the help desk receives on a monthly basis. Six months after the FAQs are implemented, the help desk can create a current metric. If the current metric indicates that the number of Word-related "how to" questions has gone down considerably, it can be surmised that the FAQs are a success. Although less tangible, the help desk could also show the number of **page hits**—Web page visits—the FAQs are receiving, or use exit polls to show that the FAQs are being used and that customers consider them helpful. On the Internet, exit polls combine questions such as "Was this information helpful to you?" with Yes and No buttons that customers can use to provide feedback.

Several techniques can be used to determine the cost of or to show the cost savings realized by an improvement initiative. Two of the most common techniques are to calculate a labor savings or to calculate and use cost per contact.

TIP In many companies, improvement opportunities will never be acted on unless they are shown to have clear financial benefits, even if some of those benefits are intangible. Knowing a variety of ways to justify improvement opportunities will enable you to gain acceptance for a greater number of ideas and more quickly obtain approval for ideas.

Calculating a Labor Savings. The expression, "Time is money," is particularly true in the business world where labor often represents a company's single greatest expense. For example, labor and benefits usually represent 60% to 80% of a help desk's overall costs. Saving time, for example, by reducing the help desk's workload through automation or by providing self-services via the Web, will in turn, save money.

Figure 7-12 illustrates the savings that can be realized by shifting calls from the help desk to Web-based self-services. This example estimates that implementing an automated Web-based system for password resets will result in a 75% reduction in the number of password reset requests made to the help desk via the telephone.

Cost/Data Element	Actual Data
Number of password reset requests per month	1,000
Average duration of calls requesting password resets	2 minutes
Total duration of calls requesting password resets (minutes)	2,000 minutes
Total duration of calls requesting password resets (hours)	33 hours
Average hourly rate for level one analysts	$19/hour
Total cost of password resets via telephone per month	$627/month
Total cost of password resets via telephone per year	$7,524/year
Estimated percentage of password reset requests to be automated	75%
Labor savings by automating password resets	$5,643/year

Figure 7-12 Labor savings by automating password resets

This is, of course, a simplistic example. For the savings to be accurate, a cost benefit analysis (discussed in the Advanced Business Skills for Technical Professionals section later in this chapter) must be performed that considers the cost of implementing the Web-based system, training the help desk staff and customers on how to use the system, marketing the service to customers, and so forth. When a quick estimate of labor savings is desired, however, this simple formula illustrates how a small set of data elements can be used to communicate a labor savings in financial terms.

NOTE According to the Association for Support Professionals' 2004 Technical Support Salary Survey, the median salary for a level one support technician is $40,000. The $19 hourly rate for level one analysts used in Figure 7-12 is derived from this figure. To calculate an hourly rate, start with an annual salary (in this case, $40,000), then divide by 2,080 (52 weeks X 40 hours = 2,080 work hours in a year).

When calculating savings, accurate data are important. When actual data are not available, industry standard data such as the hourly rate previously discussed can be useful. Cost per contact is another metric that can be calculated using actual data or industry standard data.

NOTE Companies often look for "industry standard" metrics that they can use as a starting point when establishing goals and determining costs and benefits. Such metrics can be difficult to find, however, because no one organization represents the support industry as a whole. Organizations such as the Help Desk Institute (**www.helpdeskinst.com**), META Group (**www.metagroup.com**), Service & Support Professionals Association (**www.thesspa.com**), STI Knowledge, Inc. (**www.stiknowledge.com**), and supportindustry.com (**www. supportindustry.com**) all provide, some for a fee, their version of metrics such as cost per contact. Typically, they determine metrics by surveying their members or clients and by conducting surveys via the Internet.

Calculating and Using Cost Per Contact.

Cost per contact is a financial measure frequently used in the support industry. **Cost per contact**, historically called cost per call, is the total cost of operating a help desk for a given time period (including salaries, benefits, facilities, and equipment) divided by the total number of contacts received during that period. A **contact** is a communication to or from the help desk, such as a telephone call, e-mail, fax, or Web request.

NOTE　Contact volume is frequently used to calculate costs and create metrics such as cost per contact. Contact volume is the total number of contacts received during a given period of time. To obtain an accurate contact volume, it is imperative that help desks implement technology that can be used to capture contact data. For example, ACDs and e-mail response management systems can be used to capture the number of telephone calls and e-mail messages received. In the absence of these technologies, help desk analysts must log all contacts in the help desk's incident tracking and problem management system. Logging all contacts provides the help desk with the data needed to produce meaningful metrics and to perform trend and root cause analysis.

Some companies also calculate **cost per unit**, the total cost of operating a help desk for a given time period (including salaries, benefits, facilities, and equipment), divided by the total number of units (such as devices and systems) supported during that period. Figure 7-13 shows the average cost per contact for telephone calls and e-mails according to a survey conducted by supportindustry.com ("2004 Service and Support Metrics Survey," www.supportindustry.com, May 2004).

The results of this survey are similar to the results of a survey conducted by the Help Desk Institute (HDI). Based on a survey of its members, HDI determined the following average cost per contact for the following channels: phone, $28.19; e-mail, $20.66; and self-service, $8.25 ("Help Desk Institute 2003 Practices Survey," Help Desk Institute, 2003).

A study by STI Knowledge also estimates cost per contact and shows that cost per contact increases dramatically when calls are escalated. It estimates the following average range of cost per contact at each level: level zero, $2 to $11; level one, $15 to $30; level two, $50 to $75; level three (on-site support), $100 ("The Enterprise Service Desk—A Roadmap to Success," STI Knowledge, Inc., 2002). This range illustrates how moving problems from level three to level one or level zero and eventually to elimination can result in real cost savings to an organization.

Cost per contact is an extremely useful metric that can be used in a variety of ways. For example, some companies use cost per contact to benchmark their services against other help desks or the industry average. **Benchmarking** is the process of comparing the help desk's performance metrics and practices to those of another help desk in an effort to identify improvement opportunities. Companies may also use cost per contact to compare the cost of operating their help desk to a service agency (outsourcer).

Average Cost Per Telephone Call		
Choice	Percent	Graph
$0–$10	17.2%	
$10–$15	15.6%	
$15–$20	20.3%	
$20–$25	14.4%	
$25 and above	32.8%	
Total Responses:	100%	

Average Cost Per E-Mail		
Choice	Percent	Graph
$0–$10	35.9%	
$10–$15	14.1%	
$15–$20	10.9%	
$20–$25	17.2%	
$25 and above	21.9%	
Total Responses:	100%	

Figure 7-13 Average cost per contact

Meaningful goals and metrics, communicated in financial terms, enable the help desk team to justify opportunities and demonstrate improved performance. Presentations are often used to communicate the help desk's achievements and gain needed support and commitment for additional improvement initiatives.

USING PRESENTATIONS TO COMMUNICATE

Presentations are an important form of communication in today's business world. They are used daily to convey information, promote the benefits of ideas and opportunities, and win approval for those ideas and opportunities. For professionals, presentations are an important way to build credibility, and the ability to make presentations can greatly influence a person's standing in his or her company, community, and industry.

NOTE For help desk professionals, presentations provide an invaluable opportunity to promote the help desk and communicate its value to the business. Presentations can also be used to demonstrate the important role the help desk plays in terms of collecting, using, and disseminating data and information that can be used by the entire organization to continuously improve.

Designing and Making Presentations

Making a presentation is a great fear for many people. In fact, it has been said that people fear making presentations more than spiders, snakes, and even death. Although making presentations can be nerve racking, they are inevitable if you want to communicate your ideas and, what is more important, have those ideas accepted and acted upon. Presentations are a form of public speaking and are used in many different types of situations, such as those listed in Figure 7-14.

- Facilitated workshops
- Meetings
- Sales presentations
- Seminars
- Speeches
- Training sessions
- One-to-one

Figure 7-14 Types of presentations

Although the setting in which these presentations are made may vary, they all have one thing in common: the audience members are being brought together for a reason. For example, their approval is needed to move forward on a project. Their input is needed to formulate an action plan. You need to make the audience aware of something or teach them something.

Just as the audience members are being brought together for a reason, there is a reason you are making the presentation. For example, you have an idea that you want to advance. You have information that others want to hear. You have knowledge or skills that your audience members want to learn. Simply put, you are the expert. You have been asked to give this presentation, or you have decided to give this presentation, for a reason, and you need to accept that fact.

Knowing the purpose of your presentation and repeating over and over "I am the expert" may not eliminate the fear and anxiety that often accompanies making a presentation. They are critical first steps, however, and cannot be overlooked. If you have great ideas, you have to be willing to get up and communicate those ideas to other people. If you need people to commit resources to a project, you have to be willing to ask for that commitment and explain the benefits to your audience. To be successful in today's business world, you have to communicate, communicate, communicate.

Although making a presentation is not an exact science, there are proven steps you can take to ensure success. Completing the steps listed in Figure 7-15 will give you the confidence needed to work through your fears and do your best.

Step 1. State your objective

Step 2. Know your audience

Step 3. Design the presentation

Step 4. Rehearse the presentation

Step 5. Deliver the presentation

Step 6. Learn from the experience

Figure 7-15 Proven steps for a successful presentation

The following sections explore each of these steps in detail. These steps represent a methodical approach that can be used whether you are making a 5-minute presentation or a 45-minute presentation. These steps can also be used regardless of the type of presentation you are making or the size of your audience.

Step 1. State Your Objective.   A clearly stated objective has many benefits. For example, it helps you to determine whether a presentation is needed. People often complain that they are asked to attend too many meetings. If writing a memo will meet your objective, do not ask people to take time out for a presentation. If a presentation is needed, however, a clearly stated objective will help you focus your thoughts and the thoughts of your audience. A clearly stated objective also enables you and your audience to measure the success of your presentation. If you give a great presentation but fail to meet the stated objective, you may not get the results you seek and your audience will most likely be dissatisfied. In other words, a clearly stated objective enables you to set and manage your audience's expectations.

A single sentence should be all you need to state your objective. If you need more than one sentence, you may be trying to achieve more than you can realistically in a single presentation. The exception to this rule would, of course, be extended presentations such as seminars and training sessions. The key is to be realistic about the results you are trying to achieve. Persuading people to radically change their work habits or to adopt an expensive new technology may require more than one presentation.

> Obtain approval from management to assemble a team and explore the use of remote control technologies.
>
> Inform help desk analysts about new procedures for handling e-mail contacts.
>
> Communicate the status of a project and obtain management commitment to dedicate resources to upcoming activities.

Step 2. Know Your Audience.   This step is critical and greatly influences all future steps. Making a presentation to a group of your peers is different than speaking to a group of managers or to a group of customers. This steps requires that you determine what is important to your audience members. Do they want you to get to the point quickly? Do they want you to back up your material with statistics? Do they want you to cover a subject in-depth? If you do not know your audience, you cannot answer the questions that audiences most often ask: "How does this affect me?" and "How does this benefit me?"

Knowing your audience also involves understanding the background of your audience. For example, if you are giving a technical presentation and your audience is not technical, you will have to use basic terminology or define the terminology you are using. If part of your audience's primary language is not the language you speak, you may need to adapt your vocabulary, slow your rate of speech, or have a translator available. It is also a good idea to avoid idioms and speak in relatively short sentences that are limited to a single idea.

When in doubt, ask. Ask the person who entrusted you to make the presentation about your audience. Ask people who have made a presentation to your audience in the past to give you their advice. One size does not fit all when making presentations. The more you know about the needs of your audience, the greater your success.

NOTE

Learning about your audience may prompt you to rethink or refine your objective and vice versa. For example, presenting an in-depth overview of a new process to management is typically not a good idea. Management will want a summarized view with a statement of benefits. Conversely, making a presentation to your peers that is aimed at obtaining funding for a new project will not produce the desired result. Your peers will want to know how much of their time the project will take and whether the project has management's commitment.

Step 3. Design the Presentation.   Designing a presentation is like writing a story. It needs to have a beginning, a middle, and an end. In presentations terms, these components are referred to as the introduction, the body, and the closing. One of the best ways to design a presentation is to begin with an outline. Preparing an outline will help you organize your thoughts and develop a logical flow of ideas.

When demonstrating a system, such as a new e-mail response management system or a new Web-based system, introduce your demonstration by describing the system's users and its benefits. Technical professionals sometimes make the mistake of diving straight into a demonstration without selling the benefits of the system. Even when your objective is to teach people how to use a system, begin with an explanation of why to use the system.

Once you have an outline, research your topic and collect facts that support your objective. Showing that you have done your homework builds credibility with audience members. Be specific. Quote sources. Include current statistics. Incorporate into your presentation stories that show your experience and knowledge of the topic. When appropriate, include the findings of other experts in the field.

Once you've done your research, you can begin to develop visual aids that support and communicate your ideas. Visual aids are important. They should not, however, be your presentation. People quickly become bored when a presenter stands in front of a room and simply reads the presentation word-for-word from the slides. The audience wants you to share (depending on the nature of the presentation) your knowledge, experience, observations, or recommendations, and back that up with visual aids.

An effective technique is to anticipate the questions your audience may ask and use visual aids to answer those questions. Common questions include:

- **Who?**—Use organization charts or correct department or division names to communicate who, for example, will benefit from a new technology or be affected by a new system.
- **What?**—Use bullets or numbered lists to answers questions such as, "What are the risks?" and "What are the benefits?"
- **When?**—Use Gantt charts to communicate schedules or a sequence of events. A Gantt chart is a horizontal bar chart that provides a graphic illustration of a schedule.
- **Where?**—Use maps or drawings of buildings to communicate the scope of a project, system, or service.
- **Why?**—Use bullets or numbered lists to answers questions such as, "Why is a new system needed?" or "Why is it a good time to offer new services?"
- **How?**—Use tables, charts and graphs to answer questions such as, "How much?" and "How many?"

Figure 7-16 shows the various visual aids that can be used to answer these questions.

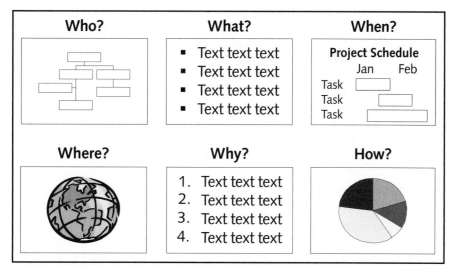

Figure 7-16 Sample visual aids

Once you have created your visual aids, conduct a preliminary walk-through of your presentation. This enables you to fine-tune the sequence of your visual aids. You may also decide you need more, or have too many, visual aids for the time allotted. The most successful presenters use their oral or storytelling skills to transition seamlessly from one visual aid to the next.

Step 4. Rehearse the Presentation. There's an old expression: "Practice makes perfect." Rehearsing your presentation is a critical step for a number of reasons. First, you must make sure that you can cover your material in the time allotted. Your audience will quickly lose interest or may have to leave if you run over the time allotted. Your audience typically expects you to leave time for questions as well. What this means is that you must fine-tune your presentation until it is just right. Not too long. Not too short. This is not an easy task, but it does get easier with practice.

TIP

It is better to have your presentation run a little short than a little too long. Preparing a shorter-than-needed presentation ensures you can cover all your material in the allotted time and also allows time for questions and answers. When rehearsing, time your presentation so you know where you should be at the halfway point of your allotted time. That way, if you are running behind while delivering your presentation, you know to pick up the pace a bit and make up for lost time. If you are running ahead of schedule, you can add an example or two, which you prepared during your rehearsal, to elaborate points along the way.

Keep in mind that rehearsing is different than memorizing. Although you may want to memorize your introduction and your closing because they are critical to setting audience expectations, it is better to memorize only the key points you want to make during the body of your presentation. Some people write their key points on a piece of paper or on index cards so they have them if they need to refer to them as a reminder. If you try to memorize every word, you may become flustered if you are interrupted by a question or forget a key point. Furthermore, you may bore people if you do nothing but read from your notes or visuals aids. Rehearsing your presentation several times will give you confidence in your knowledge of the material and enable you to fine-tune your notes and visual aids to the point where they are most effective.

Step 5. Deliver the Presentation.   This is the scary part for some people. Although making a presentation may seem scary, it is not a life or death situation. It is, however, a situation for which you can prepare.

Prior to your presentation, take the time to make a final check of your equipment and the site. If you need a computer to make your presentation, make sure that one is available or that your personal computer will work with any audio visual equipment already at the site. If you need other visuals aids, such as a flip chart or a white board, make sure those are available. Make sure water is available that you can use to calm your nerves and lubricate your throat during your presentation. There is nothing worse than walking into a room five minutes before making a presentation and realizing that the site is not ready. Do yourself a favor, and double check every detail. That way you can spend the five minutes prior to your presentation greeting your audience and using calming techniques such as deep breathing and positive self-talk: "I am the expert!"

Keep in mind that for many people, delivering the presentation is actually the fun part. These people will often admit that they were scared the first time they made a presentation. They may even still become a bit anxious prior to a particularly important presentation. For people who are willing to take the risk, however, the rewards are worth it. Remember, the audience wants to hear want you have to say, and you are the best person to say it.

When making a presentation, be confident. After all, you've done your homework. Also, be enthusiatic. Know that if you do not appear to be confident in your recommendations or excited about the benefits of a project, you cannot expect your audience to be either. Look from one audience member to the other. In even the toughest rooms, you will find people who are nodding in agreement with your message or listening closely to what you have to say. When people smile in response to your enthusiasm, smile back.

Standing stiffly behind a microphone or lectern will magnify your nervousness. Although you want to avoid pacing back and forth, move around a bit and interact with your visual aids and the audience. Try not to stand in front of your visual aids or turn your back to the audience.

For many presenters, handling questions is the most challenging part of making a presentation. One reason is that answering questions in the course of a presentation can throw off your timing. If this is a concern, and time is a considerable constraint, politely ask your audience at the start of the presentation to hold their questions until the end.

> Ladies and gentlemen, in the interest of time, please hold all of your questions until the end.

If you run out of time for questions at the end, let the audience know that you will be happy to answer their questions offline.

> I'm sorry we ran out of time for questions. I am happy to stay and answer your questions. Or, my e-mail address is on your handout.

When possible, try to handle questions when they are asked. Remember, however, to answer the question asked and only the question asked. Then get back to your presentation. If an audience member asks a complex question that you know you are going to answer shortly, politely ask the audience member to hold his or her question until the appropriate point in your presentation.

> That's a great question and I'm going to cover the answer shortly.
> Could I ask you to hold that question and I'll come back to it shortly?

When possible, acknowledge the person's question when you get to the appropriate point in your presentation and stay with the question until you know it is answered fully.

> Here's the answer to Jane's question about metrics.
> As I recall, there was a question about the project schedule. Here is the schedule. . . .

Handling questions when they are asked can be challenging. People sometimes ask questions that seem irrelevant or perhaps even hostile. Do your best to answer all questions politely and briefly. If necessary, remind the audience of the presentation objectives and any time constraints you may be facing. It is your responsibility to keep the presentation on track.

NOTE Audience members usually expect to receive a handout. The handout may simply be a copy of your presentation or it could be a booklet or report. When appropriate, provide a simple handout that includes Web links that audience members can use to obtain additional details.

Presenters usually distribute handouts at the start of their presentation so audience members can follow along and take notes. However, there are situations where presenters may opt to distribute the handouts at the end of the presentation, such as when the handout is a comprehensive report that you want audience members to read offline. The key is to let audience members know when and if they will be receiving a handout so they can take notes accordingly.

Step 6. Learn from the Experience.   Many lessons can be learned from making presentations. Most people who have made more than two presentations will tell you that sometimes they go well and sometimes they don't. Most of the mistakes that occur when making presentations are the result of overlooking one of the steps discussed earlier. Take time after each presentation to evaluate your performance and determine how you can improve. If evaluations are provided, view the feedback you receive as constructive and figure out what you can do to improve.

Presentation evaluations can be harsh and you may be blamed for factors out of your control. For example, people may complain that the room was too hot or too cold or that there wasn't enough coffee. Accept responsibility about what you can change and pass other feedback on to the appropriate party. Don't take it personally!

Some people are born communicators and find making presentations invigorating. Others may not enjoy making presentations at first, but find they do get easier in time. Whether or not you enjoy making presentations, presentation skills are essential if you want to educate, inform, obtain information from, build consensus with, and communicate with others.

Author Susan Jeffers wrote a great book called *Feel the Fear and Do It Anyway* (Ballantine Books, 1987). Although her book is not specifically about making presentations, the sentiment very much applies. The only way to overcome your fear of making presentations is by getting up and making presentations. The good news is, the more often you present and the more varied the setting, subject matter, and audience are, the more comfortable you will become.

In today's competitive workplace, making presentations is an important business skill—one of the many business skills you must acquire if you want to get ahead.

Advanced Business Skills for Technical Professionals

Advanced business skills such as managing projects, conducting a cost benefit analysis, and calculating ROI are critical skills for more senior technical professionals. Although the need for these skills may vary from company to company, even a basic understanding of these concepts will enable you to make the most of learning and growth opportunities. For example, you can learn about managing a project by participating on a project team. Or, you can gain a better understanding of techniques such as cost benefit analysis and ROI by simply learning to communicate costs and benefits in financial terms.

Like technical skills, business skills training is only effective when it is reinforced in the workplace. Understanding how to do something is not the same as actually doing it. Many technical professionals acquire their business skills on the job. For example, they may participate on a project team and learn about managing projects. Or, they may be asked to justify an idea and learn how to compare the costs and benefits of a proposed solution. To excel at advanced business skills, technical professionals require a blend of formal training and experience. In other words, simple observation is not enough. Some study, even if only self-study, is needed along with experience. This is particularly true in the case of a skill such as project management.

Managing Projects

In today's business world, change is constant and it is occurring at an increasingly rapid pace. What this means is that people working in a help desk are continuously exposed to projects. A **project** is a distinct unit of work aimed at producing a specific result or end product. Projects can be small, such as installing a new computer, or quite large, such as moving an office or developing and installing a new business application. Help desk professionals may complete projects by, for example, creating a set of new FAQs for the help desk's Web site. Or, they may support the end product of a project, such as a new or enhanced system.

NOTE Help desk professionals may also initiate projects. To initiate projects, analysts must first sell their ideas to management using the techniques previously discussed such as using data and information to quantify their ideas, communicating the benefits of their ideas in financial terms, and using presentations to market their ideas to management.

NOTE For larger projects, a business case is often used to justify the initiation of a project. A business case is a report that describes the business reasons that a change is being considered. Typically, a business case provides a description of the current ("as is") environment along with an assessment of what is right about the environment and what needs to be improved. A business case also describes a proposed future ("to be") environment along with a roadmap of changes that must be made to achieve the desired state. The risks of both maintaining the current environment and pursuing the proposed environment are discussed. A business case is typically prepared by a business analyst. A business analyst is an individual who is skilled at working with end users to determine their needs. A business analyst may be an employee of the company or an independent consultant.

To be successful, technical professionals must understand project management concepts and tools. As working on a project typically involves working on a team (discussed in Chapter 12), they must understand the roles that people play within a project and they must understand how to work successfully with others on the project team.

Early in their careers, help desk analysts are typically on the receiving end of projects. In other words, they learn about the project when it is nearing completion. For example, the help desk learns about a new accounting system when the Programming department is preparing to install the system and deploy it to the Accounting department. Or worse, they learn about the system the day after it is installed and customers start calling the help desk for assistance. Because they have not been involved in the project since its inception, help desk analysts sometimes find it difficult to understand why a project is being managed in a certain way. Learning about project management concepts enables you to better understand how projects are managed and the critical factors that enable project success.

Project management is the process of planning and managing a project. All projects, regardless of their size, require some planning and have the following:

- A clearly defined scope
- Well-defined deliverables
- Clearly defined acceptance criteria
- An established start date
- An established end point

Project planning begins with a written definition of the project's **scope**, which is a general description of the work to be done. The project scope serves as an agreement between the customer of the project and the supplier about the project's end product and includes a description of the acceptance criteria to be used to evaluate the project's success. **Acceptance criteria** are the conditions that must be met before the project deliverables are accepted.

Failing to clearly define and manage project scope is one of the most common reasons that projects fail. Managing customer expectations when working on a project is just as important as it is when delivering customer services. Failing to manage customer expectations can lead to scope creep, and will ultimately lead to customer dissatisfaction. Scope creep describes unplanned changes to a project's scope. Some scope creep is normal and beneficial. Left unchecked, however, scope creep can quickly exhaust a project's financial, human, and technological resources and extend its schedule. To minimize scope creep, many companies have a project change control process in place for reviewing and approving scope changes. This is particularly important when scope changes result in the need for additional resources, such as time and money.

.In the case of small projects, the project scope may be as simple as a request that is submitted and approved via the company's request management process. For larger projects, the project scope is typically defined by a project planning committee made up of project stakeholders. A **project stakeholder** is a person or group who is involved in or may be affected by project activities. For larger projects, the project scope is documented and includes the following:

- **Project overview.** An overview of the project and of the business need driving the project.
- **Project deliverables.** The physical items to be delivered as a result of the project, such as products, systems, services, reports, and plans.
- **Project objectives.** The measurable goals in terms of time, money, and quality that the project must achieve to be considered successful.
- **Considerations and concerns.** A description of all considerations and concerns identified during the development of the project scope.
- **Change control plan.** A description of how the project scope will be managed and how agreed changes will be incorporated into the project deliverables.

Once documented, the project scope must be approved by the project sponsor. The **project sponsor** is the person who has ultimate authority over the project. The project sponsor provides or secures funding for the project, provides high-level guidance and direction to the project team, resolves issues when necessary, approves scope changes, and approves major deliverables. The project sponsor is responsible for ensuring that the project is aligned with the organization's business goals, but is not typically involved in the day-to-day activities of the project. That is the responsibility of the project manager. The project manager is the person who leads the project team and is assigned the authority and responsibility for overseeing the project and meeting the project's objectives. The project manager is selected after the project scope is defined and approved

Not all projects require a team. Some projects, particularly smaller projects, may be completed by a single individual. In such cases, that individual is the project manager. He or she may not be assigned that title, but he or she assumes the responsibilities. The individual's manager will typically serve as project sponsor, although, again, he or she may not be assigned that title. Project manager responsibilities include:

- Developing and maintaining a project plan
- Directing project activities
- Creating project status reports
- Preparing and participating in project reviews
- Resolving project plan deviations
- Resolving and escalating, if necessary, issues that pertain to the project to management
- Administering project change control (that is, managing changes to the project scope)

One of the project manager's most important responsibilities is developing and maintaining a project plan. A project plan is a summary document that describes the project, its objectives, and how the objectives are to be achieved. For smaller projects, the project plan may consist of scheduling a request submitted via the help desk's incident tracking and problem management system and documenting a simple To Do list in the request record.

> *If you are failing to plan, you are planning to fail.* Tariq Siddique

For larger projects, a much more formal approach is taken. With larger projects, an important component of the project plan is a task-oriented breakdown of the work to be done, also known as a **work breakdown structure.** As illustrated in Figure 7-17, the work breakdown structure is used to logically arrange the tasks to be completed and define milestones. A **milestone** is a key, or important, event in the life of a project. The work breakdown structure is also used to assign resources to tasks, create schedules, and estimate costs.

Project Plan						
Task Name	January	February	March	Est. Start	Actual Start	Actual End
Project approved	◉				1/3	1/3
Project meetings	Kickoff ▲ ◆	Review ▮ ◆	Review ▲		1/8	3/1
Define project scope	◆				1/9	1/9
Define system requirements	◆ ◆				1/9	1/12
Evaluate hardware / software		◆ ◆			1/12	1/19
Select hardware / software		◆			1/22	1/22
Develop system		◆━◆			1/26	2/9
Develop training		◆━◆			1/26	2/9
Test system		◆━◆			2/12	2/23
Deliver training			◆━◆		2/26	3/12
Implement system			◉		3/17	3/17

Figure 7-17 Sample project plan

Many software products are available that can be used to create and manage project plans. Some of the most popular products include Milestones Simplicity by KIDASA Software, Inc. (**www.kidasa.com**), TurboProject by IMSI (**www. turboproject.com**), Microsoft Project by Microsoft (**www.microsoft.com**), and SureTrak Project Manager by Primavera Systems (**www.primavera.com/ products/sure.html**). These products provide the ability to create project plans along with reports and charts that can be used to communicate project status.

A critical project manager responsibility is communicating on a regular basis with the project sponsor, project stakeholders and their management, project team members and their management, and all other interested parties. Project status reports are an important communication tool and typically include the following:

- Accomplishments this period
- Accomplishments planned next period
- Resources required next period
- Considerations and concerns
- An updated project plan

With smaller projects, project status may be reported via the help desk's incident tracking and problem management system. For larger projects, status reports are typically submitted in writing and periodically via presentations. Ongoing communication is critical to a project's success. Communications must occur before, during, and after the project to ensure stakeholders and all parties affected by a project understand its purpose and goals. This is sometimes a difficult concept for technical professionals to understand. A busy technical professional may think "I got the work done. I don't have time to sit and do a bunch of paperwork about it." Failing to communicate, however, will almost always result in mismanaged expectations and dissatisfaction.

People with strong technical skills are sometimes assigned the role of project manager because their skills are highly important to a project. The fact that a person is highly technical does not mean that he or she knows how to be a good project manager. Furthermore, not all technicians enjoy doing the work that project managers are required to do, such as developing project plans and communicating project status. Learning about project management concepts and tools will enable you to assess your abilities and determine how you can best contribute to a project team. Some people prefer to serve as a project team member, rather than as project manager. Other people enjoy the project manager role and strive to continuously improve their project management skills.

Technical professionals can learn a lot about project management by simply observing how projects are run and by trying to understand the keys to project management success. They can also learn a lot by being an active participant when working on a project team. Rather than simply focusing on the tasks you have been assigned, try to understand the bigger picture and how your piece fits into the puzzle. Try to understand the constraints that may be placed on the project by the project's scope and how the project manager is containing that scope.

If you are interested in being a project manager, take advantage of any training that is offered where you work, or seek out self-study opportunities. You can also ask a seasoned project manager to serve as your mentor. Many project managers hone their skills by serving as a deputy, or assistant, to another project manager. This technique enables you to gain an understanding of how projects are run, without bearing all of the responsibility. Once you have a better understanding of how projects are run, you can begin initiating projects aimed at implementing your ideas.

WWW Project management certification programs enable people to enhance and demonstrate their project management skills. The most recognized and valued certification programs are the Project+ certification offered by CompTIA (**www.comptia.com/certification/project/default.aspx**) and the Project Management Professional (PMP) certification offered by the Project Management Institute (PMI) (**www.pmi.org/prod/groups/public/documents/info/pdc_pmp.asp**). Both of these programs require knowledge of project management concepts and practical project management experience. Individuals passing the Project+ certification must have 2,000 hours of on-the-job practical experience. CompTIA's Project+ can serve as a standalone certificate or as a stepping stone toward PMI's PMP certification, which requires 4,500 hours of experience.

JOE LEGGIERO

INFORMATION TECHNOLOGY CONSULTANT

ATLANTA, GEORGIA

Joe Leggiero has more than 18 years of experience in managing professional services and systems integration. He began his career as a system developer for IBM mainframe systems. After working with a team of developers on a large project, he soon became a team leader. Building on team leader experiences led him to become a project manager and, in time, an independent consultant. As an independent consultant, he specializes in helping organizations make better use of technology and processes to improve enterprise operations. He has worked with large corporate clients, small businesses, and software publishers to design and implement technology and business process solutions. Joe Leggiero shares his thoughts on building a professional career.

A career is a journey of experiences. Each experience is a building block to the next position, the next opportunity, or the next level of responsibility. Every decision, good or bad, will influence the direction of your career and provide opportunities for personal growth and rewards.

In the business world, ethical behavior, strong effort, respect for others, dependability, and integrity are timeless characteristics of a professional. Business skills such as communicating with others, managing conflict, and handling criticism are also timeless skills. They help you deal with others and maintain an atmosphere of cooperation.

Companies measure employees based on their contributions to corporate goals. Being a professional requires working with others to achieve those goals. To do this, professionals must strive to understand and learn from the uniqueness of others. They must work hard to resolve conflicts quickly so those conflicts do not get in the way of working together. Professionals must also be able to accept feedback and criticism, and view both as tools for personal growth, not as a personal attack. Understanding others and graciously accepting feedback and criticism are essential, but difficult, business skills to learn.

On your career journey, as in life, learning never ends. Throughout your career, you will meet people who have years of experience using the very skills you seek. Ask questions. Use the knowledge these more experienced people have acquired through the years. Use the research skills that you learned in school to keep your knowledge current and to continuously expand your skills. Apply the business skills that you have learned and a good work ethic to every new situation you encounter. For example, in any technical position, problem-solving skills are important and universal. You don't have to re-learn these skills for each new position or technology. You must simply adapt your skills to the new situation. Employers are always looking for individuals who can apply their knowledge and experience to new situations. Your ability to continuously draw from your portfolio of skills will help determine your value as an employee and will influence your ability to advance in a career.

Selecting and building a career is not easy. People who are unsure about their career path can still build a foundation of business skills as they are trying to decide on a college major or a career. For example, don't underestimate the value of courses heavy in communications, psychology, and writing when building the foundation for a professional career. Many of us start our careers working for a company in an entry-level position. A key to success is understanding that every position, even an entry-level position, offers the opportunity to acquire business skills. For example, you can learn about setting and achieving career goals, working in a team setting, and what it takes to be a leader.

At some point you will need to decide if you want to pursue a technical career path or a management career. Your business skills will apply within each career path. For example, on a technical path, communication skills may be used to describe the benefits of a technical solution. On a management path, communication skills may be used to explain goals and the importance of meeting those goals. Both paths require the ability to evaluate and communicate costs and benefits. The bottom line here is that although technical skills can become obsolete, you can use most of the business skills you learn along the way regardless of the career path or profession you choose.

Whether pursuing a technical or managerial career path, at some point you may be presented the opportunity to assume a leadership position. That position may involve becoming a team leader, or it may involve serving as a project manager. People are typically chosen to be team leaders because they've demonstrated the ability to get things done and management believes they can provide guidance to others. First-time team leaders soon find that influencing others requires a new set of skills. For example, team leaders must learn to solve business problems, as opposed to technical problems, and they must learn to motivate and empower others. Some people excel as team leaders and go on to become successful managers and executives. For others, a team leader role convinces them to stay on a technical career path and solve problems with technology instead of with people and schedules.

Some people build leadership skills by becoming a project manager. Project managers use structured methods to plan and direct projects. Being a project manager involves assuming greater responsibilities, taking ownership of your actions and the actions of project team members, and recognizing and learning from failures or successes. It means helping others succeed at their tasks by helping them manage their time and resources. Experience as a team leader will help you in your role as project manager, but it is not required. A broad range of business skills are required. For example, project managers must understand and be able to justify the business goals of projects. They must also be able to communicate, manage conflict, and provide constructive feedback and criticism. Sound familiar?

The journey of your career will have many challenges, triumphs, and setbacks. While you cannot control the outcome of each situation, the decisions that you make will be based on what you learn along the way. The more you learn from each experience along the way, the more apt you will be to avoid making mistakes or missing opportunities in the future.

I have found that combining timeless professional characteristics with previous experience and a continuous quest for knowledge is the formula for building a successful professional career.

Conducting a Cost Benefit Analysis

Senior technical professionals, help desk team leaders, and help desk managers increasingly are required to quantify proposed projects using an advanced technique called cost benefit analysis. Cost benefit analysis compares the costs and benefits of two or more potential solutions to determine an optimum solution. **Cost benefit analysis** can be as simple as deciding to replace a failing cathode ray tube (CRT) monitor with a liquid crystal display (LCD) flat screen monitor. Although the cost of the LCD flat screen monitor may be greater than that of the CRT monitor, the benefits such as a larger viewing screen, high resolution graphics, resistance to glare, and a smaller footprint justify the cost for many people, particularly when the user spends a considerable amount of time in front of his or her computer. In this example, once the decision is made to purchase a LCD flat screen monitor, a second cost benefit analysis must be performed to compare available monitors. That analysis must take into consideration factors such as the reputation of the manufacturer, the size and weight of the monitor, and so forth. Once the costs and benefits are compared, a specific monitor is selected.

A cost benefit analysis can also be quite complex and require considerable time and skill. This is particularly true when a proposed solution represents a significant investment, such as implementing a new incident tracking and problem management system, or a significant culture change, such as implementing ITIL-compliant processes. Because of the time and skill required, the cost of performing a complex cost benefit analysis can be considerable. As a result, companies typically offer guidelines that determine the level of detail required in a cost benefit analysis. These guidelines take into consideration factors such as the size, cost, and impact of the proposed solution.

In its simplest form, a cost benefit analysis uses only financial costs and financial benefits. Financial costs may be one time (nonrecurring) costs or they may be ongoing (recurring). Figure 7-18 shows sample costs and benefits.

Note that many of the costs and benefits reflected in Figure 7-18 are expressed in monetary values and can therefore be measured precisely. However, a more sophisticated approach to cost benefit analysis attempts to place a financial value on intangible costs and benefits. This can be highly subjective. For example, what is the value of increased customer satisfaction? Although companies may be able to demonstrate increased customer satisfaction, for example, by surveying customers, showing its connection to the company's bottom line can be difficult.

As shown in Figure 7-18, some companies assign a numeric value to intangible benefits. For example, maximum benefit is assigned a value to 3, average benefit is assigned a value of 2, and nominal benefit is assigned a value of 1. This numeric value can then be used for comparison purposes.

Costs	Alternative 1	Alternative 2
Personnel costs such as payroll costs, including overtime benefits and expenses. *Note:* Nonrecurring costs include activities such as project planning and management, solution design, development, and implementation. Recurring costs include end-user education and training, end-user support, and system maintenance activities.	$	$
Hardware costs such as computers, peripheral devices such as printers and scanners, and network devices. *Note:* Hardware costs include the one-time cost of purchasing equipment as well as recurring maintenance and upgrade costs.	$	$
Software costs such as operating system software, application software, productivity tools, and monitoring tools. *Note:* Software costs include the one-time cost of purchasing software as well as recurring maintenance and upgrade costs.	$	$
External services such as outsourcing services, voice and data communication services, and professional services (consultants). *Note:* External services costs may include the one-time use of consultants as well as recurring services such as outsourcing services.	$	$
Facility costs such as office space, security and utilities. *Note:* Nonrecurring facility costs may include temporary quarters for the project team as well as recurring costs associated with housing personnel and equipment.	$	$
Total Costs	$	$
Benefits		
Increased profits	$	$
Decreased costs	$	$
Total Benefits	$	$
Net Benefits (Total Benefits – Total Costs)	$	$

Figure 7-18 Sample costs and benefits

Intangible Benefits	Numeric Value (NV)	
Increased customer satisfaction	NV	NV
Improved communication	NV	NV
Net Intangible Benefits (Total Numeric Value)	TNV	TNV

Figure 7-18 Sample costs and benefits (continued)

Intangible benefits are important and must be taken into consideration. This is particularly true in the support industry where intangible benefits, such as those listed in Figure 7-19, can determine whether a help desk succeeds or fails.

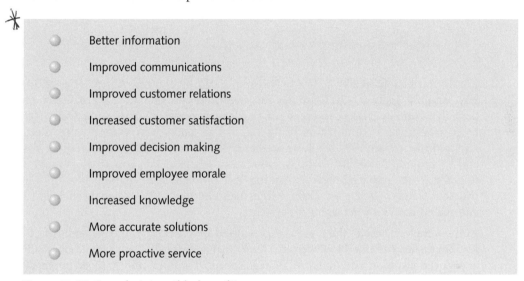

- Better information
- Improved communications
- Improved customer relations
- Increased customer satisfaction
- Improved decision making
- Improved employee morale
- Increased knowledge
- More accurate solutions
- More proactive service

Figure 7-19 Sample intangible benefits

When insufficient data prohibits expressing an intangible benefit in financial or numeric terms, the judgement and experience of the individual or team performing the cost benefit analysis are used to determine the value of intangible benefits.

NOTE When estimating benefits, care must be taken to identify the benefits for the recipients of a proposed solution and for any organizations involved in delivering or supporting the proposed solution. For example, implementing a new remote control system will benefit help desk customers, help desk staff, and level two service providers.

The end result of a cost benefit analysis is the identification of the best solution to a business problem, given two or more proposed solutions. Simply put, it answers the questions:

- Which of the proposed solutions is the best solution?
- Is the proposed solution worth the cost?

The key to whether a solution is worth the cost lies in the goals of the organization. Each company must decide what the benefits (tangible and intangible) are worth to their organization.

Calculating Return on Investment

Another technique used to assess the worth of a project is to calculate its return on investment. **Return on investment (ROI)** is a technique that measures the total financial benefit derived from an investment—such as a new technology project—and then compares it with the total cost of the project. The following is the standard formula used for simple ROI calculations:

ROI = Net Benefits / Project Investment

Like a cost benefit analysis, ROI in its simplest form uses only financial costs and benefits. For example, Figure 7-20 illustrates the estimated cost savings to be realized when a help desk that handles 24,000 contacts per year transitions customers away from 100% phone-based services to a combination of phone, e-mail, and self-services via the Web. Industry-standard metrics are used to illustrate the expected savings. To achieve these costs savings, and to provide flexibility to its customers, this help desk plans to implement a $75,000 upgrade to its existing incident tracking and problem management system. The upgrade provides features such as an automated e-mail interface, a Web-based self-help tool, and an automated password management system.

In this simple example, the cost savings realized by reducing the cost per contact more than justifies the investment. However, it is likely that additional benefits could be quantified, such as reduced abandon rate, reduced average speed of answer, and reduced average wait time. **Abandon rate** is the percentage of abandoned calls compared to the total number of calls received. An **abandoned call** is a call where the caller hangs up before an analyst answers. **Average speed of answer (ASA)** is the average time it takes an analyst to pick up an incoming call. **Average wait time**—also known as **average queue time**—is the average number of minutes a caller waits for an analyst after being placed in the queue by an ACD.

As shown in Figure 7-20, ROI typically states the return on investment in percentage terms.

ROI% = Net Benefits / Project Investment X 100

Calculating ROI can be much more complex, however, because benefits can also be intangible. As with performing a cost benefit analysis, intangible benefits can be difficult to define and express in financial terms. They are important, however, and must be taken into consideration.

Contact Method	Usage Percent	# of Contacts	Cost Per Contact	Cost
Pre-Investment				
Phone	100%	24,000	$28.19	$676,560
Post-Investment				
Phone	65%	15,600	$28.19	$439,764
E-mail	25%	6000	$20.66	$123,960
Self-service	10%	2400	$8.25	$19,800
Total cost				$583,524
Total annual savings				$93,036
Total first year investment (upgrade to existing incident tracking and problem management system)				($75,000)
Total first year benefits in savings				$18,036
Annual ROI percentage (Benefits / Investment * 100)				124%

handwritten annotation: Total Annual ÷ Total first year investment × Total first year

Figure 7-20 Sample ROI calculation (incident tracking and problem management system upgrade)

For example, take the case of a small five-person help desk. The help desk supports customers at both the corporate headquarters (which is where the help desk resides) and at a second office across town. At least weekly, a member of the help desk team drives to the remote office to diagnose and repair problems that could not be diagnosed over the telephone or via e-mail. Customers are frustrated by the time it takes to have their problems resolved. The help desk team is frustrated because the drive to the remote office is time-consuming and stressful. On average, the drive takes two hours (round trip) and is through a high-traffic area. Driving to the remote office is also costly and team members are spending an average $20 per month on gas and tolls. In such a scenario, the tangible and intangible benefits of implementing a $200 remote control software package are considerable. As illustrated in Figure 7-21, a quick calculation of time savings and expenses shows that a return on the $200 investment could be realized within months.

This is, of course, a simplistic example. For the ROI to be accurate, other costs and benefits should be considered, such as the costs associated with implementing the system and the benefits in terms of increased productivity realized by customers and help desk staff, increased first contact resolution, and decreased average time to resolution.

In this scenario, intangible benefits such as increased customer satisfaction and improved employee morale are not reflected in the ROI calculation. These benefits are important, however, and may outweigh the financial benefits. Customer and employee complaints, customer and employee satisfaction surveys, and judgement and experience on the part of decisionmakers can be used to quantify these intangible benefits.

Monthly travel time per analyst (2 hours @ $19 per hour X 4 trips)	$152.00
Monthly expenses per analyst ($20 per trip X 4 trips)	$80.00
Total monthly expenses	$232.00
Eliminating one trip per month (total monthly expenses / 4 weeks)	$58.00
Total annual savings (one trip per month X 12 months)	$696.00
Total first year investment (remote control software cost)	$(200.00)
Total first year benefits in savings	$496.00
Annual ROI percentage (Benefits / Investment * 100)	248%
Payback period in months (Investment / Benefits * 12 months)	4.9

Figure 7-21 Sample ROI calculation (remote control software implementation)

As shown in Figure 7-21, some companies also determine the time it takes to recover an investment when calculating ROI. The period of time over which the benefits of an investment are received is known as the payback period.

Payback Period = Project Investment / Net Benefits X 12 Months

Some companies establish guidelines relative to the use of payback period when making purchasing decisions. For example, if the payback period is less than six months, purchase the product immediately. If the payback period is greater than six months, consider the purchase in light of other budget expenditures. If the payback period is greater than one year, consider the purchase in a future budget.

NOTE   Calculating ROI has many benefits, including greater credibility for IT and better IT and business alignment. According to a survey conducted by CIO Insight Magazine, 84% of CIOs say they calculate ROI for initial justification of IT projects. Of the survey participants, 68% say their ROI practices have had a positive effect on IT and business alignment ("How Well Do You Work with the Business?" CIO Insight, www.cioinsight.com, April 2004).

ROI can be a complex and time-consuming calculation and is therefore typically reserved for larger technology investments. In its simplest form, however, ROI is a useful way to communicate the worth of even a small investment. Simply put, ROI answers the questions:

- What do I get back (in return) for the money I am being asked to spend (invest)?
- Is the return worth the investment?

IT professionals and business analysts are increasingly being asked to answer the question, "What is the ROI?" In practice, this is a difficult question to answer. The answer becomes easier, however, as you develop the business skills needed to identify and communicate costs and benefits in financial terms.

The business world has changed and technical professionals must change as well. By acquiring and using business skills, technical professionals can expand their opportunities and have more control over their careers. Rather than always being told what to do and how to do it, technical professionals with business skills can propose new and better solutions and participate fully in bringing their ideas to life.

CHAPTER SUMMARY

❐ Whether a person works for a small company or a large corporation, some business skills are useful and increasingly required. Many business skills relevant to technical professionals such as listening, communicating, and writing are basic business skills and can be learned on-the-job, through self-study, or in the classroom. These skills, along with skills such as customer service, process management, problem solving, project management, conflict management, and time management, are relatively universal and can be used regardless of a person's chosen profession. Skills such as financial management and human resources management are also important and become more important as people advance in their careers.

❐ People working in a help desk hear day-in and day-out from customers who are having trouble using technology. As a result, they have a unique opportunity to support the goals of business by using what they learn from customers to eliminate or minimize the impact of problems and identify improvement opportunities. To do this, technical professionals must learn to use data to identify and quantify improvement opportunities and to use techniques such as trend and root cause analysis. They must also learn how to use goals and metrics, communicated in financial terms, to state the expected benefits of their ideas and to justify improvement initiatives.

❐ Presentations are an important form of communication in today's business world. Although making presentations can be nerve racking, they are inevitable if you want to communicate your ideas and, more important, have those ideas accepted and acted upon. Making a presentation is not an exact science, but there are proven steps that can be taken to ensure success. The more often you present and the more varied the setting, subject matter, and audience, the more comfortable you will be.

❐ Advanced business skills such as managing projects, conducting a cost benefit analysis, and calculating return on investment (ROI) are increasingly critical skills for more senior technical professionals. Although the need for these skills may vary from company to company, even a basic understanding of these concepts will enable you to make the most of learning and growth opportunities. To acquire these skills, some study, even self-study, is needed, along with experience.

❏ The business world has changed and technical professionals must change as well. By acquiring and using business skills, technical professionals can expand their opportunities and have more control over their careers. Rather than always being told what to do and how to do it, technical professionals with business skills can propose new and better solutions and participate fully in bringing their ideas to life.

KEY TERMS

abandon rate — The percentage of abandoned calls, compared to the total number of calls received.

abandoned call — A call where the caller hangs up before an analyst answers.

acceptance criteria — The conditions that must be met before the project deliverables are accepted.

anomaly — A deviation or departure from the average or the norm.

average queue time — See average wait time.

average speed of answer (ASA) — The average time it takes an analyst to pick up an incoming call.

average wait time —The average number of minutes a caller waits for an analyst after being placed in the queue by an ACD; also known as average queue time.

baseline — A metric used to show a starting point.

benchmarking — The process of comparing the help desk's performance metrics and practices to those of another help desk in an effort to identify improvement opportunities.

budget — The total sum of money allocated for a particular purpose (such as a project) or period of time (such as a year).

business — A commercial enterprise or establishment; also used to describe a person's occupation, work, or trade, for example, "He is in the computer business," or "She is in the accounting business."

business analyst — An individual who is skilled at working with end users to determine their needs.

business case — A report that describes the business reasons that a change is being considered.

change control plan — A description of how the project scope will be managed and how agreed changes will be incorporated into the project deliverables.

contact — A communication to or from the help desk, such as a telephone call, e-mail, fax, or Web request.

contact volume — The total number of contacts received during a given period of time.

cost — An amount paid or the expenditure of something, such as time or labor.

cost benefit analysis — A technique that compares the costs and benefits of two or more potential solutions to determine an optimum solution.

cost effectiveness — A metric that ensures a proper balance between the cost of service on one hand, and the quality of service on the other.

cost per contact — Historically called cost per call; the total cost of operating a help desk for a given time period (including salaries, benefits, facilities, and equipment), divided by the total number of contacts received during that period.

cost per unit — The total cost of operating a help desk for a given time period (including salaries, benefits, facilities, and equipment), divided by the total number of units (such as devices and systems) supported during that period.

customer satisfaction — The difference between how a customer perceives he or she was treated and how the customer expects to be treated.

effectiveness — How completely and accurately services are delivered.

efficiency — How quickly services are delivered.

employee satisfaction — How satisfied an employee is with his or her job.

ethics — The rules and standards that govern the conduct of a person or group of people.

exit poll — A measurement technique that, on the Internet, combines questions such as "Was this information helpful to you?" with Yes and No buttons that customers can use to provide feedback.

Gantt chart — A horizontal bar chart that provides a graphic illustration of a schedule.

industry knowledge — Business skills that are unique to the industry or profession the help desk supports, such as accounting or banking.

intangible — A characteristic that is difficult to measure precisely.

IT and business alignment — A process aimed at ensuring that information technologies support corporate goals and objectives.

milestone — A key, or important, event in the life of a project.

nonprofit — A company established for charitable, educational, or humanitarian purposes rather than for making money; also known as not-for-profit.

page hit — A Web page visit.

payback period — The set period of time over which the benefits of an investment are received.

project — A distinct unit of work aimed at producing a specific result or end product.

project deliverables — The physical items to be delivered as a result of project, such as products, systems, services, reports, and plans.

project management — The process of planning and managing a project.

project manager — The person who leads project team and is assigned the authority and responsibility for overseeing the project and meeting the project's objectives.

project objective — A measurable goal in terms of time, money, and quality that the project must achieve to be considered successful.

project overview — An overview of the project and of the business need driving the project.

project plan — A summary document that describes a project, its objectives, and how the objectives are to be achieved.

project sponsor — The person who has ultimate authority over a project.

project stakeholder — A person or group who is involved in or may be affected by project activities.

quality — How well services meet customer expectations.

resolution data — Details about how a problem was resolved, including the fields required to track service level compliance and perform root cause analysis, such as the person or group who resolved the problem, resolution description, date and time resolved, customer satisfaction indicator, date and time closed, and root cause.

return on investment (ROI) — A technique that measures the total financial benefit derived from an investment—such as a new technology project—and then compares it with the total cost of the project.

scope — A general description of the work to be done to complete a project.

scope creep — A term used to describe unplanned changes to a project's scope.

service industry knowledge — Business skills that are specific to the customer service and support industry, such as understanding the importance of meeting customers' needs and knowing how to manage their expectations.

status data — Details about a problem that are used to track problems not resolved at level one, including problem status (such as assigned, awaiting parts, resolved, closed), the person or group assigned, date and time assigned, and priority.

tangible — A characteristic that is capable of being measured precisely.

turnover rate — The ratio of the number of workers who had to be replaced in a given period of time to the average number of workers.

work breakdown structure — A task-oriented breakdown of the work to be done.

REVIEW QUESTIONS

1. List two reasons that business skills are useful and increasingly required.

2. What are two factors that influence the business skills and knowledge required for a help desk job?

3. Describe three ways that people can learn business skills.

4. Individuals who want to advance in the support industry must move from knowing how to _____ technology to how to _____ technology to achieve business goals.

5. What is IT and business alignment?

6. List the four most common data categories captured by help desks.

7. How are customer records linked to problem records?

8. Describe two ways that customer data are used.

9. Describe two ways that problem data are used.

10. Describe two ways that status data are used.

11. Describe two ways that resolution data are used.

12. Define the term trend analysis.

13. Trends can be positive or _____.

14. Why is it important to eliminate the root cause of problems?

15. What is a budget?

16. True or False? Quality is a tangible characteristic.

17. Why are intangible characteristics difficult to measure?

18. Why is a balanced set of goals important?

19. How do you calculate an hourly rate from an annual salary?

20. Define the term cost per contact.

21. What are three benefits of having a clearly stated objective when designing and making presentations?

22. What do you need to know about your audience when designing and making presentations?

23. True or false? Rehearsing a presentation involves memorizing every word you want to say.

24. What are two ways to handle questions when making a presentation?

25. True or False? Understanding how to do something is the same as actually doing it.

26. What is a business case?

27. List five elements that all projects share regardless of their size.

28. What is scope creep?

29. What are two of the project manager's most important responsibilities?

30. What is a cost benefit analysis?

31. A cost benefit analysis answers what two questions?

32. The key to whether a solution is worth the cost lies in _____.

33. Define the term ROI.

34. ROI answers what two questions?

DISCUSSION QUESTIONS

1. How important is it for technical professionals to acquire business skills? What skills are most important? What skills are most transferable from one job to another?

2. Consider the characteristics typically used to create metrics: cost, customer satisfaction, efficiency, effectiveness, employee satisfaction, and quality. Which of these characteristics are tangible and why? Which are intangible and why? Which are the easiest to measure and why?

3. Technical professionals often have a "just do it" philosophy. Are project management skills and a disciplined approach to projects really needed in today's fast-paced
business world?

HANDS-ON PROJECTS

Project 7-1

Learn about business skills. Interview a friend or family member who is in a senior
technical or management position. Ask this person how he or she developed business skills
such as understanding and speaking the language of business, using data to solve business
problems, making presentations, managing projects, and conducting a cost benefit analysis.
How important does this person feel it is to have business skills? What other skills does this
person feel are needed to be successful in today's business world? Summarize what you
learned from this interview in two or three paragraphs.

Project 7-2

Learn about the language of business. Visit the Web site of the company where you
work or where you would like to work and click on the About Us link (or a comparable
link such as Welcome or Corporate Information). What language does the company use
to describe its mission and its goals? Is the company not-for-profit or for-profit? What can
you learn about the industry that the company is in and its vision for the future relative to
that industry? What, if any, industry-specific terms are used to describe the company.
Summarize what you have learned about this business in two or three paragraphs.

Project 7-3

Learn how data is captured and used. Go to the Web site of one of the popular incident tracking and problem management systems listed in the following table. Download
and install a demonstration or trial version of the system to learn more about data fields
captured by help desks. Explore the Web site and demonstration version of the system you
select, and then prepare a table or spreadsheet that shows what data fields the system collects for each of the data categories: customer data, problem data, status data, and resolution data. Also, provide a paragraph or two describing how the data is used—for example,
the types of reports that can be created, the types of metrics that can be produced, the types
of knowledge base searches that can be performed, and so forth.

Product and Vendor	URL
Clientele HelpDesk by Epicor	www.clientele.com
DKHelpDesk by DKSystems	www.dksystems.com
Enterprise HelpDesk by PeopleSoft	www.peoplesoft.com/corp/en/products/ent/crm/ module/helpdesk.jsp

Product and Vendor	URL
HelpSTAR by HelpSTAR.com	www.helpstar.com
HEAT by FrontRange Solutions	www.frontrange.com/heat
Action Request System by Remedy (Remedy also offers Magic Service Desk for mid-sized businesses and HelpDeskIQ for small businesses)	www.remedy.com/solutions
Track-It by Intuit	www.itsolutions.intuit.com
ServiceCenter by Peregrine	www.peregrine.com/products/servicecenter.asp
Unicenter ServicePlus Service Desk by Computer Associates	www3.ca.com/Solutions/SubSolution.asp?ID=4085

HANDS-ON PROJECTS

Project 7-4

Evaluate and debate performance characteristics. Choose two classmates or collegues to work with. Each of you selects one of the following performance characteristics: efficiency, effectiveness, or quality. List the pros and cons of focusing on this single performance characteristic. For example, list the pros and cons of focusing only on how efficiently the help desk is performing while ignoring its effectiveness or the quality of its services. Hold a debate about these characteristics with your classmates. For example, each classmate could present the merits of a single performance characteristic and state why he or she believes that characteristic is more important than the others. You could then end the debate by summarizing the pros and cons of focusing on a single performance characteristic.

HANDS-ON PROJECTS

Project 7-5

Report on a trend. Everywhere you look, studies are being conducted that produce a trend. It seems you cannot watch a television news show or read a magazine without hearing or seeing the phrase "Studies show that. . . ." Select a topic in which you are interested—it could be sports, cooking, gardening, the Internet, and so forth. Search for and explore a Web site or read a magazine that specializes in the subject you have selected and find a trend. Prepare a brief report that describes the trend and explains your perspective on factors that are influencing the trend.

HANDS-ON PROJECTS

Project 7-6

Identify presentation tips and techniques. Assemble a team of at least three classmates. Discuss the topic of using presentations to market your ideas. Develop a list of reasons why people fear making presentations. Using your list, prepare a second list of 10 practical tips and techniques that people can use to minimize the anxiety associated with making presentations. Share your tips and techniques with the class.

Project 7-7

Present the status of a project. Practice makes perfect. To practice your presentation skills, prepare and present to the class a brief (five-minute) presentation that provides the status of a "project" in which you are currently involved. The project could be acquiring and preparing a new laptop for school or work, an upcoming celebration (such as a wedding or graduation) or moving into a new home. Use the format of a project status report as your outline.

Project 7-8

Learn about project management software. Go to several Web sites of the project management software vendors mentioned in this chapter. Download demonstration or trial versions for two systems. Complete the demonstrations or explore the trial versions. Prepare a table or spreadsheet that compares the features and benefits of the two products you have selected.

Project 7-9

Perform a cost benefit analysis. Many people who perform cost benefit analyses on a regular basis tend to call it "shopping around." Think of an acquisition you have been considering. For example, you may be thinking about acquiring a digital camera, a PDA, or a fairly expensive gift for a friend or family member. Complete the following steps:

1. Document the goal you are trying to achieve.

2. Produce a table that shows all of the costs (purchase price, monthly service fee, time to set up, and so forth) and benefits of two or more of the products you want to purchase.

3. Analyze the costs and benefits (tangible and intangible) and select a product.

4. Document the reason for your decision.

CASE PROJECTS

1. Root Causes of Hardware Problems

You are the team leader at a help desk that recently installed a new incident tracking and problem management system. This system provides the ability to capture the root cause of problems. You have decided to begin by tracking the root cause of hardware problems. Prepare a list of root causes for hardware problems. For each root cause, identify at least one proactive way to prevent this type of problem from recurring.

2. Tips for Effective Charts and Graphs

You would like to begin using charts and graphs to communicate ideas you have for improving help desk services. Search the Web or go to your local library and learn more about how to effectively use charts and graphs to present information. For example, how can you use color to enhance your charts and graphs? How can you use labels to provide additional information about the data being presented? Prepare a list of 10 tips for creating effective charts and graphs.

3. ROI Presentation

Your team leader wants you to help prepare a presentation aimed at convincing the help desk manager to invest in remote control software. Prepare three slides that show the intangible benefits of remote control software to customers, the help desk team, and level two service providers. (Hint: Refer to the section "Technical Writing Best Practices" in Chapter 6 for practical tips and techniques about writing with lists and being consistent.)

8

CUSTOMER BEHAVIOR, CUSTOMER LOYALTY, AND EXCEPTIONAL SERVICE

Objectives

◆ Describe customers' buying behavior relative to their basic needs.

◆ Distinguish between customer satisfaction and customer loyalty.

◆ State the relationship between customer expectations and customer perceptions.

◆ Describe methods companies use to measure customer satisfaction.

In a business sense, customers can be considered as assets. Most companies regard assets as items that must be protected and whose value must be maintained and even maximized over time. From the customer's viewpoint, virtually all customer service activities, from billing accuracy to courtesy and accessibility of personnel, are prime components of excellent customer service. The trend in customer behavior and attitude is to expect that excellent customer service will be provided during all customer contacts.

Because recent data show that 40 percent of even satisfied customers will defect to a competitor, companies that are intent on retaining customers must cultivate loyalty by establishing a common ground and showing concern for customers through listening and using humor.[1] Contrary to popular belief, increased technology isn't the way to create customer loyalty. In fact, the more high-tech the business world becomes, the more challenging it is to build customer rapport. Despite their obvious conveniences, e-mail, voicemail, fax machines, PDAs, and other technological devices take attention away from customers. These gadgets eliminate the human touch needed to build long-term customer relationships.

[1]Laura Michaud, "Beyond Customer Satisfaction," *Expert Magazine* (August 14, 2003): 15.

UNDERSTANDING CUSTOMER BEHAVIOR

The primary objectives of perfect customer service are to experience repeat business and to increase business from current customers. These goals require specific knowledge about customers' behavior—why they buy, how they buy, and particularly what causes them to return and increase their purchases over time. Thinking like a customer isn't easy. In fact, many companies are unable to do it. Today's customers want choices, but they want them to be relevant to what they need to accomplish.

Although the reasons consumers buy vary considerably, they are derived from four basic needs that each of us has, regardless of our industries or businesses.

1. *The need to be understood.* Emotions, customs, and language barriers can get in the way of properly understanding the needs of customers. Every effort should be made to work with these challenges.

2. *The need to feel welcome.* That first impression a customer gets from service professionals is critical. Anyone who is made to feel like an outsider when doing business with a company will probably not return for future goods and services.

3. *The need to feel important.* Little things mean a lot. Acknowledgment, name recognition, and eye contact make a person feel important and appreciated.

4. *The need for comfort.* People need physical comfort— places to wait, rest, talk, or do business. They also need psychological comfort—the assurance and confidence they will be taken care of properly and fairly.

Organizations that understand customer behavior and make the transition to customer-centric service are characterized in two ways: (1) the organization is regarded by customers as easy to buy from or deal with, and (2) the organization depends on systems and processes (not speeches and slogans) to see that its service fits the customer's needs at a price the customer is willing to pay.

> **Ethics/Choices**
> *If you were being verbally "beaten up" by a customer for an issue you knew was caused by a colleague who was just fired last week, would you tell the customer who caused the problem? Explain.*

In various industries, excellent service is often driven by customer behaviors and needs. Some examples are:

1. The retail business. A customer-oriented retail organization provides a wide variety of merchandise, convenient shopping hours, parking, reasonable policies on returns and exchanges, and availability of trained, courteous sales and service professionals.

2. The consumer direct-marketing or mail-order business. The nature of this business requires a high degree of customer trust and, in general, centers on immediate access to advertised products, prompt delivery, a liberal exchange and return policy, and hassle-free dealings that occur from a distance.

3. The banking and financial services business. This area has shown tremendous advances in customer service recently, with its automatic teller machines, interactive phone systems for handling account queries, and increased availability and higher skill levels of customer service personnel. In addition, customers receive faster turnaround on loans and quick resolution of money problems through immediate access to the financial institution's website links.

Our basic needs drive our decisions to buy from certain companies, while not buying from others.

EARNING CUSTOMER LOYALTY

The customer is king. This phrase has become something of a mantra for retailers during the last several years, but many fail to support it with their behaviors or policies. Customer-centricity has become the new, challenging, competitive battlefield. The only way to survive in the current marketplace is by building a wide base of loyal customers, and the only way to do that is by tailoring the shopping experience to customer wants and needs as much as possible.

In companies across America, a disconnect between intentions and reality may be driving away customers. Often, companies do not live up to customer expectations. Incredibly, the disappointments that customers experience are frequently the result of expectations that the company has set up for itself. For example, customers are routinely surprised because many businesses fail to meet their own promised deadlines, fail to back up their products adequately, provide only limited availability of their advertised products, or provide inconsistent product service and support after the sale. Clearly, customer loyalty is not earned in these ways.

How Loyalty Is Earned

Profound changes have transformed the business world. Ask most managers what is different in today's economy, and they will tell you that markets are more crowded with global competitors, and attracting and retaining customer attention is harder than ever. An increased capacity to produce products and information has created an overcrowded marketplace, as more and more companies compete for the same customers.

Interestingly enough, a momentous shift has occurred: we have, in effect, entered an age of customer scarcity. The end result of this shift is that customers have become the most precious of all economic resources to businesses. Earning and keeping their loyalty, therefore, is tremendously valuable to successful companies.

Many companies today are maximizing the loyalty and the purchasing behavior of their customers by offering customer rewards programs. The popularity of loyalty programs among today's consumers is evident in multiple industries in the United States. According to an October 2004 poll commissioned by Maritz Loyalty Marketing, nearly 90 percent of Americans actively participate in some type of loyalty program, including credit card, retail store, and airline rewards programs, and most consumers are enrolled in more than one. Further, research indicates that more than half of those surveyed are more loyal to companies that offer rewards programs.[2]

Companies that have earned customer loyalty get the results they want—increased and consistent sales revenues.

[2]Gail Sneed, "Do Your Customers Really Feel Rewarded?" *Target Marketing* (September 2005): 41.

Customers tend to stay with organizations that enable them to experience positive, meaningful, and personally important feelings, even if an organization cannot always provide everything customers want or cannot solve all their problems. Most people shift from one supplier to another because of dissatisfaction with service, not price or product offerings. The service provider's responsibility is to manage the emotions in customer service exchanges.

According to Technical Assistance Research Programs, Inc. (TARP), a Washington, DC, consulting firm, 68 percent of customers who go elsewhere do so because of a perception of indifference.[3] Indifference in this regard means that customers believe their loyalty is wasted on a company that doesn't care whether they remain customers. Thus, they vote with their feet and walk out the door, seldom or never to be seen again. Establishing lasting customer relationships can be extremely difficult, because one bad experience—or even a mediocre one—can cause a customer to take his or her business to a competitor.

An equation for keeping customers—not exactly a secret, considering the multitude of books on the topic— goes as follows: Take a good, first reaction with the customer; add in reliability, a quick response time, quality services and products, plus empathy; and you end up with a satisfied customer. Take away any of these factors and customer loyalty will begin to wane. Figure 8–1 lists some tips that are useful to earn repeat business from customers.

There is a cost benefit of building customer loyalty. Companies that frequently and periodically survey their customers to find out how happy they are and what suggestions they have to offer to improve products and services are doing the right thing. Some corporations and retailers that have taken these steps and, thus, have earned the right to experience deep customer loyalty are GE, Microsoft, Intel, Yahoo!, Home Depot, Wal-Mart, Nordstrom's, L.L. Bean, and Amazon.com. These are some companies that actively seek out from their customers better ways to serve them. Ultimately, the entire purpose of improved service is to honor customers by caring enough to meet their needs. Loyalty is earned when intentions and reality blend and become one. Customer-centric organizations do whatever it takes to avoid any type of customer turnoff.

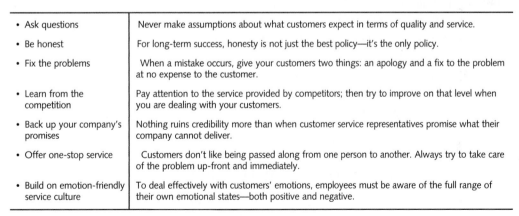

• Ask questions	Never make assumptions about what customers expect in terms of quality and service.
• Be honest	For long-term success, honesty is not just the best policy—it's the only policy.
• Fix the problems	When a mistake occurs, give your customers two things: an apology and a fix to the problem at no expense to the customer.
• Learn from the competition	Pay attention to the service provided by competitors; then try to improve on that level when you are dealing with your customers.
• Back up your company's promises	Nothing ruins credibility more than when customer service representatives promise what their company cannot deliver.
• Offer one-stop service	Customers don't like being passed along from one person to another. Always try to take care of the problem up-front and immediately.
• Build on emotion-friendly service culture	To deal effectively with customers' emotions, employees must be aware of the full range of their own emotional states—both positive and negative.

Figure 8-1 Tips to Earn Repeat Business from Customers

[3]Joan Fox, "How to Keep Customers from Slipping through the Cracks," *The Small Business Journal* (May 2001): 2.

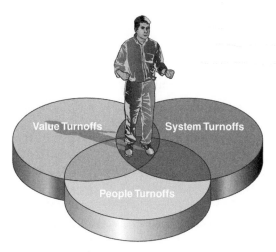

Figure 8–2 What Drives Customers Away?

Customer Turnoffs

Attracting replacement customers is an expensive process, because research indicates that it costs five times as much to generate a new customer as it does to keep an existing one. Unfortunately, few companies even track customer retention rates, much less inquire about what issues might be driving their customers away. Could it be fear about discovering the answers that prevents businesses from ever asking the question "What turns you off as a customer?"

If asked, customers would probably cite three categories of turnoffs, illustrated in Figure 8–2.

1. *Value turnoffs.* When a customer says, "I didn't get my money's worth on this product," this is a value turnoff. Value turnoffs include inadequate guarantees, a failure to meet quality expectations, and high prices relative to the perceived value of the product or service.

2. *System turnoffs.* These irritations arise from the way a company delivers its products or services. When transactions are unnecessarily complicated, inefficient, or troublesome, customers experience system turnoffs. For example, employees who lack the knowledge to answer customer questions and organizations that have just one person capable of fulfilling a key function are symptomatic of system failures. So are voicemail menus that are unnecessarily complicated. Slow service, lack of delivery options, cluttered workplaces, unnecessary or repetitive paperwork requirements, poor product selection, and inadequate reordering processes are additional examples of system turnoffs.

Why Do Customers Defect from Established Relationships?
1. They don't know where or how to complain to the supplier.
2. They are too busy and can't, or won't, take the time to resolve concerns they have.
3. They consider complaining to be an annoyance that they would rather avoid.
4. They don't believe the company will do anything about it anyway.
5. They don't see any direct value or benefit to them from complaining.
6. They fear some post-complaint hostility or retaliation on the part of the company.
7. They can get what they want from a competitor, so switching is easy.

Steps to Reduce Defections
1. Make it easy for customers to complain.
2. Train CSRs to use good questioning techniques to uncover complaints.
3. Get resolution to customer problems more quickly.
4. Positively acknowledge every complaint as soon as possible.
5. Enforce a closed-loop complaint management system in which complaints are routinely gathered and analyzed for insights.

Figure 8–3 Why Customers Defect and Approaches to Reduce Defections

 3. *People turnoffs.* These are the turnoff occurrences most often associated with poor customer service. Examples include showing lack of courtesy or attention, using inappropriate or unprofessional behavior, and projecting an indifferent attitude. In short, any behavior that conveys a lack of appreciation, care, or consideration for the customer is a people turnoff.

According to Jill Griffin and Michael Lowenstein, co-authors of Customer WinBack, customers defect from an established relationship for seven primary reasons. Figure 8–3 itemizes these reasons and goes on to suggest approaches companies can take to reduce customer defections.

Don't pass blame. When a customer calls with a problem you personally did not create, don't rush to point out, "I didn't do it" or "It's not my fault." Instead of dodging the issue or blaming someone else, immediately apologize for the customer's inconvenience and take action to resolve it.

OFFERING EXCEPTIONAL CUSTOMER SERVICE

Exceptional customer service is in the eye of the beholder—the customer. How does the customer determine whether a company has provided exceptional customer service? It usually depends on two factors: the customer's expectations and his or her perceptions. **Customer expectations** are what a customer wants before a transaction. Typically, a customer forms expectations from several sources: advertising, previous experience, word of mouth, and the competition.

Customer perceptions, in contrast, are created during and after a transaction. A customer's perception is based on how actual service measures up to his or her expectations. If customers get more than they expected, the end result is **exceptional customer service.** However, if customers get anything less than they expected, they perceive a performance gap; in that gap lies customer disappointment. Disappointed customers will leave an organization and take their business elsewhere, and poor customer service is responsible for much of the disappointment experienced by customers.

In practice, what does exceptional customer service really mean? Perhaps it happens when a company seriously tries to determine what makes it truly unique and what makes its customer experience better than that of its competitors. Keep in mind also that when you define what better customer service means for your customers, that definition is based on how they feel now; this doesn't necessarily mean that the definition won't change in the future. In other words, defining exceptional customer service is an ongoing, fluid process.

Focus on Best Practices

Ritz-Carlton is the only service company to have won the prestigious Malcolm Baldrige National Quality Award twice—in 1992 and again in 1999. Receiving this industry-honored distinction was certainly not by accident. Every day at the chain's 57 hotels, all 25,000 Ritz-Carlton employees participate in a 15-minute "lineup" to talk about one of the basics. For example, Basic #14 states, "Use words such as 'Good morning,' 'Certainly,' 'I'll be happy to,' and 'My pleasure.' Do not use words such as 'O.K.,' 'Sure,' 'Hi/Hello,' 'Folks,' and 'No problem.'" The lineup ritual makes the hotel one of the few large companies that sets aside time for a daily discussion of its core values.

Further, if you are employed by Ritz-Carlton, the hotelier will spend about $5,000 to train you. First, you'll get a two-day introduction to the company values (it's all about the service), including the credo (again, service) and the 20 Ritz-Carlton basics (you got it—service!). Next comes a 21-day course focused on job responsibilities, such as a bellman's 28 steps to greeting a guest. Each employee carries a plastic card imprinted with the credo and the basics, as well as the "employee promise" and the three steps of service.

Step 1: "A warm and sincere greeting. Use the guest's name."

Step 2: "Anticipation and fulfillment of each guest's needs."

Step 3: "Fond farewell. Give a warm good-bye and use the guest's name."

For those reasons, strong organizations stay in touch with their customers on a regular basis and are not afraid to receive negative comments. In fact, they welcome negative comments that help them improve. Complaining is not only appropriate, but necessary. Why? Because it lets businesses know where they have room for improvement. When businesses know what they should improve and then make these improvements, they bring in more customers, resulting in more sales. Good companies fully recognize that it is infinitely better to have customers tell their complaints to the company's service representatives than to tell them to someone else.

The Value of Exceptional Customer Service

Exceptional customer service matters. Customers who experience world-class customer service return for more products and services and are less likely to shop around. Knowing what is on the customer's mind, therefore, is the smartest thing a business can do. Successful companies focus on what the customer is saying and then tailor their products or services to meet customer needs.

Profits and customer service go hand in hand. The value and economic effects of exceptional customer service are realities businesses are recognizing. According to a myriad of customer service surveys and resulting statistics, on average,

- Most people tell 10 other people about great service they have received (and are willing to pay more just to have), but will tell up to 20 people about poor service they have gotten.
- Depending on the industry, it costs between 2 and 20 times more to gain a new customer than it does to satisfy and retain a current one.
- Ninety-five percent of the customers whose problems are fixed quickly continue to do business with the company.

Paying attention to the finer points throughout a buying transaction is that special touch that makes a company stand out from the crowd. Some of the most effective extras are really very basic concepts of conducting good business, although customers are often surprised when these actions take place. Little details that contribute to exceptional customer service include:

- Treating customers respectfully and courteously at all times.
- Greeting customers by name and promptly answering their questions. (If you can't answer promptly, get back to the customer with an answer as quickly as possible.)
- Standing behind your product or service and doing whatever it takes to right a customer service concern in a manner that is fair to both sides.

Moment of truth is a term coined by Jan (Yon) Carlzon of Scandinavian Airlines Systems (SAS) in turning around his company as a result of a tremendous loss of profits in 1981.

Simply put, a moment of truth is an episode in which a customer comes in contact with any aspect of the company, however remote, and thereby has an opportunity to form an impression. This **moment of truth** happens in a very short time period, from 7 to 40 seconds. That is the amount of time you, as a CSR, have to make a good impression on your customer. This impression will guide the rest of the encounter.

If the moment is favorable, the whole interaction will be pleasant. If it is not, a positive customer relationship has been tarnished. Carlzon's idea is that, if his company's 10 million passengers had an average contact with five SAS employees, the company had 50 million unique, never-to-be-repeated opportunities, or "moments of truth." With these moment-of-truth events, the company recovered from an $8 million loss to a profit of $71 million in two years.

TIP

Customers with high expectations— sometimes referred to as tough, demanding customers—make a business better. The secret is to use these situations as opportunities to maximize customer retention and improve customer services.

Critical First Impressions

According to an old saying, "You never get a second chance to make a first impression." Nowhere is this more applicable than in business situations, whatever the industry, because how you initially communicate with people is key to your overall and continued success. In general, most consumers prefer to spend their money where they are treated well.

Research suggests that when two individuals meet for the first time, they take only four minutes to decide whether to continue the relationship. Evidently, this decision is based on certain assumptions. Perhaps the scariest truth of all is that this initial impression usually lasts a lifetime. If the first interaction with a customer is poor, even if a fairly good relationship ensues, the brain remembers that very first impression.

Successful companies examine and evaluate their customer service program regularly in order to establish a baseline standard for serving customers. A **baseline standard** is the minimum level of service it takes to satisfy customers under ordinary circumstances. Here are some examples of practices that constitute a baseline:

- Greet all customers just after entering your business.
- When possible, use a customer's name.
- Ask a customer about his or her visit.
- When asked, walk the customer to the product and place the item in his or her hand.
- Return voice and e-mail messages within 12 to 24 hours of receipt.

Positive first impressions are critical. Several types of communication can be used to create a positive first impression: in person at the physical place of business (both the environment and the way in which people are greeted); by telephone, voicemail, and e-mail; through printed materials; and by the way you present yourself and your company outside the office. First impressions are also influenced by a customer service representative's personal habits. When a CSR's hair is groomed, hands and fingernails are clean, clothing is appropriate and clean, and general actions reflect professionalism on the job, these practices send a positive impression to those who do business with your company.

Indicative of our age of quick response time, returning calls promptly, delivering products or services quickly, and using modern technology to decrease response time are also smart business moves. Each of these actions helps to create superior first impressions, because customers simply are not willing to wait. Beware of using on-hold time to deliver information about your business. A waiting customer can easily take offense at being forced to endure your advertising or your taste in music. If at all possible, have enough phone lines (and enough people to answer them) so that callers don't get a busy signal or get put on hold for longer than 45 seconds.

In making a favorable first impression, a good rule of thumb is to consistently exceed customer expectations. Keep in mind, however, that a positive first impression isn't going to do much good in the long run if a subsequent negative experience eclipses it. The best way to maximize the value of a positive first impression is to reinforce it with extraordinary approaches to customer service and other favorable experiences throughout the course of future interactions. Empowering employees to solve customer concerns is a critical component to making a great first impression.

Empowerment

Empowerment, defined as giving somebody power or authority, must follow a top-down model that conveys authority through the ranks to frontline staff members. It enables them to make administrative decisions based on corporate guidelines. It means that employees should never have to tell a customer "no." When an employee can do whatever he has to do on the spot to take care of a customer to that customer's satisfaction, not to the company's satisfaction, that is empowerment, because if the customer doesn't win, the company loses.

One significant benefit of empowerment is the elimination of nearly all multilevel problem solving that involves management. Scores of managers talk about empowerment, but many more have difficulty putting it into practice. Too often, they don't really understand what empowerment is. To many managers, empowerment is giving employees the authority to make a decision to take care of the customer—as long as the action they take follows the rules, policies, and procedures of the organization. Some would interpret this to mean there actually is no empowerment. True empowerment means employees can bend and break the rules to do whatever they have to do to take care of the customer.

 Undeliverable promises can do more harm than saying "no" to a customer.

TIP

Empowerment is an important aspect of legendary customer service for any business. Having a team of empowered employees who are afraid to make a decision is as bad, if not worse, than not having an empowerment program at all. When employees make a customer-related decision, the greatest concern for many of them is that they will be reprimanded—or worse, fired—for making what management sees as a bad decision.

For empowerment to work, employees should know they won't be fired if they make an error and that it's okay to make mistakes in the process of working to win customer satisfaction. Once empowered, customer service representatives have the responsibility to exercise that authority when the need arises. Ultimately, an empowered staff reduces the amount of time customers spend reaching satisfactory conclusions and has far-reaching effects in keeping a customer who would consider going elsewhere for your product or service.

Ethics/Choices

Time after time, when entering the employee break room, you overhear other CSRs talking about how bad the management is at your company—specifically, your manager. What is your reaction to this situation? Would you enter the discussion to express your personal views, ignore the discussion, or try to reason with your coworkers and advise them against spreading negative thoughts? Explain.

Extraordinary Approaches to Customer Service

To go beyond client satisfaction, make every effort to exceed your clients' expectations, every time. An age-old rule that is followed by customer-savvy organizations is to "under promise and over deliver." For example, if you think it will take two months to complete a project, quote a two-month time frame. If you get the job done a week or two early, you have under promised and over delivered. Tactics such as these empower people in the organization by giving them freedom to act in customers' best interests, and they yield enormous dividends for the company.

Stellar customer service is a mindset that defines each company's culture. It is pervasive, visible to others, and everyone's responsibility. Obviously, this unity of purpose begins with hiring and training the right people, but it also requires organizations to keep the basic company functions in superior shape, so that CSRs do not get bogged down by the grind of cleaning up problems, correcting errors, or being on the defensive with customers. The following six actions can help improve performance and apply extraordinary approaches to customer service.

1. *Decide who you are and what you can deliver.* It's important to know what you can and cannot provide. Make sure you are true to your company's mission. Decide who you want to provide exemplary service to. Decide what you want to deliver and deliver it well.

2. *Decide who your customers are and what they want.* What you think customers should value might not be what they really value. Make sure you are in sync with customer interests and concerns.

Explain

3. *Deliver more than you promise.* Make sure you give your customers more than they request, but, when doing so, ensure it is something they will value.

 4. *Review your rules.* Look at both formal and informal rules. Some rules might have evolved from previous customer encounters in your company. Examine which rules obstruct serving your customers' needs and get rid of them, if possible. Make every effort to favor the customers' needs over internal needs.

 5. *Celebrate your diversity.* Some employees might be difficult to work with, but they might be the best fit with some customers. Empower them. They might become your best employees.

6. Treat your employees as you expect them to treat your customers. Treat your employees with respect. Put yourself in their shoes. Make them feel special. Make time for them. The result will be that they will treat customers the same way. In business, this idea is referred to as the **mirror principle,** which says, your employees won't treat customers better than you treat your employees.

In this discussion about what exemplary customer service is, it is perhaps prudent to examine what service is not. Service is not easily managed, because so many factors make it unpredictable and difficult to control fully. The following characteristics of service contribute to this complexity; therefore, when focusing on serving customers in the best way, remember these realities, which can cause dilemmas for CSRs:

- Customer service happens instantaneously and right in front of the customer.
- Customer service is created and delivered at the same time.
- Service must be individualized for each customer; it cannot be standardized or routinely applied universally.
- The perception of the customer may not be the same perception as that of the service providers.
- Often, customer requests are complex and unique, and cannot be speedily resolved.
- Different customers have different needs; further, the needs of the same customers change constantly.
- Complete customer service requires others in your organization to support you; it requires customer service teamwork, with everyone committed to the same goal.

 If a company doesn't take care of its customers, some other company will.

MEASURING CUSTOMER SATISFACTION

The case for maximizing customer satisfaction is a strong one, because a customer base will remain if it is built on trust, quality, timely service, and product excellence. Although superior customer satisfaction is the goal, it is difficult to measure. Satisfaction, like quality, is in the eye of the beholder. What is the best way to measure customer service and satisfaction? The answer is simple—ask your customers. Having customers tell you specifically what you are doing right, what you are doing wrong, and how you can improve critical areas of your business is the single and most accurate means of determining how well you are meeting their needs.

Benefits to the Customer

Several ways exist to gather customer feedback: surveys and assessments, focus groups, and interviews. When conducted at six-month and yearly intervals, these are all first-rate methods for generating qualitative and quantitative information for sound decision making and appropriate changes to the way a business operates. Customer feedback can help companies increase service quality, innovation, and most important, customer retention. This feedback meets one or any number of the objectives that follow:

- Finding and acting on the issues which lead to innovation, employee or customer turnover, or other key outcomes
- Motivating and guiding change efforts and identifying the most promising opportunities for improvement
- Recording a baseline from which progress can be measured
- Creating a consensus on priorities or issues to be dealt with
- Providing a two-way communication with employees or customers

The traditional methods to gauge customer satisfaction are to conduct periodic customer surveys via telephone, direct mail, the Internet, and e-mail. Some problems inherent in the use of these approaches are that they are often slow, expensive, imprecise, and not always helpful for getting at the root of deviations in customer satisfaction. In a perfect world, customer satisfaction data should be reliable, viewed in real time, tied to specific CSRs, and cost a fraction of traditional third-party surveys.

A faulty belief exists in the marketplace that the mere collection of data will result in improvement. That's probably because, in years past, just the act of conducting a survey had some positive impact on customer satisfaction and loyalty, but the bar has been raised. With a smarter base of customers who have greater expectations of service, companies can no longer ask whether customers are satisfied without acting in a personalized way on the responses they receive. The process of asking customers to set the standards for the level of service they expect from a company

- Helps the company set realistic goals and monitor trends.
- Provides critical input for analyzing problem areas.
- Assists the company in monitoring progress toward improvements.
- Keeps the company close to its customers.

Benefits to the CSR

You cannot change what you don't measure, understand, and acknowledge. Customer service representatives and their managers, therefore, pay more attention to performance standards that are measured because they then know what to expect. Customer-focused measurements are needed because they explain reasons for lost sales, retention problems, time-consuming and costly complaints, and cost redundancies.

Without measurable performance standards, employees are left to guess what good service is. When that happens, customers become disappointed. The following are some examples of measurable customer service standards that good companies implement:

- Answering telephones by the third ring
- Serving hot food at a temperature of at least 140 degrees
- Smiling and greeting all guests within 10 feet of you
- Responding to each shopper so that he or she does not stand in line more than two minutes
- Offering bellman or concierge service to every hotel guest
- Speaking professionally to clients and avoiding the use of slang expressions

How do you ask customers if your service goals are in line with their service expectations? The easiest way is to have a customer response system in place. You can use several methods, such as comment card surveys, post-episodic surveys, automated call surveys, or mail surveys, to name a few.

COMMENT CARD SURVEYS Hand the card to the customer at the end of the transaction. Ask the customer to please take a moment to complete the survey, as it will be useful to your company in determining how well you are meeting his or her needs.

POST-EPISODIC SURVEYS A new feedback concept gaining popularity with perceptive companies is the post-episodic survey. **Post-episodic surveys** gather information from customers after they have completed a business transaction such as opening a new account or getting a car serviced at a dealership. Essentially, this is a satisfaction survey dealing with just one service episode. Surveys are usually conducted by phone within 24 to 48 hours of the transaction. Post-episodic surveys are valuable when you want to measure improvement in customer service, develop further insight into the needs and expectations of your customers, or identify best practices.

AUTOMATED CALL SURVEYS This survey uses specific software that is integrated with the customer call center's system. After the caller has elected to bypass self-service and speak with an agent (usually by pressing "0"), the caller is asked to participate in a survey after the call. Typically, they are instructed to press "1" for "yes" and "2" for "no." Callers respond via entries on the touch-tone pad. Some systems accept verbal responses. Usually, between 5 and 10 percent of callers will agree to participate in the survey.[4]

MAIL SURVEYS Include a cover letter explaining the reasons for your survey. Address a short survey to the person who interacted with your company and include a postage-paid return envelope.

OTHER METHODS Electronic surveys, in-store shopper surveys, and onsite interviews can also be effective. In addition, create a forum for customer service representatives to provide anecdotal, subjective feedback from customers about product features, functionality, and pricing.

Finally, nobody knows what customers are thinking better than CSRs do. Examples of customer response methods are shown in Figure 8–4.

Business in Action
BEN & JERRY'S

The consumer services manager at Ben and Jerry's Homemade, Inc., describes how "euphoric service" can move customers from mere satisfaction of purchasing their ice cream into passionate loyalty like this: "Customer satisfaction is only a feeling— an attitude—that does not predict future customer performance, because satisfied customers will still purchase from your competitor. Customer loyalty, on the other hand, is a behavior. When you make a personal connection with your customers and let them know that you hear what they're saying, and then prove it by being responsive to their needs, you're building loyalty that influences behavior. Loyalty is always going to be based on relationships, and that's what you want."

CONCLUDING MESSAGE FOR CSRs

To be sure, it takes more than "the customer is always right" rhetoric to satisfy today's diverse customers. Customers are not always right, but customers are always emotional. They always have feelings—sometimes intense, other times barely perceptible—when they make purchases or engage in business transactions. When unhappy CSRs in an organization are out of touch with their own feelings, they cannot provide emotional competence or use emotional connections to increase customer loyalty.

---

[4]Dick Bucci, "The New Best Way to Measure Customer Satisfaction," *Call Center Magazine* (November 2005): 44.

Customer Comment Card
YOUR CONCERN IS OUR CONCERN

Please provide your comments
in the space below.

_____
_____
_____
_____
_____
_____
_____
_____
_____
_____
_____
_____
_____
_____
_____
_____
_____
_____

We appreciate your input, because it helps
us serve you better. Thank you.

HOW ARE WE DOING?
To help us improve our commitment to you, please take a moment
to respond with your reactions to our service.

Please rate us on a scale of 1–5 using the following system:

5 Outstanding	Friendliness	5 4 3 2 1
4 Exceeds Expectations	(For example, how courteous was our sales staff?)	
3 Meets Expectations	Timeliness	5 4 3 2 1
2 Dissatisfied	(For example, was our sales staff able to assist you promptly?)	
1 Unacceptable		
	Helpfulness	5 4 3 2 1
	(For example, did our sales staff offer suggestions?)	
	Overall satisfaction	5 4 3 2 1

Comments: _____

Completed by: _____

Figure 8–4 Two methods that survey customers' expectations and satisfaction with products and services

If you want loyal customers, don't just stop at customer satisfaction, because basic service delivery isn't enough in today's marketplace. Here is something to think about: when a company loses a customer, it does not lose one sale, but a lifetime opportunity of profitability with that individual. The question becomes "What could that customer have been worth?" To determine the average lifetime value of customers, first estimate how much they will spend with your company on an annual basis, and multiply it by the number of years they could potentially use your products and services. For example, if an average customer spends $100 a month, 12 months a year, for 10 years, their average lifetime value is $12,000. Now add on the value of all the new customers that your loyal customer will refer to your company. You can easily see how increasing customer retention and loyalty translates into huge increases in profitability and long life to any company.

SUMMARY

- The primary mission of perfect customer service is to experience repeat business and to increase business from current customers.
- Earning customer loyalty is critical, because today's economy has an increased capacity to produce products and information; therefore, an excess in the marketplace is inherent as more and more companies compete for the same customers.
- Customer expectations are what a customer wants before a transaction; customer perceptions are created during and after a transaction.
- In terms of making a favorable first impression, a good rule of thumb is to exceed customer expectations consistently, because first impressions are formed within the first four minutes of customer contact.
- Because of a smarter customer base that has greater expectations, companies can no longer use survey techniques to ask whether customers are satisfied, without acting on the responses they receive.

KEY TERMS

baseline standard
customer expectations
customer perceptions
empowerment
exceptional customer service
mirror principle
moment of truth
post-episodic surveys

CRITICAL THINKING

1. In what ways do the four basic needs described in this chapter relate to the reasons people buy from certain companies?

2. Describe an experience you have had or have heard about that demonstrates excellent customer service.

3. Are customer satisfaction and customer loyalty the same in meaning? Why or why not?

4. Of the three types of customer turnoffs—value turnoffs, system turnoffs, and people turnoffs— which do you feel is the most often violated by organizations? Why?

5. In your own words, explain the relationship between customer expectations and customer perceptions.

6. Do you agree with the statement "You never get a second chance to make a first impression"? Why or why not?

7. Are the reasons customer service is difficult to manage just excuses for poor customer service or are they reasonable? Explain.

8. If you were the president of a retail organization, what methods would you use to measure customer satisfaction? Why?

ONLINE RESEARCH ACTIVITIES

Project 8–1 Measuring Customer Satisfaction

Assume you are doing a report on surveys that measure customer satisfaction. Use the Internet to locate examples of published information from business journals and business-oriented websites. List the results of your search, including the URLs, of current information you might use in your report.

Project 8–2 Customer Loyalty and Retention

The big push at On-Time Technology Products is to increase sales by doing whatever it takes to retain customers and increase customer loyalty. In the technology business, however, Vice President Woo, who is in charge of customer relations, realizes that because of many good ideas and outstanding competitors, it might be prudent to do some research on the Internet. He specifically wants to survey how customer loyalty is achieved—especially as it applies to the technology industry.

Go to the Amazon website and locate three books on customer loyalty and customer retention. Enter your findings in the following table to inform Mr. Woo which recently published books are available and those you would recommend, along with a brief description of each.

Title and Author	Price	Brief Description of Book
1.		
2.		
3.		

HANDS-ON PROJECTS

Project 8–3 Moment of Truth Examples

A moment of truth is an episode in which a customer comes in contact with any aspect of the organization, however remote, and thereby has an opportunity to form an impression. In other words, a moment of truth

- Consists of any interaction with a customer.
- Determines a customer's perception of your service.
- Requires judgment, skill, and understanding by the CSR.
- Occurs in less than 40 seconds.

Look at the list of customer-oriented industries in column 1. In column 2, write down specific actions a customer service professional can make to improve a moment-of-truth experience as it relates to each industry. For informal research, ask another adult if they have had a moment-of-truth experience in the past week and if so, have the person describe it. Be prepared to share your findings and written ideas as part of a class group discussion.

How to Create Positive Moments of Truths for Customers (for example, Smile)

1. Hotel	• • •
2. Restaurant	• • •
3. Retail store (for example, Wal-Mart)	• • •
4. Airline (for example, Southwest Airlines)	• • •

Project 8–4 Customer Turnoffs Discussion

You are sitting in the lunchroom at On-Time Technology Products with two other CSRs, Rosie and Doug. It's Friday and everyone is looking forward to the weekend, but Doug is relating a customer problem he has just experienced and is asking how you and Rosie would have handled it. You discuss it, then the discussion moves to other examples of situations that turn customers off and how each of you would handle those situations. Listed below are three major customer turnoffs, which are not specific to the technology industry.

1. Waiting in line while the CSR is chatting with a coworker

2. Red tape—such as refunds, credit checks, and adjustments on account

3. A company's failure to stand behind their products or services

Pair up with a classmate and role-play each of the given situations that can turn customers off. In a class discussion, be prepared to state how you, representing a specific company, might address each scenario in a positive way.

Project 8–5 The Mirror Principle

Helen Harrison, marketing director of a major manufacturing plant on the east coast, was driving back from a noon chamber of commerce meeting and was reflecting on a statement made by the luncheon speaker. The speaker described the mirror principle by saying, "Your employees won't treat your customers better than you treat your employees." Given the increasingly fragile employee morale, decrease in sales, and increase in customer service complaints at the plant over the past six months, Helen is wondering whether this is what is happening in her company.

1. If you were Helen, in what ways would you translate your feelings into an action plan for improvement?

_____

_____

_____

2. What steps would be included in your action plan to turn these problematic customer service issues around?

_____

_____

_____

HANDS-ON PROJECTS

Project 8–6 Customer Service Satisfaction and the Budget

It is budget time at On-Time Technology Products, and Mr. MacGibson is seeking input from employees in order to develop a realistic budget for next year. One budgeting change he is considering is to increase the amount of money allocated to the customer service department by 8 percent. Sam Brown, Vice President of Sales, has advised him that just committing more resources to customer service will not necessarily increase customer satisfaction and loyalty. Nonetheless, Mr. MacGibson needs more input and has asked you and the other CSRs to respond to the following three customer service situations in order to acquire more information as he prepares the budget.

Set up a class panel discussion to address these questions:

1. In what ways could a higher budget assist On-Time Technology Products to make credits and adjustments to customer accounts easier?

_____

_____

_____

2. In what ways could a higher budget assist On-Time Technology Products in providing information and answers to customers in a more timely way?

_____

_____

_____

3. Can allocating more money to a department really solve customer service problems? Why or why not?

_____

_____

_____

CHAPTER 9

AN OVERVIEW OF ETHICS

As you read this chapter, consider the following questions:

- ◆ What is ethics, and why is it important to act according to a code of principles?
- ◆ Why is business ethics becoming increasingly important?
- ◆ What are corporations doing to improve business ethics?
- ◆ Why are corporations interested in fostering good business ethics?
- ◆ What approach can you take to ensure ethical decision making?
- ◆ What trends have increased the risk of using information technology unethically?

Quote

Man, when perfected, is the best of animals, but when separated from law and justice, he is the worst of all.

—Aristotle

Vignette
Parent Company of Philip Morris Strives for Integrity

"Nothing is more important than our commitment to integrity—no financial objective, no marketing target, no effort to outdo the competition. Our commitment to integrity must always come first," said Louis C. Camilleri. Coming from the CEO of Altria Group, the parent company of Philip Morris of tobacco fame, such a statement might give pause to many Americans. Yet, Camilleri was referring to a massive initiative to establish a corporate code of conduct among Altria enterprises.

Led by Camilleri, the board of directors, and senior officers, the Altria Compliance and Integrity program has searched for ways to ensure that the code filters down to its employees at all levels. Employees receive customized handbooks that are translated into their native languages and cover information they need to know. Managers receive much more information about the code than their workers. Online courses focus on specific risks and on-the-job scenarios. Employees also watch skits staged with professional actors, answer questions, and engage in discussions with managers and other workers.

At the same time, Altria encourages employees to report violations of the code. Not only can employees approach the Human Resources Department and other departments, they can call a 24-hour Integrity Helpline and voice concerns anonymously. The helpline provides translation services for more than 100 languages. Altria's policy states that employees can be disciplined and even fired for retaliating against anyone who has made a complaint in good faith.

Altria conducts annual audits to determine risk and review best practices. Compliance and Integrity managers have also met with more than 150 employees to help shape the content of their code, which includes such goals as producing accurate records, protecting company assets, and dealing with customers honestly. Altria appears committed to implementing this code. Yet one goal—responding to society's expectation of Altria—may prove increasingly challenging to a company whose products include a carcinogen known to cause approximately 87 percent of all lung cancer deaths in the United States.

What Is Ethics?

Each society forms a set of rules that establishes the boundaries of generally accepted behavior. These rules are often expressed in statements about how people should behave, and they fit together to form the **moral code** by which a society lives. Unfortunately, the different rules often have contradictions, and you can be uncertain about which rule to follow. For instance, if you witness a friend copy someone else's answers while taking an exam, you might be caught in a conflict between loyalty to your friend and the value of telling the truth. Sometimes, the rules do not seem to cover new situations, and you must determine how to apply the existing rules or develop new ones. You may strongly support personal privacy, but in a time when employers track employee e-mail and Internet usage, what rules do you think are acceptable to govern the appropriate use of company resources?

The term **morality** refers to social conventions about right and wrong that are so widely shared that they become the basis for an established consensus. However, one's view of what is moral may vary by age, cultural group, ethnic background, religion, and gender. There is widespread agreement on the immorality of murder, theft, and arson, but other behaviors that are accepted in one culture might be unacceptable in another. For example, in the United States it is perfectly acceptable to place one's elderly parents in a managed care facility in their declining years. In most Middle Eastern countries, however, elderly parents would never be placed in such a facility; they remain at home and are cared for by other family members.

Another example concerns attitudes toward the illegal copying of software (piracy), which range from strong opposition to acceptance as a standard approach to business. In 2003, 36 percent of all software in circulation worldwide was pirated, at a cost of $29 billion to software vendors. The highest piracy rates were in Vietnam and China, where 92 percent of the software was pirated. In the United States, the piracy rate was 22 percent.

Even within the same society, people can have strong disagreements over important moral issues—in the United States, for example, issues such as abortion, the death penalty, and gun control are continuously debated, and both sides feel their arguments are on solid moral ground.

Definition of Ethics

Ethics is a set of beliefs about right and wrong behavior. Ethical behavior conforms to generally accepted social norms, many of which are almost universal. However, although nearly everyone would agree that lying and cheating are unethical, what constitutes ethical behavior on many other issues is a matter of opinion. For example, most people would not steal an umbrella from someone's home, but a person who finds an umbrella in a theater might be tempted to keep it. A person's opinion of what represents ethical behavior is strongly influenced by a combination of family influences, life experiences, education, religious beliefs, personal values, and peer influences.

As children grow, they learn complicated tasks—walking, riding a bike, writing the alphabet—that they perform out of habit for the rest of their lives. People also develop habits that make it easier to choose between what society considers good or bad. **Virtues** are habits that incline people to do what is acceptable, and **vices** are habits of unacceptable behavior. Fairness, generosity, honesty, and loyalty are examples of virtues, while vanity, greed, envy, and anger are considered vices. People's virtues and vices help define their **value system,** the complex scheme of moral values by which they live.

The Importance of Integrity

Your moral principles are statements of what you believe to be rules of right conduct. As a child, you may have been taught not to lie, cheat, or steal or have anything to do with those who do. As an adult who makes more complex decisions, you often reflect on your principles when you consider what to do in different situations: Is it okay to lie to protect someone's feelings? Can you keep the extra $10 you received when the cashier mistook your $10 bill for a $20 bill? Should you intervene with a coworker who seems to have an alcohol or chemical dependency problem? Is it okay to exaggerate your work experience on a résumé? Can you cut some corners on a project to meet a tight deadline?

A person who acts with **integrity** acts in accordance with a personal code of principles—integrity is one of the cornerstones of ethical behavior. One approach to acting with integrity is to extend to all people the same respect and consideration that you desire. Unfortunately, this consistency can be difficult to achieve, particularly when you are in a situation that conflicts with your moral standards. For example, you might believe it is important to do as your employer requests and that you should be fairly compensated for your work. However, if your employer insists that you not report recent overtime hours due to budget constraints, a moral conflict arises. You can do as your employer requests or you can insist on being fairly compensated, but you cannot do both. In this situation, you may be forced to compromise one of your principles and act with an apparent lack of integrity.

Another form of inconsistency emerges if you apply moral standards differently according to the situation or the people involved. To be consistent and act with integrity, you must apply the same moral standards in all situations. For example, you might consider it morally acceptable to tell a "little white lie" to spare a friend some pain or embarrassment, but would you lie to a work colleague or customer about a business issue to avoid unpleasantness? Clearly, many ethical dilemmas are not about right versus wrong but involve choices between right versus right. For example, it is right to protect the Alaskan wildlife from being spoiled, and it is right to find new sources of oil to maintain U.S. reserves, but how do you balance these two concerns?

The remainder of this chapter provides an introduction to ethics in the business world. It discusses the importance of ethics in business, outlines what businesses can do to improve their ethics, points out that good ethics is not always good business, provides advice for creating an ethical work environment, and suggests a model for ethical decision making. The chapter concludes with a discussion of ethics as it relates to information technology (IT) and provides a brief overview of the remainder of the text.

ETHICS IN THE BUSINESS WORLD

Risk is the product of multiplying the likelihood of an event by the impact of its occurrence. Thus, if the likelihood of an event is high and its potential negative impact is large, the risk is considered great. Ethics has risen to the top of business agendas because the risks associated with inappropriate behavior have increased, both in their likelihood and their potential negative impact.

Several corporate trends have increased the likelihood of unethical behavior. First, greater globalization has created a much more complex work environment that spans diverse societies and cultures, making it much more difficult to apply principles and codes of ethics consistently. For example, numerous U.S. companies have garnered negative publicity for moving operations to third-world countries where employees work in conditions that would not be acceptable in most developed parts of the world.

Employees, shareholders, and regulatory agencies are increasingly sensitive to violations of accounting standards, failures to disclose substantial changes in business conditions to investors, nonconformance with required health and safety practices, and production of unsafe or substandard products. Such heightened vigilance raises the risk of financial loss for businesses that do not foster ethical practices or run afoul of required standards. For example, Enron's accounting practices hid the real value of the firm, and in late 2001 the energy company was forced to file for bankruptcy. The case was notorious, but many other recent scandals have occurred in IT companies in spite of safeguards that were enacted as a result of the Enron debacle:

- The U.S. Securities and Exchange Commission (SEC) filed fraud charges against WorldCom in June 2002 for inflating its earnings by $11 billion. The stock peaked at $64.50 in June 1999 and dropped to less than $1 per share three years later. WorldCom eventually became the largest bankruptcy in U.S. history after Chairman Bernard Ebbers resigned and the extent of the fraud was revealed. (It since has emerged from bankruptcy under the name MCI Inc. to become the object of an acquisition war between Qwest and Verizon Communications, which Verizon eventually won.) Under a judgment released in May 2003 by a U.S. District Court in New York, MCI was required to pay a civil penalty of $1.51 billion to defrauded shareholders and bondholders, although the amount was reduced to $500 million under terms of a bankruptcy settlement. Ebbers was convicted in March 2005 of helping to orchestrate the massive accounting fraud. In addition, 10 members of the WorldCom board of directors avoided trial by agreeing to pay a total of $18 million on top of the $250 million they lost when the stock collapsed.

- Qwest Communications International Inc., the primary local phone provider in 14 western states, had been under investigation by the SEC since 2002. On the same day that Ebbers was convicted, the SEC charged former Qwest CEO Joseph Nacchio and six other executives with orchestrating massive financial fraud from April 1999 to March 2002. In 2000, the company allegedly misstated that $3 billion from a one-time sale was a recurring revenue in order to ensure a merger with US West. Qwest executives allegedly reaped tens of millions of dollars in profit while hiding the scheme from investors and the public.

- In 2004, Adelphia Communications Corp. founder John Rigas and his son Timothy were convicted in federal court on charges of conspiracy, bank fraud, and securities fraud. They were charged with hiding $2.3 billion in debt at the cable company, deceiving investors, and stealing company cash to line their own pockets. Although most of the fraud took the form of hidden debt, the trial provided examples of excessive extravagance that has marked other white-collar trials. The prosecutor alleged that Rigas ordered 17 company cars and the company purchase of 3600 acres of timberland for $26 million to preserve the pristine view outside his Coudersport home.

- Several former Computer Associates (CA) executives pleaded guilty to civil and criminal fraud and obstruction of justice for systematically recording sales revenue before contracts were finalized, inflating CA's financial results by about $2.2 billion during 2000 and 2001. The scandal eventually led to the resignation of Sanjay Kumar, the company's CEO, in April 2004. In May 2005, the company said that a continuing review of its accounting practices turned up more improperly recorded transactions from 1998 through 2001. This required CA to restate its financial reports again, reducing revenue in prior periods by up to $110 million in aggregate. (For more on the CA scandal, see the Cases section at the end of the chapter.)

These cases have led to an increased focus on business ethics. Read the following Legal Overview to find out more about one attempt by the U.S. Congress to improve business ethics.

Legal Overview
The Sarbanes-Oxley Act

The U.S. Public Company Accounting Reform and Investor Protection Act of 2002—better known as the Sarbanes-Oxley Act or simply SOX—was enacted in response to public outrage over several major accounting scandals, including those at Enron, WorldCom, Tyco, Adelphia, Global Crossing, and Qwest, plus numerous restated financial reports that clearly demonstrated a lack of oversight within corporate America. The sponsors, Senator Paul Sarbanes (D-Maryland) and Representative Michael Oxley (R-Ohio), wanted to renew investors' trust in corporate executives and their financial reports.

Sarbanes-Oxley Act Section 404, Management Report on Internal Control over Financial Reporting, states that annual reports must contain a signed statement by the CEO and CFO attesting that the information in any SEC filing is accurate. The company must also submit to an audit to prove that it has controls in place to ensure accurate information. The penalties for false attestation can include up to 20 years in jail and significant monetary fines for senior executives. As a result, CEOs and CFOs, their staff, and others spend significant time and energy to document and test internal control processes. The average company spends an estimated 0.1 percent of annual revenues to conform to SOX; for example, a company with annual sales of $10 billion will spend about $10 million, including employee time, fees for outside resources, and software.

A key provision of the act was the creation of the Public Company Accounting Oversight Board (PCAOB). The PCAOB provides oversight for auditors of public companies, including establishing quality control standards for company audits and inspecting the quality controls at audit firms under its oversight. The PCAOB is made up of five full-time appointed members and is overseen by the SEC.

The act attempts to ensure that internal controls or rules are in place to govern the creation and documentation of financial statements. However, it is not specific; for example, it does not define a required set of internal control practices or specify how a business must store records. It simply describes which records to store and for how long. The legislation not only affects the financial side of corporations, it affects IT departments that must store a corporation's electronic records. The act specifies that a firm must have adequate controls, but not necessarily automated controls. Thus, a company can decide whether to make a significant investment in technology that automates its manual processes or make a smaller investment in additional people to double-check everything manually. The SEC set a deadline of November 15, 2004, for the rule to take effect, but problems didn't surface until companies began to file their annual reports and 10K reports in the first quarter of 2005. On March 2, the SEC extended the deadline to July 15, 2006, for small and midsized companies and foreign firms.

In November 2004, SunTrust Banks Inc. became one of the first companies to report an accounting problem that made it impossible to meet its SOX reporting requirements. The firm said an internal audit had found numerous errors in the loan loss allowance calculations for its first and second quarters that were not immediately investigated and corrected. Additional problems revealed inadequate internal control procedures, insufficient validation and testing, and a failure to detect errors in the allowance calculations. The bank had to restate its first- and second-quarter 2004 financial results, and three employees were fired.

In March 2005, more than a dozen companies reported deficiencies with their internal accounting controls, forcing them to delay the filing of annual reports to regulators. The share prices of most of these companies dropped substantially after they disclosed that they needed more time to file audited financial reports with the SEC. These companies joined some 500 others that told shareholders they couldn't ensure their financial reports were accurate and reliable under the new rules.

Because IT systems are used to generate, change, store, and disseminate data, the IT organization must build controls that ensure the information stands up to audit scrutiny. Critical elements include controls that ensure the overall performance and integrity of financial systems, business process applications, and other applications. The audit emphasizes segregation of duties to avoid potential fraud—for example, the same person cannot generate a purchase order and approve its payment—and limiting the authorization to perform critical functions to a few people; for example, only people in quality control should be able to release products that are placed on hold, pending the results of quality tests. The audit also requires companies to document who performs specific roles within the system. In the future, the SEC might revise its interpretation of SOX, creating additional work for IT organizations.

Why Fostering Good Business Ethics Is Important

Corporations have at least five reasons for promoting a work environment in which they encourage employees to act ethically when making business decisions:

1. To gain the goodwill of the community

2. To create an organization that operates consistently

3. To produce good business

4. To protect the organization and its employees from legal action

5. To avoid unfavorable publicity

Gaining the Goodwill of the Community

Although organizations exist primarily to earn profits or provide services to customers, they also have some basic responsibilities to society. Many corporations recognize these responsibilities and make a serious effort to fulfill them. Often, they declare these responsibilities in a formal statement of their company's principles or beliefs. Their socially responsible activities include making contributions to charitable organizations and nonprofit institutions, providing benefits for employees in excess of any legal requirements, and choosing economic opportunities that might be more socially desirable than profitable.

The goodwill that socially responsible activities create can make it easier for corporations to conduct their business. For example, a company known for treating its employees well will find it easier to compete for the best job candidates. On the other hand, companies viewed as harmful to their community may suffer a disadvantage. For example, a corporation that pollutes the air and water may find that adverse publicity reduces sales, impedes relationships with some business partners, and attracts unwanted government attention.

Creating an Organization That Operates Consistently

Organizations develop and abide by values to create a consistent approach that meets the needs of their stakeholders—shareholders, employees, customers, suppliers, and the community. They need to emphasize workplace issues that affect their corporate strengths, weaknesses, opportunities, and threats. Although each company's value system is different, many share the following values:

- Operate with honesty and integrity, staying true to corporate principles.
- Operate according to standards of ethical conduct, in words and action.
- Treat colleagues, customers, and consumers with respect.
- Strive to be the best at what matters most to the company.
- Accept personal responsibility for actions.
- Value diversity.
- Make decisions based on facts and principles.

Good Ethics Can Mean Good Business

In many cases, good ethics can mean good business and improved profits. Companies that produce safe and effective products avoid costly recalls and lawsuits. Companies that provide excellent service maintain their customers instead of losing them to competitors. Companies that develop and maintain strong employee relations suffer less turnover and enjoy better employee morale. Suppliers and other business partners often prefer to work with companies that operate in a fair and ethical manner.

Likewise, bad ethics can lead to bad business results. For example, many employees can develop negative attitudes if they perceive a difference between their own values and the values stated or implied by an organization's actions. In such environments, employees often act to defend themselves against anticipated punishment or retaliate against poor treatment. A bad ethical environment destroys employee commitment to organizational goals and objectives, creates low morale, fosters poor performance, erodes employee involvement in corporate improvement initiatives, and builds indifference to the organization's needs.

Protecting the Corporation and Its Employees from Legal Actions

In 1991, the U.S. Justice Department published sentencing guidelines that suggested more lenient treatment for convicted executives if their companies had ethics programs. Fines for criminal violations can be lowered by up to 80 percent if the organization has implemented an ethics management program and cooperates with authorities. These measures are covered in Chapter Eight of the Federal Sentencing Guidelines for Organizations.

The following list briefly describes the key features an organization must implement to show it has an effective program of compliance and ethics.

- Identify its core beliefs, which need to include a commitment to complying with the letter and spirit of the law and ethical conduct.
- Understand the strengths and weaknesses of its culture and organizational capacities.
- Scan its business environment, presumably on an enterprise-wide basis, to determine what pressures the organization faces, especially the risk of criminal conduct and violating other applicable laws, and more broadly, to gather benchmarking data to compare to industry standards and best practices.
- Determine, relative to its goals and objectives and baseline data of its prior performance, what outcomes should be expected of the program.
- Identify targets and measurable indicators of expected program outcomes.
- Design, implement, and enforce a program that will "exercise due diligence to prevent, detect, and report criminal conduct and otherwise promote an organizational culture that encourages ethical conduct and a commitment to compliance with all applicable law."
- Regularly evaluate its program to determine if it is effective, and capture what the organization learns along the way.

Avoiding Unfavorable Publicity

The public reputation of a company strongly influences the value of its stock, how consumers regard its products and services, the degree of oversight it receives from government agencies, and the amount of support and cooperation it receives from business partners. Thus, some companies are motivated to build a strong ethics program to avoid negative publicity. If an organization is perceived as operating ethically, customers, business partners, shareholders, consumer advocates, financial institutions, and regulatory bodies will regard it more favorably.

Companies that operate unethically often suffer negative consequences and bad publicity. A recent example involves the Federal National Mortgage Association (Fannie Mae), which helps low-income and middle-income Americans finance home mortgages. The Office of Federal Housing Enterprise Oversight (OFHEO) began investigating Fannie Mae in September 2004 and found serious accounting problems, including earnings manipulation and poor internal controls. The SEC ordered Fannie Mae in December 2004 to restate its earnings back to 2001, a correction estimated at $9 billion. In February 2005, the OFHEO reported additional problems with accounting for securities and loans and improper practices to spread the impact of income and expenses over time. As a result, several Fannie Mae executives were forced out by the board of directors and changes were made in its staff of 1400 information systems and services workers. Fannie Mae stock dropped below $58 per share on the New York Stock Exchange (NYSE) by March 2005, their lowest level in more than four years and 30 percent below a high of nearly $80 in March 2004.

Improving Corporate Ethics

The risks of unethical behavior are increasing, so the improvement of business ethics is becoming more important. The following sections explain some of the actions corporations can take to improve business ethics.

Appointing a Corporate Ethics Officer

Corporate ethics can be broadly defined to include ethical conduct, legal compliance, and corporate social responsibility. The primary functions of a corporate ethics policy include setting standards, building awareness, and handling internal reports—tasks that are either not consolidated or handled well in many organizations. As a result, many organizations pull these functions together under a corporate officer to ensure that they receive sufficient emphasis and cohesive treatment.

The **corporate ethics officer** is a senior-level manager who provides vision and direction in the area of business conduct. Ethics officers come from diverse backgrounds such as legal staff, human resources, finance, auditing, security, or line operations. Their role includes "integrating their organization's ethics and values initiatives, compliance activities, and business conduct practices into the decision-making processes at all levels of the organization." Typically, the ethics officer tries to establish an environment that encourages ethical decision making through the actions described in this chapter. Specific responsibilities include "complete oversight of the ethics function, collecting and analyzing data, developing and interpreting ethics policy, developing and administering ethics education and training, and overseeing ethics investigations."

The presence of a corporate ethics officer has become increasingly common. There is even a professional association, the Ethics Officer Association (EOA), for managers of ethics, compliance, and business conduct programs. "The EOA provides ethics officers with training and a variety of conferences and meetings for exchanging best practices in a frank, candid manner." As of March 2005, there were more than 700 EOA member companies, including the well-known IT companies shown in the following list.

Adelphia Communications Group	Intel
AOL Time Warner	MCI
AT&T	Microsoft
BAE Systems	Oracle
British Telecom	QUALCOMM
Cingular Wireless	Qwest
Computer Associates, International	Sprint
Dell Computer	Sun Microsystems
Hewlett-Packard	Texas Instruments

However, simply naming a corporate ethics officer does not automatically improve ethics; hard work and effort are required to establish and provide ongoing support for an organizational ethics program.

Ethical Standards Set by Board of Directors

The board of directors is responsible for the careful and responsible management of an organization. In a for-profit corporation, the board's primary objective is to oversee the organization's business activities and management for the benefit of all stakeholders, including shareholders, customers, suppliers, and the community. In a nonprofit corporation, the board reports to a different set of stakeholders, particularly the local communities that the nonprofit serves.

The board fulfills some of its responsibilities directly and assigns others to various committees. The board is not normally responsible for day-to-day management and operations; these responsibilities are delegated to the organization's management team. However, the board is responsible for supervising the management team.

Directors of the company are expected to conduct themselves according to the highest standards of personal and professional integrity. Directors are also expected to set the standard for company-wide ethical conduct and ensure compliance with laws and regulations.

As you learned earlier in this chapter, the passage of Sarbanes-Oxley led to significant reforms in the content and preparation of disclosure documents by public companies. Section 406 of the act requires public companies to disclose whether they have codes of ethics and to disclose any waivers of those codes for certain members of senior management. The SEC also approved significant reforms by the NYSE and NASDAQ that, among other things, require companies listed on these exchanges to have codes of ethics that apply to all employees, senior management, and directors.

Establishing a Corporate Code of Ethics

A **code of ethics** highlights an organization's key ethical issues and identifies the overarching values and principles that are important to the organization and its decision making. The code frequently includes a set of formal, written statements about the purpose of the organization, its values, and the principles that guide its employees' actions. An organization's code of ethics applies to its directors, officers, and employees. The code of ethics should focus employees on areas of ethical risk relating to their role in the organization, provide guidance to help them recognize and deal with ethical issues, and provide mechanisms for reporting unethical conduct and fostering a culture of honesty and accountability in an organization. The code of ethics helps ensure that employees abide by the law, follow necessary regulations, and behave in an ethical manner.

A code of ethics cannot gain company-wide acceptance unless it is developed with employee participation and fully endorsed by the organization's leadership. It must also be easily accessible by employees, shareholders, business partners, and the public. The code of ethics must continually be applied to a company's decision making and emphasized as an important part of its culture. Breaches in the code of ethics must be identified and treated appropriately so that its relevance is not undermined.

Establishing a code of ethics is an important step for any company, and a growing number have done so

In March 2005, Business Ethics magazine rated U.S.-based, publicly held companies using a statistical analysis of corporate service to seven stakeholder groups—employees, customers, community, minorities and women, shareholders, the environment, and non-U.S. stakeholders. The top IT company, based on performance between 2000 and 2004, was Intel Corporation, the world's largest computer chip maker. Intel's code of ethics is summarized in the following paragraph.

Honest and ethical conduct, including the ethical handling of actual or perceived conflicts of interest between personal and business relationships, is our rule every day and for all that we do. If we are to maximize the value we create for our stockholders, it is the personal responsibility of each of us to: (1) comply with applicable laws (including statutes, controlling case law, agency regulations and orders, and other administrative directives) and Intel guidelines, (2) employ technical excellence and integrity to do the best we can to provide timely, accurate and understandable reporting of actual and forward-looking financial information, (3) employ our business processes and guidelines to do the best we can to base our business decisions on sound economic analysis (including a prudent consideration of risks), and (4) safeguard and utilize our physical, financial, and intellectual property assets to the best and most prudent effect.

A more detailed version of Intel's code of ethics is spelled out in a 22-page document that offers employees guidelines designed to deter wrongdoing, promote honest and ethical conduct, and comply with applicable laws and regulations. Intel's code of ethics also expresses its policies regarding the environment, health and safety, diversity, nondiscrimination, supplier expectations, privacy, and business continuity.

Conducting Social Audits

An increasing number of companies conduct social audits of their policies and practices. In a **social audit,** companies identify ethical lapses they committed in the past and set directives for avoiding similar missteps in the future. For example, each year Intel sets socialresponsibility goals and tracks results against those goals. Intel's annual report on its socialresponsibility efforts shares the information with employees, shareholders, investors, analysts, customers, suppliers, government officials, and the communities in which Intel operates. Here are a few highlights from its 2003 report:

- Intel contributed more than $100 million in cash gifts worldwide.
- Global waste recycling teams exceeded their goals by recycling more than 66 percent of chemical waste and 74 percent of solid waste worldwide. These totals represented 40,000 tons of materials recycled.
- Intel has trained more than 1.5 million teachers in 33 countries to use technology effectively and improve student learning.
- Intel remained at world-class levels of health and safety performance.

Requiring Employees to Take Ethics Training

The ancient Greek philosophers believed that personal convictions about right and wrong behavior could be improved through education. Today, most psychologists agree with them. Lawrence Kohlberg, the late Harvard psychologist, found that many factors stimulate a person's moral development, but one of the most crucial is education. Other researchers have repeatedly supported these findings—people can continue their moral development through further education that involves critical thinking and examining contemporary issues.

Thus, a company's code of ethics must be promoted and continually communicated within the organization, from top to bottom. Organizations should show employees examples of how to apply the code of ethics in real life. One approach is through a comprehensive ethics education program that encourages employees to act responsibly and ethically. Such programs are often presented in small workshop formats in which employees apply the organization's code of ethics to hypothetical but realistic case studies. For example, Procter & Gamble requires all its employees to take a workshop on the topic of principle-based decision making, based on principles in the corporate code of ethics. Workshop participants must decide how to best respond to real-life ethical problems, such as giving honest and constructive feedback to an employee who is not meeting expectations. Employees are also given examples of recent company decisions made using principle-based decision making. Not only do these courses make employees more aware of a company's code of ethics and how to apply it, the courses demonstrate that the company intends to operate in an ethical manner. The existence of formal training programs can also reduce a company's liability in the event of legal action.

Including Ethical Criteria in Employee Appraisals

Employees are increasingly evaluated on their demonstration of qualities and characteristics that are stated in the corporate code of ethics. For example, many companies base a portion of their employee performance evaluations on treating others fairly and with respect, operating effectively in a multicultural environment, accepting personal accountability to meet business needs, continually developing themselves and others, and operating openly and honestly with suppliers, customers, and other employees. These factors are considered along with more traditional criteria used in performance appraisals, such as an employee's overall contribution to moving the business ahead, successful completion of projects, and maintenance of good customer relations.

When Good Ethics Result in Short-Term Losses

Operating ethically does not always guarantee business success. Many organizations that operate outside the United States have found that the "business as usual" climate in some foreign countries can place them at a significant competitive disadvantage.

For example, a major global telecommunications company faced significant competitive disadvantages by consistently applying its corporate values to its South American business. Although the organization's code of ethics prohibited the practice of financially "influencing" decision makers on project bids, its competition did not play by the same rules. As a result, the company lost many projects and millions of dollars in revenues. Senior management argued in favor of integrity and the consistent application of corporate ethics, reasoning that situational ethics was wrong and that the practice could be hard to stop once it was started. Their hope was that good ethics would prove to be good business in the long term.

Creating an Ethical Work Environment

Most employees want to perform their jobs successfully and ethically, but good employees sometimes make bad ethical choices. Employees in highly competitive workplaces often feel pressures from aggressive competitors, cutthroat suppliers, unrealistic budgets, minimum quotas, tight deadlines, and bonus incentives for meeting performance goals. Employees may also be encouraged to do "whatever it takes" to get the job done. Such environments can make some employees feel pressure to engage in unethical conduct to meet management's expectations, especially if there are no corporate codes of conduct and no strong examples of senior management practicing ethical behavior. Table 9-1 shows how management's behavior can result in unethical employee behavior, and Table 9-2 provides a manager's checklist for establishing an ethical workplace; to each question in the latter table, the preferred answer is yes.

Employees must have a knowledgeable and potent resource with whom they can discuss perceived unethical practices. For example, Intel expects employees to report suspected violations of its code of ethics to a manager, the Legal or Internal Audit Departments, or a business unit's legal counsel. Employees may also report violations anonymously through an internal Web site dedicated to ethics. Senior management at Intel has made it clear that any employee can report suspected violations of corporate business principles without fear of reprisal or retaliation.

How management can affect employees' ethical behavior

Managerial behavior that can encourage unethical behavior	Possible employee reaction
Set and hold people accountable for meeting "stretch" goals, quotas, and budgets	"My boss wants results, not excuses, so I have to cut corners to meet the goals my boss has set."
Fail to provide a corporate code of ethics and operating principles to guide decision making	"Because there are no guidelines, I don't think my conduct is really wrong or illegal."
Fail to act in an ethical manner and set a poor example for others to follow	"I have seen other successful people take unethical actions and not suffer negative repercussions."
Fail to hold people accountable for unethical actions	"No one will ever know the difference, and if they do, so what?"
When employees are hired, put a 3-inch binder titled "Corporate Business Ethics, Policies, and Procedures" on their desks. Tell them to "read it when you have time and sign the attached form that says you read and understand the corporate policy."	"This is overwhelming. Can't they just give me the essentials? I can never absorb all this."

Manager's checklist for establishing an ethical work environment

Questions	Yes	No
Does your company have a corporate code of ethics?	☐	☐
Was the corporate code of ethics developed with broad input from employees at all levels within the organization, and does it have their support?	☐	☐
Is the corporate code of ethics concise and easy to understand, and does it identify the values you need to operate consistently and meet the needs of your stakeholders?	☐	☐
Do all employees have easy access to a copy of the corporate code of conduct, and have they all signed a document stating that they have read and understood it?	☐	☐
Do employees participate in annual training to reinforce the values and principles that make up the corporate code of ethics?	☐	☐
Do you set an example by communicating the corporate code of ethics and actively using it in your decision making?	☐	☐
Do you evaluate and provide feedback to employees on how they operate with respect to the values and principles in your corporate code of ethics?	☐	☐
Do you seek feedback from your employees to ensure that their work environment does not create conflicts with the corporate code of ethics?	☐	☐
Do employees believe that you are fair, and do they seek your advice when they see coworkers violating the company's code of ethics?	☐	☐
Do employees have an avenue, such as an anonymous hotline, for reporting infractions of the code of ethics?	☐	☐
Are employees aware of sanctions for breaching the code of ethics?	☐	☐

Ethical Decision Making

Often in business, the ethically correct course of action is clear and easy to follow. Exceptions occur, however, when ethical considerations come into conflict with the practical demands of business. Dealing with these situations is challenging and can even be risky to one's career. How, exactly, should you think through an ethical issue? What questions should you ask, and what factors should you consider? This section lays out a seven-step approach that can help guide your ethical decision making; however, the process is not a simple, linear activity. Keep in mind that information you gain or a decision you make in one step may cause you to go back and revisit previous steps.

The seven steps are summarized in the following list and explained in the following sections:

- Get the facts.
- Identify stakeholders and their positions.
- Consider the consequences of your decision.
- Weigh various guidelines and principles.
- Develop and evaluate options.
- Review your decision.
- Evaluate the results of your decision.

Getting the Facts

Innocent situations can often become unnecessary controversies because no one bothers to check the facts. For example, you might see your boss receive what appears to be an employment application from a job applicant and then throw the application in the trash after the applicant leaves. This would violate your company's policy to treat each applicant with respect and to maintain a record of all applications for one year. You could report your boss for failure to follow the policy or you could take a moment to speak directly to your boss. You might be pleasantly surprised to find out that the situation was not as it appeared. Perhaps the "applicant" was actually a salesperson promoting a product for which your company had no use, and the "application" was marketing literature.

Identifying the Stakeholders and Their Positions

A **stakeholder** is someone who stands to gain or lose from how a situation is resolved. Stakeholders often include others besides people who are directly involved in an issue. Identifying the stakeholders helps you better understand the impact of your decision and could help you make a better decision. Unfortunately, it may also cause you to lose sleep from wondering how you may affect the lives of others. You may recognize the need to involve stakeholders in the decision and thus gain their support for the recommended course of action. What is at stake for each stakeholder? What does each stakeholder value, and what outcome does the stakeholder want? Do some stakeholders have a greater stake because they have special needs or because the company has special obligations to them? To what degree should they be involved in the decision?

Considering the Consequences of Your Decision

You can view the consequences of a decision from several perspectives. Often, your decision directly affects you, although you must guard against thinking too narrowly and focusing on what is best for you. Another perspective is to consider the harmful and beneficial effects your decision might have on the stakeholders. A third perspective is to ask whether your decision will help the organization meet its goals and objectives. Finally, you should consider the decision's impact on the broader community of other organizations and institutions, the public, and the environment. As you view problems and proposed solutions from each of these perspectives, you may gain additional insights that affect your decision.

Weighing Various Guidelines and Principles

Do any laws apply to your decision? You certainly don't want to violate a law that can lead to a fine or imprisonment for yourself or others. If the decision does not have legal implications, what corporate policies or guidelines apply? What guidance does the corporate code of ethics offer? Will any of your personal principles affect your decision?

Philosophers have developed many approaches to deal with moral issues. Four of the most common approaches, which are summarized in Table 9-3 and discussed later in this section, provide a framework for decision makers to reflect on the acceptability of their actions and evaluate moral judgments. People must find the appropriate balance between all applicable laws, corporate principles, and moral guidelines to help them make decisions.

Philosophical theories for ethical decision making

Approach to dealing with moral issues	Principle
Virtue ethics approach	The ethical choice best reflects moral virtues in yourself and your community
Utilitarian approach	The ethical choice produces the greatest excess of benefits over harm
Fairness approach	The ethical choice treats everyone the same and shows no favoritism or discrimination
Common good approach	The ethical choice advances the common good

Virtue ethics approach.   Virtue ethics focuses on how you should behave and think about relationships if you are concerned with your daily life in a community. It does not define a formula for ethical decision making, but suggests that when faced with a complex ethical dilemma, people either do what they are most comfortable doing or what they think a person they admire would do. The assumption is that people are guided by their virtues to reach the "right" decision. A proponent of virtue ethics believes that a disposition to do the right thing is more effective than following a set of principles and rules and that people should perform moral acts out of habit, not introspection.

Virtue ethics can be applied to the business world by equating the virtues of a good businessperson with those of a good person. However, businesspeople face situations that are peculiar to business, so they may need to tailor their ethics accordingly. For example, honesty and openness when dealing with others is generally considered virtuous; however, a corporate purchasing manager who negotiates a multimillion dollar deal might need to be vague in discussions with competing suppliers.

A problem with the virtue ethics approach is that it doesn't provide much of a guide for action. The definition of virtue cannot be worked out objectively; it depends on the circumstances—you work it out as you go. For example, bravery is a great virtue in many circumstances, but in others it may be foolish. The right thing to do in a situation depends on which culture you're in and what the cultural norm dictates.

Utilitarian approach.   This approach to ethical decision making states that you should choose the action or policy that has the best overall consequences for all people who are directly or indirectly affected. The goal is to find the single greatest good by balancing the interests of all affected parties.

Utilitarianism fits easily with the concept of value in economics and the use of cost-benefit analysis in business. Business managers, legislators, and scientists weigh the benefits and harm of policies when deciding whether to invest resources in building a new plant in a foreign country, to enact a new law, or to approve a new prescription drug, respectively. A complication of this approach is that measuring and comparing the values of certain benefits and costs is often difficult, if not impossible. How do you assign a value to human life or to a pristine wildlife environment? It can also be difficult to predict the full benefits and harm that result from a decision.

Fairness approach.   This approach focuses on how fairly actions and policies distribute benefits and burdens among people affected by the decision. The guiding principle of this approach is to treat all people the same. However, decisions made with this approach can be influenced by personal biases toward a particular group, and the decision makers may not even realize their bias. If the intended goal of an action or policy is to provide benefits to a target group, other affected groups may consider the decision unfair.

Common good approach.

This approach to decision making is based on a vision of society as a community whose members work together to achieve a common set of values and goals. Decisions and policies that use this approach attempt to implement social systems, institutions, and environments that everyone depends on and that benefit all people. Examples include an effective education system, a safe and efficient transportation system, and accessible and affordable health care.

As with the other approaches to ethical decision making, there are complications. People clearly have different ideas about what constitutes the common good, which makes consensus difficult. In addition, maintaining the common good often requires some groups to bear greater costs than others—for instance, homeowners pay property taxes to support public schools, but apartment dwellers do not.

Developing and Evaluating Options

In many cases, you can identify several answers to a complex ethical question. By listing the key principles that apply to the decision, you can usually focus on the two or three best options. What benefits and harm will each course of action produce, and which alternative will lead to the best overall consequences? The option you choose should be ethically defensible and should meet the legitimate needs of economic performance and the company's legal obligations.

Reviewing Your Decision

Is the decision consistent with your personal values as well as those of the organization? How would coworkers, stakeholders, business partners, friends, and family regard your decision if they knew the facts of the situation and the basis for your decision? Would they see it as right, fair, and good? If you belonged to any of the other stakeholder groups, would you be able to accept the decision as fair?

Evaluating the Results of Your Decision

After the organization implements the decision, monitor the results to see if it achieved the desired effect and observe its impact on employees and other affected parties. This evaluation will allow you to adjust and improve the process for future decisions.

ETHICS IN INFORMATION TECHNOLOGY

The growth of the Internet, the ability to capture and store vast amounts of personal data online, and greater reliance on information systems in all aspects of life have increased the risk of using information technology unethically. In the midst of the many IT breakthroughs in recent years, the importance of ethics and human values has been underemphasized—with a range of consequences. Here are some examples that raise public concern about the ethical use of information technology:

- Today's workers might have their e-mail and Internet access monitored while at work, as employers struggle to balance their need to manage important company assets and work time with employees' desire for privacy and self-direction.
- Millions of people have used peer-to-peer networks to download music and movies at no charge and in apparent violation of copyright laws.

- Organizations contact millions of people worldwide through unsolicited e-mail (spam) at an extremely low cost.
- Hackers break into databases of financial institutions and steal customer information, then use it to commit identity theft, opening new accounts and charging purchases to unsuspecting victims.
- Students around the world have been caught downloading material from the Internet and plagiarizing content for their term papers.
- Web sites plant cookies or spyware on visitors' hard drives to track their Internet activity.

This book is based on two fundamental tenets. First, the general public has not realized the critical importance of ethics as they apply to IT; too much emphasis has been placed on the technical issues. However, unlike most conventional tools, IT has a profound effect on society. IT professionals need to recognize this fact when they formulate policies that will affect the well-being of millions of consumers and have legal ramifications.

Second, in the corporate world, important technical decisions are often left to the technical experts. General business managers must assume greater responsibility for these decisions, but to do so they must be able to make broad-minded, objective, ethical decisions based on technical savvy, business know-how, and a sense of ethics. They must also try to create a working environment in which ethical dilemmas can be discussed openly, objectively, and constructively.

Thus, the goals of this text are to educate people about the tremendous impact of ethical issues in the successful and secure use of information technology; to motivate people to recognize these issues when making business decisions; and to provide tools, approaches, and useful insights for making ethical decisions.

SUMMARY

What is ethics, and why is it important to act according to a code of principles?

Ethics is a set of beliefs about right and wrong behavior. A person who acts with integrity acts in accordance with a personal code of principles. Integrity is one of the cornerstones of ethical behavior.

Why is business ethics becoming increasingly important?

Ethics in business is becoming more important because the risks associated with inappropriate behavior have grown in number, complexity, likelihood, and significance.

What are corporations doing to improve business ethics?

Corporations can appoint a corporate ethics officer, set ethical standards at a high organizational level, establish a corporate code of ethics, conduct social audits, require employees to take ethics training, and include ethical criteria in employee appraisals.

Why are corporations interested in fostering good business ethics?

Corporations want to protect themselves and their employees from legal action, to create an organization that operates consistently (because good ethics can be good business), to avoid negative publicity, and to gain the goodwill of the community. Being ethical, however, does not always guarantee business success.

What approach can you take to ensure ethical decision making?

One approach involves seven steps: get the facts of the issue, identify the stakeholders and their positions, consider the consequences of the decision, weigh various guidelines and principles, develop and evaluate various options, review the decision, and evaluate the results. This is not a linear process; some backtracking and repeating of previous steps may be required.

What trends have increased the risk of using information technology unethically?

The growth of the Internet, the ability to capture and store vast amounts of personal data online, and greater reliance on information systems in all aspects of life have increased the risk of using information technology unethically. In the midst of the many IT breakthroughs in recent years, the importance of ethics and human values has been underemphasized—with a range of consequences.

SELF-ASSESSMENT QUESTIONS

Your instructor can provide the answers to the self-assessment questions.

1. Habits that incline people to do what is acceptable are called.

2. Integrity is a cornerstone of ethical behavior and is the practice of acting in accordance with one's own code of principles. True or False?

3. Increased corporate globalization is one of several trends that have made it more difficult to apply principles and codes of ethics consistently. True or False?

4. Which of the following companies has not been charged with serious accounting irregularities?

   Qwest

   MCI

   Adelphia

   Intel

5. Corporations need to operate consistently so that they can promote an ethical work environment by encouraging employees to act ethically when making business decisions and by supporting them when they do. True or False?

6. The sentencing of organizations for violating federal law changes periodically and is now covered in Chapter Eight of the Federal Sentencing Guidelines for Organizations, which provides for lesser punishment if the organization can demonstrate that it had an "effective compliance and ethics program." True or False?

7. The highlights an organization's key ethical issues and identifies the overarching values and principles that are important to the organization and its decision making.

8. In a, companies set goals for social responsibility, define improvement programs, and track progress toward meeting their goals.

REVIEW QUESTIONS

1. Define the word *ethics* and the term value system.

2. What trends have increased the need for organizations to foster an ethical environment?

3. In what ways do good ethics engender good business?

4. Briefly summarize the key provisions of Section 404 of the Sarbanes–Oxley Act. How might it affect the accounting practices of an organization?

5. What are the key reasons that corporations need to promote an ethical work environment?

6. The goodwill that socially responsible activities create can make it easier for corporations to conduct their business. Explain what this means, and provide an example.

7. Identify specific actions that corporations can take to improve business ethics.

8. What is the purpose of a corporate code of ethics?

9. What is meant by principle-based decision making?

10. What pressures might be placed on employees that make it difficult for them to perform ethically?

11. Outline and briefly discuss a seven-step approach for ethical decision making.

12. Identify several areas in which the increased use of IT has raised ethical concerns.

DISCUSSION QUESTIONS

1. Can you recall a situation in which you had to deal with a conflict in values? What was it? How did you resolve this issue?

2. Is every action that is legal also ethical? Can you describe an action that is legal but ethically wrong? Is every ethical action also legal? Is the law, not ethics, the only guide that business managers need to consider? Explain.

3. What is the role of the board of directors in establishing an ethical workplace?

4. Do you think it is easier to establish an ethical work environment in a nonprofit organization? Why or why not?

5. This chapter discusses four approaches to dealing with moral issues. Identify and briefly summarize each one. Do you believe one perspective is the most important? Why or why not?

6. Is it possible for an employee to be successful in the workplace without acting ethically?

7. What are the key elements of an effective corporate ethics training program?

8. Identify and briefly discuss a recent example that illustrates the negative impact of using IT unethically.

WHAT WOULD YOU DO?

Use the seven-step approach to ethical decision making to analyze the following situations and answer the questions.

1. You and your 10 project team members are working on a new information system for your firm. You have heard a rumor that when the project is completed, the system's ongoing maintenance and support will be outsourced to another firm. The original implementation plan called for at least three team members to work full time on system support and maintenance. Should you break this news to your team? What should you do?

2. You are the customer service manager for a small software manufacturer. The newest addition to your 10-person team is Aubrey, a recent college graduate. She is a little overwhelmed by the volume of calls, but is learning fast and doing her best to keep up. Today, as you performed your monthly review of employee e-mail, you were surprised to see that Aubrey is corresponding with employment agencies. One message says, "Aubrey, I'm sorry you don't like your new job. We have lots of opportunities that I think would much better match your interests. Please call me and let's talk further." You're shocked and alarmed. You had no idea she was unhappy, and your team desperately needs her help to handle the onslaught of calls generated by the newest release of software. If you're going to lose her, you'll need to find a replacement quickly. You know that Aubrey did not intend for you to see the e-mail, but you can't ignore what you saw. Should you confront Aubrey and demand to know her intentions? Should you avoid any confrontation and simply begin seeking her replacement? Could you be misinterpreting the e-mail? What should you do?

3. While mingling with friends at a party, you mention a recent promotion that has put you in charge of evaluating bids for a large computer hardware contract. A few days later, you receive a dinner invitation at the home of an acquaintance who also

attended the party. Over cocktails, the conversation turns to the contract you're managing. Your host seems remarkably well-informed about the bidding process and likely bidders. You volunteer information about the potential value of the contract and briefly outline the criteria your firm will use to select the winner. At the end of the evening, the host surprises you by revealing that he is a consultant for several companies in the computer hardware market. Later that night your mind is racing. Did you reveal information that could provide a supplier with a competitive advantage? What are the potential business risks and ethical issues in this situation? Should you report the conversation to someone? If so, who should you talk to and what would you say?

4. You have just completed interviewing three candidates for an entry-level position in your organization. One candidate is the friend of a coworker who has implored you to "give his friend a chance." The candidate is the weakest of the three but has sufficient skills and knowledge to adequately fill the position. Would you hire this candidate?

5. A coworker calls you at 9 a.m. at work and asks for a favor. He is having trouble this morning and will be an hour late for work. He explains that he has already been late for work twice this month and that a third time will cost him four hours pay. He asks you to stop by his cubicle, turn his computer on, and place some papers on the desk so that it appears he is "in." You have worked on some small projects with this coworker and gone to lunch together. He seems nice enough and does his share of the work, but you are not sure what to tell him. What would you do?

Cases

CASE PROJECTS

1. Is There a Place for Ethics in IT?

On March 15, 2005, Michael Schrage published an article in CIO magazine entitled "Ethics, Schmethics" that stirred up a great deal of controversy in the IT community. In the article, Schrage proposed that "CIOs should stop trying to do the 'right thing' when implementing IT and focus instead on getting their implementations right." Ethics, Schrage argued, had become a buzzword much like quality in the 1980s, and that the demand for ethical behavior interferes with business efficiency.

Schrage gave a few scenarios. For example, a company is developing a customer relationship management (CRM) system, and the staff is working very hard to meet the deadline. The company plans to outsource the maintenance and support of the CRM once the system is developed. There is a good chance that two-thirds of the IT staff will be laid off. Would you disclose this information? Schrage answered, "I don't think so."

Schrage asked readers in another scenario, "How about deliberately withholding important information from your boss because you know that its disclosure would provoke his immediate counterproductive intervention in an important project?" Schrage said he would do it; business involves competing values, he argued, and trade-offs must be made to keep business operations from becoming paralyzed.

Schrage was hit with a barrage of responses accusing him of being dishonorable, short-sighted, and lazy. Other feedback provided new perspectives on his scenarios that Schrage hadn't considered. For example, Kathleen Dewey, an IT manager at Boise State University, argued that doing the right thing is good for business. Not disclosing layoffs, she argued, is a trick that only works once. Remaining employees will no longer trust the company and pursue jobs where they can feel more secure. New job applicants will think twice before joining a company with a reputation for exploiting IT staff. Other readers responded to the scenario by suggesting that the company maintain loyalty by offering incentives for those who stayed or providing job placement services for departing employees.

Addressing the second scenario, Dewey suggested that not giving the boss important information could backfire on the employee. "What if your boss finds out the truth? What if you were wrong, and the boss could have helped? Once your boss knows that you lied once, will he believe you the next time?"

Another reader, Gautam Gupta, had actually worked under an unproductive, reactive, meddling boss. He suggested confronting the boss about the problem at an appropriate time and place. In addition, as situations arose that required Gupta to convey important information that might elicit interference, he developed action plans and then made firm presentations to his boss. The boss, he assured Schrage, will adapt.

Gupta, Dewey, and others argued that CIOs must consider a company's long-term needs rather than just the current needs of a specific project. Others argued that engaging in unethical behavior, even for the best of purposes, crosses a line that eventually leads to more serious transgressions. Some readers suspected that Schrage had published the article to provoke outrage. Another reader, Maikel Marrero, agreed with Schrage, arguing that ethics has to "take a back seat to budgets and schedules" in a large organization. Marrero explained, "At the end of the day, IT is business."

Questions:

Discuss how a CIO might handle Schrage's scenarios using the virtue ethics approach, the fairness approach, the utilitarian approach, and the common good approach.

Discuss the possible short-term losses and long-term gains in implementing ethical solutions to each of Schrage's scenarios.

Must businesses choose between good ethics and financial benefits? Explain your answer using Schrage's scenarios or your own examples.

CASE PROJECTS

2. Computer Associates Is Forced to Clean up Its Act

On July 5, 2000, Erika Miller of the Nightly Business Report announced, "While most of the nation was preparing for Fourth of July fireworks, Computer Associates quietly released a bombshell of its own." The company had issued a warning that its first quarter earnings for fiscal year 2001 would fall short of expectations. The forecast had been for a $0.55 profit per share, but the company said it expected an actual profit of no more than $0.16 per share. Stock prices dropped 43 percent, from $51 to $29.50, in a single day.

Miller reported, "The company blames the shortfall on weak European sales, a slowdown in its mainframe business, and delays in several large contracts," but the real reason was quite different and would plague the company for years to come.

According to the Securities and Exchange Commission (SEC), executives at Computer Associates (CA) practiced a fraudulent accounting method between January 1998 and September 2000. CA would keep the books open after the quarter ended and report revenue from contracts that had not yet been signed. This method, called the "35-day month," allowed them to meet quarterly earnings expectations and artificially raise stock prices. The SEC maintains that first, second, third, and fourth quarter earnings for fiscal year 2000 were inflated by 25 percent, 53 percent, 46 percent, and 22 percent, respectively. When CA changed auditors and came under increasing scrutiny, they altered their accounting methods, precipitating the July 2000 crash.

The conspiracy involved an array of CA employees from the Finance and Sales departments to top executives. As news of the scandal leaked, CA was pummeled with class actions, the Standard and Poor's Rating Service placed the company on its CreditWatch list, and the SEC indicted CA executives. What seems difficult to understand is why one of the world's largest software companies would sink to criminal practices.

The answer may lie in an earlier scandal. According to a 1995 agreement, founder Charles Wang, cofounder Russel Artzt, and former CEO Sanjay Kumar were to receive 20.25 million shares if stock prices closed at or above $53.30 for 60 days within a 12-month period—by the end of the year 2000. The lure of this reward may have motivated the executives to conspire to maintain artificially high stock prices. Not only did CA institute a "35-day month," it engaged in other shady dealings that allowed it to meet estimated quarterly earnings. In early 2000, after the stock prices reached the required benchmark, the three tried to cash in their shares. Irate shareholders sued the company and forced the executives to return $560 million.

The attempt to cash in these stock options brought CA and its accounting practices under closer scrutiny. In February 2002, pressure mounted and CA elected Walter Schuetze, former SEC Chief Accountant, to the Board of Directors. He led an independent investigation that initially concluded in September 2002 that CA had not violated accepted accounting principles. By 2003, however, the Sarbanes-Oxley Act (passed in July 2002) and increased media scrutiny aroused by the Enron scandal was affecting companies across the nation. Chief financial officers (CFOs) had to answer to the CEO and to stronger boards composed of independent directors. Companies were instituting more oversight and better controls. In October 2003, Schuetze revealed that—upon further investigation—his committee had discovered irregularities. CA's CFO was forced to step down, and Kumar himself later resigned. The board also asked other senior executives involved in the scandal to resign.

In the meantime, the SEC and the federal government are looking to prevent accounting fraud in the future by imposing the harshest measures possible on violators. In June 2005, the SEC expanded its charges against Kumar, accusing him of paying hush money in the form of a $3.7 million contract to a CA client who had learned of CA's fraudulent accounting practices. The Sarbanes-Oxley Act provides for stiffer punishment—longer prison sentences and higher fines. CA may not see the end of the scandal for years to come, which could serve as a considerable disincentive for other companies to follow in CA's footsteps.

Questions:

Why do you think Walter Schuetze reversed his initial finding that Computer Associates committed no accounting irregularities?

Research the Web to identify other accounting irregularities employed by Computer Associates beyond the use of a "35-day month."

Do you think a company can commit widespread accounting fraud without the knowledge of lower-level managers in the Accounting and Finance departments?

CASE PROJECTS

3. McKesson HBOC Accused of Accounting Improprieties

HBO (named for founders Huff, Barrington, and Owens) & Company was formed in November 1974. The company quickly made a name for itself by delivering cost-effective patient information and hospital data collection systems. Its premiere product, MEDPRO, was designed to be the most cost-effective system in the industry. MEDPRO helped hospital administrators track patient admissions, discharges, emergency room registrations, order communications and results reporting, scheduling, and data collection.

The company went public in June 1981 under the NASDAQ stock symbol HBOC. Its fast growth in sales and profits made it a favorite of investors throughout the 1990s, and its stock rose more than a hundredfold between October 1990 and October 1998. Much of its growth came through acquisitions of other companies.

On January 12, 1999, McKesson Corporation, one of the largest distributors of prescription drugs in the United States, completed a merger with HBO & Company by exchanging shares of common stock. At the time, the two companies had a combined market value of more than $23 billion.

Just three months after the merger, McKesson HBOC, Inc. announced that its auditors had discovered accounting irregularities at HBOC during a routine annual review. The problems were uncovered when McKesson's accounting firm, Deloitte & Touche, mailed a survey to several clients and asked them to report the actual amount of goods and services they had purchased from the company. Several of the amounts returned by clients did not match what HBOC had recorded. As a result, McKesson HBOC, Inc. had to restate earnings for the last four quarters. When the restatement of earnings was announced in April 1999, shares of the company plunged from $65 to $34 in a single day. The restated results were as follows:

Quarter Ending	REVENUE (in millions)			NET INCOME (in millions)		
	Originally Reported	As Restated	% Overstated	Originally Reported	As Restated	% Overstated
3/98	$393.1	$376.8	4.3%	$64.9	$45.6	42.3 %
6/98	$376.7	$308.1	22.3%	$75.6	$23.5	221.7 %
9/98	$399.6	$330.5	20.9%	$83.7	$16.5	407.3 %
12/98	$469.0	$381.0	23.9%	$59.6	$8.5	601.2 %
3/99	$431.9	$402.6	7.3%			

Some believed that certain HBOC managers, seeking to ensure that the company would meet or beat analysts' expectations for sales and profits, had used several innovative approaches to report financial results. Throughout 1998, it was alleged that HBOC allowed more than a dozen hospitals to buy HBOC software or services with conditional "side letters" that enabled the hospitals to back out of the sales. It was further alleged that these side letters were not shared with the auditors and that the associated sales were reported as complete, violating accounting rules. In at least one case, a hospital canceled a purchase HBOC had booked.

Additional allegations were made that, to bolster its results, HBOC agreed to questionable sales with two other large computer companies. In September 1998, two days before the end of HBOC's quarter and just weeks before HBOC and McKesson agreed to merge, HBOC signed to buy $74 million in software from Computer Associates (CA), supposedly for resale. CA, a software manufacturer for large companies, bought $30 million in HBOC software in return, also supposedly for resale. The deals were split into separate contracts, neither of which made reference to the other. In the two years following its purchase of HBOC's software, CA neither used nor distributed any of the $30 million in HBOC software products, according to a court indictment. Similarly, HBOC had sold only a fraction of the $74 million in CA software it bought.

It was also alleged that McKesson HBOC, Inc. and Data General, a computer hardware maker based in Massachusetts, had agreed to a similar deal in March 1999. Data General disclosed to auditors that what appeared to be a simple $20 million purchase of HBOC software had a side agreement that essentially ensured Data General would never have to pay for it.

Investors and analysts had no idea these problems would be so costly. McKesson first said it had found $42 million in sales from its HBOC unit that had been improperly booked. Eventually, however, $327 million in overstated revenue and $191 million in overstated income were uncovered from 1997 to 1999.

In one of the drug industry's largest corporate shakeups, the board of McKesson HBOC, Inc. ousted some of its top executives over the accounting irregularities. In July 1999, the U.S. Attorney's Office for the Northern District of California and the SEC started investigations. In addition, 53 class actions, three derivative actions, and two individual actions were filed against the company and its current or former officers and directors. Two former top executives of HBOC were indicted in July 2000 and accused of costing investors more than $9 billion, one of the largest financial frauds in American history.

In October 2003, former HBOC president Albert Bergonzi pleaded guilty to two counts of securities fraud charges. In a plea agreement, prosecutors dropped nine other charges and Bergonzi agreed to cooperate in the government's case against another McKesson executive, Richard Hawkins. Bergonzi was the fourth former senior HBOC executive to plead guilty to charges stemming from the scandal. In January 2005, McKesson agreed to pay $960 million to settle a federal class action, but numerous other suits remain.

Questions:

Make a list of the parties that were hurt by the use of nonstandard accounting practices at HBOC. Identify the harm suffered by each party.

As you read this case, was there a clear point at which ethical wrongdoings became legal wrongdoings? If so, when?

What would motivate HBOC managers to use nonstandard accounting procedures to report increased revenues and earnings?

END NOTES

National Cancer Center Institute, www.cancer.gov/statistics.

"Compliance and Integrity," Altria Web site, www.altria.com/responsibility/4_2_complianceandintegrity.asp.

Weiss, Shari, "Case Study: Developing An Ethical Company, Compliance Pipeline," www.compliancepipeline.com/showArticle.jhtml?articleID=165701047, July 8, 2005.

Weiss, Todd R., "Study: Global Software Piracy Losses Totaled $29B in 2003," *Computerworld*, www.computerworld.com, July 7, 2003.

Lawson, Stephan, "MCI Settles Fraud Charges with SEC," *Computerworld*, www.computerworld.com, May 20, 2003.

Eichenwald, Kurt, "Ebbers' Verdict A Sign: Juries Blame the CEO," *Cincinnati Enquirer*, page D1, March 16, 2005.

Kadlec, Daniel, "A Wake-Up Call for Directors," *Time*, www.time.com, January 17, 2005.

Shore, Sandy, "SEC Suit Charges Fraud at Qwest," *Cincinnati Enquirer*, page D2, March 16, 2005.

Associated Press, "Adelphia Founder John Rigas Found Guilty," MSNBC News, www.MSNBC.com , July 8, 2004.

Gross, Grant, "Update: Kumar Leaves CA," *Computerworld*, www.computerworld.com, June 4, 2004.

Cowley, Stacy, "CA Shows Revenue Growth as Turbulent Fiscal Year Ends," *Computerworld*, www.computerworld.com, May 27, 2005.

Full text of Sarbanes-Oxley Act, frwebgate.access.gpo.gov/cgi-bin/getdoc.cgi?dbname=107_cong_reports&docid=f:hr610.107.pdf.

"Sarbanes-Oxley Act," whatis.com at searchcio.techtarget.com, March 30, 2005.

Bruno, Joe Bel, "Accounting Compliance Spurs Investors' Fears," MSN Money, news.moneycentral.msn.com, March 17, 2004.

Hoffman, Thomas, "IT Managers Brace to Meet Ongoing Sarbanes-Oxley Compliance Demands," *Computerworld*, www.computerworld.com, August 2, 2004.

Holder, Tony and Mindak, Mary, "Overall Analysis of Stock Price Reactions, Disclosure Level and Significant Issues Related to SOX 404," University of Cincinnati, March 17, 2005.

Pham, Duc, "Sarbanes-Oxley: Technical Enforcement of IT Controls," *Computerworld*, www.computerworld.com, July 20, 2004.

Weiss, Todd R., "Accounting Problem at SunTrust Could Delay Sarbanes-Oxley Filing," *Computerworld*, www.computerworld.com, November 16, 2004.

Johnson, Kenneth, "Federal Sentencing Guidelines: Enterprise Risk Management," *Ethics Today Online*, www.ethics.org/today/, Volume 3, Issue 3, December 2004.

Johnson, Kenneth W., "Federal Sentencing Guidelines: Enterprise Risk Management," Ethics Resource Center 2004-09, Article ID 864, www.ethics.org/resources/article_detail.cfm?ID=864.

"Two Top Execs at Fannie Mae Forced Out," *SmartPros Accounting*, accounting.smart pros.com/x46295.xml, December 22, 2004.

Gordon, Marcy, "New Problems Found in Fannie Mae Accounting," MSN Money, news.moneycentral.msn.com, February 23, 2005.

"What is an Ethics Officer," Web site of Ethics Officer Association, www.eoa.org/Whatis.asp, March 17, 2005.

"What is an Ethics Officer," Web site of Ethics Officer Association, www.eoa.org/Whatis.asp, March 17, 2005.

Harned, Patricia, "A Word from the President: Ethics Offices and Officers," *Ethics Today Online*, www.ethics.org/today/, Volume 3, Issue 2, October 2004.

Home page of Ethics Officer Association, www.eoa.org , March 17, 2005.

Intel Web site, Corporate Compliance, www.intel.com/intel/finance/docs/ CBP%20-%20Ethics%20and%20Compliance.pdf, March 19, 2005.

Intel Press Release, "Intel Reports on Corporate Social Responsibility Performance," www.intel.com/pressroom/archive/releases, May 27, 2004.

Sources for Case 1

Schrage, Michael, "Ethics, Shmethics," CIO, www.cio.com/archive/031505/ethics.html, March 15, 2005.

"Ethics, Shmethics, Readers Comments," CIO, www.cio.com/comment_list.html?ID=3308.

Sources for Case 2

"Computer Associates' Earnings Warning Computes Big Losses On Wall St.," Nightly Business News Web site, www.nightlybusiness.org/transcript/2000/trnscrpt070500.htm, July 5, 2000.

"SEC Files Securities Fraud Charges Against Computer Associates International, Inc., Former CEO Sanjay Kumar, and Two Other Former Company Executives," Press Release 2004-134, U.S. Securities and Exchange Commission Web site, www.sec.gov/news/press/2004-134.htm, September 22, 2004.

Berniker, Mark, "Computer Associates Sacks Execs," Internetnews.com, www.internetnews.com/bus-news/article.php/3089691, October 9, 2003.

Cowley, Stacy, "Prosecutors Revise Indictment of Ex-CA CEO Kumar," Network World, www.computerworld.com/governmenttopics/government/legalissues/story/0,10801,96096,00.html, June 30, 2005.

Sources for Case 3

Morrow, David J., "The Markets: Market Place; McKesson to Restate Earnings for 4 Quarters and Stock Falls 48%," www.nytimes.com, April 29, 1999.

Berenson, Alex, "Two Ex-Executives Are Indicted In Fraud Case," www.nytimes.com, September 29, 2000.

"Suit Contends Board of McKesson Knew of Problems at HBO," www.nytimes.com, November 15, 2000.

McKesson HBOC, Inc., Form 10-Q filed with Securities and Exchange Commission for quarter ended December 31, 2000, www.edgar-online.com.

McKesson HBOC, Inc., Form 10-K Annual Report for the year ended March 31, 1999, filed with Securities and Exchange Commission, www.edgar-online.com .

"Bergonzi Pleads Guilty to HBOC Fraud," Health Data Management, www.healthdatamanagement.com , June 30, 2005.

United States Attorney's Office, Northern District of California, www.usdoj.gov/usao/can/press/html/2003_06_04_mckesson.html , June 30, 2005.

CHAPTER

10

ACHIEVING HIGH CUSTOMER SATISFACTION

In this chapter you will learn:

◆ The role the help desk plays in delivering quality technical customer support

◆ How to manage, meet, and exceed customer expectations

◆ The mix of skills needed for a career in technical customer support

---

Technology pervades our lives. People of all ages, backgrounds, and skill levels use computers at work, at school, and increasingly at home. This growing use of computing technology results in an enormous need for technical support. Many companies meet this need by setting up help desks. A help desk is a single point of contact within a company for managing customer problems and requests and for providing solution-oriented support services. Companies worldwide know that they must provide high-quality customer service and support if they want to survive in today's fiercely competitive business environment. The help desk plays an extremely important role in delivering that service and support. An integral component of the help desk is people. Having the right people on a help desk facilitates high customer satisfaction. Finding and keeping people who enjoy working with technology and helping customers is a great challenge facing companies.

Historically, the help desk was considered a stepping stone to other professions within the computer industry. Today, the help desk has been elevated to a profession in and of itself and provides a tremendous opportunity for people who want to pursue an exciting career in the technology field. Because the help desk is such a critical part of any customer-oriented business, people who possess the skills needed to deliver quality customer service and technical support are extremely valuable and somewhat rare.

To work in a help desk, you must possess a mix of skills, including business skills, technical skills, soft skills, and self-management skills. You must understand the characteristics of quality customer service and technical support. Finally, you must understand that how you interact with each and every customer influences that customer's perception of your company and its products and services.

DELIVERING QUALITY TECHNICAL CUSTOMER SUPPORT

The information age is upon us, and the technology we employ to obtain and use information has found its way into every aspect of our lives. For the average person, it can be a challenge to keep that technology up and running and get it to do what he or she wants and needs it to do. A person may turn to any number of help desks for support. For example, when at home, a person may contact the particular company that manufactured her computer or the company that publishes a software package she uses. When at work, she may contact her company's help desk for aid using programs that are unique to her company. A person working as a help desk analyst may even contact other help desks, such as a vendor's help desk for assistance in diagnosing a hardware, software, or network problem. How a help desk treats people influences their level of satisfaction and perception of the entire company and its products. People's level of satisfaction with and perception of a company can determine whether that company succeeds or fails.

Customer Support and the Help Desk Role

The term *help desk* was coined in the late 1970s; however, the technical support industry has changed dramatically since that time as has the role of the help desk. Established originally simply to screen calls, today's help desk serves as a key part of any technical support organization. **Technical support** refers to the wide range of services that enable people and companies to continuously use the computing technology they acquired or developed. Technical support services include: installing the hardware, software, network, and application components that enable technology users to do their work; keeping the system in good repair; upgrading hardware and software when needed; and providing customer support. **Customer support** includes services that help a customer understand and benefit from a product's capabilities by answering questions, solving problems, and providing training. A customer is a person or organization that buys products or services or might buy products or services in the future.

Customer service and support organizations come in all shapes and sizes and deliver a wide range of services. These organizations can be either a company, or a department within a company devoted to customer service and support. One type of customer service and support organization is **a call center**, which is a place where telephone calls are made, or received, in high volume. The term **contact center** is being used increasingly to refer to a call center that uses technologies such as e-mail and the Web in addition to the telephone to communicate with its customers. Examples of call centers and contact centers include airline reservation centers, catalog ordering centers, and home shopping centers.

The help desk and the support center (discussed below) are also customer service and support organizations. Help desks and support centers typically handle technology-oriented problems and questions, whereas a call center handles a wide range of problems and questions that may or may not be technology-oriented.

The name support organizations use for help desks varies from one company to the next. Help desk has historically been the most popular. Other common names include customer service center, customer support center, IT support, and support services. Service desk is increasingly being used as well.

Although this book focuses on the help desk and the support center, many of the concepts covered in this book apply to any organization devoted to customer service and support. Skills such as listening, creating a positive telephone image, improving your writing skills, and handling difficult situations are important in any profession, but are particularly important when dealing with customers.

The help desk makes a significant contribution by providing a single point of contact for all technical and customer support services, delivering value to customers, and capturing and distributing information. Because people working in a help desk have daily contact with customers, they enjoy a unique opportunity to capture an enormous amount of information about customers' wants and needs. Successful help desks share this information with customers, managers, and other groups within the organization that are involved in supporting customers.

The help desk and these other support groups are often structured in a series of levels, an approach commonly known as a multi-level support model. In a **multi-level support model**, shown in Figure 10–1, the help desk refers problems it cannot resolve to the appropriate internal group, external vendor, or subject matter expert. Level one is the help desk because it is the first point of contact for customers. If the level one help desk cannot resolve an incident, it hands off the incident to the next highest level, level two. Level two might consist of a development group for a particular software application, a network support group, or an expert in a particular application. If level two cannot resolve the problem, then it hands off the problem to level three, which is usually a software vendor, a hardware vendor, or a subject matter expert. A subject matter expert (SME) is a person who has a high level of experience or knowledge about a particular subject. The goal of this multi-level support model is to have the help desk resolve as many problems as possible at level one. This approach ensures the most efficient use of level two and three resources.

Figure 10–1 Multi-level support model

NOTE

In the context of a multi-level support model, customers solving problems on their own using self-services is known as level zero. Self-services such as users guides and owners manuals, a help desk Web site that contains answers to frequently asked questions (FAQs), and online help systems that provide solutions to known problems empower customers to support themselves. Empowering customers to help themselves increases customer satisfaction because customers can get the help they need when they need it. Self-services also benefit support organizations because they are a cost effective way for the help desk to assist large numbers of customers while freeing human resources to work on more complex problems and requests.

NOTE

Not all help desks require three levels of support. Technology and a broader scope of responsibilities are making it possible for many level one help desks to function at a much higher level than in the past, thus eliminating the need for a third level. Also, it is not uncommon for smaller help desks to have only two levels of support. This is particularly true in organizations that support primarily off-the-shelf computer software products. In those organizations, if a level one analyst cannot resolve a problem, he or she contacts the appropriate software vendor.

Historically, the level one help desk delivered customer support services, while the level two groups handled technical support services such as repairing systems and upgrading hardware and software when needed. As the support industry has evolved, that division of responsibilities has changed. Many companies have consolidated their support services into a support center. A **support center** is a help desk with a broader scope of responsibility and with the goals of providing faster service and improving customer satisfaction. Customer satisfaction improves when solutions are delivered quickly. Solutions are delivered quickly when the help desk has the ability and the authority it needs to handle problems and requests. Transitioning technical responsibilities to the support center makes it possible for it to achieve both of those goals.

Remote support technologies, such as asset and configuration management systems, remote control and monitoring systems, and software distribution systems, have also enabled the enhanced help desk to absorb many customer-related activities from other support groups, such as field services and network support. By expanding its responsibilities to include activities such as network monitoring and network and system administration, the help desk can be more proactive and timely because it doesn't have to engage other groups to perform these tasks. **Network monitoring** involves using tools to observe and control network performance to prevent and minimize the impact of problems. **Network and system administration** involves activities such as setting up and maintaining user accounts, ensuring that the data the company collects is secure, and performing e-mail and database management.

The technical support services that a company delivers as well as how and by whom those services are delivered vary according to company size, company goals, and customer expectations. The help desk contributes significantly to its company or department by serving as the first point of contact for all technical support services and by ensuring that customer problems and requests are resolved as quickly and cost-effectively as possible.

A number of membership organizations and associations provide information, guidance, and networking opportunities to support professionals. The most recognized are:

Organization	URL
The Association of Support Professionals	www.asponline.com
The Help Desk Institute	www.thinkhdi.com
Service & Support Professionals Association	www.thesspa.com
STI Knowledge	www.stiknowledge.com

Components of a Successful Help Desk

A successful help desk plays an important role in providing quality technical customer support. A successful help desk also is made up of many tightly integrated components. Each component relates to the others in some way and, together, these components enable the help desk to satisfy customers. The components of a successful help desk include:

- **People.** The staff and structure a company or department puts in place to support its customers by performing business processes. The principle roles played by people who work in a help desk include the **front-line service providers** who interact directly with customers and help desk management personnel. Although titles and job descriptions vary from one help desk to the next, front-line service provider positions include dispatcher or call screener, level one analyst, and level one specialist. Depending on the size of the organization, help desk management positions include help desk supervisor or team leader, help desk manager, and senior help desk manager.

Several supporting roles such as knowledge engineer, technical support, and training are also becoming more important and more commonplace in the help desk. A **knowledge engineer** develops and oversees the knowledge management process and ensures that the information contained in the help desk's knowledge base is accurate, complete, and current. A **knowledge base** is a collection of information sources such as customer information, documents, policies, and procedures, and incident resolutions. Technical support involves maintaining the hardware and software systems used by the help desk. Training ensures the help desk team receives training that addresses the business, technical, soft, and self-management skills they need.

- **Processes.** Interrelated work activities, or tasks, that take a set of specific *inputs* and produce a set of specific outputs that are of value to a customer. **Value** is the perceived worth, usefulness, or importance of a product or service to the customer. The consistent use of processes leads to customer confidence and employee satisfaction because customers and help desk employees know what and how something needs to be done. Some common processes found in a help desk include problem management, request management, and service-level management.

- **Technology.** The tools and systems people use to do their work. Help desk employees and managers use technology to perform processes. They also use technology to capture, use, and share information about their customers and their work. Help desks increasingly use technology to automate routine tasks such as password resets and to deliver solutions simultaneously to large numbers of customers through, for example, a mass mailing. Some tools found in a typical help desk include incident-tracking and problem-management systems, knowledge-management systems, telephone systems, and Web-based systems.

- **Incident-tracking and problem-management systems** are the technology used to log and track customer problems and requests. These different types of customer transactions—that is, problems and requests—are often called **incidents** or issues. By logging all customer incidents, the help desk prevents the most common customer complaint, which is that incidents are lost or forgotten. Furthermore, when analysts log incidents in an incident-tracking or problem-management system, they can use the many features these tools provide to track incidents from start to finish. For example, many incident-tracking and problem-management systems generate alerts that remind analysts to periodically contact customers with status updates when incidents cannot be resolved immediately. Many systems also allow analysts to access a knowledge base.

- **Information.** Data that are organized in a meaningful way. People need information to do their work. For example, help desk analysts need information about customers and the details of their problems to provide support. Management needs information to evaluate team and individual performance and identify improvement opportunities. For example, help desk managers need information that tells them how quickly, completely, and accurately services are delivered. Other groups within the organization need information about the company's customers. For example, a company's Research and Development department needs information about how customers are using the company's products and services and how customers would like those products and services to be improved. Without data, help desks have trouble creating the information required to understand customer needs and expectations and measure customer satisfaction. Consequently, successful companies consider information a resource in the same way that well-trained employees, well-defined processes, and well-implemented technology are resources. Types of data captured by help desks include customer data, incident data, status data, and resolution data.

TIP   When working in a help desk, you must understand that customers, managers, and coworkers use the data you collect on a daily basis to create information. The knowledge gained by analyzing this data can be used to increase customer satisfaction, enhance productivity, improve the quality of products and services, increase the efficiency and effectiveness with which services are delivered, and create new products and services. Chapters 6 and 7 explore the help desk analyst's role in capturing data.

People are by far the most important and expensive component of a help desk. Finding qualified people to deliver quality customer support is a great challenge being faced throughout the support industry. People are the most important component because customers are people who have feelings and expectations that only other people can understand. In fact, customers do not buy products or services so much as they buy expectations. Customer **expectations**, results that customers consider reasonable or due to them, are a moving target, and it is this movement that makes it so difficult for companies to get and stay ahead. Customer expectations are a moving target for a number of reasons. As customers become more comfortable using technology, they become more demanding of the support they require. Also, as companies improve the quality of the services they deliver, the standard that represents great service gets redefined. When companies consistently deliver a high level of service, that high level becomes the standard, making it extremely difficult, and sometimes quite costly, for companies to go beyond what customers have come to expect. Companies must manage and, when possible, exceed customers' expectations to compete in today's business world. The best companies listen rigorously to their customers' suggestions and complaints in an effort to fully understand their customers' wants and needs. Those companies communicate what they can do to customers and work hard to ensure they deliver the products and services customers really want and need; not products and services they think their customers want and need.

Customers have expectations not only about what a product can do, but also about what the company can do to enable them to fully use that product. This is particularly true in the world of high technology where customers increasingly use customer service and technical support to differentiate between companies and their products. Vendors are constantly striving to duplicate the features offered by their competitors. Companies that gain a competitive edge through product innovation can quickly lose that edge when a competitor publishes its next release. In other words, the products themselves can be very similar at any point in time. Companies that deliver excellent service—that is, they meet and exceed their customers' expectations—can use that excellent service, as well as a great product, to maintain their competitive edge. Also, the more complex and pervasive technology becomes, the more people crave personalized service and support. This notion is summed up in the phrase "high tech, high touch"; the more technological (high tech) the world becomes, the more people desire one-to-one personalized (high touch) service and support. Companies that deliver excellent customer service work hard to treat every customer as an individual. They pay attention and attend to the details of each customer's need.

Delivering high touch service can be very costly, so most companies also strive to deliver "low touch" services that meet and exceed their customers' expectations. Self-services offered through the Web, such as knowledge bases, FAQs, and online forms that can be used to submit problems and requests, are excellent examples of low touch ways that companies use technology to support customers, 24 hours a day, 7 days a week.

NOTE Technology is increasingly being used to make customers feel that they are getting personalized service, even when the services being delivered are low touch. For example, many Web sites enable users to create a profile to specify personal preferences and some use cookies to identify users and track their preferences. A cookie is a very small text file created by a Web server that is stored on a user's computer either temporarily for that session only or permanently on the hard disk. When a profile or cookie is present, the Web server remembers who you are and displays information that you requested or that is relevant.

Benefits of Quality Customer Support

Companies that deliver excellent customer support receive substantial benefits, as do their employees. Some of those benefits are very tangible, such as return business and the positive word-of-mouth that leads to new business. These then lead to higher sales and profits. Industry recognition is another benefit, and many companies are striving to be recognized as "world class." A **world class** company has achieved, and is able to sustain, high levels of customer satisfaction. World class companies often reap the benefit of customer loyalty. Loyal customers are willing to pay slightly more for products and suffer minor inconveniences, such as temporarily living without a feature that a competitor's product has, in exchange for excellent service.

NOTE Establishing and maintaining a help desk can be costly, and the cost is even greater when a company strives to achieve world class status. Not all companies are able or willing to invest in the help desk. When working in a help desk, you must promote the benefits of quality customer support and show that you understand and are committed to satisfying your customers' needs and expectations. Chapter 7 explores the business skills you can use to communicate the value of help desk services.

A less-tangible benefit of quality customer support is customer feedback. Companies that deliver great service often receive customer feedback about how they can improve their service even more: "This is great, but you know what would be even better . . ." Companies that deliver poor service don't receive that kind of feedback because a very small percentage of dissatisfied customers complain. Most dissatisfied customers just walk away and don't come back.

Service providers need to understand that customer complaints are a good thing, and they need to be responsive to and even encourage complaints. Companies that make it easy for customers to complain by, for example, conducting customer satisfaction surveys, will receive a greater number of complaints. Technology is also making it easier for customers to complain when, for example, a company provides a link on its Web site or an e-mail address that can be used to provide feedback. The challenge is for companies to collect and analyze the feedback that customers provide and take action to improve their services. Companies that are receptive to customer feedback often are given an opportunity to further improve or a second chance when they fall down. Companies that deliver poor service or fail to listen to their customers do not typically receive that second chance; customers just take their business elsewhere.

Another benefit of quality customer support is the very real phenomenon that happy customers result in happy employees, who in turn create more happy customers. Some companies believe that if they treat their employees well, their employees in turn will treat their customers well. Regardless of who came first, the happy customer or the happy employee, companies that are committed to delivering high-quality service and support derive many benefits, and those benefits are often passed on to their employees.

The most obvious benefits that companies pass on to their employees are reward and opportunity. For example, companies are increasingly offering their employees "pay for performance" plans that are tied to customer satisfaction. Some companies offer profit-sharing plans that enable employees to directly benefit when the company is doing well. Some companies offer bonuses to employees who consistently go the extra mile for their customers. Job security is another benefit, and although few companies guarantee life-long jobs, people with the right mix of skills are highly employable and can more easily find work.

> *One of the most important principles of success is developing the habit of going the extra mile. Napoleon Hill*

Employees also derive intrinsic benefits from supporting customers, for example, the pride and satisfaction that comes from helping other people. People who enjoy the technical customer support field also tend to demonstrate a strong sense of purpose. They know the role they play is important to their customers and their company and they take it very seriously.

✳Trends Influencing the Help Desk

An irreversible dependence on technology has prompted customers to demand ever-cheaper, better, and faster support services. This huge demand for support, coupled with a shortage of information technology (IT) professionals, has created a tremendous career opportunity in the field of customer service and technical support. According to the United States Department of Labor, computer support is projected to be among the fastest growing occupations through the year 2012 ("Computer Support Specialists and System Administrators," U.S. Department of Labor Bureau of Labor Statistics, February 2004).

The help desk offers—and for the foreseeable future will continue to offer—considerable opportunities to people who want to be a part of this dynamic and growing industry. As help desks evolve, they face many challenging business trends. Many of these trends, listed in Figure 10–2, have resulted in elevating the help desk to a more strategic role within companies and help desk professionals to a valued and rewarded position.

- 24 × 7 support
- Fee-based support
- Global support
- Help desk as a profession
- Increased dependence on technology
- Mobile workforce support
- Multi-channel support
- Outsourcing
- Web-based support

Figure 10–2 Help desk industry trends

Each of these trends affects how help desks are run and the opportunities they present to help desk analysts.

24 5 × Support.   Customers are challenging companies to provide **24 × 7 support**, which means that help desk services are provided 24 hours a day, 7 days a week. The need to support an increasingly self-sufficient customer base, a global customer community, a mobile workforce, or a part of the business that operates around the clock, such as a manufacturing facility, leads to this demand for continual support.

This 24 × 7 support trend creates many opportunities for help desk professionals. It creates positions for help desk analysts as well as positions for team leaders and supervisors. Companies that provide 24 × 7 support often employ three work shifts: a day shift, a mid-day (or mid) shift, and a night shift. The hours of these shifts vary from company to company.

Companies that provide 24 × 7 support may also offer very flexible schedules for their employees. For example, people may work ten hours per day for four days and then have three days off. Or, they may work part-time, such as 20 hours per week. These scheduling alternatives help accommodate the needs of people who want to continue their education, have family demands, and so forth.

24 × 7 support does not, however, mean that help desk analysts must be on-site at all times. Some help desks use their phone system to transfer callers to analysts who work at home or to instruct callers about how to obtain emergency support if needed—typically by using a pager to contact an on-call analyst.

Increasingly, help desks direct customers to their Web site after hours where they can help themselves, submit a problem or request, or obtain the status of an outstanding problem or request. This trend toward self-service creates opportunities for people who assume supporting roles in the help desk. For example, the help desk's technical support staff maintains the help desk's Web site and makes it possible for customers to gain access to Web-based self-services after hours. Knowledge engineers also make it possible for customers to get answers to FAQs and search knowledge bases for solutions after hours.

For some companies, demand for support may be fairly light after hours. As a result, support may be provided by a service agency (see the section on Outsourcing later in this chapter), by an on-call employee, or through the Web. Customers may not receive the same depth of service after hours that they receive during normal business hours. Most customers are satisfied, however, if they can at least find answers on their own, submit a request to obtain service during normal help desk business hours, or obtain support in the event of an emergency.

Fee-Based Support.   With **fee-based support**, customers pay for support services based on usage. Historically, help desks have been **cost centers**, in which the budget items required to run the help desk are considered a cost (or expense) to the company. Some help desks, however, are run as **profit centers**, in which the help desk must cover its expenses and, perhaps, make a profit by charging a fee for support services. Some organizations, particularly internal help desks, establish the help desk as an overhead expense; each department in the company is assessed a fee based on how great its need is for help desk services. An **internal help desk** responds to questions, distributes information, and handles problems and service requests for its company's employees. Other organizations, particularly external help desks, establish detailed pricing structures that allow customers to choose free services such as self-help services delivered through the Web, fee-based standard services, or premium services. An **external help desk** supports customers who buy its company's products or services.

NOTE

Some external help desks provide pre-sales support, meaning that they answer questions for people who have not yet purchased the company's products or services and may take orders and respond to billing inquiries. Most external help desks provide traditional post-sales support, which involves helping people who have purchased a company's products or services. The role of the external help desk is evolving as companies start to fully appreciate that positive customer experiences help sell products and services. These companies recognize the enormous contribution the help desk makes by capturing and sharing customer feedback with the appropriate groups in the company. The companies can then use this information to develop new and more desirable products and services. External help desks are continuously being challenged to build customer relationships and contribute to corporate growth and profitability.

Whether run as a cost center or profit center, help desks are under increasing pressure to analyze and control their costs, market the value of their services, and—without alienating customers—charge a premium for "customized" services.

People entering the help desk industry need to be aware of this trend and determine whether and how their employer, or prospective employer, charges for support. A company's policy on this practice greatly influences how analysts account for their time and effort as well as how they interact with customers. For example, analysts who work at help desks that charge for services are typically required to verify that a customer is entitled to support before they begin working on a problem. They may also be required to account for every activity they perform throughout the day so those activities can be billed to the customers. Help desk managers value people who understand that the help desk is a "business within a business" that must justify its existence and that can be run profitably.

Global Support.   Some companies are being challenged to support customers anywhere in the world. This demand for **global support** may be caused by the need to support a large company that has foreign divisions and subsidiaries, or by the need to support customers who are doing business with the company through the Web. Companies providing global support must address the culture, language, and legal issues that come with working in an international market. There are several ways they can do that, including:

- **Regional, in-country help desks.** Traditionally, large companies establish multiple, in-country help desks that each provide localized support. These in-country help desks provide highly personalized service because they understand issues such as language, culture, and local expectations. Some companies prefer this highly personalized form of support even though it can be expensive. To mitigate their costs, these companies may require that all help desks use the same processes and technologies. Each help desk may also produce a standard set of metrics or, performance measures, that are forwarded to the corporate headquarters for review. Conversely, some companies allow each help desk to establish its own processes and technologies and focus only on its own needs and the needs of its customers.

- **Follow the sun support.** Follow the sun support means that companies establish several help desks (typically three); each on a different continent, and as one help desk closes, another opens and begins supporting customers. For example, consider a company that has help desks in the United States, the United Kingdom, and Australia. When the United States completes its normal business day, it transfers support to the help desk in the United Kingdom. When the United Kingdom completes its business day, it transfers support to the Australian help desk, which transfers support back to the United States when its day is done. These help desks use common tools and processes and can share common data sources such as knowledge bases and asset and configuration management databases. The advantage of this approach is that the company is able to leverage technology and maximize its return on investment (ROI), while analysts within each help desk can deliver personalized service to their customers—that is, service that addresses issues such as language and culture. Large, multi-national companies often take a follow the sun approach.

- **One global support desk.** One global support desk means that one physical help desk provides 24 7 support. This approach tends to be less costly than follow the sun support because companies are not required to set up and staff multiple facilities, nor are they required to replicate their processes and technologies across multiple sites. These companies must, however, address issues such as language and culture, and they must also determine how to deliver localized support when necessary. For example, a help desk may need to determine how to ship a replacement laptop to a mobile worker in another country. Companies that need to provide global support but lack a large support staff, such as a small Web-based company, often opt to have a single global support desk.

Regardless of how companies provide global support, this trend presents a number of opportunities for people pursuing a help desk career. First, companies that provide global support often operate 24 hours a day, 7 days a week, which means more job opportunities. Second, people with the right skills may be given the opportunity to travel and gain experience working abroad. Third, global support often requires people who speak multiple languages and understand the cultural issues that are unique to a particular part of the world. For example, in Germany people consider it rude to address someone by their first name prior to being given permission. In the United States, however, people rarely use last names anymore. Also, although some companies provide information and deliver support through the Web in English only, others offer a choice of languages. These companies depend on their analysts to translate solutions and publish them in a variety of languages. Companies that provide global support value and are willing to reward people who understand cultural differences and can read and write as well as speak multiple languages. Rewards may include higher salaries and perks such as the opportunity to telecommute or travel abroad.

Help Desk as a Profession. Historically, the help desk was considered a stepping stone to other professions. Today, a number of trends indicate that the help desk has been elevated to a profession in and of itself. For example:

- According to the Help Desk Institute, a networking forum for help desk professionals, 66.3% of help desks report to a chief information officer (CIO) or senior executive. This shows the importance of help desks within companies.

- Some companies are creating new team leader and supervisor positions within the help desk in recognition of the need to provide feedback, coaching, and counseling to front-line staff. As a result, more management positions are available.

- Turnover, considered a serious issue by 69% of HDI members in 2002, is viewed as serious by only 2.3% in 2003 ("Help Desk Institute 2003 Practices Survey," Help Desk Institute, 2003). Although this trend is somewhat influenced by a tight economy, it also reflects the fact that companies have been working hard in recent years to retain the knowledge and experience of seasoned analysts. According to HDI members, nearly 41% of their level one analysts remain in the help desk for three to five years. An additional 19% remain for more than five years. Historically, employees remained in help desks for less than two years.

- Individual and site certification programs are increasingly being used by help desk managers and help desk analysts to demonstrate their business, technical, soft, and self-management skills. There are two types of certification programs available to help desk professionals: *technical certifications* that are vendor specific and *help desk certifications* that are vendor neutral. Help desk certifications enable companies to certify the individual managers and analysts within their help desk or their entire help desk. Figure 10–3 describes the leading help desk certification programs available to help desk professionals:

These certification programs enable individuals to focus on and demonstrate that they possess the industry knowledge and soft skills needed to deliver excellent customer support, and enable help desks to benchmark their practices against industry best practices. A **best practice** is an innovative process or concept that moves a company or department to a position of improved performance.

Certification programs can be costly and time-consuming to complete successfully, and so individuals and help desks that become certified truly exemplify world class service providers. Certification represents industry recognition and the ability to demonstrate a level of competency based on industry best practices. Help desk certification also offers individuals and sites education about the support industry—how it works and how help desks and individuals within help desks contribute to their company's strategic business goals. As a result, individuals and sites that complete help desk certification programs gain a bigger picture perspective than technical certification programs tend to offer.

That does not mean that technical certification programs aren't important and valuable. Many individuals are opting to obtain technical certification from third-party vendors. Technical certification programs range from entry-level programs such as CompTIA's A+ program to more advanced programs offered by vendors such as Microsoft, Cisco, Oracle, Novell, Sun, HewlettPackard, and IBM. To ensure technical certifications retain their value, these vendors continuously update their programs and work hard to prevent

- **Help Desk Institute Certification.** Help Desk Institute certification is an open, standards-based, internationally recognized certification program for help desk professionals (**www.thinkhdi.com/certification/individualCertification**). Certification levels include Customer Support Specialist (CSS), Help Desk Analyst (HDA), and Help Desk Manager (HDM).

- **Service & Support Professionals Association (SSPA) Certification.** The SSPA individual certification training program is designed to prepare support professionals at all levels to perform within industry standards and to earn international certification (**www.thesspa.com/programs/certifications/indiv.asp**). The five levels of SSPA individual certification available include Customer Service Qualified, Certified Support Professional, Certified Support Specialist, Certified Support Manager, and Certified Support Executive. The SSPA also offers the Support Center Practices (SCP) site certification program that evaluates help desk performance relative to 11 major criteria such as people programs, total quality management, productivity tools, and performance metrics (**www.thesspa.com/programs/certifications/site.asp**). SSPA's programs are geared to companies that provide external customer support.

- **STI Knowledge Certification.** STI Knowledge offers help desk certification (**www.stiknowledge.com/certification_advisory/courses.asp**) for help desk analysts, managers, and directors. These certification programs involve a stringent testing process that includes a three-hour written exam along with an oral exam or a specific help desk project. Certification levels include Certified Help Desk Professional, Certified Help Desk Manager, and Certified Help Desk Director. STI Knowledge also offers the Core 2000 certification program, which enables companies to certify their entire help desk (**www.stiknowledge.com/certification_advisory/comp_certification.asp**).

Figure 10–3 Help desk certification programs

cheating. Many of these vendors also recognize and in some cases require completion of other programs. For example, Microsoft accepts CompTIA's A+, Network+, Security+, or Server+ certifications in lieu of passing elective exams for its Microsoft Certified Systems Administrator (MCSA) certification. Novell requires CompTIA's IT Project+ certification for its Master Certified Novell Engineer (MCNE) certification.

To learn more about available certification programs, go to **www.gocertify.com**.

In early 2004, Microsoft released its first certification exam designed specifically for help desk professionals. The Microsoft Certified Desktop Support Technician (MCDST) credential provides individuals the ability to prove they have the skills needed to successfully support end users and to successfully troubleshoot desktop environments running on the Microsoft Windows operating system (**www.microsoft.com/learning/mcp/mcdst/requirements.asp**).

Although becoming certified does not automatically guarantee an individual will be hired or promoted, being certified does enable individuals to distinguish themselves from other job candidates and may make them eligible for raises or bonuses. According to a study conducted by *Certification Magazine*, on average, certification brought a 15.1% salary increase to IT professionals in 2003, versus a 7% increase in 2002 ("*Certification Magazine* Salary Survey," *Certification Magazine*, December 2003).

To read a summary of *Certification Magazine's* Salary Survey, go to www.certmag.com/articles/templates/cmag_feature.asp?articleid=523&zoneid=1

Some companies have a formal policy about raises for certification, whereas others leave it to the discretion of the employee's manager. Some companies pay a one-time bonus—typically between $250 and $1,000—to employees who become certified.

One of the most common incentives is for companies to pay for the training and for the cost of the exam that leads to certification. Many companies pay for certification to reward their employees, and they view it as a way to retain people who have the skills needed to support today's sophisticated technology environments. As this cost can be substantial, some companies require individuals to sign a contract that requires them to stay at the company for a specified period of time once they become certified. Employees who choose to leave the company before that time may be required to reimburse the company all or a portion of the certification cost.

Some companies also reward individuals who demonstrate that they are applying the lessons learned through certification and sharing those lessons with others. For example, some companies compare metrics before certification—such as first contact resolution and customer satisfaction—to metrics after certification, in an effort to validate, quantify, and ultimately reward an increase in a person's level of competence.

Certifications are becoming a necessary credential for help desk professionals. Managers value people who dedicate the time and effort necessary to get certified. As a result, certified individuals often get better jobs, receive higher salaries, and advance more quickly.

Increased Dependence on Technology.   A trend that has led to a great demand for support is our increased dependence on computing technology and on technology in general. In the business world, even the smallest businesses tend to use computers to manage some aspect of their operations. Children regularly use computers in class and often need one to do their homework. At home, many people use computers to manage their personal finances, research vacation destinations and make travel arrangements, or run a home-based business. Many people would not think of leaving home without a cell phone, laptop, or a handheld computing device such as a personal digital assistant. A **personal digital assistant (PDA)** is a small mobile handheld device that provides computing and information storage and retrieval capabilities for personal or business use. This increased dependence on technology, coupled with a constant barrage of new technologies, not only creates job opportunities, it also requires people in support positions to continuously update their skills.

Also, the ubiquitous computing wave is beginning to arrive. **Ubiquitous computing** is an environment where people have access to their information and computing systems from public shared access points, such as airports, hotel rooms and lobbies, libraries, retail stores, and supermarkets. As illustrated in Figure 10–4, access to these computing devices will be much like today's access to automated teller machines (ATMs).

Figure 10–4 Ubiquitous computing devices

We can only guess how this need to ensure access whenever and wherever customers want it will impact the support industry. You can be sure, however, that the demand for support will be great while this technology is maturing.

Mobile Workforce Support.   A growing mobile workforce is another reason that many help desks are experiencing an increased demand for support. According to International Data Corporation (IDC), the number of mobile workers in the United States will increase from 92 million in 2001 to 105 million by 2006. This means that roughly 66% of the U.S. workforce will be working in a mobile capacity ("U.S. Mobile Workforce to Grow," International Data Corporation, July 2002). IDC estimates there will be more than 20.1 million mobile workers in Europe by 2005, up from 6.2 million in 2000 ("Western European Teleworking: Mobile Workers and Telecommuters, 2000–2005," International Data Corporation, October 2001).

The variety of mobile and wireless devices and applications and the speed at which individuals are adopting these devices make supporting mobile workers particularly challenging for help desks. Gartner, Inc. estimated that by 2004, 60% of office workers will carry or own at least three mobile devices. This constant barrage of new technologies and a lack of standards in this area are causing help desks to realize that they must assess the skills of their staff, redesign their business processes, evaluate their tools, and rethink their data and information needs in order to address mobile computing requirements.

Increasingly, help desks are helping to define standards in terms of which mobile devices and applications best serve the needs of users and ensure the security of corporate data assets. Help desks are also modifying Service Level Agreements (see Influencing Customer Perception) to include mobile computing policies and procedures, and address asset management and configuration issues such as when and how to swap out failing devices with usable devices.

Multi-Channel Support.   For years, most help desks have offered customers alternatives to the telephone such as voice mail, e-mail, and some Web-based support. These various routes of communication to and from the help desk are typically called **channels**. Help desks have historically viewed the telephone as the "official" support channel. Accordingly, help desks required analysts to log all or most telephone calls, and telephony-centric metrics such as average speed of answer and abandon rate were the primary measures used to gauge help desk performance. Alternate support channels were often handled informally— for example, they might not have been logged—and few, if any, metrics were captured.

Several factors are causing help desks to look at multi-channel support differently now.

1. Customers are increasingly using alternate channels, prompting help desks to realize that they must handle these support channels in a more formal manner. All contacts must be logged, and metrics such as response time must be used to ensure that all contacts are handled in a timely manner.

2. Customers' expectations relative to alternate channels are changing, particularly relative to response time. Customers increasingly expect help desks to respond to e-mail messages and Web submissions in a more real-time manner—that is, within minutes or hours, as opposed to days.

3. Customers are increasingly willing to use technologies such as the help desk's Web site or e-mail and pick up the telephone only when they need additional or immediate help.

Herein lies the trend. Web technology is becoming more and more ubiquitous. Help desk Web sites are becoming more robust and real time. **E-mail response management systems** are enabling help desks to manage high-volume chat, e-mail, and Web form messages in much the same way that telephone systems enable help desks to handle telephone calls. As a result, many help desks are encouraging customers to move to these "lower touch" technologies and away from more costly telephone service.

This approach can result in increased customer satisfaction if the technologies are implemented effectively. Smart help desks know that customers will embrace their Web site only if its content is current, well organized, and easy to use. They also know that customers will embrace e-mail only if their inquires are answered in a timely manner and the responses are clear and concise. These same help desks also know that some customers are still going to prefer using more traditional channels such as the telephone to obtain support.

As a result, help desks face the challenge of ensuring that they are capturing the data needed to efficiently and effectively manage the various support channels they offer to customers. This means they must determine how best to integrate the various tools needed to capture this data, such as telephone systems, e-mail systems, incident-tracking and problem-management systems, and Web-based systems, to name just a few. Help desks must also begin to produce meaningful metrics such as response time and cost per contact relative to each channel they offer. They must understand that when sites are well designed, Web-based contacts cost less than contacts that involve analysts, but they are not free. Companies must bear the cost of maintaining their Web sites and they must work hard to keep them useful and up to date, or customers will return to the telephone. Companies must also understand that telephone contacts will increasingly cost more, because they represent complex and unique problems that typically cannot be resolved using self-services.

NOTE Multi-channel support requires help desks to determine how best to utilize each of the components of a successful help desk: people, processes, technology, and information. Many companies are taking the first step toward meeting this challenge by redesigning their business processes. By redesigning their business processes, help desks are able to determine how best to utilize their existing people and technology before hiring new people or acquiring new technology. Help desks can use information to determine which processes need to be redesigned, or designed, and they can also use information to measure the efficiency and effectiveness of their new processes.

NOTE Companies struggling to redefine their business processes are increasingly looking to ITIL for guidance. The Information Technology Infrastructure Library (ITIL) is a set of best practices for IT service management. The ITIL consists of a series of books that gives guidance on IT service management topics. Two of the main topics covered are service support and service delivery. Together, the service support and service delivery topics cover 10 disciplines or processes that are responsible for the provision and management of effective IT services. ITIL is the most widely accepted approach to IT service management in the world and is used by companies such as Microsoft and Hewlett-Packard. Many vendors that publish help desk incident-tracking and problem-management systems have also been working hard in recent years to make their products ITIL compliant. As a result, the ITIL philosophy and vocabulary are quickly becoming familiar to help desk management and staff.

Outsourcing. Many of the trends discussed previously such as 24 7 support, global support, increased dependence on technology, and mobile workforce support are prompting continued growth in help desk outsourcing. **Outsourcing** is when companies have services, such as help desk services, provided by an outside supplier (service agency or outsourcer), instead of providing them in-house. According to a study conducted by the Help Desk Institute, more of its members have plans to increase their level of outsourcing (16.9 %) than decrease their level of outsourcing (6.6%) ("Help Desk Institute 2003 Practices Survey," Help Desk Institute, 2003). Factors that prompt companies to consider outsourcing include outsourcer experience, flexibility such as an outsourcer's ability to accommodate peak periods, seasonal call volumes, or after-hours call volumes, and the opportunity to leverage an outsourcer's investment and use of new technologies. Frequently, companies are partnering with service agencies to deliver high-quality support services at a reduced cost.

NOTE Outsourcing requires that the two companies involved—the service agency and the company that hires it—work closely together to define the services to be delivered and the expected level of performance. Companies that outsource services must continuously monitor performance to ensure that the service agency is meeting its commitments and satisfying the company's customers. Ongoing communication between the two companies is critical to make certain that trends are identified and acted on and that every effort is made to determine why problems occur and how they can be prevented.

The desire by companies to outsource all or some support services—fueled primarily by pressure to reduce costs and improve services—has spawned a tremendous increase in the number of companies that offer help desk outsourcing services. It has also sparked tremendous interest in the area of offshore outsourcing. **Offshore outsourcing** is when a company has services, such as help desk services, provided by an outside supplier (service agency or outsourcer) that is located or based in a foreign country.

Organizations worldwide are looking to decrease the cost of technical support services. To do this, many companies in the United States, Europe, and Asia are contracting with service agencies in countries such as India, China, and Mexico whose wages tend to be lower than those in, for example, the United States. In addition, countries such as India, for example, have a well-educated workforce of young professionals who possess the technical skills needed for technical customer support. As a result, companies are able to considerably reduce the labor costs associated with delivering technical support while gaining access to a highly skilled workforce. Because wages typically make up the greatest portion of a company's budget, the savings are considerable.

The risks, however, are considerable as well. For example, the culture, language, and legal issues involved in offshore outsourcing are considerable (see the section on Global Support later in this chapter). Other risks include privacy, security, time zone differences, geopolitical factors that may be influencing a country or region of the world, and potential customer backlash.

Some risks are not as great as they have been in the past. For example, although technological concerns would have prohibited offshore outsourcing in the past, improved voice and data networks now make it possible for companies to safely move support services overseas. Telephone systems can seamlessly transfer callers to an offshore facility and data networks allow analysts to interact with customers through technologies such as e-mail and the Web.

NOTE

Offshore outsourcing is a hotly debated subject worldwide. Company executives who are being pressured to reduce costs cannot ignore the financial advantages of moving IT jobs to a locale with a lower cost of labor. IT professionals fear the trend because it can mean the loss of high-paying jobs. Customers can become frustrated if they encounter language or culture differences, and they may also resent the moving of jobs overseas. Given all the pros and cons, the reality is that offshore outsourcing is an option that companies will continue to explore because it is an inevitable outcome of globalization. In the business sense, globalization means operating around the world. Although many large companies have been operating around the world for decades, advances in communication, transportation, and technology have made it considerably easier and more cost effective for even small companies to do business worldwide.

Whether outsourcing offshore or domestically, help desk managers and executives must work hard to fully understand the pros and cons of outsourcing. Help desk professionals must find ways to reduce costs, increase productivity, and most important, satisfy their customers in an effort to reduce the risk of losing their jobs. Help desk professionals must also continuously upgrade their business, technical, soft, and self-management skills in order to create the greatest opportunities for themselves—perhaps by working for a company that provides help desk outsourcing services.

An important consideration with help desk outsourcing is that "one size does not fit all." Many companies—45% of HDI members—do not outsource and do not plan to outsource (Help Desk Institute 2003 Practices Survey," Help Desk Institute, 2003). Of those that do outsource, some companies outsource all of their support services. Others outsource a portion of their services, such as after-hours support, hardware support and repair, or off-the-shelf PC software support. Some companies outsource support for industry standard hardware and software products such as Windows so they can dedicate their resources to supporting systems developed in-house.

Help desk service agencies offer a variety of technical support services. Outsourcers can act as an external help desk, such as when they provide support for original equipment manufacturers (OEMs); or they can act as an internal help desk, such as when they provide support for the employees of a company. Consequently, because they offer many jobs that provide a lot of flexibility, service agencies represent a great opportunity for people who want to pursue a help desk career. Each outsourcer needs the right number of people with the right skills to support its clients at the right time. Outsourcers are constantly looking for people who have great customer service skills along with the necessary mix of business and technical skills to satisfy their customers' needs, which naturally vary considerably from one customer to the next. As a result, people have the opportunity to work with a diversity of customers while being employed by one company. Outsourcers often base raises and bonuses on people's performance and ability to satisfy customers. The best and the brightest people are regularly rewarded and promoted. Service agencies also tend to offer flexible work hours and even the opportunity to work on a contract basis. This means that people who want to work for a time and then take time off (for example, to go to school or to care for a child or family member) have the opportunity to do so as long as they give the service agency adequate notice.

 Some of the largest providers of help desk outsourcing services include: CompuCom Systems, Inc. (**www.compucom.com**), Electronic Data Systems Corporation (**www.eds.com**), International Business Machines Corporation (IBM) (**www.ibm.com**), SafeHarbor Technology Corporation (**www.safeharbor.com**), STI Knowledge, Inc. (**www.stiknowledge.com**), and Sykes nterprises, Inc. (**www.sykes.com**).

People working in help desks tend to be frightened by the prospect of outsourcing because it can result in the loss of jobs. However, successful outsourcing creates job opportunities for the external service agency, which they may then offer to help desk employees. It is not uncommon for companies to allow a service agency to hire qualified members of their help desk staff when it takes over support because knowledge about the customer community is very important. This is particularly true when a company decides to **insource** its support services, which means the service agency employees who deliver support services are physically located at the company's facilities. Companies may insource for security reasons, or because they want to leverage an existing investment in technology. Whether a company outsources or insources its support services, people with the right skills are valued.

Web-Based Support. Customers have come to expect support organizations to offer Web-based services such as knowledge bases, FAQs, Web forms that can be used to submit problems and requests, and so forth. This trend has and will continue to have a considerable impact on the support industry because the Web is changing the way support is delivered and the skills required to deliver it.

A common misconception is that Web-based services eliminate the need for help desk analysts. For example, some companies believe that if they provide self-services such as FAQs and solutions to known problems on the Web, customers will find the answers on their own and the company can downsize its help desk. Although it is true that some companies may be able to downsize their help desks, there will always be a need for qualified analysts. Some customers simply prefer to speak with a human being, whereas others want to interact in real time with analysts online. Also, new technologies are being introduced regularly that arrive with a whole new set of questions and problems. Finally, complex problems require the attention of people with strong problem-solving skills or perhaps even a team of resources working together to identify a resolution. Help desk analysts—not technology —accommodate these varying customer requirements.

Companies that deliver Web-based support cannot eliminate all other channels of support. Companies that make it difficult to call or contact the help desk through other channels such as the telephone will quickly find themselves isolated from their customers.

Although Web-based support does not eliminate the need for qualified help desk analysts, it does change the skills they must have and the types of problems and requests they resolve. Because customers can handle their simpler problems through the Web, they contact the help desk with their more complex problems. As a result, good problem-solving skills are increasingly important for analysts. Writing skills have greater importance because analysts: (1) use these skills to interact with customers through e-mail and Web-based systems, and (2) contribute to the written information that customers access on the Web. Internet skills such as the ability to use browsers, find content online, and use Internet-based diagnostic tools such as remote control systems also are increasingly imperative.

Web-based support also creates a need for people to develop, maintain, and support the help desk's systems. Roles such as technical support and knowledge base administration have greater importance as help desks rely more heavily on their support systems, and use these systems to collect and maintain content for their Web sites. Help desks also need people to embrace trends such as self-healing, mass-healing, and assisted service, and to evaluate and deploy the technologies that enable these services. **Self-healing systems** are hardware devices and software applications that have the ability to detect and correct problems on their own. **Mass-healing systems** enable help desks to detect and repair problems across the entire enterprise. For example, mass-healing systems provide help desks with the ability to detect and eliminate viruses that may be infecting the company's networked PCs. Help desks also need people to evaluate and deploy assisted services such as remote control systems that enable analysts to diagnose and correct problems, provide training, and distribute software to customers via the Web.

Web-based support does not reduce the need for a well-trained, professional help desk staff. It does, however, free analysts to handle more challenging problems and work on projects aimed at increasing help desk efficiency and enhancing customer self-sufficiency.

All of these trends influence the availability and the quality of opportunities within the support industry. Companies are striving to attract and retain people who possess and want to use both technical and interpersonal skills. Companies are also seeking people who work well with others, whether they are customers or members of other support groups within the company.

The Help Desk Analyst's Role in the Service Delivery Chain

Recall that there are two principal types of help desks: internal help desks and external help desks. An internal help desk responds to questions, distributes information, and handles problems and service requests for its company's employees. Each employee is considered an internal customer, a person who works at a company and at times relies on other employees at that company to perform his or her job. A company can have any number of internal help desks that employees contact for support. For example, employees may contact the Human Resources department when they have questions about their medical insurance or other employee benefits. They may contact the Facilities department to have office fixtures installed or repaired. And, they may contact the company's IT department when they need help with the hardware and software they use to accomplish their work.

An external help desk supports customers who buy its company's products or services. An **external customer** is a person or company that buys another company's products or services. For example, most companies that manufacture hardware and publish software packages have external help desks to support their customers. Many computer stores offer help desk services to customers who purchase products or equipment at the store. And, as discussed earlier, some service agencies offer fee-based help desk services to external customers.

If you are not supporting the external customers of your company, you are supporting someone who is. In other words, by delivering great service to an internal customer, you enable that person to—ultimately—deliver great service to the company's external customers.

The relationship between internal and external customers is tightly linked. For example, every interaction the internal help desk has with an internal customer affects that person's ability to provide excellent service to his customers, who may be the external customers of the company. Conversely, the support an external help desk receives from other people or groups within the company (such as the internal help desk or the Sales, Marketing, Field Services, and Research & Development departments) greatly affects its ability to support the company's external customers. This concept, shown in Figure 10–5, is known as a customer service delivery chain.

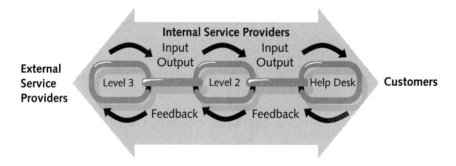

Figure 10–5 Customer service delivery chain

The customer service delivery chain shows the relationship that exists between customers, internal service providers, and external service providers. Feedback is used to communicate customer expectations through the service delivery chain. Using the feedback as a guide, internal service providers receive input from other service providers, and deliver output to other service providers, until the expected service is delivered to the customer. Sometimes, external service providers are engaged by internal service providers in an effort to meet the customer's expectations. A help desk analyst, a level two service provider, or a level three service provider may contact a vendor for help resolving a particularly difficult problem. The internal service provider at that point becomes the vendor's customer. The vendor will have its own customer service delivery chain that must now work together to meet its customer's expectations.

The customer service delivery chain illustrates that all of the departments within a company—all of its internal service providers—are interdependent and must work together to deliver services to external customers. Even departments that do not interface directly with customers perform work that results in the delivery of services to external customers. Because of this, each and every role in a company's service delivery chain adds value and must be respected and supported.

Day in and day out everyone can be considered at times a customer and at other times a service provider. For example, a coworker may ask you to provide information needed to complete a project. In this case, you are the service provider and your coworker is the customer. Later in the day, you may ask this same coworker to help you solve a problem; now you are the customer and your coworker is the service provider. Whether a customer or a service provider, you must respect that each person with whom you interact has a role to play—a job to do—and you must strive to understand the other's needs and expectations. Ultimately, the job each of you does leads—through the customer service delivery chain— to the delivery of service to the company's external customers. As a result, you must also strive to understand your external customers' expectations. Typically, how your efforts contribute to meeting those expectations will be communicated in the form of your job description and feedback relative to your job performance.

One of the best ways to become an excellent service provider is to pay attention when you are the customer.

Customer-oriented companies understand and nurture each of the customer–service provider relationships that make up their customer service delivery chain. They understand that every link is important and that the chain is only as good as its weakest link. These companies also realize that productivity and profit gains are possible only when the help desk, whether it is an internal help desk or an external help desk, is seen as a strategic corporate resource. How customers perceive the entire company, that is, the entire service delivery chain, is influenced every single time they interact with the help desk—meaning, each and every time they interact with you!

INFLUENCING CUSTOMER PERCEPTION

Customer satisfaction reflects the difference between how a customer perceives he or she was treated and how the customer expects to be treated. This reality is one of the things that makes supporting customers a challenge. It is common knowledge that two people who experience the same event will perceive the event differently. For this reason, help desks must work hard to manage their customers' expectations by clearly defining their mission, spelling out their services and policies, and continuously assessing their mission, services, and policies in light of their customer's needs. To do this, some companies have established Service Level Agreements with their customers. A **Service Level Agreement (SLA)** is a written document that spells out the services the help desk will provide the customer, the customer's responsibilities, and how service performance is measured. These agreements are an excellent way to manage customer expectations because they spell out exactly what services can and cannot be delivered.

NOTE

According to the Help Desk Institute, nearly 80% of its members have SLAs with some or all of their customers ("Help Desk Institute 2003 Practices Survey," Help Desk Institute, 2003). The reason most help desks have SLAs is that they realize that they can't keep pace with customers' rising expectations. SLA negotiations ensure that the help desk understands its responsibilities and that customers understand their responsibilities. While negotiating SLAs, the help desk and the customer discuss the company's cost to meet the customer's expectations to ensure that the company does not exceed the benefit that customers will obtain from a service. Consequently, help desks use SLAs as a tool for managing customer expectations and, when possible and appropriate, enhancing customer self-sufficiency.

As illustrated in Figure 10–6, SLAs must take into consideration every group in the company's customer service delivery chain or customer expectations will not be met. For example, if the company guarantees a customer that certain types of problems will be resolved in two hours, and one of the groups in the service delivery chain cannot respond within two hours, the customer's expectations will not be met.

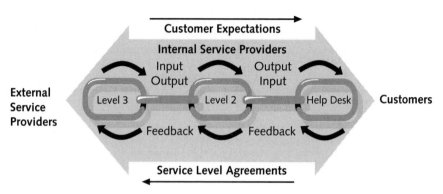

Figure 10–6 Impact of SLAs on the customer service delivery chain

SLAs are an excellent way to influence customer perception because they show how well the help desk is meeting customer expectations. Furthermore, the help desk does not have to guess at what customers expect—they know what customers want and need because it is all clearly defined in the SLAs. Figure 10–7 shows a sample help desk SLA.

SLAs can be quite complex, or they can be simple one-page documents such as the sample shown in Figure 10–7. For example, an SLA between a company and a service agency that provides help desk outsourcing tends to be quite complex because it is typically viewed as a contract. It will provide measurable performance metrics for all parties involved and may provide for incentives or penalties based on performance. On the other hand, an SLA between a help desk and a department in a company may be fairly simple, and used primarily to clarify expectations and responsibilities.

NOTE

An increasing number of help desks have SLAs with internal (level two and level three) support groups and with external vendors. Like SLAs with customers, these agreements are an excellent way to ensure that all parties involved understand their respective responsibilities.

ABC HELP DESK
SERVICE LEVEL AGREEMENT

This document is an agreement between the ABC help desk and its customers. This Service Level Agreement (SLA) has been designed to promote a common understanding about the services the help desk provides and customer responsibilities relative to those services. This document also describes how service level performance is measured

Parties: The *help desk* provides a single point of contact for the ABC IT department. *Customers* are ABC employees who seek technical support services from the ABC IT department.

Responsibilities: The *help desk* provides first level support to customers using the processes and technology implemented by the ABC IT department. The help desk also facilitates second and third level support by engaging resources as needed to resolve problems beyond the scope and authority of the help desk. *Customers* obtain service using the processes and technology implemented by the ABC IT department and described in this document. Specifically, ABC employees must contact the help desk when support services are needed.

Hours of operation: The help desk is available to ABC employees 24 hours a day, 7 days a week.
- During *normal business hours*—Monday through Friday 7 a.m. to 8 p.m.—customers can contact the help desk and speak directly with an analyst
- *After-hours*—8 p.m. to 7 a.m. weekdays, weekends, and holidays—customers can access the help desk's Web site. For *severity 1* problems only, customers can contact the help desk and obtain support from on-call analysts who carry pagers.

Contact methods: Customers can use the following methods to obtain support:
- Telephone—Customers can contact the help desk by calling **(555) 555-4357**. Every effort will be made to answer all calls within one (1) minute. Following a brief introduction, customers may hear a system outage message. This message is broadcast only when a severity 1 problem exists. Customers are then prompted to:
    - o Press 1 to report a new problem or request
    - o Press 2 to obtain the status of an outstanding problem or request
- Voice mail—Voice mail is offered to customers who call the help desk during normal business hours after a two (2) minute delay. Customers can use this option in lieu of waiting in the queue. Voice mail messages will be answered within thirty (30) minutes during normal business hours.   **Note:** Customers calling with a severe problem are encouraged to wait in the queue. Voice mail messages left after hours will be answered the next business day.
- E-mail—E-mail messages sent to **helpdesk@abc.com** will be answered within one (1) hour during normal business hours. E-mails sent after-hours will be answered the next business day.
- Internet—The help desk's Web site at **helpdesk.com** provides forms that can be used to submit problems and requests. Problems and requests submitted via the help desk's Web site are automatically logged in the help desk's incident tracking system and are handled according to their severity. The Web site also provides self-services such as FAQs, a solution knowledge base, a password reset utility, and access to remote diagnostic and control utilities.

Problem severity levels: Problem severity reflects the impact of a problem on the ABC business and as such, when and how the problem must be solved. Help desk analysts and customers will work together to determine problem severity using the following guidelines:

Severity	Business Impact	Target Resolution Time
1	System or device down, business halted.	1 hours
2	System or component down or level of service degraded, business impacted.	4 hours
3	Not critical, customer can wait.	12 hours

This agreement is effective through December 31st of the current year and will be evaluated and republished yearly or as needed.

Figure 10–7 Sample help desk SLA

Understanding Customer Needs and Managing Expectations

Managing expectations in today's rapidly and radically changing business world is indeed a challenge. It is not hard to understand why. Expectations are influenced by many factors and vary from one person to another, one situation to another, and even one day to another. Although the varying nature of customer expectations may make it seem that satisfying customers is an impossible task, Figure 10–8 lists three things you can be certain customers will want.

- Responsiveness
- A caring attitude
- Skill

Figure 10–8 Customer needs

Each of these characteristics of excellent customer support addresses a particular customer need, and ignoring any one of these characteristics can cause customer dissatisfaction.

- **Responsiveness.** Responsiveness refers to the help desk's ability to: (1) be available when customers need help, and (2) make it easy for customers to obtain help. Responsiveness involves answering the telephone promptly or responding to voice mail and e-mail inquiries within the time frame promised. For example, some companies guarantee that all voice mails will be returned within 30 minutes and all e-mail inquiries will be answered within 24 hours. Given these options, customers can decide whether they want to wait on the telephone line for an analyst or send an e-mail for a less immediate response. Responsiveness also involves anticipating customers' support needs and, when possible and practical, providing self-services through the Web. Unfortunately, some help desks do not seem very responsive. They are not available when they say they will be, or their hours of operation do not match the needs of their customers. They implement complex telephone systems that have long menus with numerous confusing options and no easy way to reach a "live" person or, they offer a telephone number that more often than not connects customers to a voice mailbox where they can leave a message. Customers often perceive that these messages go unanswered because they have left a message or messages in the past and those messages have gone unanswered. Optimally, responsive help desks have hours of operation that are comparable to the business hours during which their customers are most likely to need support. They also set up technology in a way that is easy for customers to navigate and that actually adds value to the interaction. For example, some telephone systems capture information about the customer and use that information to transfer the customer to the help desk analyst best suited to handle the customer's problem or request. Some Web sites provide customers the ability to automatically check for software updates and download software patches. Simply put, responsiveness refers to the help desk's ability to be there for customers.

■ A caring, positive, and helpful attitude goes a long way to keeping customers satisfied. One of the biggest reasons that customers choose to stop doing business with a company is that they feel an attitude of indifference. In other words, no one made the customers feel that the company wanted to satisfy their needs. Although the help desk may not always be able to give customers exactly what they want, when they want it, there is always something the help desk can do. It can take the customer's request and log it in its incident-tracking system so the request is not lost or forgotten. It can take ownership of the customer's request and ensure the request is forwarded to the person or group that can satisfy it. If nothing else, it can let the customer know where to obtain help. Customers occasionally contact the help desk with questions about a product or system that the help desk does not support. What the help desk can do in those situations is give the customer the name and telephone number of the person or group that does support the product. In other words, the help desk must be willing to assist customers in any way it can.

> *Your customers don't care how much you know until they know how much you care. Gerhard Gschwandtner*

■ **Skill.** Skill refers to the help desk's ability to quickly and correctly resolve customer problems and requests. Given today's complex technology and sophisticated, demanding customers, it is not enough for help desk analysts to be polite, perky, and caring. Help desk analysts must also be efficient and knowledgeable. They must have the ability and authority to solve problems or know exactly how to get problems solved. If customers perceive the help desk cannot help, they will simply go around it. They may turn to peer-to-peer support, a practice where users bypass the formal support structure and seek assistance from their coworkers or someone in another department whom they believe can help. They may find out who in their company or department can help and contact that person directly. Other times, they may simply give up and take their business elsewhere. The help desk must convince customers that contacting the help desk is the fastest, cheapest, and best way to obtain a solution. They must be able to handle any request that comes their way.

 To satisfy customers, the help desk must be there, be willing, and be able.

TIP

Although these characteristics may seem very nice and "fluffy," they are actually very measurable. Most companies use metrics to evaluate the performance of their help desk in all or some of these areas. Figure 10–9 shows some of the metrics that help desks use to ensure they understand their customers' expectations and are meeting their customers' needs.

Be There

✓ Answer the telephone within 20 seconds.

✓ Respond to voicemail messages within 30 minutes.

✓ Respond to all e-mail messages within 4 hours.

✓ Maintain a monthly average abandon rate of less than 5%.

Be Willing

✓ Answer the telephone with a smile on your face.

✓ Gather the facts and approach each problem in a methodical fashion.

✓ Speak clearly and use terms your customer can understand.

✓ Accurately assess the severity of problems you must escalate.

✓ Take ownership and track 100% of problems to closure.

✓ Maintain a high customer satisfaction rating.

Be Able

✓ Use all available resources in an effort to resolve problems and requests.

✓ Resolve 75% of reported problems and requests.

✓ Resolve or escalate 100% of problems and requests within the time required for the stated severity.

✓ Assign 100% of escalated problems and requests to the correct level two group.

Figure 10–9 Sample help desk customer satisfaction metrics

Metrics are used to measure the help desk's responsiveness and its ability to demonstrate a caring attitude and skill. Metrics enable each and every member of the help desk team to know how well they are meeting their customer's needs and managing their expectations. In addition, metrics provide help desk analysts the information needed to determine what else they can do to satisfy their customers.

Help desks use data captured by tools and technology to produce these metrics. They also use techniques such as customer satisfaction surveys and monitoring. **Customer satisfaction surveys** are a series of questions that ask customers to provide their perception of the support services being offered. **Monitoring** is when a supervisor or team leader listens to a live or recorded call, monitors an analyst's data entry and key strokes during an e-mail or chat session, or sits beside an analyst to measure the quality of an analyst's performance during a customer contact.

Ron Muns
CEO AND FOUNDER
HELP DESK INSTITUTE
COLORADO SPRINGS, COLORADO
WWW.THINKHDI.COM

Ron Muns is an international leader in the help desk and customer support industry and is frequently quoted on key issues and concerns. He has more than 25 years of experience as the founder of Help Desk Institute (HDI), as a software engineer, as the creator of several successful commercial software products, as a consultant with an international accounting firm, and as an IT strategist. HDI is the leading membership organization for support professionals worldwide.

Customer expectations go up every year. Customers want technologies and services that are cheaper, better, and faster. They want technologies that are aligned with their business goals, not technology just for technology's sake. When they click to open an application or use technology, they want it to work right away and to work correctly. If the technology doesn't work, customers increasingly expect an immediate answer. When they get the answer, it better solve the problem. Simply put, real-time support of technology is no longer a nice-to-have, it is a must-have. Companies that are not continuously improving their level of service in an effort to meet these rising expectations are getting behind.

The help desk plays a strategic role by providing quick responses to customer incidents as well as by storing data about those incidents in one place. Advanced help desk organizations use this data to identify quality improvement opportunities that focus on their customers' productivity. Organizations can no longer assume that customers want to call the help desk, or even that help desks can afford to handle every customer inquiry via the telephone. Customers are increasingly willing to embrace self-help, self-diagnostic, and self-healing technologies. In other words, customers are willing to help themselves, but they want it their way. Access to information about customers' wants and needs, and the ability to use that information to continuously provide improved products and services, have given the help desk a more prominent position within the eyes of both the IT and general business worlds.

Working in a help desk offers tremendous opportunity to individuals who are dedicated to meeting and exceeding customer expectations. To seize this opportunity, you must enjoy the fact that a lot of things are happening all at one time and that things are constantly changing. You must develop an awareness of different types of customers and understand that each customer needs to be handled in a different manner: Try to understand people and where they're coming from. Try to appreciate the fact that although customers are becoming more technically savvy, they are at times going to be confused and need assistance as new tools and services are constantly introduced. Acknowledge the fact that every customer who contacts the help desk wants to believe that he or she is your only customer. Listen to what your customers are saying and involve them in determining how support is delivered. Listening is and always will be one of the most important skills that analysts must possess. You must listen not only to how customers describe a technical problem, but listen for their needs and expectations as well.

In the support industry, some things will never change. For example, customers will always want more than can be delivered. A lot has changed and is changing, however, and you have the opportunity make a real difference as we head into the future. Put yourself in your customers' shoes. Learn what they do and figure out how to help them do it cheaper, better, and faster. That's all they expect!

Demonstrating a Positive *Can Do* Attitude

Delivering high-quality customer support is incredibly challenging for a number of reasons. One, customers are people whose feelings and expectations can change from minute-to-minute. Two, customers today are more sophisticated and demand cheaper, faster, and better service. Three, technology is increasingly complex and changes so rapidly that it can be difficult for help desk analysts to keep up. Although these factors may tempt you to consider the possibility of satisfying customers in a hopeless scenario, remember, there is always something you can do.

A can do attitude means that rather than telling a customer what you cannot do, you tell them what you can do. A subtle distinction, for sure, but it goes a long way toward satisfying customers. That is, customers perceive that they have been helped.

> *There is little difference in people but that little difference makes a big difference. The little difference is attitude. The big difference is whether it is positive or negative.* Author Unknown

To be successful, help desk analysts must learn to strike all negative phrases from their vocabulary. For example, rather than telling a customer "We don't support that product," an analyst can say, "What I can do is give you the telephone number of the company that supports that product." If you were the customer, wouldn't being pointed in the right direction satisfy you more than simply hearing "We can't help?"

Saying no is one of the most difficult things for help desk analysts to do. This is because many of us grew up hearing phrases such as "The Customer Is King" and "The Customer Is #1." Although the spirit of these phrases lives on, the execution is often much more difficult and costly than companies expect. In today's competitive marketplace, few companies have the resources to give customers everything they want, when they want it. Rather, companies are trying to maximize their resources and provide a high level of service, even if it means limiting the scope of their services. For example, many companies are establishing standards in terms of the products they support, rather than supporting all of the possible products their customers may want to use. In doing so, the help desk can acquire the training, tools, and talent needed to support that limited set of products. If the help desk tried to be all things to all people, its resources would quickly be stretched too thin and its entire level of service would decline.

A common phrase is "The Customer Is Always Right." Unfortunately, companies have found that customers are not always right. For example, a customer may install a product that conflicts with your company's product and then ask, "What are you going to do about it?" Or, a customer may download a document from the Web that contains a virus and corrupts their system. Again, they turn to the help desk for support. Should the help desk support customers in these situations? Absolutely, because, although the customer may not always be right, they are always the customer. Your company's policies will spell out what you can do in these situations.

When facing these challenging situations, a can do attitude will always serve you well. Sometimes it is necessary to say "no" to customers. Sometimes it is impossible to respond as quickly as customers would like when they have a problem. A can do attitude enables you to give customers this information without offending or alienating them. Throughout this book, you will learn how to maintain a can do attitude day in and day out, and how that attitude will positively influence not only your interactions with customers, but each and every person with whom you come into contact each day.

Going the Extra Mile

Are satisfied customers loyal? Not necessarily. Satisfying a customer simply means that the company has fulfilled the customer's need. The customer contacted the help desk with a problem and that problem was resolved. If the help desk solves problems consistently, will customers contact the help desk when they have a need in the future? Yes. Will they, however, rave about the service they received, thus attracting new customers? Not necessarily. Figure 10–10 shows reasons companies lose customers.

As shown in Figure 10–10, feeling an attitude of indifference is the number one reason that customers choose to do business with another company. The scary part is that customers

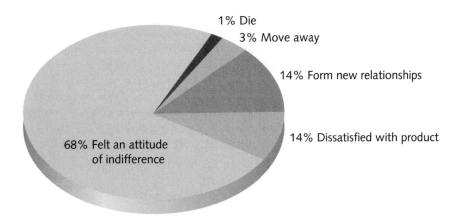

Figure 10–10 Common reasons companies lose customers

don't always tell you how you're doing, but they will tell others when they are dissatisfied. According to some estimates:

- 96% of unhappy customers never speak up.
- 13% of dissatisfied customers will tell their story to 20 other people.
- 5% of unhappy customers will just take away their business.

Although it is sometimes hard to listen to complaints day in and day out, these statistics illustrate why it is so important to thank customers who provide feedback.

> **TIP** Complaining customers are giving you and your company an opportunity to improve. Listen carefully!

How, then, do companies generate customer loyalty? How do companies go beyond customer satisfaction, to customer delight? Companies must go the extra mile—and give a little something extra. Most help desks define boundaries of what analysts can do to delight their customers. For example, some help desks authorize analysts to make exceptions to company policies in certain situations. Other help desks authorize analysts to waive product shipping charges or offer a free product upgrade in certain situations. Those situations are typically clearly spelled out. These boundaries are important. Without boundaries, the cost of going the extra mile might quickly deplete the company's profits.

> **TIP** Most customers understand that products can fail and human beings can make mistakes. How a company handles those situations ultimately determines whether customers remain loyal or take their business elsewhere. Companies that train employees to quickly take responsibility, empathize with what the customer is experiencing, and offer a viable solution can retain even the most dissatisfied customer.

In technical support, just as in customer service, it is often the little things that delight customers—the unexpected. Two key ways to delight customers are to: (1) save them time, and (2) enhance their self-sufficiency. For example, you can save customers time by teaching them a faster or easier way to use their computer, such as clicking the right mouse button or setting up shortcuts on their desktop. You can enhance customer self-sufficiency by teaching them how to maintain their system and prevent problems by performing maintenance tasks, such as backing up their data and using utilities such as Microsoft ScanDisk and Miscrosoft Disk Defragmentor (Defrag). Taking a few minutes to teach customers a simple trick or a way that they can diagnose and perhaps fix problems on their own comes back to you tenfold in customer goodwill.

> *Goodwill is the one and only asset the competition cannot undersell or destroy.*
> Marshall Field

DEVELOPING THE RIGHT MIX OF SKILLS

The support industry is evolving and companies are continuously changing the ways they do business in an effort to gain customer loyalty. This dynamic business climate represents a tremendous opportunity for people who possess the mix of skills needed to meet the help desk's expanding responsibilities. Figure 10–11 shows the principle skills needed to work successfully at a help desk.

Business skills

Technical skills

Soft skills

Self-management skills

Figure 10–11 Principle help desk skills

Each of the help desk roles, such as dispatcher, level one analyst, level one specialist, and help desk manager, requires a specific set of skills. The level of skill and experience required will vary from company to company, but most companies will explore a job candidate's qualifications in each of the following categories:

- **Business skills.** These are the skills people need to work successfully in the business world, such as the ability to understand and speak the language of business (business knowledge); the skills that are unique to the industry or profession the help desk supports, for example, accounting skills or banking skills (industry knowledge); and also the skills that are specific to the customer service and support industry, for example, understanding the importance of meeting customer's needs and knowing how to manage their expectations (service industry knowledge).

- **Technical skills.** These are the skills people need to use and support the specific products and technologies the help desk supports. Technical skills also include basic computer and software literacy.

- **Soft skills.** The skills and personality traits that people need to deliver great service, such as listening skills, verbal communication skills, customer service skills, problem-solving skills, writing skills, and the ability to be a team player.

- **Self-management skills.** The skills, such as managing stress and time, that people need to complete their work effectively, feel job satisfaction, and avoid frustration or burnout. Self-management skills also include the ability to get and stay organized and to continuously and quickly learn new skills.

Filling front-line positions with people who have the right mix of skills is one of the most difficult challenges facing help desk managers today. People who have very strong interpersonal skills—that is, soft and self-management skills—may lack the technical skills required to support today's increasingly complex technology. People with strong technical skills may lack the skills such as patience and empathy that are needed to support customers with varying skill levels. Some people prefer a more hands-on approach to technical support and may be more comfortable working in a field service role away from the front line. The employee and the company benefit when the right skills are matched with the right position.

When hiring people for front-line positions, companies look for people with positive, *can do* attitudes who genuinely enjoy helping other people and enjoy solving problems. Companies also look for individuals who are team-oriented and enjoy working with other people. This is because of the general belief that technical skills can be developed more easily than interpersonal skills. Companies are willing to provide technical training to individuals with good interpersonal skills and a customer service orientation. Also, technology is constantly changing and technical skills must be continuously updated. This does not mean that technical skills are unimportant. At times, companies may hire people with very strong technical skills and then provide extensive customer service training. Or, companies may need people who have a very specific business skill or technical skill that would take an extensive amount of training to develop, so they hire people who already possess that skill. Smart companies let their customers' needs and expectations drive their hiring decisions. For this reason, people who understand that all of these skill sets—business, technical, soft, and self-management—are important will create for themselves the greatest opportunity.

 Contrary to popular belief, interpersonal skills can be developed, but people must be willing to work at them.

TIP

Companies worldwide know they must deliver high-quality customer support, or lose business to their competition. These companies are seeking people who have the mix of skills and the desire needed to satisfy as well as delight customers day in and day out. The rapidly growing support industry represents a tremendous opportunity for people who want to use all of their skills: business, technical, soft, and self-management. To seize this opportunity, you must understand the characteristics of excellent technical customer support and remember at all times that you are supporting people using technology, and not just technology. Those people will have needs and expectations that will take all of your skills to meet and exceed.

This book focuses on the soft skills and self-management skills, and touches briefly on the business skills needed to pursue a successful career in technical customer support. Although the business skills and the technical skills you may choose to develop are wide-ranging and diverse, soft skills and self-management skills are somewhat universal. It is possible to build a solid foundation of these latter skills from which you will always be able to draw.

Skills such as listening, communication, and stress-management skills are excellent "life" skills that will serve you well regardless of your chosen profession.

CHAPTER SUMMARY

- ❑ The pervasive nature of increasingly complex computing technology has created a tremendous demand for technical support. The help desk is the first point of contact for this support. How people are treated by the help desk influences their level of satisfaction and how they perceive the entire company and its products. To be successful, a help desk must effectively utilize all of its assets: people, processes, technology, and information. People are by far the most important component because customers are people who have needs and expectations that only other people can understand.

- ❑ An irreversible dependence on technology has prompted customers to demand ever-cheaper, better, and faster support services. This huge demand for support, coupled with a shortage of information technology (IT) professionals has created a tremendous career opportunity in the field of customer service and technical support. Trends such as the need to provide 24 7 support, fee-based support, global support, help desk as a profession, increased dependence on technology, mobile worker support, multi-channel support, and Web-based support are influencing the direction in which the help desk industry is heading. Each of these trends affects how help desks are run and the opportunities they present to help desk analysts.

- ❑ Managing customer expectations is a challenge, but you can be certain that customers want the help desk to be there, be willing, and be able. Even when it seems customer expectations cannot be met, you can avoid offending or alienating customers by demonstrating a can do attitude and by going the extra mile. A can do attitude means that rather than telling a customer what you cannot do, you tell them what you can do.

❑ The support industry is evolving and the dynamic nature of this industry represents a tremendous opportunity for people who possess the right mix of skills. Skills needed include business, technical, soft, and self-management. This book focuses on the soft and self-management skills, and touches briefly on the business skills needed to pursue a successful career in technical customer support. These skills are somewhat universal and will serve you well throughout your life and career.

KEY TERMS

24 × 7 support — Help desk services that are provided 24 hours a day, 7 days a week.

best practice — An innovative process or concept that moves a company or department to a position of improved performance.

business skills — The skills people need to work successfully in the business world, for example, the ability to understand and speak the language of business (business knowledge); the skills, such as accounting skills or banking skills, that are unique to the industry or profession the help desk supports (industry knowledge); and also the skills that are specific to the customer service and support industry, for example, understanding the importance of meeting customers' needs and knowing how to manage their expectations (service industry knowledge).

callcenter — A place where telephone calls are made, or received, in high volume.

can do attitude — Telling a customer what you are able to do rather than what you cannot do.

caring attitude — A help desk's ability to communicate that it wants to satisfy its customer's needs.

channel — A route of communication to and from the help desk.

contact center — A call center that uses technologies such as e-mail and the Web in addition to the telephone to communicate with its customers.

cookie — A very small text file created by a Web server that is stored on a user's computer either temporarily for that session only or permanently on the hard disk.

cost center — A help desk in which the budget items required to run the help desk are considered a cost (or expense) to the company.

customer — A person who buys products or services or with whom one must deal.

customer satisfaction — The difference between how a customer perceives he or she was treated and how the customer expects to be treated.

customer satisfaction surveys — A series of questions that ask customers to provide their perception of the support services being offered.

customer support — Services that help a customer understand and benefit from a product's capabilities by answering questions, solving problems, and providing training.

e-mail response management systems — Systems that enable help desks to manage high-volume chat, e-mail, and Web form messages in much the same way that telephone systems enable help desks to handle telephone calls.

expectations — Results that customers consider reasonable or due to them.

external customer — A person or company that buys another company's products or services.

external help desk — A help desk that supports customers who buy its company's products or services.

fee-based support — An approach wherein customers pay for support services based on usage.

front-line service providers — People who work in a help desk who interact directly with customers and help desk management personnel.

global support — Support for customers anywhere in the world; may be a result of the need to support a large company that has foreign divisions and subsidiaries, or a result of the need to support customers who are doing business with the company through the Web.

help desk — A single point of contact within a company for managing customer problems and requests and for providing solution-oriented support services.

incident — A customer transaction—that is, a problem or a request; also called an issue.

incident tracking and problem management systems — The technology used to log and track customer problems and requests (incidents).

information — Data that are organized in a meaningful way.

Information Technology Infrastructure Library (ITIL) — A set of best practices for IT service management.

insourcing — When service agency employees who deliver support services are physically located at the facilities of the company that hired them to provide support services.

internal customer — A person who works at a company and at times relies on other employees at that company in some way to perform his or her job.

internal help desk — A help desk that responds to questions, distributes information, and handles problems and service requests for its company's employees.

knowledge base — A collection of information sources such as customer information, documents, policies and procedures, and incident resolutions.

knowledge engineer — A person who develops and oversees the knowledge-management process and ensures that the information contained in the help desk's knowledge base is accurate, complete, and current.

mass-healing systems — Systems that enable help desks to detect and repair problems across the entire enterprise.

metrics — Performance measures.

monitoring — When a supervisor or team leader listens to a live or recorded call, monitors an analyst's data entry and keystrokes during an e-mail or chat session, or sits beside an analyst to measure the quality of an analyst's performance during a customer contact.

multi-level support model — A common structure of help desks, where the help desk refers problems it cannot resolve to the appropriate internal group, external vendor, or subject matter expert.

network monitoring — The use of tools to observe and control network performance in an effort to prevent and minimize the impact of problems.

network and system administration — Activities such as setting up and maintaining user accounts, ensuring the data that the company collects are secure, and performing e-mail and database management.

offshore outsourcing — When a company that has services, such as help desk services, provided by an outside supplier (service agency or outsourcer) which is located or based in a foreign country.

outsourcing — When a company that has services, such as help desk services, provided by an outside supplier (service agency or outsourcer), instead of providing them in-house.

peer-to-peer support — A practice where users bypass the formal support structure and seek assistance from their coworkers or someone in another department whom they believe can help.

people — The component of a help desk that consists of the staff and structure put in place within a company or department to support its customers by performing business processes.

personal digital assistant (PDA) — A small mobile handheld device that provides computing and information storage and retrieval capabilities for personal or business use.

post-sales support — The help desk assists people who have purchased a company's product or service.

pre-sales support — The help desk answers questions for people who have not yet purchased the company's products or services and may take orders and respond to billing inquiries.

processes — Interrelated work activities, or tasks, that take a set of specific inputs and produce a set of specific outputs that are of value to a customer.

profit center — A help desk that must cover its expenses and, perhaps, make a profit by charging a fee for support services.

responsiveness — The help desk's ability to (1) be available when customers need help, and (2) make it easy for customers to obtain help.

self-healing systems — Hardware devices and software applications that have the ability to detect and correct problems on their own.

self-management skills — The skills, such as stress and time management, that people need to complete their work effectively, feel job satisfaction, and avoid frustration or burnout. Self-management skills also include the ability to get and stay organized and to continuously and quickly learn new skills.

Service Level Agreement (SLA) — A written document that spells out the services the help desk will provide the customer, the customer's responsibilities, and how service performance is measured.

skill — The help desk's ability to quickly and correctly resolve customer problems and requests.

soft skills — The skills and personality traits that people need to deliver great service, such as listening skills, verbal communication skills, customer service skills, problem-solving skills, writing skills, and the ability to be a team player.

subject matter expert (SME) — A person who has a high level of experience or knowledge about a particular subject.

support center — A help desk with a broader scope of responsibility and with the goals of providing faster service and improving customer satisfaction.

technical skills — The skills people need to use and support the specific products and technologies the help desk supports.

technical support — A wide range of services that enable people and companies to continuously use the computing technology they acquired or developed.

technology — The tools and systems people use to do their work.

ubiquitous computing — An environment where people have access to their information and computing systems from public shared access points, such as airports, hotel rooms and lobbies, libraries, retail stores, and supermarkets.

world class — A company that has achieved, and is able to sustain, high levels of customer satisfaction.

value — The perceived worth, usefulness, or importance of a product or service to the customer.

REVIEW QUESTIONS

1. Why is there a tremendous need for technical support?

2. What is a help desk?

3. What influences customers' level of satisfaction and how they perceive a company and its products?

4. How is technical support different than customer support?

5. What are the goals of a multi-level support model?

6. How is a support center different than a help desk?

7. What are the components of a successful help desk?

8. Customer expectations are _____.

9. Why do companies have a hard time meeting and exceeding customer expectations?

10. List three benefits that companies derive when they deliver excellent customer support.

11. List three benefits that employees derive when they work for a company that delivers excellent customer support.

12. List two reasons that customer support is projected to be one of the fastest growing occupations through the year 2012.

13. What are four ways that companies provide 24 × 7 support?

14. True or false? Only help desks that are run as profit centers are under pressure to analyze and control their costs and market the value of their services.

15. What are three ways that companies provide global support?

16. List and describe the two types of certification programs available to help desk professionals.

17. How do help desk certifications enable individuals to gain a bigger picture perspective than technical certifications tend to offer?

18. What are three ways that help desks can ensure that mobile devices and applications meet the needs of users and ensure the security of corporate data assets?

19. Which of the following support channels will be used in the future?

    a. telephone

    b. e-mail

    c. Web

    d. all of the above

20. List three reasons, other than reduced cost, that companies outsource their help desk services.

21. List three skills that are increasingly important for people in a help desk to have in order to provide Web-based support.

22. Why are roles such as technical support and knowledge base administration important to help desks that provide Web-based support?

23. What are the two principal types of help desks?

24. List three types of companies that provide external customer support.

25. What is the most important link in a customer service delivery chain?

26. A customer service delivery chain is only as good as its _____.

27. What is customer satisfaction?

28. What is a Service Level Agreement?

29. What three characteristics of excellent customer support can the help desk count on customers wanting?

30. Name three ways that companies produce the metrics needed to measure their performance.

31. Rather than telling a customer what you cannot do, tell them what you _____.

32. Is a customer always right?

33. What turns a satisfied customer into a loyal customer?

34. What are two things that help desk analysts can do to delight customers?

35. What are the four principle skills needed to work successfully at a help desk?

36. Which of the four principle skills are universal or life skills?

DISCUSSION QUESTIONS

1. Generally speaking, high-touch service is where people receive service that is highly personalized and low-touch service is where people help themselves. Some would say that high-touch services are better than low-touch services. Do you agree or disagree? Explain why.

2. Ubiquitous computing is an environment where people have access to their information and computing systems from public shared access points, such as airports, hotel rooms and lobbies, libraries, retail stores, and supermarkets. What impact do you think the arrival of ubiquitous computing will have on the support industry?

3. A common perspective is that soft and self-management skills such as listening, communication, and stress management are innate. In other words, you are either born with them or you are not. Do you agree or disagree? Explain why.

HANDS-ON PROJECTS

Project 10–1

Evaluate technical support needs. The average person may contact any number of help desks for support. Talk to at least three friends or classmates who use computers about their experiences with technical support. Ask each person the following questions:

❑ Have they ever contacted a help desk for support?

❑ What were their expectations when they contacted the help desk?

❑ Were their expectations met?

❑ Did they receive "high touch" service?

❑ Did they use any "low touch" services?

Write a one-page report that summarizes each experience and presents your conclusions about each experience.

Project 10–2

Learn about help desk certification. Search the Web to locate an organization that certifies help desk professionals or select one of the organizations discussed in this chapter. Visit the organization's Web site and then determine the following:

❑ What levels of certification are available?

❑ What skills are certified?

❏ What must you do to get certified?

❏ What are the benefits of being certified?

Write a report that summarizes what you have learned about certification from visiting this Web site.

Project 10–3

Learn about help desk outsourcing. Search the Web to locate three organizations that provide help desk outsourcing services or select three of the help desk outsourcing companies mentioned in this chapter. For each company, visit its Web site and then write a paragraph that answers the following questions:

❏ What services do they deliver?

❏ What do they consider standard services, and what do they offer as optional services?

❏ How do they distinguish themselves from their competition?

❏ What do they say about their staff?

❏ What do they say about their hiring practices?

❏ What do they say about satisfying their customers?

Project 10–4

Understand the service delivery chain. Day in and day out we are all at times a customer and other times a service provider. Think about your experiences as a customer and as a service provider during the past week or so. Write a paragraph describing your experiences as a customer. For example, contacting a company for technical support or going to a store to purchase needed equipment. Were your expectations for service and support met? What did the service provider do well? How could the service provider have done better? Write a second paragraph describing your experiences as a service provider. For example, assisting customers at the company where you work or helping a friend or family member with a project. Do you feel you met your customer's expectations? What did you do well? How could you have provided better service?

Project 10–5

Compare perceptions and expectations. Describe in a paragraph or two a situation where your perception of an event was different than what you expected. Include, if possible, a description of how a person with you had a different perception and different expectations. For example, you go to Mardi Gras in New Orleans expecting it to be fun and exciting and find that you are actually overwhelmed by what you perceive is the unruly nature of the crowd. On the other hand, your friend has a great time and can't wait to go back next year.

Project 10–6

Discuss customer needs and expectations. Assemble a team of at least three of your classmates. Assume the perspective of an office-based worker and discuss each of the three things you can count on customers wanting: responsiveness, a caring attitude, and skill. Discuss the ramifications if any one of these customer needs is not consistently met. Assume the perspective of a mobile worker, and repeat the discussion. Are the ramifications different if any one of these customer needs is not consistently met? Write a brief summary of your findings and discuss them with the class.

Project 10–7

Demonstrate a *can do* attitude. Sometimes we forget that in life, there is always something you can do. For the next 24 hours, write down any negative phrases you catch yourself using, such as "I can't," "It's not my job," and "There's nothing I can do." For each situation, restate the negative phrase in a positive way. Place your list of negative and restated phrases somewhere easy to locate.

Project 10–8

Assess your interpersonal skills. When hiring people for front-line positions, companies look for people with good interpersonal skills and a customer service orientation. Write down your answers to the following questions:

❑ Do I have a positive attitude?

❑ Do I enjoy helping other people?

❑ Do I enjoy solving problems?

❑ Do I consider myself a team-oriented person?

❑ Do I enjoy working with other people?

CASE PROJECTS

1. Way Cool, Inc.

Way Cool, Inc. has hired you to determine how it can minimize costs in terms of customer service and support. Its focus is on its product, a state-of-the-art virtual reality game that is extremely popular and attracting new users each day. The company wants to invest as much as possible in developing its game and as little as possible in terms of providing support. In fact, the company believes the game is so easy to use that support is unneeded and is thinking of eliminating customer support services all together. Prepare a brief report that outlines the pros and cons of minimizing the company's investment in support. Suggest ways the company can minimize its costs without eliminating support services altogether. Also suggest ways the company can ensure its minimized services are meeting customers needs.

2. Bill's Cyber Cycle Shop

Bill, the owner of Bill's Cyber Cycle Shop, has hired you to help survey his customers and determine whether his business is meeting its customer's needs. Bill wants his customers to perceive that his staff is there, willing, and able to support customers when they need help ordering bicycles and associated accessories from his Web site. Draft a customer satisfaction survey that Bill can use to measure his customer's satisfaction. Remember, he wants to know if customers perceive his staff as responsive, if they demonstrate a caring attitude, and if they have the skill needed to answer customer inquiries.

3. Bayside Unlimited

You work for a help desk that supports the internal employees of Bayside Unlimited. Your boss has asked you to identify any resources the help desk can use to improve the quality of its support services. Search the Web to locate organizations your help desk can join or magazines your help desk can subscribe to to learn more about the help desk industry and how other companies run their help desks. Prepare a report of your findings; include the name and a brief description of each organization and magazine you found along with the URL of its associated Web site.

CHAPTER

11

ATTITUDE, ANGRY CUSTOMERS, AND RELATIONSHIP BUILDING

Objectives

◆ Describe a customer-oriented attitude.

◆ Recognize situational examples that elicit rage reactions in customers.

◆ Identify actions CSRs can take to ensure delivery of comprehensive customer services.

◆ Describe the customer service benefits of the teamwork approach in organizations.

Customer expectations have a power in and of themselves. Learning to define, meet, and exceed those expectations is essential to customer satisfaction. As all the management and quality consultants will tell you, "The customer is king," because the customer remains the final judge of quality. The customer sets the standard for excellent service. The customer keeps a business in business.

All customers—internal and external—place different values on service, attitude, and performance. Therefore, find out exactly which areas are most important to the customer you are currently serving. Customer expectations must be realistic and attainable. Being able to define, meet, and exceed those expectations on a regular basis is the key to personal service performance, business growth, and customer satisfaction.

339

A CUSTOMER-ORIENTED SERVICE ATTITUDE

Think about the last time you visited a restaurant. What do you remember about it? Is your strongest memory of the food or of the service you received? Most of us say the service, even though we consciously believe we are going to a restaurant to get a good meal.

Management guru Peter Drucker put it best when he said, "The purpose of business is to create a customer." The logic follows that business is not about making sales, or even making profits. Those come naturally when you create customers—and keep them. Employees who give exceptional customer service have a positive, can-do attitude. They treat customers honorably and know it's essential to their success.

The **American Customer Satisfaction Index (ACSI)**, established in 1994 by the Business School at the University of Michigan, tracks trends in customer satisfaction and provides valuable benchmarking insights of the consumer economy for companies, industry trade associations, and government agencies. In the first quarter of every year, the ACSI measures customer satisfaction with the quality of products and services in energy utilities, airlines, express delivery, U.S. Postal Service, hospitals, hotels, fast-food restaurants, cable and satellite TV, and telecommunications services. After nudging upwards the previous quarter, the ACSI rose to 74.1 in the first quarter of 2006, its largest jump since 2003.[1]

The Power of a Positive Attitude

It may sound simplistic, but the first step toward creating an appropriate customer-oriented attitude is to begin thinking positive thoughts about yourself and others. What we see depends more often than not on what we look for. The second step is to reflect those thoughts in positive self-talk. **Self-talk** happens inside us, whether we are aware of it or not. We all talk to ourselves, and this self-talk can have a tremendous effect on our attitudes. Positive self-talk can help each of us build a positive, winning attitude.

Conversely, negative self-talk can do just the opposite. For example, we become our own worst enemies by telling ourselves things like "I'll never be any good at this" or "I look terrible today." We feel better if we replace those thoughts with statements such as "I'm sure I can do this with just a little practice" or "I look and feel great today."

A positive attitude is not necessarily something you are born with. Even if your attitude is negative from time to time, you can change and create a positive customer attitude that is helpful and dedicated to being outstanding. Today's customers perceive good service as added value. In other words, you need to add something extra to the product or service that is delivered.

Customers can sense positive energy, and the result is that they too come away feeling positive. The late Dr. Norman Vincent Peale had this to say about positive thinking: "You can make yourself sick with your thoughts, and you can make yourself well with them. A positive emotion is created by positive thoughts and images."

---

[1]"Consumer Willingness to Spend Beyond Means May Exceed Ability, According to American Customer Satisfaction Index," (May 16, 2006). www.theacsi.org.

A positive attitude is not only about choosing to have a good outlook through good times and bad, but also about learning to love what you do. Think of the successful people you know and you may agree that most are passionate about what they do, are rarely affected by negativity, and tend to enjoy their work. Having a positive attitude will help you make the best of almost any situation.

It's true that you can never have absolute control over what occurs in your company and in your personal life. But the attitude with which you choose to greet the day, approach your work, and respond to the people around you is fully within your control. A positive workplace attitude is reflected when you believe in your company, its products or services, its people, and in yourself. It should culminate in making the customer feel your belief from your words and actions.

Ethics / Choices

Carolyn, a CSR you work with, is having a difficult day. You have overheard her on two occasions sounding short with customers on the phone and are aware that your company is randomly monitoring customers' calls. Would you pull Carolyn aside to talk with her about your concerns?

TIP

Negative self-talk affects your attitude and interferes with your ability to develop an emotional connection with your customer.

The Customer's Attitude and You

In the real world, CSRs serve customers who display a variety of attitudes. For example, some customers are

1. *Comfortable.* Customers who believe their needs and expectations will be met.

2. *Indecisive.* Customers who cannot make up their minds or may not even know what they want.

3. *Insistent.* Customers who make demands and require you to take immediate action.

4. *Irate.* Customers who are angry and need to blow off steam before you can begin to work with them.

Your attitude toward a customer is not the only factor that can affect the outcome of that customer contact. When some other aspect of your life is bothering you, it can affect the way you interact with others. Whether your negative thoughts are based on something that happened to you earlier that day or on your negative expectations regarding a particular customer, replace them with positive ones, such as "I'm eager to help" or "Problem

Statement	Reason
1. "We don't offer that."	It's fine to say "no"; however, how you say "no" is all-important. For example, when you have to turn away a customer, recommend where the product or service can be found.
2. "All sales are final."	Your business should have a reasonable return policy and warranty plan. This sends a clear message to customers that you believe in what you are selling.
3. "I don't know who does that."	Business is lost, and this type of response frustrates customers. Employees must be familiar with who does what at a business or at least have immediate access to people who do have this knowledge.
4. "Sorry, that's our policy."	Customers faced with this statement will be annoyed at the lack of creativity a company shows in resolving their problems. Be flexible and helpful with customers who deserve a break.
5. "Tell us what you think."	Unless you are prepared to react to all varieties of feedback, be careful with this statement. A survey to assess customer satisfaction can be designed by companies to handle complaints as well as compliments.
6. "It will be ready tomorrow."	Unless you are sure it will be ready as promised, don't make this commitment. It is smarter to under promise and over deliver.
7. "I don't know."	Don't use that phrase unless you follow it with the phrase "but I will find out for you." Admitting you don't have the answer is fine and can actually improve your credibility, as long as you make an effort to get the answer for the customer.

Figure 11–1

solving is something I'm good at." Sometimes, on "off days," we say things we later regret. Figure 11–1 describes seven statements you should never say to customers.

The following list offers some survival tips to help keep your attitude up:

- Engage in positive self-talk. Practice healthy thinking. Do not clutter your mind with negatives.
- Get a calming object. Use a photo, cartoon, small stuffed animal, or positive notes in your work area that remind you "this too shall pass."
- Focus on successes rather than negatives. Track the things that go right.
- Use your break time effectively. Do something to keep yourself going, something that relaxes you and clears your mind. For example, listen to music, take a short walk, do some yoga stretches, or read. Do not use your free time for complaining to others.
- Develop a buddy system at work. Learn from each other and share the load.

As a CSR, do whatever it takes to avoid customer rage confrontations.

- Keep in mind your overall goals. When the details of work or a particular customer situation are getting you down, step back and look at the big picture.
- Be kind to yourself. Exercise, volunteer, spend time with friends and family, and do other things that add value to your life.
- Take your sense of humor to work. Take your work seriously, but don't take yourself seriously. Learn to laugh at yourself.

Ethics / Choices

Do you feel that service professionals have a choice whether to be rude or kind to others? Explain.

---

*CUSTOMER RAGE

Imagine these scenarios:

- Driving to work one morning, someone cuts you off in traffic. A little while later, you can't get someone to wait on you in a store when you run in for a pack of gum. Finally, you call your insurance agent but are unable to get a live person on the phone to answer a question. Before you know it, you're behaving rudely to somebody else.
- More than 25 times over the past couple of weeks, you've dialed your cell phone provider's customer service department, asking for help. Each time you had to ensure that the cell phone was fully charged, you would not be interrupted, and you had the time available to complete the call. Even after you were placed on hold for more than 20 minutes, no one responded to your call.

- When calling the bank, you provided your account number at the time of the automated phone greeting by using your touch-tone phone. You were passed off three times to another live agent, who asked you for the same information you'd already given.

- A CSR told you that she understood and sympathized with your problem and that she would refund your money (or fix the product) if she could, but unfortunately, she was powerless to do so. The computer system wouldn't permit her to help you. Then she said, "You are the tenth person with this problem today. We've asked management to fix this, but they never listen to us."

- You buy a software program hoping it will save you time, but it doesn't work. After combing the company's website for 10 minutes to find a telephone number, you call, only to be greeted by the company's seven-layer voicemail system. Once you finally get someone on the line, he insists that you are the one who created the problem and puts you on hold while finding someone who might be qualified to answer your questions.

Many frustrating situations can lead to customer rage. With \customer rage \comes an increasing number of irritated consumers who are taking out their anger on the CSRs they are dealing with. According to a customer rage survey released in November 2005, 15 percent of shoppers surveyed who received unsatisfactory service actually sought revenge for their suffering. Luckily for frontline customer service representatives, just 1 percent reported actually exacting vengeance (the details of which were not divulged in the study). A more composed 33 percent admitted to raising their voices, while 13 percent said they used profanity when interacting with CSRs.

The findings of the report, conducted by Customer Care Alliance in collaboration with the W. P. Carey School of Business at Arizona State University, show that the relationship between sellers and shoppers is rocky at best. Of the 1,012 survey respondents, 70 percent experienced customer rage, relating that their most serious consumer problem in the past year made them "extremely" or "very" upset. Most consumers characterize the service they get as "acceptable" or "average," and according to the report, more people say it is getting worse instead of better.[2]

Providing customer service seems as if it should be a matter of common sense. But many different things can go wrong. Although no one condones over-the-top behavior that sometimes accompanies customer rage, many of us have witnessed it as the unfortunate result of poor service.

Customers don't become dissatisfied because of problems. Customers become dissatisfied with the way problems are handled. Dealing ineffectively with a complaint can ruin brand or company loyalty. Putting the wrong person in front of a customer is ineffective and bears enormous costs. Add the loss of the lifetime value of a customer to the cost of hiring and replacing an employee, and your bottom line becomes affected. What can you do? Develop a real plan for problem resolution. Put the right people in place, make sure they are well

---

[2]Dayana Yochim. "Customer Rage Is on the Rise," *The Motley Fool* (November 3, 2005).

trained to listen and offer apologies when appropriate, and give them the authority to offer solutions. These actions show customers that you have a trained staff ready to help them.

Some companies give employees the authority to make customers happy. With these guidelines, customer care representatives are empowered to make decisions on the spot—to give exchanges, credits, or refunds, or even to get a customer something else by having a "no-hassle" policy whereby customers can return products at any time for any reason.[3]

DELIVERING COMPREHENSIVE SERVICE

Serving customers well is not a case of "us versus them," but rather a win–win situation. When common goals with your customer are established, you are both working toward something you agree is worthy. When you reach those goals, you are both satisfied. Moreover, if you don't reach them, the customer feels that at least you tried and gave an honest effort.

When a customer complains, you need to take corrective action as soon as possible. If the customer complains directly to you, avoid being defensive or judgmental. Do not attempt to explain why the problem occurred. The customer is not particularly interested in reasons for poor service or who is to blame. Customers want to know they are being heard and that their comments are valued. Most of all, they want the problem resolved. Remember, when a customer perceives that he or she is not being served well, that is the customer's reality.

If a word or a phrase isn't common knowledge, don't use it with a customer. Always speak distinctly, or you risk failing to connect with the customer.

TIP

Delivery of Services

Often, customer service representatives have to deal with customers who perceive services they receive through a **filter**, or screen. Such a frame of reference can depend on one or more factors.

- How the customer feels that day
- Experiences the customer has had that day
- Experiences the customer has had in the past with the CSR or the company
- Experiences the customer's friends or family members have had with employees in the company
- The setting, environment, and circumstances of the current interaction

---

[3]Elaine Appleton Grant, "Top 10 Ways to Fail at Customer Service," *Momentum*, the Microsoft® newsletter (December 1, 2005).

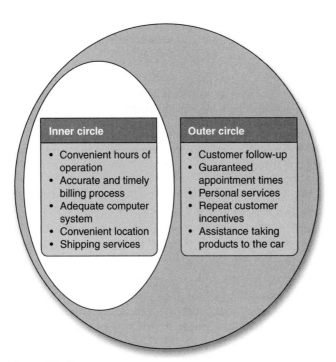

Figure 11–2

All things being equal, there is little difference between one organization's product over its competitor's. Customer service is the variable. One small action can make all the difference to a customer on a particular day. In the case of customer service, we can look at delivery of services similar to those in Figure 11–2. The concept of delivery of services can be represented by two circles—one within the other.

The inner circle is made up of the basic services and products an organization and its competition provide. Customers expect the services shown in the inner circle: convenient hours of operation, accurate and timely billing processes, adequate computer systems, convenient locations, and shipping services. In contrast, the outer circle allows a company to showcase its organization, to set itself apart from the competition by providing elements that exceed customers' expectations: customer follow-up, guaranteed appointment times, personal services, repeat customer incentives, and assistance taking products to the car.

Outer-circle service is extremely important. This is where you can separate yourself from the competition. Your inner circle may be perfect because you do everything the customer expects, but what you do might not be enough to guarantee that the customer will come back on a regular basis. Without strong outer-circle service, you may not be offering the customer anything special enough to set you apart from the competition.

---

[4]Bill Brooks, "It's All about People—All the Time," *Agency Sales* (September 2005): 35.

Service, a critical business function, is driven primarily by the mindset, perspective, and abilities of the people who perform the activities. Granted, you can provide people with better tools, improved systems, enhanced delivery methods, improved facilities, and all the rest. But the bottom line is simple—good people get good results, better people get better results, and superior people get superior results. Only accomplished service providers can turn the correct phrase, make the proper decision, take ownership of problems, and go out of the way to do the right thing. And, in the final analysis, those are the things that determine long-term business success—or failure.[4]

CSRs and the Adversity Quotient®

Paul Stoltz, author of the book *Adversity Quotient @ Work*, states that companies should hire customer service representatives who have a high adversity quotient (AQ®). An **adversity quotient** is a precise, measurable, unconscious pattern of how people respond to adversity. According to Stoltz, companies need to hire customer service representatives who are not only nice but also resilient and who have high AQs. Unless CSRs learn how to maintain control and be energized by tough problems, adversity will take its toll on them and negatively affect the services they provide to customers. The core elements of an adversity quotient, according to Stoltz, are control, ownership, reach, and endurance.

CONTROL CSRs who have a high AQ perceive that they have influence over adverse customer service situations. For example, if the company has a product recall, CSRs remain calm, project a positive attitude, and reassure customers that the problem will be remedied. On the other hand, low-AQ CSRs become stressed and overwhelmed by adversity.

OWNERSHIP CSRs with a high AQ hold themselves accountable for solving customers' problems. Conversely, low-AQ CSRs are likely to say, "It's not my fault."

REACH High-AQ CSRs refuse to allow negative situations to reach into other areas of their work lives. For instance, if a customer threatens to defect to a competitor, they focus on earning back the customer's loyalty, remaining upbeat no matter what. Conversely, low-AQ CSRs view the situation as hopeless and allow their feelings to have an impact on other aspects of their job.

ENDURANCE High-AQ CSRs can see beyond difficulties and retain their optimism. This gives them the endurance to hang on during adverse encounters with customers. In contrast, low-AQ CSRs reason, "Why try to endure this? It's only going to end in disaster!"[5]

Star CSRs have a number of skills and personal characteristics in common. In today's competitive marketplace, you need to do all you can to differentiate yourself in terms of providing excellent customer service. Assume the role of the CSR you want to become and answer each question in Figure 11–3 to determine how well you might stand out compared with other service providers.

[5]"Forget the Smile Training—Consider Boot Camp!" *Managing Customer Service* (April 2001): 8.

Yes	No	Question
☐	☐	1. Do you spend 60 to 70 percent of your time listening while a customer talks?
☐	☐	2. Do you smile more often than most other people?
☐	☐	3. Are you better than others at recognizing and responding to customer questions and problems?
☐	☐	4. Are you highly effective at identifying and prioritizing customer needs?
☐	☐	5. Do you tend to recommend additional products or services that meet a customer's specific needs?
☐	☐	6. Do you explain procedures in clear, concise terms?
☐	☐	7. Are you highly enthusiastic about attending customer service training seminars and classes?
☐	☐	8. Do you listen to motivational tapes and read inspirational books in your leisure time?
☐	☐	9. Do you regard yourself as generally upbeat and positive?
☐	☐	10. Do you enjoy the work you do?
___	___	Total

Figure 11-3 Do You Stand Out from the Competition?
Note: If you answered "yes" to nine or ten questions, you already have many habits of highly successful CSRs. Eight is an average score. Seven or fewer indicates that you can improve your performance.

Customer Service Rules and Guidelines

When you work for any organization, you must follow some rules and guidelines. To distinguish among these rules, we'll refer to them as red and blue rules. **Red rules** are very prescriptive, because they must be followed exactly as specified. An example of a red rule is a legal obligation to follow particular procedures exactly as outlined. Another red rule might involve safety issues federally mandated by the Occupational Safety and Health Administration (OSHA). Every employee in an organization must follow red rules.

Blue rules are optional and can be bent or modified based on the circumstances. Statements such as "We don't work after 5:00 p.m." and "Late fees cannot be waived" are examples of blue rules. They play into the old saying, "There is an exception to every (blue) rule."

Sometimes the most reasonable and prudent action is to bend the rule because it makes sense and is for the greater good of the situation and for the customer involved. In a customer-centric organization, you must clearly define both the red and blue rules, and give individual employees the discretion to change blue rules on a case-by-case basis. CSRs are empowered when working for customer-centric organizations to use their best judgment.

BUILDING A TEAMWORK APPROACH TO CUSTOMER SERVICE

What do you think of when someone mentions the word teamwork? Sports teams most often come to mind, but other situations involve teamwork as well. For example, consider the movie industry. Every time producers make a movie, they have to put together a new team that includes actors, sound and light crews, makeup artists, clothes designers, and directors, among others. All the members of the team are needed to create the finished product, a movie. In order to accomplish that goal with positive results, all the members must work together as a team.

Similarly, taking a team approach to customer service means working together as a group with common expectations and goals. Although companies focus thousands of dollars on external customer service in hopes of wooing and retaining customers, little attention is being paid to the effect poor internal customer service has on customer satisfaction. It all starts within the organization. Sooner or later the ripple effect reaches out to customers.

Internal customer service refers to service directed toward others within the organization. It refers to the level of responsiveness, quality, communication, team-work, and morale. To help strengthen internal customer service orientation, CSRs should follow these basic rules.

• Employees should never complain within earshot of customers. It gives them the impression your company isn't well run, shaking their confidence in you.

Focus on Best Practices

FedEx Corp. is ranked among the best 100 companies to work for by Fortune magazine. The Memphis-based FedEx, which has been on the list for nine consecutive years, ranked 64th and was noted as one of the most diverse companies. In addition, FedEx was ranked No. 1 in job growth, based on number of new jobs.

Frederick W. Smith, chairman, president, and CEO of FedEx, said that the ranking was a testament to "our belief in the value of our employees. Every day, their passion allows us to deliver an exceptional experience for our customers." To determine the best places to work, Fortune and the Great Place to Work Institute conducted anonymous employee satisfaction surveys and analyzed the company's policies, culture, demographics, salaries, and benefits. With annual revenues of $31 billion, FedEx Corp. employs about 30,000 in Memphis and more than 230,000 around the United States and the globe.

Source: Memphis Business Journal (January 11, 2006).

- Employees should never complain to customers about another department's employees. Who wants to patronize a company whose people don't get along with each other?

- Employees at every level should strive to build bridges between departments. This can be done through cross training, joint picnics, off-site gatherings, or creative meetings, as well as day-to-day niceties.

What does teamwork show customers? A good team approach shows that the company is organized and that everyone is moving toward a common goal of satisfying the customer. Because of shared ownership, no team member will allow the failure of one member, because the entire team will fail. When team members are accountable to each other, customers know that the final objective of the team is their satisfaction.

Customers feel special when service providers work as a team.

Teamwork Communication

Communication is one of the most important elements of a successful team. For a team to be effective, its members must communicate with each other so everyone can stay informed. Whenever a team is put together, issues such as different personalities, management styles, and company hierarchies arise. Many times, exchanging honest, open feedback is more difficult with someone you work with than with your customers. This might be because the message you have to share with a fellow worker is not a positive one.

To maintain good working relationships, any negative feedback you offer a coworker should be focused on a specific task, not on his or her personality. Also, to be constructive, any criticism you offer should be accompanied by a positive suggestion on how to improve the task. By the same token, if a teammate is doing something well, be sure to mention it. Again, focus your comments on the task. An effective customer-centric environment fosters forthright feedback and values honesty.

Benefits of Teamwork

When customer service is built with organizational teamwork as its foundation, many benefits result. One of the most important benefits is that teamwork helps break down walls that can sometimes exist between departments within organizations. Teamwork can also provide new ideas and a new slant on customer problems. Finally, teamwork can create a more effective method for delegating work and any follow-up actions that must be taken.

Because no one is an expert on everything, people need to gather knowledge from others. People who work together tend to learn things faster and retain information longer than do individuals who work alone. Teamwork creates a synergy, which means that the combined effect of the efforts of many individuals is greater than the sum of their individual efforts. With synergy, problem solving becomes more effective, and better decisions tend to be made. Figure 11–4 provides some strategies that team members can adopt to provide exceptional customer service.

BUSINESS in Action
FORRESTER RESEARCH

Forrester Research, an independent technology and market research company, has reported the 2006 Customer Advocacy Rankings in Financial Services. Based on a survey of nearly 5,000 consumers, the rankings rate 32 leading U.S. financial services firms according to the key driver of customer loyalty. Customer advocacy is the perception on the part of consumers that their financial services firm does what's best for its customers, not just for the firm's own bottom line.

For the third consecutive year, United Services Automobile Association (USAA) retained the top spot in Forrester's rankings, followed by credit unions, GEICO®, AAA, State Farm, and Vanguard. Rounding out the bottom of the 2006 list were Bank of America, Morgan Stanley, National City, Citibank, and JP Morgan Chase. The report concludes that firms with high customer-advocacy rankings are best positioned to grow in the coming years, as intense competition forces firms to focus on selling more to their existing customers rather than growing by merger and acquisition.

Source : www.forrester.com.

1. *Support your teammates with information.* Share what you know freely with your coworkers. Use huddles—brief, informal meetings—instead of formal meetings, when time is limited.

2. *Discuss new policies.* Discuss any new policies with your team and jointly create a way to explain changes to your customers in a positive way. Sometimes, using a script can ensure that everyone is consistently following the same plan.

3. *Identify areas for improvement.* Let the ideas flow without judgment in a brainstorming session. The craziest ideas sometimes turn out to be the ones that work best.

4. *Show pride in yourself and your coworkers.* Celebrate others' successes. Let the customer know you are proud of yourself, your coworkers, and your organization.

Figure 11–4

Concluding Message for CSRs

Companies sometimes make painful compromises by hiring people with less than stable work histories and less than acceptable customer service attitudes. Employers want service providers who make a commitment to getting to work on time and who are energetic, knowledgeable, kind, and efficient with customers.

Customer care representatives can provide service more consistently if four important guidelines are followed: View all customers positively; establish an emotional connection with customers by giving them your undivided attention; listen actively to all customer concerns; and take action to resolve any problems.

Summary

- The customer is the one who sets the standard for service excellence.

- When a customer complains, corrective action should be taken as soon as possible to prevent customer rage.

- The adversity quotient is the precise, measurable, unconscious pattern of how people respond to adversity.

- A good team approach shows that the company is organized and that everyone is moving toward the common goal of doing whatever it takes to satisfy the customer.

KEY TERMS

adversity quotient
American Customer Satisfaction
Index (ACSI)

blue rules
customer rage
filter
red rules
self-talk
synergy

CRITICAL THINKING

1. How would you describe the best customer-oriented attitude you've encountered relative to services you've received over the past month?

2. Name four ways that customer rage can be prevented or reduced.

3. Describe a business you've encountered in your city where you feel both its outer- and inner-level elements of customer service are excellent.

4. Do you agree that the way people handle adversity in their lives affects their service and work attitudes? Explain.

5. What are two benefits to a CSR of contributing to team efforts at work? Why do you think some service professionals prefer to work alone rather than in a team?

ONLINE RESEARCH ACTIVITIES

HANDS-ON PROJECTS

Project 11–1 Customer Rage

Assume you are doing a report on the risks of customer rage to the customer service person. Use the Internet to search for information on this topic. As a result of your search, list three items and their URLs you might include in your report.

_____

_____

_____

_____

Project 11–2 The Adversity Quotient

In the lunchroom one day at On-Time Technology Products, someone left the book *Adversity Quotient @Work* on one of the tables. Several CSRs picked it up and started talking about the usefulness of AQ when applying these concepts in the world of business. You said you felt it could apply to any aspect of our lives, including how we work, play, learn, and interact with others. Doug, on the other hand, said he felt that AQ applied only to the business world, and Ruth said that if educators could help students achieve higher AQs, then school environments would be less violent.

Use your favorite search engine to locate and read additional information about applying the adversity quotient in other venues. With a broader understanding of its multi-application, supply responses that provide information on ways that a high adversity quotient can positively influence each of the following life situations.

Life Situation	Benefit of Applying High AQs
1. In business, in general	
2. In call centers for CSRs	
3. In the home or family	
4. In schools (K–12)	

Project 11–3 Action Plan for Improving Your Attitude

Supervisor Mary Graeff has asked each CSR at OTTP to develop an action plan to improve employees' attitudes when working with customers. Give some thought to each of the situations in column 1 and respond in column 2 with an activity that would work for you.

What Can You Do to ...	
1. Convey interest in your customers?	
2. Keep your attitude positive?	
3. Remain energized and enthusiastic on the job?	
4. Learn more about the organization you work for?	
5. Take initiative when helping a customer?	

HANDS-ON PROJECTS

Project 11–4 How to Motivate the Unenthusiastic Teammate

During a weekly team meeting at On-Time Technology Products, you notice that one of your coworkers is quieter than usual. He acts as if he does not care to be involved in the team's brainstorming session.

Respond to each of the following statements with an example of what you might say to a team member who suffers from a lack of motivation.

1. Acknowledge your teammate's value.

_____

_____

2. Get to the source of the problem.

_____

_____

3. Stress the importance of team harmony.

_____

_____

HANDS-ON PROJECTS

Project 11–5 "Deal with It!"

On the first day of a four-day holiday weekend, Samantha was having a problem with her phone and needed to use her neighbor Tim's phone. When she finished talking to the customer service representative at the phone company, she was quite shocked by the service she had received. She told Tim that the CSR said she would just "have to deal with the inconvenience until Tuesday morning." Samantha ranted and raved to Tim for 20 minutes. After answering the following two questions, discuss how the conversation should have gone.

1. Does Samantha have a legitimate reason to be upset with the phone company?

_____

_____

_____

2. If this happened to you, what steps would you suggest to the phone company for improving its customer service?

_____

_____

_____

HANDS-ON PROJECTS

Project 11–6 "If There's a Rule, I'll Follow It"

Doug, a CSR for On-Time Technology Products, recently experienced a very frustrating brush with civil law concerning boundary lines between his property and a neighbor's. Everyone at work recognizes that as a consequence of this negative legal experience, Doug is a bit strict when it comes to following rules. However, the situation is beginning to affect his work, because his narrow-minded attitude is being reflected in how he treats customers.

1. In what ways do situations in someone's personal life spill over and affect attitudes on the job? Describe some examples you've observed or experienced.

_____

_____

_____

2. If you were Mary Graeff, Doug's supervisor, how would you explain to him the best way to interpret which rules he is required to follow to the letter and which ones allow him some flexibility?

_____

_____

_____

3. If Ms. Graeff were to ask you what steps you would take to help Doug overcome this attitude and get back on track with customers, what would you recommend that she do (simply talk to him, reprimand him, enroll him in training, …)?

_____

_____

_____

12

Teams and Team Players in a Help Desk Setting

In this chapter you will learn:
◆ The characteristics of a successful team
◆ The stages of growth that teams go through
◆ How successful teams manage the inevitable and normal conflict in a team setting
◆ How to understand your role in the help desk and in your company's support organization
◆ How to contribute to your team's goals
◆ The skills needed to have positive working relationships with your teammates

In the frenetic setting of a technical help desk, no single person can know everything about all the products supported and provide all the support customers need. The demands are too great. As a result, the members of the help desk must work together as team. A **team** is a group of people organized to work together toward the achievement of a goal. To be successful, all team members must understand how their efforts contribute to the attainment of that goal.

Working in a group that calls itself a team does not make a person a team player. A team player is a person who contributes to the team's success by cooperating freely and communicating openly with his or her teammates. An effective team is made up of team players who contribute special skills or a unique personal style to the team. To be a team player, you must understand your role in the help desk and your role in the company's support organization. You must know how you can contribute to your team's goals and you must support and respect the abilities of other team members and acknowledge their contributions.

WORKING AS A TEAM

Not all work requires the efforts of a team. For example, the sales profession usually requires an individual endeavor. Although a sales person's efforts may benefit the sales "team" or company, the salesperson's compensation is typically based on personal achievements. As a result, a company's salespeople often compete with one another to enhance their personal standing. In a team setting, competition is eliminated, and team members work together toward a common goal.

Technical support lends itself to a team setting for a number of reasons. These reasons include:

- **The sheer number of available products.** The technology marketplace is jammed with vendors looking to sell their product and become a market leader. Users or potential users may be tempted to say, "A printer is a printer," but each product has unique features and functionality that a help desk analyst must understand in order to support it. Although an analyst may be able to become proficient in a single product line or family of products, no one can master all of the products available today.

- **The integration of products and systems.** A dramatic increase in the number of integrated products and systems makes it even more difficult for analysts to diagnose and determine the probable source of problems. The Microsoft Office suite, which integrates products such as Word, Excel, Access, PowerPoint, and Outlook, is just one example of how tightly integrated products can be. The integration of a company's Web site with its customer management, knowledge management, and order management systems is another example. The challenge facing help desks is compounded by the fact that many of these products and systems may be supported by different level two groups. As a result, the help desk must interface with multiple groups when the source of a problem is unclear.

- **The constant and pervasive rate of technological change.** It has become virtually impossible for a single individual to be aware of and understand the changes occurring within a single market segment, such as hardware-, software-, or network-related products, much less the integration of these products throughout an entire company. Simply reading and assimilating all of the information offered in trade magazines, electronic magazines (usually called ezines), and on Web sites could constitute a full-time job. This doesn't even include putting that information into action.

- **The need for business knowledge.** Technical support is about helping people use technology to achieve business goals. Increasingly, help desk analysts are being challenged to understand the business goals of their customers so that they can help their customers use technology to achieve those goals. This means that, in addition to technical skills, analysts may possess skills and knowledge that are unique to the profession they support, such as accounting skills or banking knowledge. It is not possible or practical for all members of the help desk team to acquire every business and technical skill needed to support their customers.

Rather, team members typically specialize in different areas of the business and then work together to solve problems that span multiple specialty areas.

- **The increasing complexity of the business world.** Help desk analysts work with people of varying skill levels, education levels, and cultural backgrounds. Furthermore, help desks increasingly partner with vendors and service agencies in the course of delivering services. For example, more companies are outsourcing help desk services in an effort to deliver high-quality support services at a reduced cost. It would be extremely difficult for one help desk analyst to manage these diverse relationships and speak the many technical and nontechnical languages associated with them.

- **The need to use resources efficiently and effectively.** Managers in today's business world demand high productivity and high quality. Help desk analysts must handle requests and solve problems correctly the first time because little to no time exists to do things over. Also, analysts who lack the skills or training to perform a task that their job requires do not have the time it would take to "figure things out" on their own. As a result, help desk analysts must collaborate with teammates and other service providers to get the job done as quickly and correctly as possible.

Technical support lends itself to a team setting because the demands of the environment are simply too great for a single analyst. Instead, the members of the help desk need to work together as a team. Each analyst must maintain a high level of knowledge about the products and systems for which he or she is recognized as an expert, and at the same time show respect and support for the other members of the team. In other words, a member of the help desk team who is highly skilled in one particular product cannot discount the efforts of another team member who is not familiar with that product. That other team member may be highly experienced in another product, or may have business skills, soft skills, or self-management skills that contribute to the goals of the team.

Blake Cahill

DIRECTOR OF MARKETING & PRODUCT MANAGEMENT

SAFEHARBOR TECHNOLOGY CORPORATION

SEATTLE, WASHINGTON

WWW.SAFEHARBOR.COM

SafeHarbor Technology Corporation is a leading provider of flexible multi-channel support solutions. Since 1998, SafeHarbor's multi-client customer intelligence center has built and delivered high-quality support solutions for some of the world's leading companies. Blake Cahill describes how SafeHarbor teams with its clients to deliver effective and innovative customer support services.

SafeHarbor's clients face a universal challenge—how to provide their customers a consistent support experience across multiple channels such as e-mail, the telephone, chat, and the Web. SafeHarbor meets this challenge by studying its clients' needs and designing integrated self-service and assisted support options that let its clients' customers obtain service however and whenever they want. SafeHarbor also meets this challenge by maintaining a client-centric work environment, filled with people who understand not only how to support technology, but also how to use technology to deliver support. Rather than adopting a traditional telephone-based service model, SafeHarbor offers next-generation support services that are designed to leverage the Web. To do this, SafeHarbor incorporates the multimedia capabilities of the Web into a self-help environment that is enhanced by support analyst interaction. In other words, SafeHarbor delivers Web-based services that are enhanced by the telephone, e-mail, and chat, rather than telephone-based services that are enhanced by the Web. Companies can outsource their support services to SafeHarbor, or they can hire SafeHarbor to develop a support solution that they can then use to do support themselves.

SafeHarbor employees are offered a wealth of opportunities that span the range of skills needed to support SafeHarbor's state-of-the-art technical infrastructure and deliver its innovative support services. Job positions include support analysts, knowledge engineers, account managers, Web designers, database administrators, and IT staff. Staff members are organized into teams and each team is dedicated to supporting a specific client account and is responsible for that account's satisfaction and results. To maximize productivity, teams are also cross-trained to support multiple customer accounts.

SafeHarbor's client-oriented approach ensures that support services are aligned with its client's goals. Support analysts, knowledge engineers, account managers, and Web designers work together to develop and deliver solutions that use a language and tone that is consistent with that of their client's. SLAs, extensive training, and monthly and quarterly reviews are used to ensure a quality customer experience, regardless of the channel a customer chooses to obtain support. A customized knowledge base further ensures a consistent support experience by giving support analysts and customers access to the same information across channels. SafeHarbor's knowledge engineers use sophisticated knowledge publishing tools to design, acquire, develop, and deliver a knowledge base that support analysts and customers can access 24 hours a day, 7 days a week. Because support analysts are often encountering problems that are not found in the knowledge base, they are considered the first link in the chain of knowledge base development. When they encounter a new problem, they use workflow built into their call tracking system to document the solution. Knowledge engineers then refine the solutions (incorporating visual aids such as diagrams, screenshots, and schematics whenever possible to make the solution easier to use) and then post the solution in the knowledge base.

Support analysts and customers can then use the new solution.

This disciplined and innovative approach enables SafeHarbor to deliver high quality solutions and services at a lower cost. By collecting and analyzing data from all support channels, SafeHarbor is able to continuously improve its solutions and services, while enabling its clients to improve their products and understand customer behaviors. Powerful data warehousing and reporting tools make it possible for SafeHarbor to deliver that data back to its clients in the form of recommendations aimed at eliminating problems, improving products and services, and, ultimately, transforming the customer support experience.

SafeHarbor is working hard to revolutionize the way support is delivered to customers. This forward-looking approach results in an interesting and challenging workplace for SafeHarbor's employees. Support analysts use a myriad of tools to deliver solutions that they are actively involved in developing. By working in multi-faceted teams, employees have the opportunity to be involved in many aspects of the support delivery process. They also have a career path into other groups within the company. Extensive cross-training makes it possible for support analysts to work with varying client accounts and customers. Most importantly, employees are actively involved in helping SafeHarbor's clients meet their goals and overcome the support industry's greatest challenge. How do companies provide their customers a consistent support experience across multiple channels? It takes a team!

Characteristics of a Successful Team

Just as working in a group that calls itself a team does not make a person a team player, assembling a group of team players does not make a successful team. To be successful, a team must share the characteristics listed in Figure 12–1. Teams that do not exhibit these characteristics are often ineffective and suffer negative side effects, such as low morale, low productivity, and high stress.

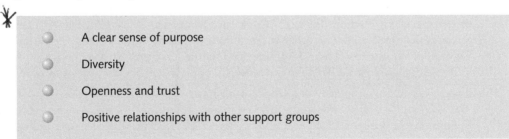

- A clear sense of purpose
- Diversity
- Openness and trust
- Positive relationships with other support groups

Figure 12–1 Characteristics of a successful team

The next sections explore each of these characteristics in detail.

A Clear Sense of Purpose.   For a help desk to be successful, the mission and goals of the team must be clearly defined and accepted by all of the team members. A help desk's **mission** is a written statement of the customers the help desk serves, the types of services the help desk provides, and how the help desk delivers those services. In other words, a mission defines who the help desk supports, what it supports, and how it provides that support. The mission then determines the type, size, and structure of the help desk. **Help desk goals** are measurable objectives that support the help desk's mission. Most help desks establish specific goals each year in an effort to clarify what analysts are supposed to focus on, eliminate conflicting goals, and encourage analysts to produce the desired results. Individual performance goals further define how help desk analysts contribute to their team's goals. **Individual performance goals** are measurable objectives for people who support the help desk's mission. Because individuals contribute to teams in different ways, individual performance goals may vary from one person to the next. However, all individual performance goals will support the help desk's goals.

NOTE   Without a clearly defined mission and goals, a help desk can fall prey to the "all things to all people" syndrome. When the help desk tries to be "all things to all people," its resources can quickly be stretched too thin and its team spirit can quickly decline.

> *The achievements of an organization are the result of the combined effort of each individual.* Vince Lombardi

Diversity.   A common misconception is that to be successful, all of the members of a team must be alike, agree on everything, and get along at all times. The reality is that the most successful teams are made up of people who have unique skills and exhibit varying approaches to teamwork. In a baseball team, for instance, each player performs a different task. One plays first base, another specializes in pitching, and so on. Each player has an area of expertise and may actually not perform well if asked to perform in an area other than his or her specialty. (Pitchers, for example, are notoriously poor batters.) Each player must also at times be a leader, and at other times follow the leader. What makes these people with varying talents a team? Their desire to play together in order to win the game. In business terms, team players must be willing to work together to achieve the team's mission and goals.

Today, when team-oriented companies consider a prospective employee, they look at the individual's personality and willingness to work in a team setting and toward team goals, as well as the person's business and technical skills. They want to ensure that the new hire will fit into the company's corporate culture and into the culture of the hiring team. Cultures vary from company to company and team to team, just as they vary from one country to the next. For example, some companies have a hierarchical culture where layers of managers coordinate and control the work of their employees. Other companies have more of a participative culture where self-directed teams coordinate and control their work with support from a team leader when needed. Furthermore, the culture of teams within a company can vary. For example, in a company with a hierarchical culture, a particular manager may encourage a participative work environment. Both companies and employees benefit when an employee's personality is compatible with a team and company's culture. This is particularly true in organizations that do not have formal management chains and strictly defined job descriptions.

> *Together Everyone Achieves More. Author Unknown*

Openness and Trust.　Communication within a team setting is just as important as communicating with customers. Team members must be willing to share their knowledge, give and receive constructive feedback, and freely express their feelings. Effective communication requires that team members are not only willing to talk, but also willing to listen. If a team member does not understand a point a coworker is making, that person must ask for clarification, paraphrase, or summarize his or her teammate's point of view to ensure understanding. Team members must also be able to rely on each other to get the job done. Although it is human nature to have a bad day now and then, team members must not impose their personal moods and problems on their coworkers. This does not mean that team members should not ask for help when they need it. In the most effective teams, members feel comfortable stating their weaknesses and looking to teammates for strength.

NOTE

Personal and professional insecurities on the part of individuals can stand in the way of teamwork. For example, a person who is insecure about his standing in a team may be hesitant to voice his opinion or share his knowledge. Or, a person who is insecure may become defensive, uncooperative, or angry when questioned about her work. People who experience insecurities must work hard to overcome their fears and have confidence in their abilities and in the abilities of others. Techniques such as positive self-talk and assertiveness training can help people overcome their insecurities and establish positive working relationships with their teammates.

TIP

To deal with an insecure person, listen to and try to understand them. Treat them with respect and interest. A positive approach may prompt the person to become more open and trusting.

Positive Relationships with Other Support Groups.　When working in a team, members are accountable not only to the other members of the team, but also to the "greater team" that constitutes the service delivery chain within their company and that includes external service providers. Successful teams have positive working relationships with other groups, such as level two support groups, the training group, the Sales and Marketing department, external service providers, and so forth. The help desk must rely on these groups to provide knowledge, tools, and credibility. When the help desk lacks credibility, customers may contact these groups directly, circumventing the help desk altogether. As a result, the help desk is unable to gain the confidence of its customers and of the other groups in its service delivery chain. Without the support of these other groups, it is unlikely that the help desk's potential will be realized and its contribution recognized.

A team leader to whom members are loyal is another characteristic of a successful team. Although a successful team can work around a poor team leader, an effective leader enables the team to achieve its full potential by removing obstacles and by sharing leadership responsibilities as needed to get the job done.

Kianna Francis
MOUSE SQUAD TEAM LEADER
GRACE H. DODGE HIGH SCHOOL
BRONX, NEW YORK

Learning to work in a team setting and on a help desk begins early for students participating in an innovative program run by MOUSE (Making Opportunities for Upgrading Schools & Education). MOUSE is a nonprofit organization funded by the local business community, private foundations, and government agencies and works with elementary, middle, and high schools to set up student-run help desks called MOUSE Squads.

Founded in 1997, MOUSE currently operates in 49 elementary, middle, and high schools in New York with recently established programs operating in Chicago, Connecticut, and Michigan. Kianna Francis, a 17-year-old junior at Grace H. Dodge High School, answers a few questions about how MOUSE Squads operate and her role as a Team Leader.

Question: What are MOUSE Squads?

Answer: MOUSE Squads (MSs) are teams of elementary, middle, and high school students recruited to set up and run a technology help desk in their schools. The MSs operate during the school day and after school to provide teachers, administrators, and students with a trained support staff to troubleshoot and solve technical problems. On average, MSs provide their schools with over 20 hours of level one technical support each week, up to 1,000 hours throughout the school year. Each Squad has an average of seven students per Squad per year.

Question: How are MSs organized?

Answer: Each MS has a Faculty Advisor who has direct responsibility for his or her school's Squad. At the start of each school year, MOUSE trains the Faculty Advisors, who in turn recruit the students who will make up the current year's Squads. Students from throughout the city come together and participate in a series of hands-on workshops where they learn how to run a technical support help desk. In addition to learning basic troubleshooting skills, students learn customer-relations skills and the role that data play in developing a technical support solution.

Students participating in the MS program can assume one or more of three roles: Technician, Team Leader, or Information Manager. All members of the Squad serve as Technicians, which means they provide an average of at least five hours of weekly service on the Help Desk and must log those hours in the Hours Log. Technicians respond to ticket requests to the best of their ability, complete scheduled maintenance projects, log ticket requests on a daily basis, and participate in weekly team meetings and required training sessions. The Team Leader is the student manager of the MS. The Information Manager manages data and information related to the MS Help Desk, in addition to his or her duties as a Technician.

Question: What are your duties as Team Leader?

Answer: In addition to my duties as a Technician, I coordinate the weekly schedule to ensure maximum Help Desk coverage, oversee responses to ticket requests, manage maintenance activities, review Help Desk data to ensure that it is being properly logged, and facilitate communication among Squad members. I also provide the Faculty Advisor with periodic updates and oversee the Help Desk's Base of Operations, which is where MS members meet and store MOUSE-related equipment.

Question: How did you become a Team Leader?

Answer: My family stresses the importance of leadership and sharing, and in school I enjoy working in groups and on group assignments. I tend to take the role of delegating tasks to others and so when I heard about the MOUSE Squad, I applied to be a Team Leader. I know that I am responsible and reliable, and I hope that as Team Leader I can help others to be the same.

Question: Tell us more about your MOUSE Squad experience.

Answer: Being on the MOUSE Squad has helped me become a better person in terms of being cooperative and learning how to take and give counsel. Because I work with a lot of guys, I am learning to be more assertive and I'm also learning how to motivate and encourage others. It can be challenging at times, for example, when we're unable to solve a problem, but we work together and get it done eventually. I feel a sense of accomplishment when we're able to complete projects and meet challenges.

Question: Do you enjoy being a part of the MOUSE Squad program?

Answer: I like it a lot now that I've gotten used to the schedule. I enjoy helping others and it makes me feel good when a problem is solved. I enjoy working with my peers on the team and I like helping the teachers, as they help us a lot. I also like that I can help my family and myself with computer problems.

Grace H. Dodge High School is one of four vocational schools in the Bronx. It offers a paralegal studies program in addition to the more conventional cosmetology, business, and health-related careers programs. Kianna is enrolled in the Academy of Finance and Accounting and plans to pursue a career in banking and finance.

Building a Solid Team

To perform at maximum efficiency and effectiveness, each team member, including the leader, must embrace the characteristics of a successful team. That is, the team must have a *clear sense of purpose*. The team leader cannot simply choose a direction and instruct the team to follow blindly. Members of successful teams are committed to the goals of the team and to each other's ability to grow and be successful. To grow, team members must embrace *diversity*. Team members must acknowledge their weaknesses, set individual goals, and take steps to improve, or rely upon, the strengths of their teammates, to get the job done. As a team, members must acknowledge the unique skills that each player contributes and seek out and accept into the team people who can fill the team's voids. When people work together this way, the sum of their efforts is invariably greater than the efforts of any one person acting alone. This is because the combined experience of the team is greater than the experience of any one team member.

> *No one can be the best at everything. But when all of us combine our talents, we can be the best at virtually anything.* Don Ward

One of the greatest challenges that a team faces is establishing methods of communication that promote *openness and trust*. This is because the team must have in place ways of communicating within the team, between individual team members, and with groups outside the team. No team stands alone. Teams must have *positive relationships with other support groups* who can provide the funds, equipment, training, and information the team needs to succeed.

A group of people cannot become a team overnight. It takes time, an open, pleasant working environment, and a willingness to work through the stages of growth that all groups experience on their way to becoming a team. Figure 12–2 introduces the Tuckman Teamwork Model. Developed by Bruce W. Tuckman, Ph.D. (*Psychological Bulletin,* 1965, pp. 63, 384-399), this model is often used to describe the developmental stages that all teams experience.

- Forming
- Storming
- Norming
- Performing

Figure 12–2   Tuckman Teamwork Model

The next sections describe the four stages of team development reflected in the Tuckman model.

Stage 1. Forming.   During this first stage, the team members are selected and the process of becoming a team begins. The team's mission and goals are defined along with the team member's roles and responsibilities. Team members often experience a range of emotions during this stage, including excitement, anxiety, and, perhaps, even fear. Little is achieved while a team is in this stage as team members get to know each other and as the team's purpose is defined. During the forming stage, team members are often on their "best behavior" and try to avoid conflict. The team leader is actively involved in this stage and provides the direction and resources the team needs to progress.

Stage 2. Storming.   During the storming stage, the team begins to face the reality of turning its mission and goals into executable action plans. Team members often begin to feel the team's goals are unrealistic and they may doubt the leader's ability to provide the team with what it needs. As the team members get to know each other, the polite facade begins to fade and they are more willing to disagree. Team members may experience frustration and self-doubt during this stage and some defensiveness and competition may occur. The team leader coaches and counsels the team during this stage and repeatedly reminds the team to stay focused on its goals.

Stage 3. Norming.   This stage represents the "calm after the storm." Team members begin to take ownership for the team's performance and they begin to have confidence in the team's abilities. They begin to feel a sense of camaraderie and they begin to exhibit team spirit. Conflict is, for the most part, avoided as team members accept and welcome feedback rather than view it as criticism. The team leader steps away from the team during this stage and gets involved only when the team asks for support.

Stage 4. Performing.   At this stage of the team's development, the team is achieving its goals and the team's members are participating fully in team activities. A spirit of cooperation and collaboration prevails, and team members trust each other and their leader. Team members feel a sense of pride and satisfaction, and the team has become a close-knit community. The team leader serves as head cheerleader and encourages the team to avoid complacency and continuously improve.

In the course of a team's development, it is inevitable that change will occur. For example, new team members will be added and old team members may leave. In the course of continuously improving, the team may rethink its mission or set new goals. The team may also be affected by changes to the company, such as a reorganization, a merger, or an acquisition of some kind. When change occurs, it can affect the team's ability to maintain or advance its current stage of growth. The best teams accept and embrace change by taking a step back to the forming stage in an effort to clarify the team's purpose and team members' roles and responsibilities. They can then move quickly through the storming and norming stages back to peak performance. Figure 12–3 illustrates the way teams continually move through the developmental stages.

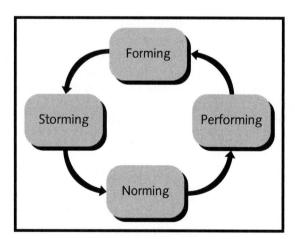

Figure 12–3 The ongoing nature of team development

Some teams never make it to the performing stage. For example, some teams avoid conflict during the storming stage and never develop the ability to deal with negative issues or achieve a consensus. A \consensus \is an opinion or position reached by all of a team's members or by a majority of its members. Conflict is inevitable in a team setting, and successful teams learn to work through it in a fair and constructive manner.

Reaching a consensus does not mean that team members agree with the majority just to avoid conflict. Typically, a consensus is reached when all team members can say that they agree with a decision or that they feel their point of view on a matter has been heard and understood, even if it has not been accepted. When a consensus is reached, some team members may still disagree with the decision but they are willing to work toward its success.

Managing Conflict in a Team Setting

Conflict is a normal part of human interaction that, when approached positively, can actually produce very creative and innovative results. In a team setting, conflict usually results from team members' varying perceptions and expectations. For example, a team member who stays late every night may resent the fact that a team member who is dedicated to his family leaves "early"—that is, on time—one or two nights a week. In a technical setting, a team member may resent the fact that a coworker has been selected to work on a choice project and as a result will be acquiring state-of-the-art skills. Another team member may feel that her technical skills are not being fully utilized and as a result are becoming stagnant. Or, a team member may feel that his accomplishments are not being acknowledged and appreciated. Conflict can even arise simply as a result of the stress that is inherent in a help desk setting. For example, a stressed team member may snap at coworkers, causing hurt feelings.

An issue is typically at the heart of a conflict. Because people often take the issue personally, they experience an emotional reaction, such as disappointment, hurt, and even anger. The best way to handle conflict is for team members to focus on the issue and not on the personalities of their teammates. Each team member must also be honest about his or her feelings, while striving to understand the feelings of his or her teammates. Engaging in a conflict is not a pleasant experience for most people. It is better, though, to resolve the issue rather than avoid it and allow it to turn into something even bigger.

Gossip is often a sign of unresolved conflict. It is best to avoid gossip by encouraging the parties who are gossiping—including yourself—to talk directly to the person or persons who are the subject of the gossip.

The following tips are helpful for resolving conflict in a team setting in a constructive manner. These tips also enable team members to maintain and perhaps even strengthen their relationship. When faced with a conflict, remember that:

- The person on the other side of the conflict has a point of view that is just as legitimate and reasonable to him or her as yours is to you. Listen actively to the other person's point of view and strive to understand his or her perspective.

- The other person may be as uncomfortable talking about the conflict or disagreement as you are. Suggest to your teammate that you want to have a positive working relationship and that you would like to find a mutually agreeable way to resolve the conflict.

- It is safer and wiser to keep to the issues of a discussion. Avoid making comments that attack your teammate's personal character or question his or her motives.

- Saying the same thing over and over will not resolve the conflict. If you feel strongly about your point of view and your teammate doesn't seem to be getting it, state your point of view in a different way, or try presenting your point of view from the other person's perspective.

- Little can be gained by discussing or debating the past. Rather than dwell on what or who caused the conflict, try to determine what can be done now and in the future to eliminate the source of conflict.

- The other person may be willing to accept a solution if you can make it sufficiently attractive. To achieve a compromise, both you and your teammate must be willing to make concessions. You must strive to identify a middle ground that you both find acceptable.

- It is okay to change your mind. Sometimes we form an opinion without having all of the facts. Should you discover through discussion that you were misinformed or that you were simply wrong, graciously acknowledge your teammate's point of view and, when appropriate, apologize for causing or prolonging the conflict.

Although it is typically best to resolve a conflict rather than avoid it, there are times when it is appropriate to delay discussing a difficult situation. It is appropriate to avoid an issue if the timing is wrong and more harm than good will come from engaging someone in a discussion. For example, the person may be highly upset or angry and, as such, incapable of having a reasonable discussion, or you may be feeling highly emotional and unable to maintain an open mind. This does not mean you should avoid the issue altogether. Doing so may lead people to perceive you don't care about the outcome or that you are unwilling to be a team player. Instead, you should choose a time when both you and the person can calmly discuss the issue and seek a resolution. Being a team player requires that people work together in an effort to resolve not only their customers' problems, but problems within the team as well.

BEING A TEAM PLAYER

Being a team player requires personal commitment and a willingness to put the needs of the team ahead of personal goals. Team players contribute to the team's success by cooperating freely and communicating openly with their teammates. This does not mean that they must abandon their personal goals to be team players. The most successful team players seek out a team setting that enables them to work toward their personal goals while contributing to the team's goals. People feel the greatest sense of job satisfaction when their skills are fully utilized and when their personal working style is acknowledged and accommodated. For example, some people like to continuously learn new skills and become bored when their work becomes routine. Other people enjoy routine and feel most comfortable when they have fully mastered the tasks they are expected to complete. A successful team is made up of a mix of people who contribute a variety of skills and personal working styles to the help desk and to the entire support organization.

Understanding Your Role in the Help Desk

A common misconception is that being a team player means going along with the crowd. Some people believe they will have to give up their individuality and become just like everyone else on the team. This is not true. For a team to succeed, all team members must understand that they have a unique role to play. The role a person plays is a sum of his or her skills, knowledge, experience, and personal style.

In his book *Team Players and Teamwork,* Glenn M. Parker writes that research indicates that there are four types or styles of team players (*Team Players and Teamwork,* 1996, p. 63). Figure 12–4 lists the four styles of team players.

Figure 12–4 Team player styles

Each of these team player styles contributes to the team's goals in different ways. For example, a *challenger* serves as the team's "devil's advocate" and often questions the team's goals, methods, and procedures. A *collaborator* is goal-oriented and is willing to do what is needed to get the job done. A *communicator* is a good listener and encourages other team members to participate in team discussions and decisions. A *contributor* is task-oriented and does everything possible to provide the team with the skills, knowledge, and information needed to achieve its goals.

Each of these team player styles serves a purpose and each shines brightest at different times during the stages of a team's growth. For example, during the forming stage, a challenger will push the team to set high standards and may question the validity of the team's goals. During the storming stage, a communicator will facilitate discussion and encourage conflict resolution. During the norming stage, a contributor will help the team stay organized and will do the research needed for the team to succeed. During the performing stage, a collaborator will encourage the team to stay focused on its goals and, when needed, revisit its goals in an effort to continuously improve.

Each team player style can become ineffective if a team player overemphasizes his or her contribution or fails to acknowledge the contributions of others. Team players must be sensitive to the needs of the team and the needs of their teammates. For example, a collaborator who jumps in and takes over a task from a coworker may believe that this is needed to get the job done. She may, however, be depriving her teammate of the opportunity to learn new skills. Furthermore, people can get "stuck in a rut," becoming a liability to the team. For example, there are times when it is no longer appropriate for a challenger to continuously question the team's goals and methods. Once a consensus has been achieved, the challenger must accept the goals and let the team move forward.

Although most people have one style that predominates, each person is capable of exhibiting all of these team player styles. In fact, they may exhibit different styles in different situations. Your challenge as a team player is to determine your personal style and use the strengths of that style to contribute to your team. Knowing your personal style will also help you to identify and overcome your weaknesses. You can also strive to embrace the strengths of the other styles, thus increasing your ability to contribute to the team. People can change and they can exhibit incredible flexibility. If you want to develop a new style in an effort to increase your effectiveness, learn more about team player styles and team dynamics. The more you know about these concepts, the more effective you can be in a team setting.

Personality tests, such as the Myers-Briggs Type Indicator (MBTI) and the Motivational Appraisal of Personal Potential (MAPP) can also be used by individuals to learn more about their work preferences and by companies to learn more about a job candidate. These test measure qualities such as motivation, temperament, learning style, and people skills. Web sites that provide information about these tests include www.myersbriggs.org, www.personalitypathways.com, and www.assessment.com.

Team players who embrace the diversity that a team setting offers are invariably happier and more successful. They continuously learn new skills from their coworkers. They become more open-minded and learn to accept, and even invite, new and challenging opportunities. They learn to respect that people are entitled to their own viewpoints and they strive to understand other people's perspectives. They enjoy the camaraderie that comes from working with others and the feeling of satisfaction that comes when a common goal is achieved.

> *Diversity: the art of thinking independently together.* Malcolm Forbes

The most successful team players value the opportunity to work with others who are equally unique. They learn to rely on other people for their knowledge, experience, and support. They appreciate and respect their teammates and want their teammates to appreciate and respect them in return. These feelings of mutual appreciation and respect also extend beyond the help desk to the entire support organization.

Understanding an Analyst's Role in the Company's Support Organization

Although each member of the help desk team plays a unique role, customers or other support groups tend to lump everyone together as "the help desk." This may not seem fair, but it is actually the essence of what makes a team a team. The help desk, as a team, has a role to play within the support organization. The help desk's mission and goals define what that role will be. The role of most help desks is to serve on the front-line between a company or department and its customers. This is a most important role. Customers form opinions of the entire company or department based on their interactions with the help desk. The help desk's performance also influences how efficiently and effectively other support resources, such as level two, level three, and external service providers, are used. Each and every member of the help desk team must embrace the help desk's mission and achieve his or her individual performance goals for the help desk team to achieve its goals.

Contributing to Team Goals

Each member of a team brings to the team a unique set of skills and a personal style. Those skills and that style are only of value if they enable the team to achieve its goals. Recall that help desk goals are measurable objectives that support the help desk's mission. Help desk goals differ from one company to the next and may vary from one year to the next, based on a company's business goals and the needs and expectations of its customers. Sample help desk goals include:

- Achieve an average four out of five rating on the annual overall satisfaction survey.
- Provide each analyst eight hours of training each month.
- Resolve 80% of reported problems at level one.
- Reduce contacts to the help desk by 5% within six months.
- Increase contacts resolved using self-services by 15% within six months.
- Reduce support costs by 5% by year end.
- Maintain a cost per contact at or below the industry average.

Recall that cost per contact is the total cost of operating a help desk for a given time period (including salaries, benefits, facilities, and equipment), divided by the total number of contacts (such as calls, e-mails, faxes, and Web requests) received during that period.

NOTE As discussed in Chapter 7, goals typically assess characteristics such as cost, customer satisfaction, efficiency, effectiveness, employee satisfaction, and quality. The best companies strive to maintain a balanced set of goals. Balanced goals are important because placing too great an emphasis on any one goal can negatively impact other goals.

Team performance is only as good as the performance of the analysts on the team. Every analyst influences the team's ability to achieve its goals and expected service levels. If every analyst in the help desk achieves his or her individual performance goals, then the team will achieve its goals. Recall that individual performance goals are measurable objectives for people who support the help desk mission. Data are needed to measure and manage both team and individual performance. Help desk analysts often create the needed data by using tools.

Some analysts mistakenly believe that management cannot measure their performance if the data is not available. The flaw in this line of thinking is that management will still measure performance; they'll simply do it without facts. In other words, management will measure performance based on what they perceive an analyst has accomplished. By capturing data and learning to use that data to create information, analysts can maximize their contribution to help desk goals and communicate that contribution to management.

Help desk tools that may be used to create metrics for individuals include an automatic call distributor (ACD), e-mail response management system, and the incident tracking and problem management system. Sample individual performance metrics captured with an ACD include:

- **Availability.** The length of time an analyst was signed on to the ACD compared to the length of time the analyst was scheduled to be signed on.

- **Average call duration.** The average length of time required to handle a call.

- **Time idle.** The average length of time an analyst was idle during a given period of time. An **idle state** means the analyst did not answer a call routed to his or her phone within the specified number of rings. When an idle state occurs, the ACD transfers the call to the next available analyst.

- **Wrap-up time.** The average length of time an analyst was in wrap-up mode during a given period of time. **Wrap-up mode** an ACD feature that prevents the ACD from routing a new inbound call to an analyst's extension.

Individual performance metrics captured with an e-mail response management system include:

- **Average handle time.** The average length of time required to handle an e-mail.

- **Average number of exchanges.** The average number of e-mail exchanges required to resolve an incident.

These metrics are combined with metrics produced using the help desk's incident tracking and problem management system. Sample individual performance metrics captured with a incident tracking and problem management system include:

Reopen %. The percentage of incidents an analyst opened back up compared to the total number of incidents closed during a given time period.

Resolution %. The percentage of incidents an analyst resolved compared to the total number of incidents that an analyst handled during a given time period.

Application of training investments. A comparison of an analyst's resolution % and reopen % before and after attending training.

Customer satisfaction is another common individual performance metric. It is captured through the results of event-driven customer satisfaction surveys. Recall that event-driven surveys are a series of questions that ask customers to rate their level of satisfaction with a recent service event. Because event-driven surveys request customer feedback on a single service event, they are an excellent way to capture information about an individual analyst's performance.

Monitoring is yet another way that companies measure the performance of individual analysts. The most effective monitoring programs provide analysts with a checklist that describes the specific criteria that supervisors or team leaders are using to measure the quality of a contact.

NOTE A metric that directly influences customer satisfaction but that can be difficult to capture is first contact resolution rate. First contact resolution rate is the percentage of contacts (such as calls, e-mails, faxes, and Web requests) resolved during a customer's initial contact compared to the total number of contacts received at the help desk for a given period of time. With telephone calls, this metric can be captured fairly easily as an analyst is able to verify a customer's satisfaction with a resolution before he or she closes the call. This metric is much more difficult to capture with e-mails because the help desk may not receive acknowledgement from the customer that a solution has worked. Many companies link customer satisfaction surveys to e-mail-delivered solutions in an effort to solicit feedback from customers.

NOTE Although not an indicator of individual performance, first contact resolution rate is also often used to measure the effectiveness of automated e-mail response management systems and Web-based knowledge management systems. Again, this metric is difficult to capture and so customer satisfaction surveys and exit polls are often used to determine the effectiveness of technology delivered solutions. Recall that exit polls combine questions such as "Was this information helpful to you?" with Yes and No buttons that customers can use to provide feedback.

Metrics are an excellent way for help desk management and staff to know whether they are achieving team and individual performance goals. It is important to note, however, that no single metric can be used to accurately measure team or individual performance. They all work together and can influence each other. The best help desks use metrics to monitor performance as well as to identify areas for improvement. For example, metrics can be used to identify the training needs of help desk analysts. They can be used to identify the need for new or improved tools or the need to refine the help desk's processes and procedures. Metrics can also be used to know when it is time to rethink the help desk's mission or revisit its goals.

Although management directs most of the performance metrics analysts must meet, you can suggest additional metrics and supply other information that further demonstrates your contribution to the team's goals. For example, you can prepare a brief report that shows how an FAQ you wrote has resulted in a reduction in the number of questions that customers have about a new product. Remember to be specific. Indicate how many questions were asked for one or two months prior to your writing the FAQ, and how many questions were asked during the month or two after the FAQ was published. Many managers try to involve their staff when establishing performance measures, and you may be encouraged to suggest ways to measure and improve team and individual performance. You can also suggest possible solutions to a problem rather than finding fault or complaining. This positive, constructive approach will really raise your standing in management's eyes. By embracing performance metrics and, when appropriate, suggesting additional performance metrics, you can show management that you are a team player.

Communicating Effectively in a Team Setting

The way people communicate in a team setting influences their relationships with their teammates and the effectiveness of the entire team. In successful teams, team players communicate freely and in ways that encourage trust and respect. Communication is bi-directional and depends on active listening. Team members not only freely share information, thoughts, and opinions, they encourage their coworkers to share as well. For example, team players:

- Originate and propose new ideas and actively encourage others to contribute their ideas.
- Articulate the team's goals and help to clarify the team's goals as needed.
- Regard conflict as a normal part of team growth and strive to resolve conflict in a positive way.
- Actively encourage teammates to participate in team activities and assert the right of each and every teammate to be heard.
- Express their feelings about issues affecting the team in a positive way and seek to understand how teammates feel about issues.

- Assume responsibility for guiding the team when their expertise or team player style is needed.
- Encourage team growth by describing the benefits to be gained by making a change.

> *Communication is the key that unlocks the door to teamwork.*
> Author Unknown

Another form of communication in a team setting is feedback. **Feedback** is communication from one team member to another about how the member's behavior is meeting the expectations of the team. Feedback is appropriate and necessary when:

- A person does something well

- A person's behavior does not appear to be aligned with the team's mission or goals

- A conflict needs to be resolved

To be effective, feedback must be delivered in a considerate, humane, and helping fashion. It must be specific and provide the recipient with a clear understanding of how his or her behavior affects the team. For example, sarcastically mumbling, "It's about time you showed up" as a chronically late coworker passes your desk does nothing to address the situation. A more appropriate form of feedback would be to let the coworker know how it affects the team when he is late. For example, "When you are late, our work stacks up and we cannot respond to our customers in the time frame they expect. It also affects our ability to take breaks and so things can get a little stressful. We really need for you to make it in on time."

> *He has the right to criticize who has the heart to help.* Abraham Lincoln

It is the responsibility of the person providing feedback to ensure the recipient received the correct message. It is the recipient's responsibility to receive the feedback in the spirit with which it was delivered. In other words, if a recipient becomes defensive or angry upon receiving feedback, it is the sender's responsibility to clarify the point he or she is trying to make and find a more positive way to communicate. In turn, the recipient must accept the fact that the person providing feedback is trying to be helpful and must try to glean from the feedback a positive message.

Interestingly enough, even positive feedback can be received negatively. For example, some people try to do their best day in and day out, and they may view a coworker's seemingly arbitrary "good job" as frivolous and patronizing. For some people, basic courtesies, such as saying "please" and "thank you," are all they ask in return for a job well done. For example, if you praise a coworker and she replies, "I'm just doing my job," you can surmise that she tends to be self-motivated. Remember, though, that people's needs can vary from one day to the next. Even a person who tends to scorn praise likes to get a pat on the back now and then. By listening actively to your coworkers, you can get a feel for their feedback preference.

For a team to be successful, everyone must participate in the feedback process. For example:

- Employees must provide feedback to other employees.
- Employees must provide feedback to supervisors and team leaders.
- Supervisors and team leaders must provide feedback to employees.
- Supervisors and team leaders must provide feedback to other supervisors and team leaders.

This feedback process is particularly important in a help desk setting. Although diversity is a hallmark of a successful help desk team, unfortunately, it can quickly lead to division unless team members communicate by providing each other with feedback. Successful teams insist that all team members share their feelings, ideas, and knowledge with the rest of the team. It is unacceptable for team members to withhold information or ideas that could be useful to the team. This includes feedback that acknowledges the efforts of a team member or that will provide a team member with information needed to improve.

TIP   The purpose of feedback is to help individuals understand their strengths and weaknesses and provide insights into aspects of their work that can be improved. To be effective, feedback must be constructive and based on behaviors, not a person's personality.

Communication in a team setting can occur formally or informally. For example, formal communication can occur during a team meeting or in the form of a publication, such as a newsletter or a procedures guide. Informal communication can occur when two or more team members interact. Teams that communicate effectively strive to use the most appropriate method of communication for each situation. For example, announcing a new team goal or a team member's promotion is handled formally to ensure that everyone affected by the announcement is kept informed and involved. On the other hand, discussing a conflict with a coworker is handled privately and informally with only the affected parties and perhaps a trusted facilitator. This enables the affected parties to feel more comfortable and thus more willing to communicate freely.

Effective communication enables teamwork. It ensures that everyone on the team knows what the team must do to succeed and what he or she must do to contribute to the team's success. Ineffective communication can cripple a team and damage the relationships that exist between team members beyond repair. It is the responsibility of each and every member of the help desk team to do all he or she can to enhance communication. Remember that a team player, by definition, contributes to the success of a team by communicating openly with teammates. Remember, too, that in an effective team setting, even conflict is viewed as a normal part of a team's functioning. Team members are encouraged to deal with conflict in a positive way by getting issues out on the table and seeking a viable solution.

What to Do When You Are New to a Team

Whether you are starting work at a new company, or simply joining a new team at the company where you work, there are a few steps you can take to quickly get oriented. Remember that when joining a new team, you have to earn your place by working hard and showing a willingness to work with others, even if you have been hired to serve as the resident expert on a particular subject. Respect and trust must be earned. You cannot assume you know what the team needs and you cannot decide what role you will play. The following steps can help you get settled into a new team as quickly as possible.

- **Meet and get to know your teammates.** As you are introduced to each of your teammates upon joining the team, make an effort to go beyond simple introductions and get to know your teammates. During your first week or two, make it a point to have a one-to-one conversation with all of your teammates. Shake their hand. Ask them what their role is, what their area of expertise is, and what projects they are working on. Ask them to help you understand how the team operates. Let them know you are looking forward to working together. Even a brief conversation will build rapport and help each of you settle into a positive working relationship.

- **Try to gain an understanding of the "big picture."** Ask your coworkers and team leader or supervisor questions and ask for any documented policies and procedures. For example, make sure you receive a copy of the help desk's mission and its goals. Make sure you understand the factors that are critical to the team's success. In other words, make sure you understand why the team exists to begin with. You also want to gain an understanding of who your customers are and where the help desk fits into the overall support organization. Ask for copies of organization charts or ask someone to draw a diagram for you that shows how the help desk relates to other departments, such as level two support groups.

- **Learn the lingo.** Every company, and even teams within a company, have their own vocabulary. They may have unique naming standards for their systems and network components or use a lot of acronyms. If available, get a glossary of terms and use it to learn the language of your new team. If a glossary of terms is not available, you may want to start one. Every time you hear a new term, write it down. Fill in the definitions as you go along. The next new team member will greatly appreciate your efforts.

- **Determine exactly what is expected of you.** It doesn't matter how hard you are working if you are not working on the right things. Failing to do what's expected of you can also create a bad first impression that may be hard to overcome. Ask your supervisor or team leader for a detailed outline of what you should be doing during the first few months that you are with the team. It takes time to learn a team's culture and it takes time to learn all of the processes, procedures, and tools you will be using to do your work. You can't fully contribute until you understand how the team operates and the role you are expected to play. Let your supervisor or team leader know that you want to be a team player and that you want to make a contribution.

- **Volunteer.** Although you want to resist the temptation to bite off more than you can chew, volunteering is an excellent way to get involved with a team. If you see an area where your expertise can be put to work, offer it, or you can offer to help out with a social or charity event that the team may be planning. Volunteering is an excellent way to let your personal interests and unique talents shine through.

Joining a team can be intimidating, especially when you are joining one that has been working together for a while. You may be tempted initially to keep your head down, do what you are told, and stay out of people's way. You'll never become a part of the team that way. A crucial element of teamwork is not only knowing what you are supposed to be doing, but also knowing what your teammates' roles and responsibilities are as well. When you first join a team it may feel as if you have blinders over your eyes. By asking questions and learning how your contributions fit into the bigger picture, you can remove the blinders and see clearly what needs to be done.

Developing Positive Working Relationships with Teammates

A help desk can be a hectic place to work. On the other hand, working in a help desk can be extremely rewarding. You have the opportunity to help other people. You can work with technology. You get to solve problems and continuously learn new skills and acquire new knowledge. Life really is good and you have the opportunity—the choice—every day of making it great. During tough times, remember that you are not alone. You are a member of a team. The following tips are designed to help you put your best foot forward in a team setting. Like the tips aimed at helping you get settled into a new team, these tips help build the respect and trust that is needed in a team setting.

- **Get to know your teammates.** You should know your teammates well enough to know their strengths and weaknesses relative to the goals of your team. You should also know what your teammates view as the priorities in their lives. For example, if a teammate's children are very important to him, learn a little about his children and ask him how they are doing now and then. If a teammate is training for a marathon, ask her how the training is going and wish her well just before the big day. You do not have to be best friends. Simply acknowledge the fact that you work side-by-side with this fellow member of the human race day in and day out. Acknowledge and embrace each person's uniqueness.

- **Extend common courtesies to your coworkers.** Simply put, say "Good morning, everyone" and "Have a good night, everybody" when you walk in and out of the door each day. Some workers slink in and out of work each day in the hopes that no one will notice that they've come or gone. Unfortunately, this approach can quickly lead to animosity. Say "Please" to your coworkers when you ask for their help and "Thank you" when you receive it. These simple phrases let your coworkers know that you respect and appreciate their time and effort. Offer to help a teammate who appears to be struggling with a difficult task.

Some people are hesitant to ask for help, but most will appreciate and accept a sincere offer. Remember that simple courtesies go a long way in creating positive working relationships and positive personal relationships as well.

- **Listen with interest to your teammates.** In other words, listen to your teammates as actively as you do your customers. The nice thing about communicating with teammates is that you often can communicate face-to-face. Be considerate. Resist the temptation to work on your computer or perform some other task when speaking with a coworker. Stop what you are doing. Make eye contact. Be attentive. If a conversation becomes too personal or lengthy, politely let your teammate know that you need to go back to work.

- **Inquire about and acknowledge your teammates' feelings.** If a usually upbeat coworker seems to be having a down day, ask if there is anything that you can do. This doesn't mean you should become a busybody, just let your coworkers know that you care about their well-being and that if there is anything you can do to help, you are willing. You don't have to be soft on people, but give them your support.

- **Share your feelings openly and honestly.** No one feels comfortable around a person who has a scowl on his or her face and yet insists that nothing is wrong, or a person who is insecure and lacking direction and yet is unwilling to ask for help. Furthermore, no one likes to hear, after an extended time, that he or she has inadvertently offended a teammate but has not been given an opportunity to repair the relationship. By sharing your feelings openly and honestly with your teammates, you create a climate of trust. Your teammates will learn to view you as fair and reasonable and will respond by being open and honest with you in return.

- **Be willing to learn and teach.** Some people set out to learn "something new everyday," a philosophy that is easily quenched in a technical support setting. Some people, unfortunately, think they know it all. Others are content to get by knowing only the bare essentials, and defer to others when problems become complex. Still others are unwilling to ask questions; they fear they will look "stupid" or that they will lose their standing as an expert. A help desk setting is an excellent place to be a perpetual student. Technology is constantly changing. Customer needs and the needs of your business are constantly changing. You will never be bored working in a help desk setting if you have an inherent sense of curiosity and are willing to say "What's that?"

 Learning is the labor of the information age.

You must also be willing to share your knowledge and experience with your coworkers. It used to be considered "job security" if a person was the only one that possessed certain knowledge or experience. In this day and age, companies are looking for people that willingly share their knowledge and cross-train their coworkers. Keep in mind also that if you are spending all of your time answering questions and handling difficult problems in a given area of expertise, you may not have the time, or the energy, you need to pursue new skills. Spread your knowledge around.

- **Recognize your teammates' achievements.** We all want to be appreciated for the work that we do and for the things we accomplish. Sincerely congratulate your teammates when they successfully complete a project or solve an exceptionally complex problem. Encourage a coworker who is studying for a certification test or who is gearing up for final exams. Teammates who are just getting started especially need to be encouraged. The first steps in any endeavor are often the hardest, and teammates who are trying to acquire new skills need your encouragement and support. A positive side effect of recognizing and acknowledging your teammates' achievements is that they will give you positive feedback in return.

- **Ask for help when you really need it.** A team cannot perform well unless each of its members is performing well. In a team setting, you cannot, and you should not, try to do everything on your own. Asking for help when you need it is not a sign of weakness. It says that you want to do things in the most efficient, effective way possible so that you contribute to the team's success. Keep in mind, though, that your teammates are just as busy as you are and may be struggling with new challenges as well. Don't be lazy. It is not okay to ask for help simply because you have let things slip through the cracks or because you want to get out of doing your homework. Effort in a team setting is as much about attitude as it is about skills and ability. Let your can do attitude shine through. Remember, too, to help your teammates when they really need it.

> *Don't worry if you're feeling confused. Worry if you're not.* Tom Peters

If you want to work on a successful team that achieves its goals and reaps the associated rewards, you cannot be an inactive or ordinary team player. You also cannot leave it up to the team leader or to the other members of the team. Each and every member of a team has to contribute. This includes and begins with you. Know your role and know your strengths. Get clear on what is expected of you and do your best to give the team what it needs. Remember, there is no "I" in team.

Chapter Summary

- ☐ Technical support lends itself to a team setting because no single person can know everything about all the products supported or provide all the support customers need. The demands are too great. A team is a group of people organized to work together toward the achievement of a goal. A team player is a person who contributes to the team's success by cooperating freely and communicating openly with his or her teammates.

- Assembling a group of team players does not make a successful team. To be successful, a team must share a clear sense of purpose, diversity, openness and trust, and positive relationships with other support groups. They must also have an open, pleasant working environment and a willingness to work through the stages of growth—forming, storming, norming, and performing—that all groups experience on their way to becoming a team. To reach the performing stage, teams must learn to work through conflict and achieve a consensus.

- Being a team player requires personal commitment and a willingness to put the needs of the team ahead of your own. This does not mean you have to give up your individuality. For a team to succeed, each team member must understand that he or she has a unique role to play. The role a person plays is a sum of his or her skills, knowledge, experience, and personal style. Team player styles include challenger, collaborator, communicator, and contributor. Each of these styles serves a purpose and each shines brightest at different times during the stages of a team's growth. Your challenge as a team player is to determine your personal style and use the strengths of that style to contribute to your team. You can also strive to embrace the strengths of the other styles, thus increasing your ability to contribute to the team.

- The help desk's mission and goals determine the role the help desk plays within the support organization. Each and every member of the help desk team must embrace the help desk's mission and achieve his or her individual performance goals for the help desk team to achieve its goals. Data are needed to measure and manage both team and individual performance. Help desk analysts often create needed data by using tools such as an automatic call distributor (ACD), e-mail response management system, and a incident tracking and problem management system. Techniques such as customer satisfaction surveys and monitoring may also be used to capture information about an analyst's performance. In addition to measuring performance, help desk managers and staff can use the data these tools and techniques provide to identify ways they can improve.

- The ways people communicate in a team setting influence their relationships with their teammates and the effectiveness of the entire team. Team members must freely share information, thoughts, and opinions and they must encourage their coworkers to share as well. Another form of communication in a team setting is feedback. To be effective, feedback must be delivered in a considerate, humane, and helping fashion. Ineffective communication can cripple a team and damage the relationships that exist between team members beyond repair. Effective communication ensures that everyone on the team knows what the team must do to succeed and what he or she must do to contribute to the team's success.

- A help desk can be a hectic place to work. On the other hand, working in a help desk can be extremely rewarding. During tough times, remember that you are not alone. You are a member of a team. If you want to work on a successful team that achieves its goals and reaps the associated rewards, you cannot be an inactive or ordinary team player. You have to contribute. Remember, there is no "I" in team.

KEY TERMS

application of training investments — A comparison of an analyst's resolution % and reopen % before and after attending training.

availability — The length of time an analyst was signed on to the ACD compared to the length of time the analyst was scheduled to be signed on.

average call duration — The average length of time required to handle a call.

average handle time — The average length of time required to handle an e-mail.

average number of exchanges — The average number of e-mail exchanges required to resolve an incident.

consensus — An opinion or position reached by all of a team's members or by a majority of its members.

feedback — Communication from one team member to another about how the member's behavior is meeting the expectations of the team.

first contact resolution rate — The percentage of contacts (such as calls, e-mails, faxes, and Web requests) resolved during a customer's initial contact compared to the total number of contacts received at the help desk for a given period of time.

help desk goals — Measurable objectives that support the help desk's mission.

idle state — An ACD state that occurs when an analyst did not answer a call routed to his or her phone within the specified number of rings.

individual performance goals — Measurable objectives for people who support the help desk's mission.

mission — A written statement of the customers the help desk serves, the types of services the help desk provides, and how the help desk delivers those services.

reopen % — The percentage of incidents an analyst opened back up compared to the total number of incidents closed during a given time period.

resolution % — The percentage of incidents an analyst resolved compared to the total number of incidents that the analyst handled during a given time period.

team — A group of people organized to work together toward the achievement of a goal.

team player — A person who contributes to the team's success by cooperating freely and communicating openly with his or her teammates.

time idle — The average length of time an analyst was idle during a given period of time.

wrap-up mode — An ACD feature that prevents the ACD from routing a new inbound call to an analyst's extension.

wrap-up time — The average length of time an analyst was in wrap-up mode during a given period of time.

REVIEW QUESTIONS

1. What is a team?

2. How does a team player contribute to a team's success?

3. What are the reasons technical support lends itself to a team setting?

4. What are the four characteristics of a successful team?

5. List the three components of a help desk mission.

6. True or False? Help desk goals are objectives that support the help desk's mission.

7. Why is it important for a help desk to have a clearly defined mission and goals?

8. In business terms, what makes people with varying talents a team?

9. Why is it important for the help desk to have a positive working relationship with other support groups?

10. List the four stages of development reflected in the Tuckman Teamwork Model.

11. How does the role of the team leader change as a team moves through these stages of growth?

12. Typically, when is a consensus reached?

13. Why does conflict usually occur in a team setting?

14. What should team members focus on when handling conflict in a team setting?

15. What is gossip often a sign of?

16. What must you remember about the other person's point of view when you are faced with a conflict?

17. How is a compromise achieved?

18. When is it appropriate to avoid a conflict?

19. Do you have to abandon your personal goals to be a team player?

20. What qualities influence the role a person plays on a team?

21. List the four types of team player styles.

22. When can a team player style become ineffective?

23. Why is it important to determine your personal team player style?

24. What two things determine the role a help desk will play in a support organization?

25. How do members of the help desk team influence the team's ability to achieve its goals?

26. What are the five most common tools and techniques that companies use to measure individual performance?

27. What are three ways that help desk management and staff can use metrics?

28. Why is communication important in a team setting?

29. What is feedback?

30. How must feedback be delivered to be effective?

31. Whose responsibility is it to enhance communication in a team setting?

32. What are five things you can do to get settled into a new team?

33. What five basic courtesies, discussed in this chapter, will help you to have a positive working relationship with your teammates?

34. Why is it important to ask for help when you really need it?

DISCUSSION QUESTIONS

1. Many people believe that because they have played on a sports team for years, for example, that they know how to be a team player at work. Is this a fair comparison? As a prelude to this discussion, consider taking the test "Are You a Team Player? at **content.monster.com/tools/quizzes/teamplayer.**

2. There is an old expression, "One bad apple spoils the bunch." Discuss traits that can get in the way of teamwork, such as negativity and insecurity. Develop a list of techniques you can use to deal with negative, insecure, and otherwise difficult people.

3. A common belief is that to achieve a consensus, someone must win and someone must lose. Another belief is that the majority rules, whether or not everyone on the team has been heard. Are these beliefs valid? Discuss the charactistics of a consensus decision and discuss ways to achieve a consensus in a team or life setting.

HANDS-ON PROJECTS

HANDS-ON PROJECTS

Project 12–1

Evaluate a team's success. Interview a friend, family member, or classmate that works in a team setting. Describe for this person the characteristics discussed in this chapter of a successful team. Ask the following questions about the person's team:

❑ Does he or she work for a successful team? That is, is the team fulfilling its mission and achieving its goals?

❑ If yes, does the team exhibit all of the characteristics discussed in this chapter? How did the team develop these characteristics?

❑ If no, what characteristics could be improved to make the team more successful?

Prepare a brief report that presents any conclusions you can draw from this interview.

Project 12–2

Determine a company's culture. Visit the Web site for the company where you work or where you would like to work. Alternatively, type "corporate culture" in your Web browser and go to the site of a company that offers information about its culture. From the Web site, determine the following:

❑ What is the company's mission or purpose?

❑ What are the company's core values?

❑ What is the company's philosophy toward (a) its customers, and (b) its employees and their work environment?

Write a one-page report that summarizes your findings.

Project 12–3

Discuss the stages of team development. Conduct a roundtable discussion within your class about the stages of team development. First, have each person in your class who is a member of a team of any kind assess the stage of development that his or her team has achieved. They may belong to a team at work, or they may be a member of a sports team or a study group. Next, ask all of your classmates who are in, for example, the forming stage to relate their current experience to the description of the forming stage discussed in this chapter. For example:

❑ What insight into the workings of their team have they gained while studying this chapter?

❑ Given what they have learned in this chapter, how do they feel they can help their team move forward or improve?

❑ What, if any, conclusions can you and your classmates draw from this discussion before moving on to the next stage of development?

Apply these questions to each of the four stages of team development. Briefly summarize the conclusions of your class. After you have finished this discussion, think of your class as a team. As a team, determine the stage of team development your class has achieved. Briefly outline the steps your team must take to achieve the next stage.

Project 12–4

Review your approach to managing conflict. Conflict is an inevitable part of human interaction. Think about a conflict that you have faced or are facing at home, school, or work. Review the tips discussed in this chapter concerning how to resolve conflict in a constructive manner. Use these tips to assess your ability to manage conflict in a positive way. Using your own words, make note of one or two of the tips you can use to improve your conflict resolution skills.

Project 12–5

Discuss team player styles. Assemble a team of three to five of your classmates. For each of the four team player styles described in this chapter, discuss the following:

❏ How does a team benefit by having a person who exhibits this team player style?

❏ How is a team impacted if a team player that exhibits this team player style becomes ineffective?

Compare the results of your discussion to the findings of other teams in the class.

Project 12–6

Learn about personality testing. On the Web, search for topics such as "personality testing," "Myers-Briggs Type Indicator," or "Motivational Appraisal of Personal Potential." Or, visit one of the following Web sites: **www.myersbriggs.org**, **www.personalitypathways.com**, or **www.assessment.com**. Determine how companies use personality testing and how you personally can use personality testing. Locate and take a free personality test. Write a short paper that describes how personality tests are used and what you learned about yourself by taking a personality test.

Project 12–7

Learn how team and individual performance are measured. Interview a friend, family member, or classmate that works in a team setting. Ask this person the following questions:

❏ How is his or her team's performance measured?

❏ How is his or her individual performance measured?

❏ Does this person feel that his or her manager has clearly communicated what he or she must do to contribute to the team's goals?

❏ Does this person feel that his or her manager uses metrics to identify improvement opportunities as well as to monitor performance?

❏ What techniques does this person use to communicate his or her achievements to management?

❏ How does this person feel about the tools he or she is required to use and the amount of data that he or she is required to provide management with regard to his or her performance? If he or she feels it is a burden, determine why.

Prepare a brief report that presents any conclusions you can draw from this discussion.

Project 12–8

Assess your communication skills. Prepare a list of the effective ways to communicate in a team setting discussed in this chapter. For each skill listed, rate yourself on a scale of 1 to 5, where 1 is very weak and 5 is very strong. Then, further assess your communication skills by answering the following questions:

❑ In what areas are your communication skills strong?

❑ In what areas can you improve your communication skills?

❑ Given what you have learned in this chapter, how can you improve your communication skills?

Project 12–9

Provide feedback. The set of questions that follows is designed to enable constructive peer feedback (*Successful Team Building*, 1992, p. 92). It could also be used to perform a self-assessment or by a team leader to evaluate each member of a team. Use this peer feedback form to:

1. Assess your skills as a team member. You can apply these questions to your behavior at work, as a member of a sports team or study group, or as a member of your class.

2. Provide feedback to a coworker. Again, this may be a coworker at work, a member of a sports team or study group to which you belong, or a classmate.

Peer Feedback Evaluation

In each category, circle the number that you believe best represents the usual behavior of [*name of team member*]:

Initiates Ideas		
10 9 8 Frequently offers ideas and solutions.	7 6 5 4 Initiates only moderately, but supports initiating by others.	3 2 1 Tends to let others take most of the initiative and often reserves support.

Facilitates the Introduction of New Ideas		
10 9 8 Actively encourages others to contribute without worrying about agreement.	7 6 5 4 Provides support for ideas with which he or she agrees.	3 2 1 Often resists the introduction of new ideas; looks for flaws.

Is Directed Toward Group Goals		
10 9 8 Often helps to identify and clarify goals for the group.	7 6 5 4 Sometimes helps the group define its goals; sometimes confuses it with side issues.	3 2 1 Tends to place priority on own goals at the expense of the group's.

Manages Conflict		
10 9 8 Regards conflict as helpful in promoting different perspectives and in sharpening the differences in views.	7 6 5 4 Generally disengages from conflict.	3 2 1 Tries to smooth over points of disagreement; plays a pacifying role.

Demonstrates Support for Others		
10 9 8 Actively encourages the participation of others and asserts their right to be heard.	7 6 5 4 Encourages certain members part of the time, but does not encourage all members.	3 2 1 Does not offer support or encouragement for other members.

Reveals Feelings		
10 9 8 Openly expresses feelings about issues; ensures that feelings parallel views.	7 6 5 4 Sometimes disguises feelings or tries to keep them to self.	3 2 1 Denies both the existence of own feelings and the importance of expressing them in the group.

Displays Openness		
10 9 8 Freely and clearly expresses self on issues so that others know where he or she stands.	**7 6 5 4** Sometimes employs tact and speaks circumspectly to camouflage real views.	**3 2 1** Is vague about views on issues, even contradictory when pressed.
Confronts Issues and Behavior		
10 9 8 Freely expresses views on difficult issues and on team members' nonproductive behavior.	**7 6 5 4** Is cautious about taking a visible position on issues and on others' actions without first ensuring widespread approval.	**3 2 1** Actively avoids issues and any conflict by talking about "safe" issues that are irrelevant to current group work.
Shares Leadership		
10 9 8 Assumes responsibility for guiding the group when own resources are needed or when problems lend themselves to his or her solving.	**7 6 5 4** Competes with other members for visibility and influence.	**3 2 1** Dominates group discussions and exerts disproportionate influence that subverts group progress.
Exhibits Proper Demeanor in Decision-Making Process		
10 9 8 Actively seeks a full exploration of all feasible options.	**7 6 5 4** Becomes impatient with a deliberate pace in generating and evaluating all options when he or she does not concur with them.	**3 2 1** Moves strongly toward early closure of discussion to vote on a preferred option.

CASE PROJECTS

CASE PROJECTS

1. Help Desk Team Leader

You were just promoted to team leader of your help desk. Research the subject of leadership and what it takes to be an effective team leader. Go to the library, search the Web, or speak to people that you respect and think of as leaders. Develop a sign that you can hang in your office that lists the three leadership qualities that you think are most important and that you want to develop. If you like, include a quotation about leadership that you consider meaningful.

2. Recognizing Achievement

You are the manager of a small help desk that is starting to perform well as a team. You have a very small budget and it is difficult for you to give people monetary rewards when they accomplish good things. You would also like the members of the team to acknowledge each other's accomplishments and not always look to you to dole out rewards. Conduct a brainstorming session with your team (choose five classmates) and identify creative ways the team can celebrate individual and team accomplishments.

3. Back to Basics

You recently began working as a help desk analyst. The help desk is very large and you are trying to become more conscious about using common courtesies, such as saying "please," "thank you," "good morning," and "good night," in an effort to build a positive working relationship with your new coworkers. You are also trying to make it a habit to use these basic courtesies whenever you interact with other people, whether they are friends, family members, coworkers, or even strangers you encounter during your day. For the next week, use these basic courtesies whenever you interact with others. Observe your feelings when people do not use these basic courtesies when interacting with you. Notice how you can influence others to use these basic courtesies by using them yourself. Discuss your observations with your classmates.

CHAPTER

13

HANDLING DIFFICULT CUSTOMER SITUATIONS

In this chapter you will learn:

◆ Why customers sometimes behave in challenging ways

◆ Proven techniques to handle irate, difficult, and demanding customers

◆ How to respond, not react, to difficult customer situations

◆ Positive steps you can take to stay calm and in control

Most customers are pleasant, calm, and appreciative of analysts' efforts. Unfortunately, there are times when customers become upset, angry, and demanding. These difficult situations can be extremely stressful. As a help desk analyst, you cannot control your customers' behavior. You can control your response to their behavior, and you can develop the skills needed to handle even the most difficult situations.

When handling difficult customer situations, it is important to be empathetic to each customer's needs. This means you must listen actively and try to understand why the customer is upset or angry. You must then acknowledge and address the customer's emotional state before you begin solving the customer's technical problem. You must also remember that you cannot take difficult situations personally. You must learn to vent your emotions, manage your stress, and stay calm and in control.

HANDLING UPSET, ANGRY, AND DEMANDING CUSTOMERS–

It would be nice if day in and day out people were pleasant and agreeable. The reality, though, is that we all have bad days. We all can become upset or even angry when things are not going our way—particularly when dealing with technology. Doesn't it seem that the closer the deadline or the greater the importance of an assignment, the bigger and more frustrating a technical problem becomes? Murphy's Law—anything that can possibly go wrong, will go wrong—seems particularly relevant when dealing with technology. Technology can be frustrating, but remember that when customers are having a problem using technology, it is your job as an analyst to help.

Most of the time, customers who contact the help desk are reasonable, pleasant, and grateful for your help. Some customers have a great sense of humor and are fun to work with. Some customers are very interesting and knowledgeable, and enjoy working together with you to solve a problem. Some customers may even teach you a thing or two, if you are open and willing to learn. However, other customer situations are more challenging. A customer who is upset may need a caring ear and a calm helping hand. A customer may be angry and want to hear an apology followed by a swift and sound resolution to her problem. A customer may even be demanding, perhaps unrealistically so, and insist that you satisfy his needs—now! The important thing to remember is that difficult customer situations are the exception, not the rule.

Because they are so stressful, difficult situations can affect your attitude and even your interactions with other customers. For example, if you receive a call or an e-mail message from an irate customer first thing in the morning, it can ruin your entire day—if you let it. That is why it is important to avoid the temptation to make sweeping statements, such as "Why is everyone being so difficult today?" or "Why are all of these customers so nasty?" These pessimistic generalizations can cause you to lose your perspective and can even influence your coworkers' attitudes. For example, a coworker who has been having a great day may begin to view things negatively.

Although it is sometimes hard to do, try to consider and treat each customer and each situation as unique. Try to put yourself in your customers' shoes and strive to fully understand their needs. This perspective will not do anything to change the behavior of angry or demanding customers, but it will enable you to control how you respond to your customers' behavior.

Understanding Customer Behavior

To understand customer behavior, you must strive to empathize with what customers are experiencing. **Empathy** involves identifying with and understanding another person's situation, feelings, and motives. Being empathetic does not mean you are responsible. For example, if a customer is screaming at you because he cannot print his report and it is going to be late, you are not responsible for the late report. The customer may have procrastinated writing the report until the deadline was reached, or he may have known there was a problem with the printer and failed to report it to the help desk. Regardless, it is your responsibility to acknowledge the fact that the customer is upset and do everything you can to help him get the report printed. Isn't that what you would want if you were the customer?

People working in a help desk often know shortcuts or have access to experts that customers do not, and so do not always fully appreciate a customer's experience. Make an effort to use the products that your help desk supports and try to experience your help desk's services. For example, rather than going directly to an expert when you have a question about how to use a new software package, call or contact the help desk as a customer would and request service. Put yourself in your customer's shoes and try to relate to the confusion and frustration everyone feels at times when dealing with technology.

Keep in mind that the frustration a customer experiences dealing with a technical problem may be compounded when he or she tries to obtain support. For example, customers who have spent a considerable amount of time trying to fix a problem on their own, perhaps by searching the help desk's Web site, may become frustrated and perhaps even angry when they are required to wait an extended period of time in a queue. Figure 13–1 lists some of the situations that may cause customers to become frustrated or angry when trying to obtain support.

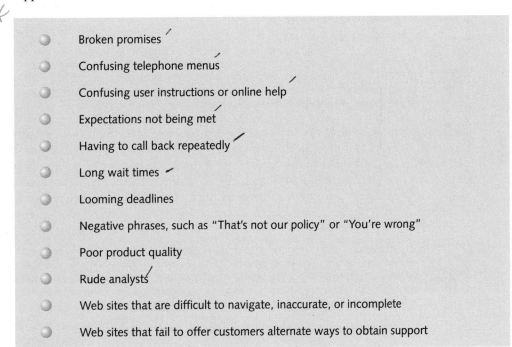

- Broken promises
- Confusing telephone menus
- Confusing user instructions or online help
- Expectations not being met
- Having to call back repeatedly
- Long wait times
- Looming deadlines
- Negative phrases, such as "That's not our policy" or "You're wrong"
- Poor product quality
- Rude analysts
- Web sites that are difficult to navigate, inaccurate, or incomplete
- Web sites that fail to offer customers alternate ways to obtain support

Figure 13–1 Situations that may frustrate or anger customers

Be aware that your company or department may be responsible for some of these situations. For example, if a customer is angry because past promises have been broken, it is imperative that you keep your promises. If a customer is confused and you realize during your conversation that a solution posted on the help desk's Web site is incorrect or incomplete, it is important that you immediately apologize for the customer's inconvenience and thank the customer for bringing the discrepancy to your attention. Work with the customer to resolve the problem and then do all you can to ensure the solution is corrected on the Web site as quickly as possible.

Remember that there is always something that you can do. For example, if customers are complaining that your company's telephone menus are confusing or they had to wait too long for you to answer the telephone, what you can do is pass each complaint on to your team leader or supervisor. You can also let customers know if there are any shortcuts they can use to move more quickly through the telephone menus.

NOTE Unmet expectations are a major source of customer frustration or anger. The help desk can minimize this frustration by setting and managing customer expectations. For example, many help desks use SLAs to set customer expectations and to communicate the help desk's policies and procedures. If customers are regularly complaining about a particular policy, take the time to document their concerns and communicate that information to management. It may be time to change the policy!

TIP Don't think that because you have reported a customer complaint once that there is no need to report it again. Management may not act on a single complaint but often will respond when they receive the same complaint from a number of customers. Take the time to document each and every customer complaint so that management has an accurate picture of the problem.

On any given day, everyone has more or less patience, awareness, and persistence. The presence or absence of these qualities invariably affects your ability to solve problems. Give your customers the benefit of the doubt; they may just be having an exceptionally bad day, or you may be the one having the bad day. Be honest. Don't blame your customers for your lack of patience or for your negative attitude. Strive to be positive and professional at all times.

TIP Pay attention when you are a customer. Consider how you feel when you receive service from someone who is having a bad day. Consider how you feel when a service provider complains to you about how busy he is or how difficult her job is. Do you care? Typically, no. You just want service. Remember that it is not your customer's fault that you are having a bad day.

Winning Over Difficult Customers

Working with difficult customers requires patience and composure. How you respond to these customers, particularly during the early moments of your conversation, will greatly influence their perception and willingness to work with you. If a customer is confused or upset, you can make the situation worse by failing to listen or by failing to empathize with the customer's situation. If a customer is frustrated, you can cause the customer to become even more frustrated or even angry by failing to communicate with positive statements. Figure 13–2 lists a step-by-step approach you can use to handle even the most difficult situation.

Step 1. Get focused

Step 2. Let the customer vent

Step 3. Listen actively

Step 4. Acknowledge the customer's emotional state

Step 5. Restate the situation and gain agreement

Step 6. Begin active problem solving

Figure 13–2 Technique for handling difficult customer situations

This section explores each of these steps and discusses some important nuances to keep in mind when practicing the steps in this proven technique.

Step 1. Get Focused.   If you sense that an interaction with a customer is going to be difficult, get yourself focused. Take a deep breath. Make sure you have a smile on your face or that you appear eager and caring. Sit or stand up straight and get your notepad ready. These are preparatory steps that you should be following prior to each customer interaction—whether on the phone or face-to-face—but they are sometimes overlooked. For example, you may be particularly busy or you may be relaxed and joking with coworkers when you answer the phone without thinking. Before you know it, the pressure is on. Rather than plowing forward unprepared, take a few seconds to relax and get focused.

Step 2. Let the Customer Vent.   An upset or angry customer has a story to tell and you must let the customer tell that story from beginning to end without interruption. If you interrupt the customer at any time, it is likely that she will start the story over. Or, the customer may have rehearsed what he is going to say and have written down several points that he wants to make. Until each point is made, the customer cannot calm down. This venting is necessary for the customer's well-being. Your challenge is to listen actively and look for cues that the customer is ready for you to begin taking control of the interaction.

Customer cues include a deep sigh or a challenging statement such as ". . . and what are you going to do about it?"

 Customers may occasionally call with a story that you have heard many times before. It is important to remember that although you have heard the story before, this particular customer is telling it for the first time and wants to be heard. Be patient and understanding. Use the opportunity to practice your active listening skills. You may hear something you did not expect!

Step 3. Listen Actively.   Recall that active listening involves participating in a conversation and giving the speaker a sense of confidence that he or she is being heard. When a customer is venting, resist the temptation to ask questions, but still communicate the fact that you are listening. Nod your head or use a verbal nod of the head to let the customer know you are listening. For example, incorporate nonintrusive verbal phrases at appropriate points in the conversation.

Uh-huh.

Go on.

I see.

I understand.

Remember also to pay attention to what is being said and how it is being said. Listen carefully for the central theme of the customer's problem or complaint. In other words, listen for the "real" problem in the customer's story. Try not to get bogged down by a customer's angry words or by what may be exaggerated statements. Take notes and be prepared to restate the customer's problem or complaint.

Step 4. Acknowledge the Customer's Emotional State.   An upset or angry customer needs to feel that you care and that you fully understand the situation before he or she can calm down. If you fail to acknowledge the customer's emotional state, it is likely that the customer will perceive that you were not listening and then become even more upset. You must acknowledge the customer's emotion, even if you do not understand why the customer has that emotion. Try to empathize with the customer or at least accept that this customer may be having a really bad day and needs your help. This is also an excellent time to respectfully use the customer's name and communicate your desire to do all you can. In other words, let the customer know you are there to help resolve his or her problem. When appropriate, sincerely apologize to the customer for any inconvenience your company may have caused.

> Miss Navarro, I'm sorry our field service engineer did not arrive at the time promised. Let me find out what happened. Would you like to hold while I contact his office, or would you like me to call you back?
>
> Mr. Boyet, I'm sorry there is a problem downloading software from our Web site. Let me walk you through the procedure.

It is imperative that you be respectful and genuine at this point of the interaction. If you use a snide or derogatory tone of voice when using the customer's name, the customer will most likely be offended. If you use an insincere tone of voice when apologizing, the customer will doubt your apology. If you don't feel that you can apologize using a sincere tone of voice, you must at least acknowledge the customer's emotion and let the customer know you will do all you can to help.

> Mr. Sheng, I understand that you are very upset. I will do everything I can to get this printer problem resolved right away.
>
> Mary, I appreciate your frustration and I want to help. Help me understand the problem you are having with your computer.

Step 5. Restate the Situation and Gain Agreement.

It is imperative that you gain the customer's agreement that you fully understand the situation and the customer's expectations about when a solution will be delivered. Fixing the wrong problem or failing to resolve the problem in the time frame the customer expects will just make the situation worse. Begin, when possible, by restating the problem in the customer's exact words. This lets the customer know that you were listening. Ask the customer to verify your understanding of the problem. Use a simple verifying statement to obtain agreement from the customer that you have heard the point he is making.

> Is that correct?
>
> Did we cover everything?

It may not always be possible or practical to restate the problem in the customer's exact words. Customers can sometimes be vague when describing a problem and problem symptoms can have multiple interpretations. In these situations, gain customer agreement by paraphrasing. Recall that paraphrasing involves using slightly different words to restate the information given by the customer. When you finish paraphrasing the problem, ask the customer to verify your understanding of the situation.

There may also be times when you need to let the customer know that you do not understand the information that he or she is providing. When doing so, avoid negative phrases that have an accusatory tone. A better approach is to ask the customer to help you understand.

> **Negative words:** You're not making any sense, or You're confusing me.
>
> **Positive words:** I'm confused. Could you repeat . . .

Step 6. Begin Active Problem Solving.

If you have been patient, clearly communicated that you care and sincerely want to help, and have gained agreement from the customer that you understand the situation, the customer should now have calmed down. This means that you can begin diagnosing the problem and developing an action plan or solution. This doesn't mean you can lose your focus. It is likely that the customer is still fragile and you may have to repeat some or all of these steps for handling a difficult customer situation before the problem is fully resolved.

Many analysts want to go straight to problem solving when a customer is upset or angry. Their thinking is that the best and fastest way to calm down the customer is to solve the problem. Solving the problem is important and will be the final outcome, but assisting and satisfying the customer is the ultimate goal. This requires that you strive to understand, acknowledge, and address the customer's emotional needs as well as the customer's technical needs. Remember that you are supporting people—living, breathing human beings—not just technology.

NOTE Each of these steps apply to handling difficult e-mail messages from customers as well. It is sometimes tempting to scan a customer's message and quickly send off a response. With e-mail, however, you do not have to reply instantaneously as you do when handling a telephone call. You can read and reread the message before formulating a reply. If the e-mail is particularly lengthy, you can print the message and underline or highlight each of the customer's questions or complaints to ensure each is addressed in your reply. Or, you can cut and paste each of the customer's questions or complaints into your reply to ensure each is addressed. If a customer's description of a problem is unclear, you can paraphrase the situation, provide a solution based on your understanding, and encourage the customer to reply if you misinterpreted the situation.

TIP Although it is important to respond promptly to all e-mail messages, take the time you need to (1) calm down, and (2) draft a positive, professional response. A good technique is to draft a reply, reread the customer's e-mail to ensure you did not miss or misinterpret any details, and then fine-tune your reply. When in doubt, ask a coworker or team leader to read the customer's e-mail and verify that your response is appropriate.

Calming Irate Customers

Customers do not start out being irate. Typically, people first experience a lesser emotion, such as frustration or confusion, which builds to anger. In most cases, these emotions can be avoided by using the technique for handling difficult customer situations previously discussed, and by the proper handling of "Moments of Truth," such as placing customers on hold, transferring customers, and so forth. There are times, however, when people run out of patience or take offense to a situation and become angry.

People experience varying degrees of anger. Some people are very slow to anger; others seem to become enraged by the slightest inconvenience. If a customer's problem or concern is addressed quickly, by using the technique for handling difficult customer situations previously described, she may not become irate. On the other hand, bypassing one or more of the steps in this technique can cause the customer to become increasingly upset or angry. It is important to listen carefully so you can accurately assess and address a customer's level of emotion.

Initially, a customer describes the inconvenience of the problem he is experiencing or his frustration with the current situation. By acknowledging the customer's frustration and communicating that you will do all you can to remedy the situation, you can calm the customer and gain the customer's confidence.

> **Customer:** I've had to wait 20 minutes to get through. Why can't you people learn to pick up the telephone?
>
> **Analyst:** I'm sorry to keep you waiting. How can I help you?
>
> **Customer:** This is the third time I've called about this printer this week. Why can't you get someone out here that will fix it right?
>
> **Analyst:** I'm sorry that your printer is still not working correctly. Let me pull up a history of the problems that you have been having so we can determine the best course of action.

If you fail to acknowledge the customer's emotion or the source of frustration, the customer may become even angrier. Very often a customer becomes angrier because he or she perceives that you do not understand and are not addressing his concern. In other words, the customer perceives that you are not listening.

> **Customer:** You're not listening. Let me say it again.
>
> **Customer:** I don't seem to be getting anywhere with you. Let me talk to your supervisor.

At this point, the customer may be starting to mistrust you. Even though you may have been listening very carefully, you have not communicated that fact to the customer. You may have acknowledged what the customer said, but not how the customer said it. The customer is either going to give you one more chance or he is going to ask to speak with someone else. Make sure you understand how to engage help at this point, if you need it. For example, some telephone systems have a "panic" button that analysts can press to get their team leader or supervisor's attention. Some analysts stand up and wave or somehow signal to a coworker or team leader that they need assistance. Do your best to handle the call, but don't be afraid to ask for help when you need it.

One situation where analysts may need help is when a customer is using particularly offensive or abusive language. Most companies have policies that dictate how to handle this type of situation. For example, many companies coach their analysts to determine if the customer is using foul language in reference to a situation or against the analyst personally. If the customer is using foul language in reference to a situation, then it is up to individual analysts to determine their tolerance level for the language. Analysts are encouraged to remember that customers will often stop using foul language after they have had a chance to vent and the analyst acknowledges the customer's emotional state (as previously discussed). If the customer is using foul language against the analyst personally, or the analyst is uncomfortable with the language, most companies advise analysts to progressively ask the customer to speak in a professional manner, as shown in Figure 13–3.

---

1. Let the customer know you want to help.
   "I am sorry there has been a problem. I will do everything I can to assist you."

2. If after venting the customer continues to use offensive language, ask the customer to speak in a professional manner.
   "I'm trying to assist you. Could you speak in a professional manner?"

3. If the customer continues to use offensive language, let the customer know you are going to take action if the language persists.
   "I appreciate your frustration [anger, concern] and I'm trying to assist you. If you cannot speak in a professional manner I will have to transfer you to my supervisor."

4. If the customer cannot speak in a professional manner, take action.
   "As you are unable to speak in a professional manner, please hold while I transfer you to my supervisor."

Figure 13–3 Technique for handling offensive or abusive language

In today's society, swearing, or cursing is increasingly commonplace. In some cases, customers may not even be aware that their language is potentially offensive. Analysts must strike a balance between empathizing with the fact that the customer is upset while giving him or her a chance to calm down, and taking abuse. Accepting foul language, whether from customers or coworkers, in essence gives the person permission to continue using the language. If you find a person's language offensive, don't be afraid to speak up. It is important to do so, however, in a professional manner that is in keeping with your company's policies.

Finally, some customers will become irate even if you have done your best. Remember that some people have unrealistic expectations or they may simply be under so much stress that they are incapable of calming down. Your challenge is to ensure that your actions do not drive customers to their irate state. It is very important to understand that customers may be responding to your behavior, or what they perceive is your behavior, when they become increasingly angry. For example, you may be using negative phrases, such as "That's not our policy" or "We don't do that," without offering the customer any options or alternatives. Keep it positive and focus on what you can do.

The Internet and e-mail make it possible for customers to voice their opinions and complaints to a wide audience any time of the day or night. Because these technologies offer a perceived layer of anonymity, customers can be quick to judge and brutal with their criticism. Successful companies accept this fact and work hard to ensure customer complaints are handled quickly and professionally.

E-mail, for example, offers a perceived layer of anonymity, and customers and service providers alike can, at times, say things they would never say to a person standing in front of them. It is important to understand that when inappropriate comments are made via e-mail, those comments can and may be forwarded to other people such as your team leader or supervisor. The best practice is to watch *what* you say and *how* you say it whether you are communicating in person, over the telephone, or in writing.

Repairing a Damaged Customer Relationship

Even the most dissatisfied customers will continue doing business with a company if their problems and complaints are consistently handled quickly and cheerfully. Companies that provide world-class customer service understand this fact and work hard to establish policies aimed at maintaining their customer's good will, even in difficult situations.

Realistically speaking, sometimes there is nothing you can do for a customer. The customer may simply have unrealistic expectations. Or, the customer may believe that a product is broken, when, in fact, the product was simply not designed to perform the function the customer requires. In this type of situation, a positive vocabularly is extremely important. Let the customer know what you can do or what the product can do. When possible and appropriate, describe to the customer any alternate ways to meet his or her needs. If the customer is still dissatisfied, let the customer know that you will document the complaint and pass it on to management. When appropriate, ask your team leader or supervisor to assess the situation and speak with or contact the customer.

As a help desk analyst, the best thing you can do is stay focused on what you can do for the customer. The worst thing you can do is make promises that you cannot keep.

You cannot assume that just because a customer seems to be happy when you complete a contact that you have regained that customer's trust. Customers often feel they have to fight for their rights and even the slightest misstep can cause a customer to once again become defensive and distrusting. Patience and consistent follow-through are required to repair a damaged relationship. Follow-through means that you keep your promises, including calling the customer back when you said you would—even if you don't have a resolution to the problem. If letting the customer know that you have not forgotten about them is the best you can do, it is better than the customer hearing nothing. Follow-through means that a field service engineer arrives on-site when promised—or calls before she is late to arrange a new arrival time. The key here is to keep customers informed and be sure they know and are comfortable with exactly what is being done to resolve their technical problem or complaint.

NOTE Proactive communication is an extremely effective way to prevent or minimize customer dissatisfaction. The best companies proactively communicate by, for example, broadcasting a message when customers can expect a longer than normal wait time when calling. Some companies send letters or e-mails to customers informing them of a problem with the company's Web site or about a product recall. Most customers appreciate being informed of a problem before they discover it for themselves.

TIP Keep the customer informed, keep the customer!

Once the problem has been resolved, it is important that you or someone from your help desk or company follow up to ensure that the customer is fully satisfied. **Follow-up** means that a help desk or company representative verifies that the customer's problem has been resolved to the customer's satisfaction and that the problem has not recurred. For example, some companies have the help desk manager or the customer's sales representative contact a dissatisfied customer in an effort to show that the company values the customer's business. In some cases, you may be the company representative contacting the customer.

Although you may feel uncomfortable following up with a customer who was very angry and perhaps, from your perspective, unreasonable, it is the only way to repair the relationship. Repairing the relationship enables both you and the customer to feel comfortable when working together in the future. Furthermore, some analysts report that when they have called or e-mailed angry customers to follow up, the customers apologized for their behavior. A customer may indicate that he was getting pressure from his boss or she was having one of those days where nothing seemed to go right. When difficult situations are handled properly, even the most disgruntled customer can become the help desk's greatest advocate.

KEEPING YOURSELF IN CONTROL

Difficult situations are inevitable when interacting with customers, so it is important to be prepared. By practicing the techniques listed in Figure 13–4, you will gain the confidence needed to stay calm and in control. Remember that you are a professional, and your job is to serve and support your customers.

- Learn to respond, not react
- Stay calm under pressure
- Get ready for your next contact

Figure 13–4 Techniques for staying in control

By responding to difficult situations in a positive, professional manner, you will gain personal confidence as well as your customers' trust and respect.

 NOTE The techniques discussed in this section are life skills that can be applied to any difficult situation, whether professional or personal. When you master these skills, you will begin to consider difficult situations less stressful as you develop a track record of handling them successfully.

Learning to Respond, Not React

Reacting is easy, especially in a difficult customer situation. Without thinking, you say or do the first thing that comes to mind. Very often, you mirror the behavior, even bad behavior, of your customer. For example, if a customer shouts, your instinct may be to shout back. If a customer is rude, you may be tempted to be rude in return. When you react without thinking, situations can quickly spiral out of control and you may say or do things you will later regret.

Responding involves making a conscious choice to control your behavior. As a professional, it is your responsibility to act in a positive, constructive way, regardless of the customer's behavior. Try to remember that a customer who is angry or upset needs your assistance just as badly as a pleasant customer who asks you nicely for help. Try to think rationally about what the customer needs and respond calmly to that need.

Practice using the proven techniques discussed in this chapter to get and keep even the most difficult situation under control. Recall that getting focused is the first step in handling a difficult customer situation. It is easy to lose your focus, so take a few seconds to calm yourself any time you feel that you are losing control. By thinking rationally and staying calm at all times, you can respond, rather than react, to your customers.

NOTE

One reason that service providers may react negatively in difficult customer situations is that they feel defensive and take the situation personally. You may think or even say "It's not my fault . . ." and you are right. It typically is not your fault and even if it is your fault (for example, you made a mistake), you cannot take the situation personally. An effective way to deal with a difficult customer situation is not to worry about who is at fault. Simply ask the customer to give you the opportunity to assist and then focus on what you can do. Do your best, learn from your mistakes, and take satisfaction in knowing that most customers appreciate your efforts.

Staying Calm Under Pressure

People experience stress and pressure differently. Some analysts can "go with the flow" and rarely become upset. Other analysts feel threatened and may panic when facing even a slightly difficult situation. Learning to stay calm under pressure requires that you learn to control your behavior. It is your job to stay in control and handle even the most difficult situations in a professional, positive manner.

Difficult situations are tough. As a human being, you can "lose your mind" on any given day in much the same way that your customers can lose theirs. This is because different sides of our brains handle logic and emotion. As is illustrated in Figure 13–5, the left side of our brain absorbs memorized data and handles linear and logical thinking. The right side of our brain handles emotion.

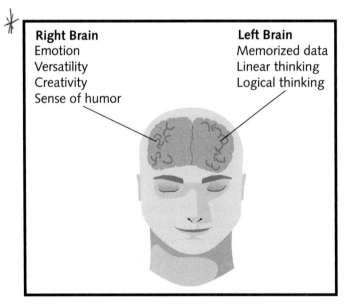

Figure 13–5 How our brains handle logic and emotion

The two sides of our brain work together; although, in most people, one side dominates the other. When we are extremely upset or angry, however, the right brain takes over. You may have heard the expression "he's not in his right mind," which implies that someone is not thinking clearly. Well, the truth is that when we are extremely upset or angry we are in our right mind. As a result, we are incapable of thinking logically as that is an activity handled by our left brain. Given the way our brains work, you can understand why you must avoid the temptation to focus only on problem solving when someone is in an emotional state. In other words, you must resist the temptation to engage the customer in left-brain activities when the customer's right brain is in control. You must first acknowledge the customer's emotional state and let the customer know that you empathize and understand his or her needs and expectations. Then, and only then, will the customer regain the capability of his or her left brain and as a result be ready to respond logically and rationally.

Recall that in most people, one side of the brain dominates the other. Determining the dominant side of your brain may be helpful to you as a help desk analyst. For example, if you are predominantly a "left-brained" person, you will tend to be a very logical thinker and may have a difficult time understanding why other people become emotional. As a result, you may try to go straight to problem solving without addressing the customer's emotional needs. Remember that this can cause the customer to become even more upset because the customer may perceive that you are not listening. Predominantly left-brained thinkers must learn to listen for and acknowledge emotion.

If you are a very "right-brained" person, you may find that you become emotional fairly quickly in a difficult situation. For example, you may find that you tend to become upset or angry when you encounter someone who is upset or angry. Remember that reacting in a negative way can cause a difficult situation to quickly escalate out of control. Predominantly right-brained thinkers must learn to control their own emotions.

Whether you are left- or right-brained, it is important that you remain calm and in control at all times. This is essential when you are interacting with a customer who is extremely upset or irate. In other words, you must maintain control of your ability to think logically. If you become upset or enraged, then neither you nor the customer is going to be able to bring the situation under control or solve the problem. One way to remain calm and in control is to learn the symptoms that you experience when you are getting upset or angry, such as the ones listed below.

- Headache
- Grinding teeth
- Concentration loss
- Nausea
- Reddening face
- Strained tone of voice
- Neck and shoulder tension

When speaking to a customer on the phone or face-to-face, the customer may notice these symptoms, and the customer's perception of these symptoms could, in fact, make the situation worse. If your voice becomes strained, the customer may perceive that you are raising your voice or shouting, or the customer may perceive that you are being rude or curt and begin to respond in a similar manner. Condition yourself to stay focused on what you have to do, and not how you feel. Figure 13–6 lists some of the techniques you can use to stay calm under pressure.

- Take a deep breath
- Sip water
- Use positive imagery
- Use positive self-talk

Figure 13–6 Calming techniques

Each technique has a different benefit, so you may want use two or more of these techniques in combination.

Take a Deep Breath.   Tension causes your chest to tighten, which in turn causes your breathing to become shallow. This can also affect your voice. For example, your voice may become high-pitched or raspy. Taking a deep breath or a series of deep breaths will lessen the tension and enable you to resume a normal breathing rate. Breathe in deeply— inhale— through your nose so that you fill your lungs and feel the release of tension, then breathe out—exhale—fully through your mouth. Remember, however, not to exhale audibly or the customer may perceive your deep breath as a sigh of weariness or a sign of frustration. For example, you may want to mute the telephone for a second or two while you take your deep breath, or, when facing a customer, you may want to take a series of smaller, less obvious breaths.

Sitting or standing up straight is another way to improve your breathing. Poor posture caused by slumped shoulders, slouching, or an ill-fitting chair makes it difficult to breathe deeply. Shallow or restricted breathing will, in time, reduce your energy and affect your attitude. Sitting up straight enables you to fully inflate your lungs and release nervous energy.

Sip Water.   Taking a sip of water will lubricate your throat and help restore your voice to its normal pitch. It will also buy you the few seconds you may need to calm yourself before you speak. Sipping water is comparable to the practice of "counting to ten" before you speak.

Use Positive Imagery.   **Positive imagery** is the act of using mental pictures or images to influence your thinking in a positive way. For example, some analysts envision themselves standing next to the customer, looking at the problem. Rather than imagining that you are pitted against the customer, this positive image enables you to remember that you and the customer are pitted against the problem, as shown in Figure 13–7. Some analysts replace the image of an angry customer with the image of someone they love and care about. Analysts who use this technique find that it enables them to remain empathetic and to better understand their customer's perspective.

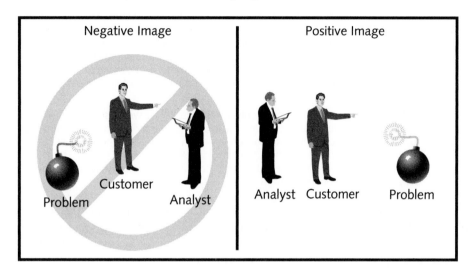

Figure 13–7 Positive imagery

Use Positive Self-Talk. **Positive self-talk** is the act of using words to influence your thinking in a positive way. The words people use, even when they are talking to themselves, influence their thoughts and attitudes. It is normal for people to talk to themselves throughout the day. Whether people are conscious of it or not, the words people use affect how they think about themselves and how they experience situations. By watching the words that you use, you can begin to notice which of your thoughts are positive and which are negative. Once you become aware of how your self-talk sounds, you can practice eliminating negative thoughts and attitudes by using positive words.

> **Negative words:** I can't handle this.
> **Positive words:** I know what to do.

When facing a difficult customer situation, use positive self-talk to remind yourself that you cannot take this situation too personally. Tell yourself that you know what to do and coach yourself to use the proven techniques discussed in this chapter to calm your customer and begin solving the problem. Train yourself to replace negative thoughts about the customer with positive thoughts. Try to maintain a positive perspective.

Negative perspective: What a jerk.

Positive perspective: This person is really upset. What can I do to help?

TIP Practice will enable you to make each of these calming techniques a habit that you will do without conscious thought. Techniques you can use to practice staying calm under pressure include role-playing with another analyst or with your supervisor or team leader. You can also record your calls and listen to them afterward, listen to other analysts' calls to learn what you can, and review a difficult call in a staff meeting to see how it could have been handled better.

TIP Difficult situations do not occur only when you are at work, so practice these techniques any time you find yourself losing control. For example, if someone is rude to you or you find yourself becoming angry, think about how you are feeling and make a conscious effort to calm yourself and regain control. The more you practice these techniques, the more confidence you will have when handling difficult customer situations.

Customers tend to respond positively when you are calm, confident, and in control. Learn to control your own emotions so that you can focus on meeting your customers' needs. Remember that you must meet your customers' emotional needs as well as their technical needs, which requires active listening and empathy.

Getting Ready for Your Next Contact

It is likely that you will find some difficult situations more draining than others. What time of day the situation occurs, your level of preparedness, and even your personal mood all influence your ability to recover from a difficult situation. Take the time you need to compose yourself before answering your next call, handling your next e-mail, or meeting your next customer. Give yourself the opportunity to let your positive, can do attitude shine through. In most cases you may just need to stand up, take a deep breath, and stretch a bit. Then you'll be ready to go. In some cases, however, you may need to follow all or some of the steps listed in Figure 13–8.

- Inform your team leader or supervisor
- Take a short break
- Avoid caffeine or other stimulants
- Employ stress-coping mechanisms

Figure 13–8 Steps for recovering from a particularly upsetting situation

You will need to follow these steps only when you feel a situation has been particularly upsetting.

Inform Your Team Leader or Supervisor.   If you are upset, it is likely that the customer may still be upset. Your team leader or supervisor needs to be informed to determine what, if any, additional steps should be taken to satisfy the customer. This will also enable you to present the facts of the situation from your perspective, enabling your team leader to have a balanced view in case the customer perceives the situation differently.

Take a Short Break.   Leave the area and catch your breath for a few moments. Take a short walk outside if you can to get some fresh air, or to the water cooler to get a drink of water. If a walk is not possible, take a minute to look out the window and observe nature. If the day is dismal, look at art or go somewhere that you can hear music. Engage as many senses as you can and try to clear your mind of negative thoughts.

Avoid Caffeine or Other Stimulants.   Caffeine is a stimulant and can increase your anxiety or exacerbate your feelings of frustration or anger. Caffeine is found in coffee, tea, cola, and chocolate. If you feel compelled to eat or drink something after a difficult situation, keep it simple. Drink a big glass of water or eat a simple snack, such as whole wheat crackers or a small handful of nuts. Give your body the time and fuel it needs to unwind.

Employ Stress-Coping Mechanisms.   Just as people experience stress in different ways, people also employ varying techniques to manage and cope with stress. For example, some analysts keep a stress ball at their desk. Some help desks have a punching bag that analysts can use. Some analysts turn to a coworker or seek out a friend who they can talk to about the situation. Try these or other stress-coping mechanisms.

Finding the humor in a situation is an excellent stress-coping mechanism. Having a sense of humor is not just about telling or laughing at jokes. It is a perspective on life that allows you to maintain a positive outlook. Laughter is a great release and people with a sense of humor tend to be more flexible and less anxious. Used inappropriately, however, humor can make a situation worse. Take care to avoid even the appearance of laughing at a customer or belittling his or her concerns. When in doubt, keep your humorous thoughts to yourself.

Remember that each and every difficult situation you handle will increase your confidence and your ability to handle future situations. As time passes, you will find these situations less stressful because you have developed the skills needed to calm your customers and gain their confidence. You will also have learned how to take care of yourself and prepare yourself for the next customer. Difficult situations are inevitable. By practicing the techniques discussed in this chapter, you can handle these situations with confidence.

CHAPTER SUMMARY

❐ Most customers are pleasant, calm, and appreciative of your efforts, but there are times when customers become upset, angry, and demanding. Although difficult customer situations are the exception, not the rule, these situations can be extremely stressful and can affect your attitude—if you let them.

❐ Proven techniques enable you to understand, acknowledge, and address the emotional needs of your customers as well as their technical needs. Consistent follow-through and follow-up enable you to maintain your customer's goodwill and repair a damaged relationship. When difficult situations are handled properly, even the most disgruntled customer can become the help desk's greatest advocate.

❐ Difficult situations are inevitable, so it is important to be prepared. By thinking rationally and staying calm at all times, you can learn to respond, not react, to these situations when they occur. One way to stay calm and in control is to learn the symptoms, such as headaches, nausea, or neck and shoulder tension, that you experience when you are under pressure. You can then use techniques, such as taking a deep breath or sipping water, to relieve these symptoms, enabling you to focus on meeting your customer's needs. Taking the time to compose yourself before you take a new call, handle a new e-mail, or meet with the next customer is also important.

❐ Each and every difficult situation you handle will increase your confidence and your ability to handle future situations. In time, you will find these situations less stressful because you have the skills needed to calm yourself and your customer and to stay in control at all times.

KEY TERMS

empathy — The act of identifying with and understanding another person's situation, feelings, and motives.

follow-through — The act of keeping your promises, including calling the customer back when you said you would—even if you don't have a resolution to the problem.

follow-up — The act of having a help desk or company representative verify that the customer's problem has been resolved to the customer's satisfaction and that the problem has not recurred.

positive imagery — The act of using mental pictures or images to influence your thinking in a positive way.

positive self-talk — The act of using words to influence your thinking in a positive way.

REVIEW QUESTIONS

1. True or False? You can control your customer's behavior. Explain your answer.

2. Do difficult customer situations happen often?

3. Why is it important to avoid the temptation to make sweeping negative statements about your customers?

4. What is empathy?

5. Does being empathetic mean that you are personally responsible for another person's situation?

6. What influences an upset or angry person's willingness to work with you?

7. What are four preparatory steps you can take prior to each customer interaction in order to get focused?

8. Why is it important to let an angry customer vent?

9. What should you be listening for when a customer is venting?

10. What can happen if you do not acknowledge a customer's emotional state?

11. What tone of voice should you use when using a customer's name or when apologizing to a customer?

12. Why is it important to gain agreement from customers that you understand their needs?

13. When handling a difficult situation, when can you begin active problem solving?

14. Briefly describe the three stages customers go through on the way to becoming irate.

15. How can you ensure your behavior is not driving a customer into an irate state?

16. How do customers want their problems and complaints to be handled?

17. Describe two ways to regain a dissatisfied customer's trust and repair a damaged relationship.

18. Why is it important to follow up with a customer who was angry?

19. How is responding to a difficult situation different than reacting?

20. What are two things you must do in order to respond, rather than react, to difficult customer situations?

21. What does the left side of the brain do?

22. What does the right side of the brain do?

23. What side of the brain takes control when you are extremely upset or angry?

24. What do you need to do if you are a predominantly left-brained service provider?

25. What do you need to do if you are a predominantly right-brained service provider?

26. What symptom that you are upset or angry is it possible for a customer to notice when you are talking on the telephone?

27. What symptom that you are upset or angry is it possible for a customer to notice when you are face-to-face?

28. List four techniques that a person can use to stay calm when facing a difficult situation.

29. What physical benefits do you derive from taking a deep breath when under pressure?

30. What benefits do you derive from taking a sip of water when under pressure?

31. What is positive imagery?

32. What kind of words can you use to eliminate negative thoughts and attitudes?

33. Why is it important to inform your team leader or supervisor that you have just handled a particularly difficult situation?

34. Why should you avoid caffeine after a stressful situation?

35. What are three things you can do in an effort to find difficult customer situations less stressful?

DISCUSSION QUESTIONS

1. Some people believe that they must be aggressive when interacting with service providers or they will not get what they want. How do you think they came to feel that way? Are they right?

2. In some organizations, management directs help desk staff to apologize any time a customer is dissatisfied—even when the customer is wrong. In other organizations, management feels that although help desk staff must always be empathetic when a customer is dissatisfied, it is only necessary to apologize when the company has clearly made a mistake. What are the pros and cons of these two scenarios? What, if any, impact could these policies have when analysts are handling difficult customer situations?

3. A common customer complaint is that a support organization failed to follow-through on promises made or follow-up to ensure a customer's satisfaction. What are some potential causes for a support organization's failure to communicate?

HANDS-ON PROJECTS

HANDS-ON PROJECTS

Project 13–1

Practice being empathetic. For the next week, note any situations you encounter or observe where someone becomes upset, angry, or demanding. Then, try to think of situations you were involved in that enable you to relate to what the people who have become upset, angry, or demanding are experiencing. For example, if the driver behind you beeps the horn as soon as the traffic light turns green, try to think of a situation when you may have been late for work or school and as a result experienced frustration with the driver in front of you. The point of this project is to simply acknowledge the fact that we are all human and we can all lose our cool on any given day. Briefly summarize the situations you observed and the personal experiences you used to empathize with each situation.

Project 13–2

Discuss situations that cause frustration or anger. Assemble a team of two or three classmates. Discuss the list of situations presented in this chapter that may cause customers to become frustrated or angry. As technology users—and therefore at times customers yourselves—discuss these situations and answer the following questions:

❑ What other situations that cause frustration or anger can your team add to this list?

❑ From the expanded list, what are the top five situations that cause technology users frustration?

❑ Select the three situations that your team feels are the greatest causes of frustration. Brainstorm a list of ways that companies can minimize the frustration that customers may experience when facing these situations. Present your ideas to the class.

Project 13–3

Discuss a difficult customer situation. Assemble a team of three to five of your classmates. Ensure that you or one of the classmates on your team has, as a service provider, faced a difficult customer situation. For example, a team member may have encountered a difficult customer situation in his or her workplace. Or, a team member may have done work for a family member or neighbor and the family member or neighbor was dissatisfied. Have the classmate describe the difficult situation to the best of his or her recollection. Discuss and document your team's answers to the following questions:

❑ What emotion was the customer experiencing?

❑ How, if at all, can you empathize with the emotion the customer was experiencing?

❑ Constructively assess the response of your classmate (the service provider) to the customer's emotional state.

❑ What, if anything, could have been done to prevent this situation?

❑ Given what you learned in this chapter, what can you learn or what conclusions can you draw from this scenario?

Project 13–4

Be objective. Unfortunately, everyone has experienced a difficult customer situation from the viewpoint of the customer. Think of a situation where you were the customer and you became upset or angry. For example, you may have received poor service in a restaurant or you may have waited on hold for an extended period of time before a customer service representative answered the telephone. Consider what you have learned in this chapter about why customers behave the way they do and how service providers can best handle difficult situations. Describe in a paragraph or two the situation and how you (the customer) or the service provider could have handled the situation better.

Project 13–5

Become aware of "broken promises." It is not uncommon for service providers to make promises to their customers that they cannot realistically keep. For example, a waiter in a restaurant may tell you he will be "back in a second" with your check. Realistically speaking, that is impossible because the "second" is up before he has even turned to retrieve your check. For the next week, pay attention to the promises that service providers make to you. Select two or three situations and briefly note your perceptions in terms of the following:

◻ When the promise was made, did you consider it realistic?

◻ Was the promise kept?

◻ How did you feel when the promise was or was not kept?

◻ Given what you have learned in this chapter, what conclusions can you draw from this exercise?

Project 13–6

Learn the predominant side of your brain. Use the following two exercises to learn whether you tend to be predominantly left- or right-brained. The first exercise is simple; the second is more comprehensive.

Exercise One—Simple Left-Brain, Right-Brain Exercise

This exercise uses the relationship between your thumbs and your brain to determine if you tend to be left- or right-brained.

1. Fold your hands together with your fingers intertwined (the way people often do when they are preparing to pray).

2. Look at your thumbs and determine if your left or right thumb is resting on top.

If your right thumb is resting on top, it is likely that you are predominantly right-brained. If your left thumb is resting on top, it is likely that you are predominantly left-brained. A fun way to validate this preference is to reverse your thumbs. That is, put the thumb that had been resting on the bottom on the top. You will typically find that it feels uncomfortable.

Exercise Two—Comprehensive Left-Brain, Right-Brain Exercise

This exercise uses your answers to a series of questions to determine if you tend to be left- or right-brained (*Brain Builders!*, 1995, pp. 332–3). Check one answer for each question.

Question	Answer	Score
1. In your opinion, is *daydreaming* (a) a waste of time, (b) an amusing way to relax, (c) helpful in solving problems and thinking creatively, (d) a good way to plan your future?	B	5
2. What's your attitude about *hunches*? (a) Your hunches are strong and you follow them. (b) You are not aware of following any hunches that come to mind. (c) You may have hunches but you don't trust them. (d) You'd have to be crazy to base a decision on a mere hunch.	A	9
3. When it comes to *problem solving*, do you (a) get contemplative, thinking it over on a walk, with friends; (b) make a list of alternatives, determine priorities among them, and take the one at the top; (c) consult the past by remembering how you handled something similar to this situation before; (d) watch television, hoping the problem will go away?	B	1
4. Take a moment to relax, put this book down, close your eyes, and put your hands in your lap, one on top of the other. Which hand is on top? (a) your right hand; (b) your left hand; (c) neither, because they are parallel?	A	1
5. Are you goal oriented? (a) True; (b) False.	A	1
6. When you were in school, you preferred algebra to geometry? (a) True; (b) False.	A	1
7. Generally speaking, you are a *very organized* type of person, for whom everything has its proper place and there is a system for doing anything. (a) True; (b) False.	A	1
8. When it comes to speaking or writing or expressing yourself with words, you do pretty well? (a) True; (b) False.	B	7
9. When you're at a party, do you find yourself more natural at listening rather than talking? (a) True; (b) False.	B	3
10. You don't need to check your watch to accurately tell how much time has passed. (a) True; (b) False.	A	1
11. When it comes to athletics, somehow you perform even better than what you should expect from the amount of training or natural abilities you have. (a) True; (b) False.	A	9
12. If it's a matter of work, you much prefer going solo to working by committee. (a) True; (b) False.	A	3
13. You have a near photographic memory for faces. (a) True; (b) False.	A	7
14. If you had your way, you would redecorate your home often, take trips frequently, and change your environment as much as possible. (a) True; (b) False.	B	1
15. You are a regular James Bond when it comes to taking risks. (a) True; (b) False.	B	3
Total Score		54
Score divided by 15		3.6

Scoring Key:

1. (a) 1 (b) 5 (c) 7 (d) 9	10 (a) 1 (b) 9
2. (a) 9 (b) 7 (c) 3 (d) 1	11. (a) 9 (b) 1
3. (a) 7 (b) 1 (c) 3 (d) 9	12. (a) 3 (b) 7
4. (a) 1 (b) 9 (c) 5	13. (a) 7 (b) 1
5. (a) 1 (b) 9	14. (a) 9 (b) 1
6. (a) 1 (b) 9	15. (a) 7 (b) 3
7. (a) 1 (b) 9	
8. (a) 1 (b) 7	
9. (a) 6 (b) 3	

1. Score each answer using the scoring key.

2. Total your points.

3. Divide your total points by 15.

The lower the number, the more left-brained you are; the higher the number, the more right-brained. For example, if your score is 1, you are an exceptionally left-brained person. If your score is 8, you are exceptionally right-brained. A score of 5 means that there is regular traffic between your left and right brain.

Project 13–7

Learn the symptoms you experience under pressure. For the next week, record the symptoms you experience anytime you are upset or angry at home or at work. Remember that you do not have to be extremely upset or irate to experience symptoms. For example, you may simply be frustrated or perhaps confused. Keep a log of the situations you encounter and the symptoms you experience. Also, note on your log any ways you may be exacerbating these symptoms, for example, by consuming an excessive amount of caffeine. Assess how you relieve these symptoms and identify any techniques you can use to stay calm in these situations. Share your experiences with your classmates and discuss how you can use the techniques discussed in this chapter to stay calm and in control.

Project 13–8

Assess your habits. Staying calm when faced with a difficult situation requires that you have good habits in place for dealing with pressure. Briefly describe a technique or techniques you use to calm yourself when facing a difficult situation. For example, is it your habit to take a deep breath or use positive self-talk? Briefly describe the benefits you derive from this habit. Given what you have learned in this chapter, what additional techniques can you incorporate as a habit?

CASE PROJECTS

1. Customer Service Script

You have been hired as a consultant to a company that wants to (1) improve its customer service, and (2) reduce the stress its staff experiences when handling difficult situations. Drawing from your experiences both as a customer and as a service provider, develop a script that illustrates a difficult situation. Prepare a series of questions you can use to prompt empathy for the customer's situation, constructive feedback for the service provider's handling of the situation, and tips and techniques for handling this situation better in the future.

2. Training Class: Respond Positively to an Angry E-Mail

Your boss has asked you to develop a handout for a training class about how to respond positively to an angry e-mail. He wants this handout to contain a customer e-mail with an obvious angry tone and several complaints that must be addressed. He also wants the handout to contain a response to the customer's e-mail that acknowledges what the customer said and how he or she said it. Prepare the handout for his review.

3. Difficult Customer Situation

A coworker has just had to handle a difficult customer situation. She thinks she could have handled the situation better and has asked for your feedback. Also, the customer hung up, in disgust, before the analyst was able to assist and she doesn't know what to do. Here's how your coworker describes the call to you:

> **Customer:** This is Jane Apponte. Let me talk to Suzie Peters.
>
> **Analyst:** I'm sorry Ms. Apponte, Suzie is on another call right now. Is there something I can do to help you?
>
> **Customer:** No, I can't wait. Interrupt her and tell her that I am waiting to speak with her.
>
> **Analyst:** I can't do that ma'am, but I can take your telephone number and have her call you back when she gets off the phone.
>
> **Customer:** That's not good enough. I have been waiting two hours for someone to get out here and fix my PC.
>
> **Analyst:** Did you call the help desk about your PC?

Customer (becoming irritated): Of course I called the help desk. Suzie told me a technician would be here within the hour and no one has shown up or called. I have a meeting in 10 minutes and I want this problem taken care of before I leave. You need to get someone out here right now!

Analyst: Do you know your ticket number?

Customer (shouting now): I don't care what the ticket number is. Get someone out here now!

Analyst: Ms. Apponte, there is nothing I can do until I know your ticket number. Please hold while I look it up. [Places customer on hold.]

Customer: [Hangs up in disgust.]

First, write out the steps that must be taken immediately to address this customer's concern. Then, write out a sample script that shows how the analyst could have handled the call better. Include in the script examples of how analysts can let their can do attitude shine through. Share and discuss your recommendations with your classmates.

14

SOLVING AND PREVENTING PROBLEMS

In this chapter you will learn:

◆ Proven techniques you can use to methodically solve problems

◆ How and when to take ownership of ongoing problems and keep customers and management informed about the status of problem resolution activities

◆ Ways to manage your workload and maintain a positive working relationship with other support groups

◆ The importance of focusing on problem prevention

To be successful, help desk analysts must be able to solve problems efficiently and effectively. A problem is an event that disrupts service or prevents access to products. Common problems include a broken device, an error message, or a system outage. Solving problems efficiently and effectively involves more than simply searching a knowledge base for known solutions. It requires a methodical approach, or process, through which analysts gather all available data, determine the probable source of a problem, and then decide on a course of action. This chapter provides a brief overview of the problem management process, but focuses on problem–solving skills.

As a help desk analyst, you need effective questioning skills and superior listening skills to be a good problem solver. Persistence is also important, because proficient problem solving requires going beyond the "quick fix" to find a permanent solution. By analyzing trends and suggesting ways to eliminate problems, you can help reduce the number of problems that customers experience and even prevent problems altogether. Problem solving is an innate skill, but it is also a skill that you can improve with practice. Improved problem-solving skills will enable you to resolve more problems, resolve problems more quickly and accurately, and, ultimately, satisfy more customers.

HOW TO SOLVE PROBLEMS METHODICALLY

Studies indicate that a high percentage of technical problems are recurring. In other words, many technical problems show up repeatedly and have already been reported to the help desk or to the product's hardware or software manufacturer. As a result, plenty of information is available for finding solutions to problems. As a help desk analyst, you can draw from your experience, access available knowledge bases, or use tools in an effort to find a solution. You can also engage other analysts or level two service providers who may have experienced the same or similar problems in the past.

The Problem Management Process

Most help desks develop processes and procedures to ensure problems are handled quickly, correctly, and consistently. A **process** is a collection of interrelated work activities—or tasks—that take a set of specific inputs and produce a set of specific outputs that are of value to the customer. A **procedure** is a step-by-step, detailed set of instructions that describes how to perform the tasks in a process. Each task in a process has a procedure that describes how to do that task. In other words, processes define what tasks to do, whereas procedures describe how to do the tasks. When multiple groups are involved in solving a problem, processes and procedures provide the framework that enables each group to understand its role and responsibilities.

Flowcharts are often used in business to outline processes. A \flowchart \is a diagram that shows the sequence of tasks that occur in a process. Table 14–1 describes the purpose of some common symbols used in flowcharts. Flowcharts are a good way to show how all the procedures involved in a process are interconnected.

Table 14–1 Flowchart symbols

Symbol	Name	Purpose
(A)	On Page Connector	Represents an exit to, or entry from, another part of the same flowchart
Task	Task	Shows a single task or operation
Predefined Process	Predefined process	Represents another process that provides input or receives output from the current process
Decision	Decision	Represents a decision point and typically has a "yes" branch and a "no" branch

Table 14–1 Flowchart symbols (continued)

Symbol	Name	Purpose
——No——▶	No result	Used in conjunction with a decision to show the next task or decision following a "no" result
Yes (↓)	Yes result	Used in conjunction with a decision to show the next task or decision following a "yes" result
Terminator (oval)	Terminator	Shows the end or stopping point of a process

One of the most common help desk processes is **problem management,** the process of tracking and resolving problems. The goal of problem management is to minimize the impact of problems that affect a company's systems, networks, and products. Figure 14–1 shows a fairly simple problem management process. This process varies from one company to the next and may be much more complex.

The problem management process begins when a problem is recognized. More specifically, it begins when a symptom is detected. A **symptom** is a sign or indication that a problem has occurred. The probable source of the problem must then be identified before problem solving can begin. The **probable source** of the problem is the system, network, or product that is most likely causing the problem. The problem management process ends when a final and permanent corrective action repairs, replaces, or modifies the source of the problem to the customer's satisfaction. The best companies take problem resolution a step further and identify the problem's root cause. The **root cause** of the problem is the most basic reason for an undesirable condition or problem, which, if eliminated or corrected, prevents the problem from existing or occurring.

It is important to distinguish the symptom and the probable source of a problem from the root cause. Each can be different. For example, if a customer contacts the help desk and indicates that she is receiving an error message each time she tries to print a report, the error message is the problem symptom. The analyst may determine that the probable source of the customer's printing problem is the software package that she is using to print. The analyst could determine this by personally routing a report to the printer to see if it prints. If it does, the analyst can eliminate the printer as the probable source. Further discussion with the customer may lead the analyst to conclude that the root cause of the problem is not, in fact, the software package that the customer is using, but the incorrect set of procedures that she is using to issue the print command.

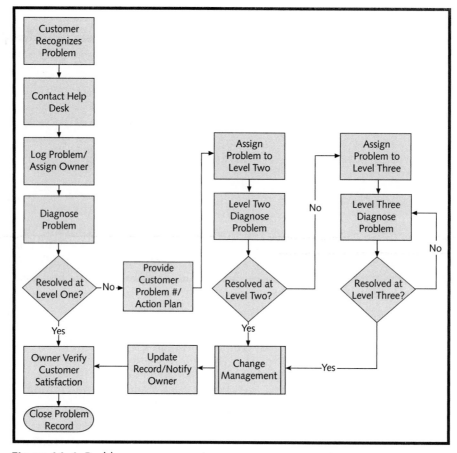

Figure 14–1 Problem management process

The terminology used to describe the problem management process can vary from one organization to the next, just as the process can vary. Increasingly, organizations are using the ITIL vocabulary to describe processes such as incident/problem management. ITIL defines incident/problem management as the resolution and prevention of incidents that affect the normal running of an organization's IT services. This includes ensuring that faults are corrected, preventing any recurrence of these faults, and the application of preventative maintenance to reduce the likelihood of these faults occurring in the first place. ITIL defines an incident as any event that is not part of the standard operation of a service and that causes, or may cause, an interruption to, or a reduction in the quality of that service. ITIL uses terms such as fault and error, or known error, to describe the incident/problem management processes. A fault is a condition that causes a functional unit to fail to perform the required function. An error, or known error, is a condition identified by successful diagnosis of the root cause of a problem when it is confirmed that a configuration item is at fault.

Sometimes called **incident management**, problem management typically also includes answering customer's questions and inquiries. Questions, \such as "How do I . . . ?", are customer requests for instructions on how to use a product. Questions occur when a product is not broken, but the customer simply needs help using it. Questions can often be solved using self-help technologies such as online help, FAQs, or a knowledge base. **Inquiries**, such as "When will my equipment arrive?", are customer requests for information. Inquiries, like questions, usually occur when the product is not broken, but the customer wants a current status report. Customers can often obtain answers to inquiries about orders or a new release of software by accessing a company's Web site. Other inquiries, such as the status of an outstanding problem, may require the assistance of an analyst who performs a lookup in a database or obtains a status from another group.

Most companies distinguish between problems, questions, and inquiries because they represent varying degrees of impact and speak differently to product and company performance. For example, a customer calling to inquire about the date for the next release of a software package may not be dissatisfied with the existing product but is just looking forward to the new version. On the other hand, a customer who gets error messages or loses data when trying to use a software package is clearly dissatisfied, and the company must try to resolve the problem quickly or risk losing that customer. Distinguishing between problems, questions, and inquiries also enables companies to determine which types of contacts are most common. They can then ensure that there are processes and technologies in place for resolving each type of contact in the most efficient, cost-effective way possible.

NOTE Most companies also distinguish between problems and requests. A **request** is a customer order to obtain a new product or service, or an enhancement to an existing product or service. Common requests include moves, adds, and changes, such as enhancing an application, installing a new PC, moving a printer, installing new software, or upgrading existing software. A different process, the request management process, is typically used to handle requests.

Companies use techniques such as trend and root cause analysis to monitor their contacts, determine how to most efficiently and effectively handle those contacts, and ultimately, how to prevent contacts. **Trend analysis** is a methodical way of determining and, when possible, forecasting, service trends. **Root cause analysis** is a methodical way of determining the root cause of problems.

NOTE Chapter 7 explores how to perform trend and root cause analysis.

The problem management process describes the overall approach to be used when handling problems within a company. Within the boundaries of the problem management process, analysts need problem-solving skills to handle each problem. The most efficient and effective way to find a solution to any given problem is to take a methodical approach. Figure 14–2 lists the basic steps to follow when solving problems.

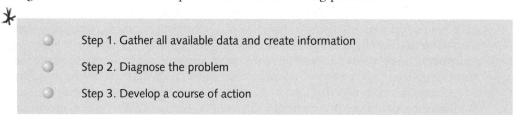

- ⬤ Step 1. Gather all available data and create information
- ⬤ Step 2. Diagnose the problem
- ⬤ Step 3. Develop a course of action

Figure 14–2 Steps to follow when solving problems

The best problem solvers condition themselves to gather and analyze all available data before drawing a conclusion.

Step 1. Gather All Available Data and Create Information

How well you perform the first step in the problem-solving process will greatly influence your ability to quickly find the correct solution. The first step is obvious: Gather all available data and create information. It takes time and effort to capture the data needed to create accurate information. It is not enough to gather data and store it in your head. You must log the data accurately and completely in an incident tracking and problem management system so managers, other help desk analysts, level two service providers, and customers can use it. Some help desks view information as a valuable resource and they use comprehensive incident tracking and problem management systems in an effort to capture as much data as possible. They can then use this data to create the information needed to justify resources, increase customer satisfaction, enhance productivity, improve the quality of products and services, deliver services more efficiently and effectively, and create new products and services. On the other hand, some help desks are so overwhelmed with their responsibilities, or so understaffed, that they capture little or no data. As a result, they have trouble creating the information needed to measure their performance and make improvements. The information needs of the help desk where you work and the complexity of the problem will influence the amount of data you are required to gather. Data to be gathered includes:

- **Customer data.** The identifying details about a customer, including the customer's name, telephone number, e-mail address, department or company name, address or location, customer number, and employee number or user ID. All of the data and text fields that describe a single customer are stored in a **customer record** in the incident tracking and problem management database. Recall that a data field is an element of a database record in which one piece of data is stored. A text field is a field that accepts free-form information. A **record** is a collection of related fields. When customer data is stored in a customer record, analysts do not have to request and key in this information every time that a customer contacts the help desk. Instead, they can access this information and simply verify key data elements such as the customer's telephone number, e-mail address, or address as needed.

- **Problem data.** The details of a single problem. They include the problem category (such as hardware or software), affected component or system (such as a printer or monitor), symptom, date and time problem occurred, contact method (such as telephone, voice mail, e-mail, Web form), date and time problem was logged, analyst who logged problem, problem owner, description, and severity. These data are also stored in fields, and all of the fields that describe a single problem are stored in a \problem record \in the incident tracking and problem management system. These fields can be used to track problems, research and track trends, or to search the knowledge base for solutions.

Customer records are linked to problem records by a unique key field, such as customer name or customer number.

One of the pieces of information you must collect from customers is a description of the problem. Many help desks capture two types of problem descriptions: a short description and a detailed problem description. A **short problem description** succinctly describes the actual results a customer is experiencing. The short description is sometimes called a problem statement.

> Error msg H536 displays when customer is logging on to accounting system. Customer is bounced back to main logon screen.
>
> Spreadsheet package fails when customer runs new macro.

Stating the short problem description is an excellent way to obtain agreement from customers that you understand the problem they are experiencing. The short problem description is often used in reports or online queries to provide an "at a glance" overview of the problem. The short problem description may also be used to search a knowledge base for solutions and may be presented in drop-down menus to enable easier and more consistent searching.

TIP Be succinct when creating the short description, but not to the point of making the description illegible. Resist the temptation to abbreviate words unless the abbreviation is widely recognized. For example, "msg" is a known abbreviation for message. Avoid acronyms and jargon unless the terms are well known to your audience. You can also eliminate words such as "and" and "the" unless they contribute considerably to the readability of the short description.

A **detailed problem description** provides a comprehensive accounting of the problem and the circumstances surrounding the problem's occurrence. The detailed problem description should contain a number of items, including:

- The result the customer expects. For example, the customer expects a report to appear on the printer.

- The actual result the customer is experiencing. For example, the report is not printing.

- Steps the customer took to get the results. For example, the customer issued a print command.

- The history or pattern of the problem. For example, this is a new report and the customer has never tried printing it before. To determine the history or pattern of the problem, you can ask the customer questions such as:

  - Does the problem occur every time the customer performs this step?

  - Does the problem only occur in certain circumstances? What are those circumstances?

  - Does the problem only occur intermittently? Under what conditions?

- Whether the problem is part of a larger problem. For example, the printer is attached to a portion of the network that is currently down.

Notice that one of the first parts of the detailed problem description is the result the customer expected. Problem solving involves asking questions until you determine why the customer's expected result did not happen.

Step 2. Diagnose the Problem

When diagnosing a problem, you are trying to determine the probable source of the problem and, ultimately, its root cause. Determining the probable source of a problem can be extremely difficult, particularly when dealing with complex technology, such as the technology found in a client-server computing environment. **Clientserver** is a computing model where some computers, known as clients, request services, and other computers, known as servers, respond to those requests. For example, consider the earlier scenario where the customer issued a print command and the report did not appear. Figure 14–3 illustrates all of the computing components that must be working correctly for the customer's report to print. This is, of course, a very simple diagram, but it is designed to show that any number of potential points of failure may need to be considered when determining the probable source of a problem.

There are many techniques that are used to diagnose problems and determine the probable problem source. Figure 14–4 lists the most common of these techniques.

Each of these techniques is useful. You may use more than one of these techniques in the course of diagnosing a problem.

Asking Questions.   Asking questions is an extremely effective way to diagnose problems. Asking questions enables you to continue gathering the data needed to identify a solution. You gain insight as to why the problem is occurring. You also gain insight about the

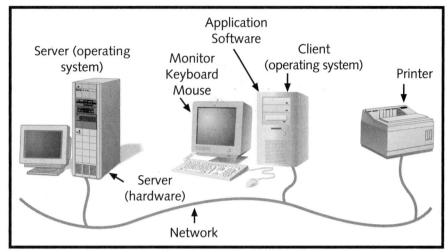

Figure 14–3 Components of a client/server computing environment

- Asking questions
- Simulating the customer's actions
- Using diagnostic tools

Figure 14–4 Problem diagnostic techniques

customer. For example, the customer's ability to answer your questions and her use of terminology when answering will provide you with insight about the customer's skill level.

When asking questions, you must listen actively to both the response your customer is giving and the emotion with which your customer is giving that response. Remember that you must acknowledge and address any strong emotions before you begin or continue active problem solving. Remember, too, that your questions must be appropriate to the customer's communication style. For example, recall that you can ask open-ended questions as needed to obtain more detailed information. To take control of the conversation, you can ask closed-ended questions that prompt short answers such as "yes" and "no."

To become an efficient problem solver, you must condition your mind to ask and obtain answers to a basic set of questions. These basic questions can help you isolate the probable source of the problem. Figure 14–5 lists these basic questions and provides a series of additional questions that you can use to obtain the data you need.

Time may not allow you to ask all of these questions in the course of diagnosing a problem. Usually, you won't have to. The goal is to condition your mind to run through these questions as the customer is relaying information. In other words, you may not need to actually ask a question in order to receive an answer. The customer may simply provide the

Basic Problem-Solving Checklist

What changed?
- ☐ Has new hardware or software been installed?
- ☐ Has old hardware or software been removed?
- ☐ Has there been a change to the way the hardware or software is configured?
- ☐ Has the customer begun using new procedures?
- ☐ Has there been a change in the customer's computing enviroment?

When was the last time it worked?

What can be used as a comparison test?
- ☐ Does it work somewhere else?
- ☐ How has it been over time?
  - The same, better, worse?
- ☐ Is the problem occurring somewhere else?
  - On one system, some systems, all systems?

Has this problem ever occurred before?

What is different and what is the same?
- ☐ What is different?
  - Are there two systems that are the same and one has a problem and one does not?
- ☐ What is the same?
  - Are there two systems that are the same and both have a problem?

Can you clearly state the problem?

Figure 14–5 Basic problem-solving questions

answer while describing the problem. You then need to ask only those questions that have not yet been addressed but still need to be answered.

Brainteasers and puzzles are an excellent way to improve your problem-solving skills. They teach you to ask questions, view problems from many different angles, and go beyond the obvious in search of a solution.

You may also have checklists available to you that provide questions more specific to the actual problem. For example, Figure 14–6 shows a problem-solving checklist that can be used to diagnose printer problems.

Printer Problem-Solving Checklist

✔	Have you ever had this problem before?	Yes/No
✔	Have you ever been able to use this printer before?	Yes/No
✔	Is this a network printer?	Yes/No
✔	Is the printer properly attached to the network?	Yes/No
✔	Have you checked the print queue status?	Yes/No
✔	Has the printer been moved recently?	Yes/No
✔	Is the printer plugged in?	Yes/No
✔	Is the printer powered on?	Yes/No
✔	Do you see a power indicator light?	Yes/No
✔	Do you see an on-line indicator?	Yes/No
✔	Does the printer have paper in it?	Yes/No
✔	Does the printer have an error code?	Yes/No
✔	Have you ever successfully printed this report?	Yes/No
✔	Has this report ever printed on this printer?	Yes/No
✔	Can you route the report to another printer?	Yes/No

Figure 14–6 Printer problem-solving checklist

These checklists may be available to you online in the form of a knowledge management system, or you and your coworkers may develop paper checklists for the different types of problems that you encounter. For example, you may have a checklist for each of the software packages that you support or for each of the types of hardware that you support, such as monitors, printers, and so forth. These checklists will help you avoid letting customers lead you to an incorrect course of action. For example, if a customer calls and indicates that his printer will not print and that he has powered it on and off and checked the paper and toner, you might "assume" that a hardware failure has occurred and escalate the problem to the field services group. By asking additional questions, you may learn that the customer was routing his report to a different printer.

 Ask your level two service providers to help you develop problem-solving checklists so that you can solve problems at the help desk, rather than escalating them to level two.

TIP

Some of the questions in this chapter may seem obvious and almost too simplistic. It is often the simple question, though, that reaps the most information. For example, if you ask a customer "When was the last time the printer worked?" and she responds, "Yesterday, before I moved it," you may have a good lead on why the problem is occurring. Asking seemingly simple questions will enable you to quickly eliminate obvious causes before moving on to more complex diagnostics.

Simulating the Customer's Actions.   Some help desks provide analysts access to the systems or software packages that their customers are using. Some help desks also have lab areas where analysts can access systems that match customers' hardware and software configurations. Analysts can use these systems to simulate a customer's actions in an effort to determine the probable source of a problem. If an analyst can perform an action successfully that a customer cannot, then the probable source of the problem is more likely in the customer's computing environment. For example, if you can access the accounting system but the customer cannot, the accounting system can be eliminated as the probable source of the problem.

The usefulness of this technique depends on the access that you have to the systems your customers use and on the policies of the company where you work. Some companies provide analysts with limited access to the systems being used by customers, in which case analysts may not be able to fully simulate customers' problems. Companies may limit access because customers are working with highly confidential information or because they are performing highly secure transactions. For example, a customer may be authorized to transfer funds in a banking setting or to change grades in an academic setting. In these situations, you may only be able to verify that the system is up and running. If the system is up and running, and you believe that the problem is occurring within the system, you will escalate the problem to a level two specialist who has the authority to perform further diagnostics within the system.

The policies of some companies include very strict standards that determine what technologies customers use. In an internal help desk setting, these standards determine the technologies available to the company's employees. In an external help desk setting, these standards represent the minimum hardware and software recommended to run a company's products without incurring problems.

NOTE It is not always possible for companies to establish or enforce technology standards. For example, some companies have customers with such diverse needs that standards would be prohibitive. Other companies, such as those that provide external support, may be contracted to support any systems that are used by their customers. An efficient, effective problem management process is imperative in the absence of standards. This is because a well-defined problem management process ensures that all problems, even problems with unfamiliar technologies, are handled quickly and consistently.

The help desk is often involved in developing technology standards. As a result, the help desk can become very familiar with the technologies it supports. For example, the help desk may be involved in testing and selecting the systems to be used within a company so they will be familiar with the systems' strengths and weaknesses. It also typically receives copies of the systems, documentation, and training, so it can simulate and solve problems more quickly.

Some companies also establish standards that determine what changes customers can make to the systems they use. For example, some companies do not allow customers to change the way their systems are configured or install personal software, such as games, on their business computers. By tightly controlling the changes that customers make to systems, the company can prevent problems that may occur as a result of an inappropriate change.

Without standards, customers may install equipment or software without the help desk's knowledge. As a result, the help desk does not have a copy of the system that can be used to simulate problems. The installation of the new system may, in fact, be causing the problem. For example, a customer may download software from the Internet that contains a virus, which may corrupt files on the customer's PC or may even destroy portions of the customer's PC. Also, without standards, customers may be able to make changes to their systems that cause problems. For example, a customer may change the PC's display settings in such a way that portions of the screen are no longer visible. Unfortunately, the customer may not remember making the change or may not recall exactly what change was made. In these cases, trying to simulate the customer's actions may be a waste of time or even impossible.

When technology standards exist, whether and how strictly those standards are enforced will vary from one company to the next. Some companies encourage customers to comply with their standards by having the help desk provide a high level of support for standard systems and little or no support for nonstandard systems. In other words, customers who choose to use nonstandard systems may be "on their own" if they have questions or problems. Although this policy of letting customers opt to use nonstandard systems without support may benefit the help desk—it is not getting calls about nonstandard systems—the company does not typically benefit in the long run. This is because the problems still occur; they are just not being reported to the help desk. When standards are enforced, the productivity of all of the groups that use and support the systems benefit. These standards benefit technology users as they receive the training they need and the number of problems they encounter is minimized. These standards benefit the help desk and other support groups, such as level two service providers, because they are supporting a limited set of systems and can acquire the training, tools, and talent needed to provide high-quality support.

ESTABLISHING TECHNOLOGY STANDARDS

Many companies establish standards that determine what hardware and software systems are used by their internal employees and, when appropriate, by their external customers. It is common for a committee to select the standard systems and define the policies that govern how the systems are used and supported. The committee typically includes representatives from all of the groups that will use and support the standard systems: Customers, the help desk, and any level two and three groups needed to support the systems are represented.

Systems undergo rigorous testing before they are selected to ensure they meet the selection criteria defined by the standards committee and to ensure the new systems are compatible with other standard systems. This testing also enables the standards committee to illustrate the benefits of implementing standard systems. Benefits of establishing technology standards include:

- A less complex environment. Rather than using two or more word-processing products, such as Microsoft Word and Corel WordPerfect, the product that best meets the company's needs is selected and implemented. As a result, customers, the help desk staff, and level two service providers are able to gain a high level of expertise in the chosen systems.

- Improved ability to share data and exchange information. Rather than converting data from one system to another, such as from a Microsoft Excel spreadsheet to a Lotus 1-2-3 spreadsheet, a single system is used. As a result, many of the problems that can occur when converting data are prevented.

- Effective training programs can be developed. Because there are fewer systems, companies have more resources available to develop and deliver high-quality training programs. The help desk receives the training it needs to support the systems, and customers receive the training they need to use the technology as efficiently and effectively as possible. Consequently, customers have fewer questions and problems, and the help desk can quickly handle questions and problems that do occur.

- Proactive support can be provided. With fewer systems, the number of isolated random problems decreases—because you have reduced the number of potential points of failure—and more common, predictable problems occur. By using trend and root cause analysis to proactively identify the likely source of potential problems, problems can be prevented. Or, their impact is minimized.

- Costs are controlled. Companies that have standards can negotiate discounts with vendors because they are purchasing software licenses and hardware for a greater number of people. For example, companies can purchase a site license, which enables all users at a given location to use a software package, rather than purchasing more costly individual licenses. Also, the costs associated with abandoning technology that does not work correctly are eliminated, as are the problems that accompanied that technology.

- The company is positioned to take advantage of state-of-the-art technology. Allowing customers to use any system they want often makes it difficult for a company to implement new technology. For example, customers who use an early version of Windows such as Windows 98 must be transitioned to a newer generation Windows operating system such as Windows XP before the company can implement the current release of Windows-based applications such as Word and Excel. Although the customers may be comfortable using the systems they have, those systems may not fit the long-term needs of the company and may be causing problems. The standards committee stays on top of industry trends and selects systems that will benefit the company now and into the foreseeable future.

It is sometimes perceived that establishing technology standards decreases the user's ability to take advantage of the latest technology trends. Although that may be true to some extent, it is equally true that the latest technologies are often plagued with problems. Establishing technology standards enables companies to create a computing environment that is more stable and less complex. That is, they create a computing environment that has fewer problems and is easier to support.

Using Diagnostic Tools.　　In addition to providing systems that analysts can use to simulate a customer's action, some help desks provide analysts with tools, such as remote control systems, they can use to diagnose problems. A **remote control system** is a technology that enables an analyst to take over a customer's keyboard, screen, mouse, or other connected device in order to troubleshoot problems, transfer files, provide informal training, and even collaborate on documents. The customer authorizes the analyst to access his or her system by keying a password. Because the analyst may be able to observe or access confidential information or transactions, some companies prohibit the use of these systems. When these systems are used, analysts can resolve many problems that would previously have required a visit to the customer's site. Most customers appreciate this technology because they do not have to wait for a field service representative to arrive. Not all customers feel comfortable with this technology, though, so it is important to ask permission and respect your customer's feelings on this matter.

Additionally, most hardware and software systems manufactured today have built-in diagnostic tools. For example, many systems come with software that can be used to automatically schedule maintenance tasks that prevent problems by cleaning up disk space and searching for and repairing data errors on the hard drive. Most systems also come with a disk that contains a diagnostic program customers can run if they encounter a problem. Some software packages include wizards that step customers through a series of diagnostic questions. Diagnostic tools can also be purchased. For example, popular antivirus packages such as Norton SystemWorks by Symantec (**www.symantec.com/sabu/sysworks/ basic/index.html**) provide the ability to schedule periodic system scans and updates in an effort to diagnose, prevent, and repair problems. Help desk analysts can prompt a customer to use these tools either while they are working with the customer or, in some cases, before the customer contacts the help desk. For example, the help desk can suggest customers use these tools on their Help Desk Quick Reference Card, or customers can be prompted to use these tools when they access the help desk's Web site. These tools can provide help desk analysts with the information they need to solve a problem, but they also can provide customers with the ability to solve problems on their own. When customers solve problems on their own, help desk analysts are freed to work on more complex and unique problems.

Some companies are exploring the use of Web-based digital agents, also known as intelligent agents or virtual agents, to diagnose and ultimately prevent problems. A digital agent is a software routine that waits in the background and performs an action when a specified event occurs. For example, when a customer asks for help at a Web site, a digital agent can interact with the customer and provide solutions in much the same way as a human. Digital agents can also take customers on a tour of a company's Web site or escalate customers from self-service to assisted service channels when needed.

Diagnostic tools are an effective way to diagnose problems. Keep in mind that using these tools may not always be an option. For example, if the network is down, access to a customer's system using a remote control system may not be possible. Or, if a hardware failure occurs, having a customer run a diagnostic program may not be possible. When diagnostic tools are not available, you can ask questions or simulate the customer's actions in an effort to identify the probable problem source.

Analysts often feel pressure to resolve or escalate problems as quickly as possible. Because of this pressure, they may draw conclusions based on insufficient information or without understanding all of the facts. In other words, they may develop a course of action based on a symptom, rather than the actual probable source. You must take the time needed to fully diagnose the problem and identify the correct probable source. Otherwise, you can waste time developing a course of action that will not permanently solve the problem. Incorrectly identifying the probable source can also damage your relationship with level two service providers. For example, a level two service provider who spends time diagnosing a problem only to learn that the problem should have been assigned to another group will often resent the interruption and may mistrust you or the entire help desk in the future.

Step 3. Develop a Course of Action

Once you have diagnosed the problem and identified the correct probable source, you then can begin to develop a course of action or action plan. The course of action may involve researching the problem further, developing a solution, escalating the problem to a level two service provider, or simply letting the customer know when to expect a more up-to-date status. It is important to note that the course of action taken will not be correct if an incorrect probable source was identified. When the correct probable source is identified, an analyst can:

- Consult printed resources (such as manuals, user's guides, and procedures), online resources (such as online help and Web sites), coworkers, subject matter experts, or the team leader in an effort to research the problem, identify a solution, or implement a solution.
- Determine if a workaround is available that can satisfy the customer's immediate need.
- Escalate the problem to the correct level two service provider or subject matter expert.
- Search a knowledge base for solutions to known problems or for policies and procedures that can be used to develop a solution.
- Search the incident tracking and problem management system for past problems that are similar or related to the current problem, which can then be used to further develop a course of action.
- Use personal knowledge to develop a solution.
- Use tools, such as remote control systems, to further diagnose the problem, identify a solution, or implement a solution.

It is important to review the course of action with the customer and ensure that the customer understands it and the time frame within which it will be executed. It is particularly important to let the customer know if the course of action or the time frame is dictated by an SLA. If the customer is dissatisfied, determine what the customer would prefer and, if possible, accommodate that preference. If you cannot accommodate the customer's preference, determine if there is an alternate course of action that will satisfy the customer's need in the interim. Record the customer's preference in the ticket and when necessary, bring the problem to management's attention.

Knowing When to Engage Additional Resources

Most help desks strive to solve as many problems as possible at level one. There are times, though, when a level one analyst needs to consult a coworker or escalate a problem to a level two service provider. For example, a customer may be reporting a very complex or unique problem, or a customer may be having a problem with a product that you have not yet been trained to support. Your first course of action is to use resources such as online help, product and procedure manuals, or a knowledge base. If these resources do not prove useful, you may turn to a coworker or level two service provider for help.

To ensure problems are solved as quickly as possible, many companies establish a **target escalation time,** which is a time constraint placed on each level that ensures problem resolution activities are proceeding at an appropriate pace. For example, a help desk's policy may state that level one should escalate problems to level two within 30 minutes. Management typically asks that analysts exercise their best judgment in following this guideline. In other words, if an analyst feels that she is close to resolving the problem, she should proceed. On the other hand, if an analyst believes that he has exhausted his capabilities and that he has used all available resources, it is time to escalate the problem.

As an analyst, you should consider the following points as the target escalation time approaches but before you escalate the problem to another service provider.

- Do I have sufficient information to clearly state the problem? Have I collected and logged pertinent details such as who, what, when, where, and how?
- Have I determined the probable source of the problem? Have I eliminated all other possibilities?
- Have I gathered and logged the information that is required by level two? If level two has provided a problem-solving checklist, has the checklist been completed and the results documented?
- What is the problem severity? Is this a problem that must be solved right away or can the customer wait?

NOTE

Recall that problem severity is a category that defines how critical a problem is based on the nature of the failure and the available alternatives or workarounds. The help desk and the customer usually work together to determine a problem's severity. The problem severity typically dictates the target resolution time of the problem. Then, a problem priority is assigned by the help desk or by the level two or level three group designated to work on the problem. Problem priority identifies the order for working on problems with the same severity. Factors that may influence the priority assigned to a problem include the number of times a problem has recurred, how long a customer's system has been down, or the terms of a customer's SLA. For example, a customer, via an SLA, may be paying for premium service that requires a quicker resolution time. Management may also increase the priority of a problem when, for example, the customer affected is a company executive, the customer has had a similar problem before that was not resolved to the customer's satisfaction, or management simply makes a judgment call and prioritizes one problem over another.

Remember that when you consult with a coworker or escalate a problem to a level two service provider, that person will expect you to be able to provide the answers to the questions previously listed. If you cannot give these answers, you may need to ask a few more questions before you seek help. With the answers to just a few additional questions, you may find that you can solve the problem on your own.

TAKING OWNERSHIP

Not every problem can be solved immediately. Contrary to how it may seem at times, most customers do understand this fact. What customers expect when a problem cannot be solved immediately is that someone take responsibility for ensuring the problem will be resolved in the time frame promised. When a help desk analyst cannot resolve a problem in the course of the initial telephone call or a problem must be escalated to a person or group outside the help desk, a problem owner is designated. The **problem owner** is an employee of the support organization who acts as a customer advocate and ensures a problem is resolved to the customer's satisfaction. When a problem owner is designated, the customer shouldn't have to initiate another call. Nor should the customer have to call around to the different groups involved in solving the problem to find out the problem's status or progress. The problem owner does that for the customer.

In many companies, the person who initially logs the problem is the owner. In other words, the help desk analyst who first handles a problem continues to follow up, even when the problem is escalated to level two or level three. Often, the analyst (problem owner) is the only person who can close the problem and does so only after verifying that the customer is satisfied. Figure 14–7 shows a sample escalation sequence where the level one analyst and the problem owner are the same person.

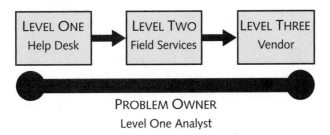

Figure 14–7 Sample escalation sequence with problem owner

In other companies, the problem owner changes as problems are escalated from one level to the next. The person designated to work on the problem must accept responsibility and agree to assume ownership of the problem before the previous problem owner transfers responsibility (ownership) to him or her.

NOTE   Problem management is known as a "closed loop process" because the customer who reports a problem must accept the solution before the problem can be closed.

Regardless of how the problem owner is established, from a customer satisfaction standpoint, it is vital that for every single problem, one person serves as an advocate for the customer. This practice ensures that problems are not lost or forgotten and that customers' needs are considered at all times.

Problem Owner Responsibilities

Taking ownership of a problem comes with specific responsibilities. The problem owner accepts responsibility for proactively ensuring that a problem is resolved to the customer's complete satisfaction, even though he or she may not actually develop or implement the solution. A problem owner:

- Tracks the current status of the problem, including who is working on the problem and where the problem is in the problem management process
- Proactively provides the customer regular and timely status updates
- When possible, identifies related problems
- Ensures that problems are assigned correctly and are not passed from level to level or group to group without any effort being made to identify a resolution
- Ensures that appropriate notification activities occur when a problem is reported, escalated, and resolved (discussed in the following section)
- Before closing a problem, ensures that all problem-solving activities are documented and that the customer is satisfied with the resolution
- Closes the problem ticket

Problem ownership does not mean that analysts focus only on problems that they own. To satisfy customers, each and every member of the help desk team must do all they can to ensure customer satisfaction. Sometimes, that means sharing ownership responsibilities. In other words, analysts:

- Help other owners when they can. For example, an analyst may have recently been to training or may be a subject matter expert and can share his or her knowledge with others.

- Update a ticket if a customer contacts the help desk to provide additional information and the owner is unavailable. A good practice is to send the owner a message or leave the owner a note if the information recorded is time sensitive.

- Update a ticket if a customer contacts the help desk for an up-to-date status and the owner is unavailable. A good practice is to note in the ticket the date and time that the customer requested a status update and the information given.

- Negotiate a transfer of ownership for any outstanding tickets if the analyst is going to be out of the office for an extended time, such as for training or vacation. A good practice is to ensure that all tickets are up-to-date and that all resolved tickets are closed before the tickets are transferred to another analyst.

Ownership is critical to the problem management process. Without it, problems can be lost or forgotten and customer dissatisfaction invariably occurs. The concept of ownership ensures that everyone involved in the problem management process stays focused on the customer's need to have the problem solved in a timely fashion and to be informed when the problem requires more than the expected time to resolve.

Providing Status Updates to Customers and Management

A problem owner has the extremely important responsibilities of promoting awareness that a problem has occurred and regularly communicating the status of problem resolution activities. These activities are known as problem notification. \Notification \informs all of the stakeholders in the problem management process, including management, the customer, and help desk analysts, about the status of outstanding problems. Notification can occur when a problem is reported or escalated, when a problem has exceeded a predefined threshold, such as its target resolution time, or when a problem is resolved.

Notification to each of the stakeholders occurs at different points and has different goals. For example, management notification is appropriate when:

- The problem is extremely severe.
- The target resolution time has been or is about to be reached.
- Required resources are not available to determine or implement a solution.
- The customer expresses dissatisfaction.

In each of these cases, notification keeps management aware of problems that might require management intervention. The goals of management notification are to ensure that:

- Management knows the current status of problems that are in an exception state, meaning that the problems have exceeded a predefined threshold. For example, the target resolution time has been exceeded, or a level two support group is not acknowledging a problem that has been assigned to it.

- Management has the information needed to oversee problems that involve multiple support groups. For example, resources from the network support and development groups are needed to resolve a problem.

- Management has sufficient information to make decisions (such as add more resources or re-assign responsibilities), follow up with the customer, or call in other management.
- Management actions are recorded in the problem record so that everyone affected by or involved in solving the problem knows what decisions management has made or what steps they took to follow up with the customer or involve other management.

These goals make sure that the customer's problem is being addressed and responded to in an appropriate time and way. Like management notification, customer notification is appropriate in specific situations, such as when:

- The analyst told the customer that he or she will provide a status at a given time, even if there has been no change in the problem's status.
- The target resolution time will not be met.
- Customer resources are required to implement a solution.
- The problem has a high severity and justifies frequent status updates.
- The customer was dissatisfied with earlier solutions.

Customer notification keeps the customer informed about the progress of the problem resolution. The goals of customer notification are to ensure that:

- The customer knows the current status of the problem.
- Customer comments or concerns are recorded in the problem record and addressed.

 These goals make sure that the customer knows that the problem is being addressed and responded to in an appropriate time and way.

Three ways that help desks deliver value are by: (1) making it easy for customers to report problems, (2) delivering solutions, and (3) taking ownership and ensuring that problems that cannot be resolved immediately are addressed in the required time frame. One of the most common complaints that help desks hear from customers is that they were not kept informed. It is important to remember that even bad news is better than no news at all. Contacting customers to let them know that the target resolution time cannot be met, and perhaps explaining the reason for any delays (such as having to order parts), is far better than having the customers hear nothing.

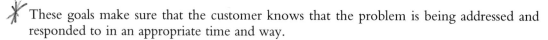

NOTE Proactive communication is the most effective way to minimize negative customer reaction and instill customer confidence when problems arise or when delays occur. Although the customer may not be happy with a delay, he or she will typically appreciate being kept informed. Customers may also accept explanations offered proactively as fact; whereas explanations offered in response to a customer inquiry may be viewed simply as an excuse.

The help desk can notify management, customers, and others by telephone, in person, with an e-mail or instant message, through a paging device, or automatically via the problem management system. How notification occurs and who is notified varies based on conditions such as the severity of the problem, who is affected by the problem, and when the problem occurs. Many help desks have documented procedures that spell out who to notify and how to notify them.

Bill Rose

SERVICE & SUPPORT PROFESSIONALS ASSOCIATION

FOUNDER AND EXECUTIVE DIRECTOR

SAN DIEGO, CALIFORNIA

WWW.SSPA.ORG

Bill Rose is one of the world's leading authorities on the process of delivering world-class software support. He founded the Service & Support Professionals Association (SSPA) in 1989 and continues to serve as its executive director. SSPA is a membership organization that provides a value-added forum where service and support professionals in the technology industry can share ideas, discuss developing trends, and network with their peers. SSPA also manages and administers certification programs for service and support professionals. Bill Rose talks about the skills needed in the support industry and trends affecting the industry.

In the support industry, three sets of skills are needed: (1) technical, (2) interpersonal, and (3) business. The support professionals who are most successful are those with strong interpersonal skills, particularly those people who can communicate effectively and appropriately with managers, coworkers, and customers.

When interacting with managers, analysts must represent the customer in a realistic fashion. When communicating customer issues to managers, analysts must demonstrate an appropriate sense of urgency. Managers don't want analysts to panic and overstate the impact of an issue; nor do they want analysts to relay an issue in a very casual manner, only to find out later that it is a big problem.

When interacting with coworkers, analysts need to remember that they are part of a team. Sometimes they need to interrupt their coworkers to ask questions. Sometimes they are interrupted and asked questions. Sometimes they have to deal with the stress of the person sitting next to them. Sometimes they have to ask for help dealing with stress. It's like family therapy. You have to stick together.

When interacting with customers, analysts must determine the customer's "level of learning," and then proceed accordingly. We have found that there are four levels of learning:

- Unconscious incompetence

- Conscious incompetence

- Conscious competence

- Unconscious competence

At the lowest level, *unconscious incompetence,* customers typically cannot articulate their problem. They will use very basic terminology or incorrect terminology, for example, "I can't get this 'doohickey' to work right." The more experienced analysts become, the more difficult it is for them to assist customers at this level. They have to be extremely patient. Customers at the *conscious incompetence* level know what they don't know. They will try to start using terminology but may use it incorrectly. Customers at this level benefit greatly when analysts reassure them and walk them through the problem-solving process step-by-step. Customers at the *conscious competence* level are often the easiest to support. They use terminology correctly and they can often clearly and correctly articulate their problem. They can also work with analysts to solve the problem. At the highest level, unconscious competence, customers are often known as "power users." They can be a challenge to support because they often feel they know more than the analysts do. They are often impatient and resent being asked "basic" questions.

You must learn to quickly assess customers' level of learning so you can communicate effectively with them. It is also important to know your level of learning so that you know when it's time to ask for help.

Many of today's young people have grown up working with computers. They have the technical skills that are needed. The question is, do they—do you—have the interpersonal skills, particularly the skills needed to support customers who are "charged up" because they are frustrated, confused, upset, or angry. Nurture your communication skills. Obtain training or attend programs such as Toastmasters (**www.toastmasters.org**) and Dale Carnegie Training (**www.dale-carnegie.com**). These skills can be developed and are worth acquiring.

Technical support is definitely a career that is here to stay. People who have the ability to communicate effectively one-on-one, over the telephone, and in writing can reap the greatest rewards. We are seeing a real shift in the way companies generate revenues. Today, greater than 80% of a software publisher's revenue comes from support maintenance and customer services. This means that CEOs are very interested in customer service and are putting programs in place to attract and retain good people. Support has become strategic to most companies' futures. We are seeing more career advancement opportunities and compensation is increasing. Even entry-level salaries are on the rise.

Building Good Relationships with Other Support Groups

Although most help desks strive to solve as many problems as possible at level one, there are times when a level one analyst needs to interact with people from other support groups, such as a field services group or a network support group. An analyst may need to escalate a problem to the support group or obtain a status update on a ticket previously assigned. The analyst may be asking for informal training or help developing a problem-solving checklist. A good relationship between the help desk and other support groups ensures that all groups can fulfill their roles and responsibilities.

It takes time and effort to build a strong relationship between the help desk and other support groups. Level one analysts must strive to continuously increase their knowledge and the efficiency and effectiveness of their problem-solving skills. This includes ensuring that all available information has been gathered and logged and that all checklists have been completed and the results logged before a problem is escalated to level two. Level two service providers must respect the help desk's role as a front-line service provider. They must acknowledge the fact that the help desk's efforts are freeing them from the need to answer the same questions or solve the same problems over and over again. They must be willing to impart their knowledge to the help desk. This enables the help desk to solve more problems at level one, while also reducing the number of problems the help desk escalates to level two. The help desk must be willing to receive that knowledge and seek assistance from level two only after using all other available resources, such as manuals, knowledge bases, and so forth.

The following techniques can be used to foster a strong relationship between the help desk and other support groups so that all groups can reap the benefits.

- **Review and understand your company's SLAs.** Recall that a help desk may have SLAs with some or all of its customers and with internal (level two and level three) support groups and external vendors. You must understand all of these agreements as they are critical in defining the roles and responsibilities of all of the support groups represented in the company's customer service delivery chain. These agreements contain information such as the services to be delivered, service hours, performance metrics, and so forth. These agreements are integral to the relationship that exists between level one and level two. For example, if there is a critical problem and the company guarantees a customer that the problem will be resolved in two hours, the help desk must notify level two immediately so that the level two service provider has an adequate amount of time to respond. Conversely, the help desk must not insist that level two drop everything else to work on a noncritical problem that does not need to be resolved for several days.

The help desk must resist the temptation to "cry wolf," or level two may become unresponsive. Understanding your company's SLAs is an excellent way to ensure everyone's expectations, including those of other support groups, are being met.

- **Provide mutual feedback.** An excellent way to enhance the relationship between the help desk and other support groups is to ask the members of each group for feedback. You will get more benefit from improving or addressing known problems than from addressing what you "think" the problems are. You can solicit feedback informally by getting feedback from someone in the support group that you know and that you trust will be constructive. The help desk team also can solicit feedback formally by, for example, preparing a survey, such as the one shown in Figure 14–8, that asks the members of other support groups for feedback. When the help desk is open to feedback, it will often find that other support groups begin to solicit and respond to constructive feedback in return.

- **Job shadowing.** Job shadowing involves working side-by-side with another person in an effort to understand and potentially learn that person's job. Job shadowing provides excellent benefits to both the help desk and support groups because each group is given the opportunity to "walk in the other's shoes." This enables both groups to gain a better understanding of the other's perspective and priorities. Job shadowing is a particularly effective way to improve your problem-solving skills. For example, job shadowing may give you the opportunity to work with a specialist to solve a complex or unique problem, or it may give you the opportunity to learn how to use new tools or to develop new checklists. As with providing mutual feedback, you can job shadow someone informally on your own, or your help desk may have a formal program in place.

- **Review incident tracking system information.** A common complaint from level two service providers is that they cannot understand the information help desk analysts give in the tickets escalated to them, or they feel the information is incomplete. Conversely, help desk analysts often complain that level two service providers do not thoroughly document the steps taken to resolve a problem. As a result, the help desk is unable to reuse the resolution when a similar problem occurs. Periodic reviews of incident tracking system information by a team of level one and level two service providers can pinpoint areas that that need to be improved. A good practice is to use real tickets during this review to illustrate and discuss examples of both poorly documented and well-documented tickets. The conclusions drawn during these reviews and the examples of well-documented tickets can be used to create new or enhanced ticket-logging procedures.

- **Communicate.** When strained relations exist between the help desk and other support groups, it is often because of poor communication. The help desk and the support groups must make sure that they communicate all appropriate information in a timely manner. For example, the help desk must let the support groups know when it typically receives its highest volume of calls or when it is receiving an unexpectedly high volume of calls. This information enables the support groups to understand the current capabilities of the help desk and the factors that influence its performance. Support groups must, in turn, let the help desk know when

Level Two Feedback Survey

The purpose of this survey is to solicit feedback that can be used to improve the quality of the services provided by the help desk. Please answer the questions below and provide constructive comments about how we can better work with your group to provide quality service to our customers and contribute to the success of the entire Technology Services organization.

Name (Optional): _____

Department (Optional): _____

1) How satisfied are you overall with the thoroughness and accuracy with which the help desk documents problem tickets assigned to your group? For example, problem description, steps taken to diagnosis the problem, resolution steps attempted, and so forth?

☐ Very Satisfied   ☐ Somewhat Satisfied   ☐ Dissatisfied

Please comment:

2) How satisfied are you overall with the help desk's ability to handle recurring problems once you have given them training, documentation, solution information, and so forth?

☐ Very Satisfied   ☐ Somewhat Satisfied   ☐ Dissatisfied

Please comment:

3) How satisfied are you overall with the accuracy with which the help desk determines the probable source of the problem and, as such, assigns problem tickets to your group?

☐ Very Satisfied   ☐ Somewhat Satisfied   ☐ Dissatisfied

Please comment:

Page 1

Figure 14–8 Level two feedback survey

Level Two Feedback Survey

4) How satisfied are you overall with the help desk's efforts to diagnose the problem prior to seeking assistance from your group?

☐ Very Satisfied ☐ Somewhat Satisfied ☐ Dissatisfied

Please comment:

5) How satisfied are you overall with the help desk's ability to record and assign the appropriate severity to problems that are reported to or discovered by it?

☐ Very Satisfied ☐ Somewhat Satisfied ☐ Dissatisfied

Please comment:

6) How satisfied are you overall with the partnership that exists between your group and the help desk?

☐ Very Satisfied ☐ Somewhat Satisfied ☐ Dissatisfied

Please comment:

7) Do you feel comfortable giving constructive feedback directly to the help desk in an effort to enhance the working relationship that exists between your group and the help desk?

☐ Yes ☐ No

Please comment:

8) What improvements have been made and what areas do you feel could be further improved between your group and the help desk?

Please comment:

Thank you for taking the time to complete this important survey.

Page 2

Figure 14–8 Level two feedback survey (continued)

they are working on a large project or when they will be shorthanded. This information will enable the help desk to appropriately manage its customers' expectations and may influence when and how the help desk escalates problems. Everyone is busy in today's business world. Timely and regular communication will circumvent misunderstandings and promote a spirit of partnership.

- **Give praise.** One of the things that makes technical customer support so tough is that you rarely hear good news. In fact, for all intents and purposes, your job is to deal with bad news. Just as you hope to receive thanks for your efforts, you can let the people who work in other support groups know that you appreciate the job they are doing. For example, if a level two service provider develops a problem-solving checklist, a representative of the help desk can send an e-mail message to the service provider's supervisor or team leader that expresses the team's appreciation. Some help desks maintain a "goody" drawer filled with snacks or toys, such as stress balls, that they can hand out to level two service providers who provide training or in some way go the extra mile. Although giving praise may seem like a small thing, it is easy to do, costs little to no money, and encourages continued goodwill. Giving praise also encourages praise in return. Praise is something we all appreciate.

Level one analysts and level two service providers must work together to ensure that problems are solved quickly and accurately. All of the support groups within a company, including the help desk, have a role to play and each must respect the other's role and responsibilities. Although it is the problem owner's responsibility to act as a customer advocate and ensure a problem is resolved to the customer's satisfaction, each and every member of the customer service delivery chain must do all they can to ensure problems are solved quickly, correctly, and permanently.

FOCUSING ON PREVENTION

Once a solution has been identified and implemented, there are still questions that need to be asked and answered. These include:

- Did the resolution solve the problem?
- Is the customer satisfied?
- Has the root cause of the problem been identified?
- Was the corrective action permanent?

If the answer to any of these question is "No," the problem cannot be considered resolved. At this point, the problem owner, assisted by coworkers, level two or level three service providers, and when appropriate, management, must determine the next steps to take.

If the answer to all of these questions is "Yes," the problem ticket can be closed once all pertinent data is captured. It is particularly important to identify the root cause. Without this data, trend and root cause analysis cannot be performed.

Some help desks have highly skilled statisticians perform trend and root cause analysis. However, it is important to remember that any or all members of the help desk team can identify and analyze trends. Very often the front-line staff can identify trends simply by considering the contacts they are receiving. For example, the help desk might notice that it is receiving many contacts about a certain system or product and bring that fact to management's attention. A trend report can then be created to validate statistically the help desk's hunch.

When working in a help desk, do not hesitate to suggest ways that problems can be eliminated. Be persistent and act on your hunches. Go beyond the quick fix and take the time to resolve problems correctly the first time. If, as a problem owner, you believe a problem has not been permanently resolved, leave the problem ticket open and engage the resources needed to determine and eliminate the root cause. Your coworkers, managers, and customers will thank you.

> *If you can't find the time to do it right, where are you going to find the time to do it over?* Author Unknown

When working in a help desk, an understanding of your company's problem management process and strong problem-solving skills are essential to your success. The problem management process and the problem-solving process both require that you systematically gather information, diagnose and solve problems, and, when necessary, engage additional resources. The problem management process also ensures that customers and managers are proactively kept informed about the status of problem resolution activities. Handling problems efficiently and effectively is important, but, ultimately, customers prefer that problems be prevented. Trend and root cause analysis can be used to prevent problems, but only if you capture accurate and complete data. When problems are prevented, you will have the opportunity to work on more complex problems and pursue new skills.

CHAPTER SUMMARY

❐ To be successful, a help desk analyst must be able to solve problems efficiently and effectively. Most help desks develop processes and procedures, such as the problem management process, in an effort to ensure that problems are handled quickly, correctly, and consistently. The goal of problem management is to minimize the impact of problems that affect a company's systems, networks, and products.

❐ Within the boundaries of the problem management process, analysts use their problem-solving skills to handle each problem. The best problem solvers condition themselves to gather all available data, create information, and methodically diagnose the problem before developing a course of action. Effective diagnostic techniques include asking questions, simulating the customer's actions, and using diagnostic tools.

❐ When problems cannot be solved immediately, customers expect someone to take responsibility for ensuring the problem is resolved in the time frame promised. The problem owner assumes that responsibility. The concept of ownership ensures that everyone involved in the problem management process stays focused on the customer's need to have the problem solved in a timely fashion and to be informed when the problem requires more than the expected time to resolve. Ownership is critical to the problem management process. Without it, problems can slip through the cracks and customer dissatisfaction invariably occurs.

❏ When working in a help desk, do not hesitate to suggest ways that problems can be eliminated and prevented. Be persistent and act on your hunches. An understanding of your company's problem management process and strong problem-solving skills are also essential to your success. These processes ensure that problems are handled efficiently and effectively. Ultimately, however, customers prefer that problems be prevented.

KEY TERMS

client/server — A computing model where some computers, known as clients, request services, and other computers, known as servers, respond to those requests.

customer data — The identifying details about a customer, including the customer's name, telephone number, department or company name, address or location, customer number, and employee number or user ID.

customer record — All of the data and text fields that describe a single customer.

detailed problem description — A comprehensive accounting of a problem and the circumstances surrounding the problem's occurrence.

digital agent — A software routine that waits in the background and performs an action when a specified event occurs.

flowchart — A diagram that shows the sequence of tasks that occur in a process.

incident management — See problem management.

inquiry — A customer request for information, such as "When will my equipment arrive?"

job shadowing — Working side-by-side with another person in an effort to understand and potentially learn that person's job.

notification — An activity that informs all of the stakeholders in the problem management process (including management, the customer, and help desk analysts) about the status of outstanding problems.

probable source — The system, network, or product that is most likely causing a problem.

problem — An event that disrupts service or prevents access to products.

problem data — The details of a single problem, including the problem category (such as hardware or software), affected component or system (such as a printer or monitor), symptom, date and time problem occurred, contact method (such as telephone, voice mail, e-mail, Web form), date and time problem was logged, analyst who logged problem, problem owner, description, and severity.

problem management — The process of tracking and resolving problems; also called incident management.

problem owner — An employee of the support organization who acts as a customer advocate and ensures a problem is resolved to the customer's satisfaction.

problem priority —The order for working on problems with the same severity.

problem record — All of the fields that describe a single problem.

problem statement — See short problem description.

procedure — A step-by-step, detailed set of instructions that describes how to perform the tasks in a process.

process — A collection of interrelated work activities—or tasks—that take a set of specific inputs and produce a set of specific outputs that are of value to the customer.

question — A customer request for instructions on how to use a product, for example, "How do I . . . ?"

record — A collection of related fields.

remote control system — A technology that enables an analyst to take over a customer's keyboard, screen, mouse, or other connected device in order to troubleshoot problems, transfer files, provide informal training, and even collaborate on documents.

request — A customer order to obtain a new product or service, or an enhancement to an existing product or service.

root cause — The most basic reason for an undesirable condition or problem, which, if eliminated or corrected, would prevent the problem from existing or occurring.

root cause analysis — A methodical way of determining the root cause of problems.

short problem description — A succinct description of the actual results a customer is experiencing; also called problem statement.

symptom — A sign or indication that a problem has occurred.

target escalation time — A time constraint placed on each level, and which ensures problem resolution activities are proceeding at an appropriate pace.

trend analysis — A methodical way of determining and, when possible, forecasting service trends.

REVIEW QUESTIONS

1. What is a problem?

2. Are most technical problems unique?

3. Define the term *process*.

4 Explain the relationship that exists between processes and procedures.

5. A(n) _____ is a sign or indication that a problem has occurred.

6. Define the term *root cause*.

7. Draw the symbol that represents a task in a flowchart.

8. Draw the symbol that represents a decision point in a flowchart.

9. Why do most companies distinguish between problems, questions, and inquiries?

10. Is the problem management process typically used to handle requests?

11. List two types of data you must gather before you can begin diagnosing a problem.

12. What is a problem statement?

13. Briefly describe the items that should be included in a detailed problem description.

14. What are you trying to determine when diagnosing a problem?

15. List three benefits that are derived by asking questions.

16. List three ways that help desks provide analysts with the ability to simulate their customers' actions.

17. Describe two situations in which you may not be able to use diagnostic tools.

18. Why is it important to determine the correct probable problem source?

19. What typically dictates the target resolution time of a problem?

20. True or False? The problem owner is the person who develops and implements the solution to a problem.

21. What can happen if no one takes ownership of a problem?

22. When can problem notification occur?

23. What are the goals of management notification?

24. What are the goals of customer notification?

25. What are two things that help desk analysts can do to build a strong relationship with their level two support groups?

26. What are two things that level two support groups can do to build a strong relationship with the help desk?

27. What four questions must be answered "Yes" before a problem can be considered resolved?

28. List three ways you can help eliminate problems when you work in a help desk.

DISCUSSION QUESTIONS

1. People with strong technical skills often feel that processes and procedures take too much time and stifle innovation. They like their freedom and feel that documenting their actions and results is a waste of time. Are they right? Discuss the pros and cons of processes and procedures versus independence and individuality.

2. In some organizations, an adversarial relationship exists between the level one help desk and some level two support groups. Discuss potential reasons for this adverse situation. Also discuss ways an adverse situation can be improved.

3. Most of us have experienced a situation where we had a fleeting thought—a hunch—that we ignored. Discuss the pros and cons of ignoring hunches. Also discuss how hunches can be used to prevent problems.

HANDS-ON PROJECTS

Project 14–1

Develop a process flowchart. Assemble a team of three to five classmates. Develop a flowchart that shows all the steps for attending a movie the entire team agrees upon. Begin the process by deciding to go to the movies and end the process by having all of the members of the team return home safely.

Project 14–2

Learn about ITIL terminology. Search the Web for sites that contain an ITIL glossary of terms such as **www.koeln-net.com/aksm/texte/Glossar_Service-Management.pdf** or **www.dream-catchers-inc.com/White%20Papers/ITIL%20Glossary%20of%20 Terms.htm.** Document the ITIL definitions for terms used in this chapter such as *problem record, severity,* and *priority.* Prepare a list of additional ITIL terms that have been used in this or previous chapters. Discuss these terms with your classmates.

Project 14–3

Tease your brain (part 1). The following letters represent something that you learned early in life, most likely before you attended first grade. Add the next two letters to the sequence and explain how these letters fit into the sequence.

O

T

T

F

F

S

S

?

?

Project 14–4

Tease your brain (part 2). The first ten letters of the alphabet have been divided into two groups. (1) What pattern differentiates the two groups? (2) Into which group would you put the letter K? (3) Into which group would you put the letter R?

Group 1: A E F H I

Group 2: B C D G J

Project 14–5

Develop a problem-solving checklist. Select a piece of computer hardware or a software package that you use regularly. Develop a problem-solving checklist that contains at least ten questions that analysts can use to diagnose problems customers may encounter when using the selected technology.

Project 14–6

Learn about remote control software. Search the Internet and access the Web site of two companies that manufacturer remote control software. Some popular vendors include Intel, Microcom, Netopia, Network Associates, Stac, and Symantec. For each of the two companies you select, summarize in a paragraph or two what you were able to learn about remote control software. Briefly describe the benefits of using these systems for both the customer and help desk analysts.

Project 14–7

Determine who to notify. A level two field service representative has just informed you that he will not meet the target resolution time for a problem that you own because another problem he is working on is taking longer than expected. The only other person who could work on the problem is in training this week. Briefly describe who you would notify and how you would minimize customer dissatisfaction in this situation.

CASE PROJECTS

1. Mind Games

You are the manager of a medium-sized help desk and have decided that you would like your staff to have some fun while they improve their problem-solving skills. Go to the library and look in books or magazines for brainteasers and puzzles that can be used to challenge your staff and encourage logical thinking. Select three brainteasers and distribute them to your staff (choose three classmates). Discuss with your staff the techniques you learned in this chapter that could be useful in solving the brainteasers. For example, what information is available? What is the expected result? What questions can you ask in an effort to determine the expected result?

2. Brownstein, Popp, and Hepburn

You work for a small law firm and have been chosen to work on a committee that will develop standards for the technologies the lawyers will be authorized to use. The lawyers where you work are very autonomous, and they resist any rules that they perceive are unnecessary. For the first meeting, each attendee has been asked to prepare a list of benefits that customers will derive as a result of establishing standards. The committee chairman hopes that promoting the benefits will lessen resistance to the new standards. Prepare for the meeting by listing the benefits that you perceive the entire company, not just the help desk, will derive by establishing technology standards.

3. Eckes Office Supplies

You have been hired as a consultant to help the internal help desk at Eckes Office Supplies improve the relationship it has with its level two support groups. In an effort to understand the dynamics of the current relationship, you have decided to survey the help desk staff and members of the level two support groups. The help desk escalates a fairly high number of problems to the network support group, so you have elected to work on that relationship first. Prepare a survey that can be used to solicit the help desk's perception of its relationship with the network support group. Your goal is to formulate questions that, when answered, will help you determine if the network support group is meeting the help desk's expectations. (*Hint:* Use the level two feedback survey presented in this chapter for ideas.)